Entrepreneurial Financial Management

Entrepreneurial Financial Management

An Applied Approach

THIRD EDITION

Jeffrey R. Cornwall
David O. Vang
Jean M. Hartman

M.E.Sharpe
Armonk, New York
London, England

This book is dedicated with love and gratitude to our families.

Library of Congress Cataloging-in-Publication Data

Cornwall, Jeffrey R.
  Entrepreneurial financial management : an applied approach / by Jeffrey R. Cornwall, David O. Vang, and
Jean M. Hartman. — 2nd ed.
      p. cm.
Includes bibliographical references and index.
ISBN 978-0-7656-2726-1 (pbk. : alk. paper)
1. Business enterprises—Finance. 2. Entrepreneurship. I. Vang, David O. II. Hartman, Jean M. III. Title.

HG4026.C637 2009
658.15—dc22   2008049001

Printed in the United States of America

The paper used in this publication meets the minimum requirements of
American National Standard for Information Sciences
Permanence of Paper for Printed Library Materials,
ANSI Z 39.48-1984.

♾

SP (p) 10   9   8   7   6   5   4   3   2

Contents

Preface   ix

1. **Introduction**   **3**
   The Importance of Knowing the Numbers   3
   Measuring Success   4
   What Is Entrepreneurial Financial Management?   5
   What Makes Entrepreneurial Finance Similar to Traditional Finance?   7
   What Makes Entrepreneurial Finance Different from Traditional Finance?   8
   How the Lack of Historical Data and Liquidity Complicates the Practice
      of Finance in Early Stage Firms   11
   Using Stakeholder Analysis to Guide Ethical Decision Making   12
   Summary   14

PART I
BUILDING A FINANCIAL FORECAST   **15**

2. **Setting Financial Goals**   **17**
   Wealth Versus Income   17
   Integrating Nonfinancial Goals into the Business   20
   The Importance of Self-Assessment   21
   The Self-Assessment Process   24
   The Business Model and Business Plan   25
   Summary   26
   Appendix 2.1. Individual Entrepreneurial Self-Assessment   28
   Appendix 2.2. Partnership and Shareholder Assessment   29

3. **Understanding Financial Statements**   **31**
   The Accounting Equation   31
   An Example   32
   Basic Financial Statements   41

The Limitations of Business Financial Statements 48
Summary 49

4. **Revenue Forecasting** **52**
Common Forecasting Mistakes 52
The Link Between the Marketing Plan and Revenue Forecasts 54
Creating Scenarios 57
The Link Between the Revenue Forecast and the Cash Flow Forecast 58
The Impact of Business Type on Revenues 59
Quantitative Forecasting Techniques 65
The Importance of Revenue Forecasting 68
Summary 69

5. **Expense Forecasting** **72**
Defining Costs 72
Cost Behavior 73
Breakeven Analysis 77
Expense Forecasting: Impact of Business Type on Expenses 78
Reducing Expenses Through Bootstrapping 83
Summary 83

6. **Integrated Financial Model** **86**
The Entrepreneur's Aspirations Reconsidered 86
Contribution Format Income Statement 87
Earnings Before Interest and Taxes 87
Inventory of Assumptions 88
Social Ventures 89
Determining the Amount of Funds Needed 89
Using the Forecasting Template to Determine the Amount
  of Funds Needed 90
Time Out of Cash 91
Assessment of Risk Sensitivity 92
Integrating Financial Forecasts into Business Plan or Funding Document 93
Summary 93
Appendix 6.1. Instructions for Using the Integrated Financial Statements
  Template 96

PART II
MANAGING THE FINANCIAL RESOURCES OF A VENTURE **121**

7. **Monitoring Financial Performance** **123**
Tracking Assumptions 123
Establishing Milestones 125
Using Numbers to Manage 126
Financial Statement Analysis 127

Ratio Analysis 129
Working with Accountants 137
Summary 138

8. Day-to-Day Cash Flow Management and Forecasting **140**
Why Is Cash Flow Different from Net Income? 140
Why Is an Accural-Based Income Statement Important? 141
How Is Cash Flow Measured? 141
Interpreting a Statement of Cash Flows: Direct Method 144
Statement of Cash Flows: Indirect Method 145
Investors' and Creditors' Use of the Cash Flow Statement 148
Effective Cash Management 149
The Emotional Side of Cash Flow Management 152
Summary 153

PART III
SOURCES OF FINANCING

155

9. **Financing Over the Life of a Venture** **157**
Common Misconceptions About Entrepreneurial Financing 157
The Diverse Nature of Business Financing 158
Financing Small Businesses with Modest Growth Potential 161
Financing High-Growth, High-Potential Ventures 162
Summary 163

10. **Start-Up Financing from the Entrepreneur, Friends, and Family** **165**
Self-Financing 165
Advantages and Disadvantages of Self-Financing 167
Friends and Family Financing 169
Structure of Funds Invested 174
Summary 174

11. **Bootstrapping** **176**
Why Bootstrap? 176
Bootstrapping Administrative Overhead 179
Bootstrapping Employee Expenses 181
Bootstrapping Operating Expenses 183
Bootstrap Marketing 185
The Ethics of Bootstrapping 190
Summary 191

12. **External Sources of Funds: Equity** **193**
Angel Investors 194
Strategic Partners 199
Private Placement 200
Crowdfunding 202

SBIC   203
The Downside of Equity Financing   203
Working with Outside Investors   204
Summary   206

13. External Sources of Funds: Debt   **208**
Short-Term Debt   208
Long-Term Debt   215
Forms of Debt Overlooked by Entrepreneurs   217
Government Funding Through SBA   217
Working with Bankers   219
The Downside of Debt   224
Developing a Financing Plan   225
Summary   226

14. Financing the High-Growth Business   **228**
Integrating Profitability into the Business Plan   229
Stages of the Firm   231
Stages of Business Funding   233
The Dark Side of Venture Capital Financing   234
Initial Contact with a Venture Capitalist   235
Initial Public Offering   237
The Process of the IPO   239
Summary   243

PART IV
PLANNING FOR THE ENTREPRENEUR'S TRANSITION   **245**

15. Business Valuation   **247**
General Concepts That Guide the Determination of Value 247
Basic Information Required for a Valuation   252
Discounted Cash Flow   254
Market Comparison Techniques   266
Summary   270

16. Exit Planning   **273**
Self-Assessment Revisited   273
The Ethical Side of the Entrepreneur's Transition   275
A Model of Exit Planning   277
Exit Options   279
The Process of Selling a Business   284
Postexit Issues   286
Summary   286

Index   289
About the Authors   301

Preface

Courses in entrepreneurial finance have expanded rapidly across the country since the first edition of this book was published. However, even with the growing number of courses, the most common approach to presenting entrepreneurial finance still tends to place too much attention on venture capital and initial public offerings. Less than 1 percent of new ventures should even consider these financing vehicles. Entrepreneurial finance is not just about raising money and creating financial statements. Entrepreneurial finance should be an integral part of the basic management of any new and growing entrepreneurial venture.

Entrepreneurial Financial Management is written from an integrated, comprehensive perspective. The authors, who come from varied backgrounds and academic disciplines, came together to write a book that reflects the real world of entrepreneurial finance that is consistent with the foundations of the disciplines of entrepreneurship, finance, and accounting. The fundamental goal of this book is to present an applied, realistic view of entrepreneurial finance for today's entrepreneurs. This book provides an integrated set of concepts and applications, drawing from entrepreneurship, finance, and accounting, that will prepare aspiring entrepreneurs for the world they will most likely face as they start their new businesses. Although venture capital and public offerings are covered in this book, they have been put in their proper perspective. Very few entrepreneurs will ever receive financing from these sources, and almost no young entrepreneurs fresh out of college are even given consideration for venture capital financing. *Entrepreneurial Financial Management* is based on practical experience, but also is informed by theory.

The book is designed for applied- and experientially-based teaching strategies for entrepreneurial financial management. Each chapter has been written with the goal of facilitating the application of its contents to real-life businesses. It is a book that can serve as a reference for entrepreneurs and aspiring entrepreneurs for years to come.

KEY FEATURES

- The structure of this book is designed to basically follow the life cycle of a new business venture. Topics are presented in the order that entrepreneurs would likely face as they begin the process of business start-up and move into growing the business.

- A comprehensive discussion of funding sources is presented in Chapters 9–14. In the second edition, these chapters were restructured to provide a better overview of the financing over the life of a venture. This section begins with an examination of financing from the entrepreneur, friends, and family. It then moves to the external sources of funding that usually come late in the life of a business. In the third edition, these chapters have been updated to reflect changes in financing at all stages and from all sources that followed the Recession of 2008. Interviews with many of the funding sources are presented in boxes labeled "In their own words" throughout these chapters.
- Numerous examples are presented throughout the text.
- A comprehensive integrated financial statements template is included with this book. This Excel tool allows for the application of many of the concepts to actual businesses. The spreadsheet can be a supplement to the process of developing both a business model and a formal business plan. Step-by-step instructions with examples are presented in Chapter 6. The financial spreadsheet templates, which include product, service, and nonprofit alternatives for social entrepreneurship business models, are all available for unlimited free downloads at Dr. Cornwall's blog site: www.drjeffcornwall.com.
- A self-assessment is included to assist student entrepreneurs in integrating their own personal aspirations into their financial and business plans. There is also a partnership assessment that helps ensure that entrepreneurs working together on a new venture understand each other's goals, aspirations, values, and work ethics.
- *Opportunities for Application* is included at the end of most chapters.

ACKNOWLEDGMENTS

The authors would like to thank the reviewers who provided constructive feedback that helped shape the manuscript as it developed through all three editions of this book. Thanks as well to Katie Thayer for her work in conducting many of the interviews used in this book. Thanks to Betsy Lofgren for her help with the first edition of this book and Joseph Ormont with the second edition.

Entrepreneurial Financial Management

1 Introduction

THE IMPORTANCE OF KNOWING THE NUMBERS

Imagine moving to a foreign country where the people speak a different language from your own. While you may be able to get by for awhile without learning the language of this country, you will be severely hampered. Asking for and receiving simple information will be a tedious and frustrating task. For example, assume you want to find a coffeehouse with a wireless hotspot. How do you get to the coffeehouse? If you make it there, how do you order an espresso? How do you get a connection to the Internet? More complex tasks are an even bigger challenge. Imagine trying to rent an apartment. What does the landlady expect from you as a tenant? The contract she is requiring you to sign is completely unintelligible to you. Even an interpreter will help only so much. He can translate, but the process is slow and certain issues in the contract lose their precise meaning during the translation. And it would be impossible to rely on an interpreter all of the time.

Accounting is called the "language of business." Much of what is communicated about a business is done in this financial language. And, yet, to many entrepreneurs this is a language as foreign to them as the language of a foreign country is to a traveler. Accountants who work with entrepreneurs often report that most entrepreneurs know very little about accounting or finance. And many of those accountants have not been trained to work effectively with entrepreneurs and their private businesses. Most accountants' training focuses on working for large publicly traded companies. The application of accounting and financial principles to entrepreneurial ventures creates unique challenges. The success of new ventures often depends on entrepreneurs having the skills and knowledge necessary to manage this aspect of their businesses.

Financial statements reveal the general financial condition of a business. How profitable is the business? Can it pay its bills on time? Can it pay its loans? What is the value of the business? All these and many more questions can be answered by the financial statements of a company. This is critical information for outsiders, such as bankers and creditors, and for insiders, such as owners and managers.

3

Financial reports also can give crucial insight into the operating effectiveness of a business. They are often critical to making the right decisions. Which products make money? Should the company add a new type of service? When should management add more employees? Can the company afford to expand right now? These are questions that are answered through the language of accounting and finance. It is a myth that entrepreneurs can answer such questions simply based on intuition or gut feel.

The language of numbers in business is also the one used to communicate with those entities and people who provide funding for businesses. Bankers, venture capitalists, and investment angels all speak this language and expect the entrepreneurs with whom they work to be fluent in the language as well. None of these sources of funding will be satisfied with reports generated by a computer. All will want to have conversations with the entrepreneur about where the business has been and where it is going, using the language of business: financial data.

Some entrepreneurs believe that they can get by with a good accountant who can speak this language for them—an interpreter, if you will. However, because this language of business is so fundamentally important to understanding any business venture, it is critical that entrepreneurs learn to speak it fluently themselves. Entrepreneurs will not have credibility with investors if they do not know the language of business. More important, they will not be able to manage their business effectively as it grows unless they understand its financial condition.

MEASURING SUCCESS

The language of business can help answer the fundamental question: How successful is the business? The language of business can assess the profitability of the business, the strength of its cash flow, its market share, and its overall financial health. All these are important measures that help ensure the survival and sustainability of an entrepreneurial venture. They are all a part of how entrepreneurs measure the success of a business (Cornwall and Naughton 2003).

However, financial measurements are not the only ways entrepreneurs assess the success of their ventures. Other measures are required in order to understand what success truly means to each entrepreneur. This is not as simple as it may first appear.

Certainly success means the ability to earn a living from a business. For most entrepreneurs, success also is measured by the ability to earn a profit from the business. Profits are important to sustain the business, to create additional income for the owners, to pay off debt, and to create value in the business (see Chapter 15 for a more thorough discussion of business valuation). Other entrepreneurs measure success through the jobs they are able to create. For many entrepreneurs, success also is measured by the ability to create balance between work and family, work and leisure, or work and community activities such as volunteering. For example, Paul Orfalea, founder of Kinko's, says, "Success in life is having kids who want to come back to visit you when they've grown up." Every entrepreneur has a unique assessment of success.

The meaning of success often is derived from the entrepreneur's personal values and personal goals. For example, Bob Thompson, founder of a highway paving business in the upper Midwest, never felt real success in his business in spite of incredible growth in sales and profits over many years. It was not until he sold his paving business and gave huge bonuses (many over $1 million) to many of his employees that he finally felt he had achieved real success. For him, success came from the ability to share the wealth from his business with those who had helped him achieve that wealth. Kate Singleton started her photography business in Nashville, Tennessee, to create a long-term sustainable income. She has no interest in expanding or growing beyond the business she can accommodate herself. She does not want to have to add employees to grow her business. Success to her is meeting her basic lifestyle needs through the income from her business. Dr. Jim Stefansic, cofounder of Pathfinder Therapeutics, defines success for this venture as the ability to market a medical device that will improve patient outcomes. He also defines success as the ability to create a satisfactory return for the company's investors (Cornwall and Naughton 2008).

To be sure, some entrepreneurs measure success solely by the profits they can put directly into their own pockets. Many of the dot-com businesses of the 1990s were criticized for this approach. Their only goal was to create enough hype to take their business public and realize a quick financial windfall. Many never created profits, and some never even created revenues, yet they were able to create wealth for themselves through a quick turn of their businesses. Likewise, the disasters of Enron, Global Crossing, and the subprime mortgage meltdown of 2007–2008 represent what can occur when people in an organization are not well versed in the language of accounting and finance and have maximization of short-term returns as their only goal.

Those in the millennial generation have two primary measures of success. The first is lifestyle. Millennials view entrepreneurship as a career path that gives them more control over their lives and as a way to create balance between their careers and their families. This is particularly true among female millennials. They also seek personal fulfillment from their entrepreneurial careers, which they do not believe they will find in a more traditional business career. It also should be noted that many in the millennial generation see entrepreneurship as a tool to help enact social change. Success for them is not measured in terms of financial outcomes, but rather outcomes that reflect improvement in social conditions.

Chapter 2 will present a process of self-assessment that is used to help entrepreneurs understand what success really means to each of them. With this understanding, they are better able to know how to measure success for each unique business.

WHAT IS ENTREPRENEURIAL FINANCIAL MANAGEMENT?

Entrepreneurial finance is typically defined simply in terms of raising funds for a business. How can an entrepreneur raise funds to support a business venture as it grows? How does the entrepreneur attract venture capital? What is the process of taking a business public? All these can be critical questions that an entrepreneur may need to address for his or her business. However, when the topic is broadened to entrepreneurial financial management, many other critical issues emerge.

Entrepreneurial financial management is defined in terms of six general activities and functions in the business. First, entrepreneurial financial management includes setting clear financial goals for the business that are consistent with the aspirations of the entrepreneur who owns the venture. What are the income and wealth goals that the entrepreneur is pursuing through the business? How will the business need to perform in order to allow the entrepreneur to realize these financial goals? As will be discussed, the focus should not be on simply growing revenues as high and as quickly as possible. Instead, the focus should be on the profit goals that help the entrepreneur reach her aspirations from the business venture. The process of setting financial goals and engineering these goals into the planning of the business will be examined in Chapter 2.

Second, using financial statements and reports to manage a growing business and to make informed decisions is a key element of entrepreneurial financial management. This is the process of becoming fluent in the language of business and being able to specifically apply this language to the unique circumstances found in each business venture. Chapter 3 will introduce the basic concepts of financial reporting, and Chapter 7 examines the process of monitoring financial performance.

Third, entrepreneurial financial management includes forecasting. The entrepreneur and his team use forecasts as a guide to assess the progress of the business and to determine how well it is meeting expected results. Forecasts also are used to communicate the potential of a business venture to outside funding sources such as banks and venture capitalists. Forecasting future financial results has been described as more art than science. However, there are tools and techniques that can drastically improve the accuracy of forecasts. Revenue forecasts (Chapter 4) should be developed hand-in-hand with the financial goals of the owners (what revenues will be required to reach the profit goals established for the business). Also, revenue goals should be consistent with data obtained through the marketing plan. Expense forecasts are discussed in Chapter 5. Chapter 6 presents a spreadsheet model for forecasting financial statements that integrates the principles of effective revenue and expense forecasting.

Fourth, entrepreneurial financial management includes effective managing of what can be *the* most precious resource: cash. Cash flow often is described as the lifeblood of a business. Cash flow management includes both long-term planning for cash needs as well as day-to-day cash flow management. Chapter 8 examines various techniques and critical issues associated with cash flow management.

Fifth, entrepreneurial financial management does include raising funds for entrepreneurial ventures. However, before racing off to obtain external funds, the entrepreneur must examine the impact of debt and equity on her ability to reach her goals throughout the life of the business. There are some creative first steps toward financing. Chapters 9 and 10 explore these issues of financing over the life of a business and start-up financing using the entrepreneur's own resources and the resources of family and friends. Additionally, if managed properly, growing businesses can often generate funds internally through the creative application of critical business functions such as marketing, staffing, operations, and so forth. Chapter 11 examines how a collection of techniques known as bootstrapping can lower expenses and reduce the need to raise outside funding. Many businesses do need external support to grow. Chapters 12–14 provide a complete overview of the various sources of external funding, including both debt and equity sources of funds.

Figure 1.1   **Model for Entrepreneurial Financial Management**

Finally, entrepreneurial financial management includes the process of how the entrepreneur exits the business that she founded. All entrepreneurs eventually leave their businesses, either through planned exits, such as selling the business, going public, or transitioning to the next generation in a family business. Some exits, such as the death of the owner or bankruptcy, are not subject to careful planning. Chapter 16 summarizes exit planning and the exit process, which, as will be seen, should actually start at the very beginning of a business venture. Chapter 15 examines business valuation.

Figure 1.1 presents the model of entrepreneurial financial management used throughout this book. As shown, the process begins with a clear understanding of the financial goals of the entrepreneur, which is used to forecast and monitor performance. This model, based on the discovery-driven planning model developed by McGrath and MacMillan (1995), includes the assumption that profit goals should be clearly established and then engineered into the plans for a new venture.

WHAT MAKES ENTREPRENEURIAL FINANCE SIMILAR TO TRADITIONAL FINANCE?

There are both similarities and differences between entrepreneurial finance and traditional corporate finance. Traditional corporate finance consists of three interrelated segments: financial markets, investments, and financial management, which are sometimes called business finance. Although this book concentrates on business finance for entrepreneurial firms, managers in such firms also need to understand the other two areas in order to succeed. While the general principles of finance apply, early-stage firms and investors have different challenges compared to well-established corporations.

Entrepreneurs need to have some understanding of financial markets, their institutions, and their structures, because either directly or indirectly the company will have to access funds from them. Conceptually, financial markets can be divided into two general segments: capital markets and money markets. Capital markets are those that offer financing with a term of one year or more. Equity financing and long-term business loans fall into this category. Such financing is very attractive for businesses that need to buy long-term (capital) assets. Capital financing also is attractive for firms that may need "patient" financing that will last as a firm develops through a stage or stages where cash flows might not be adequate to pay back the principal immediately. Conversely, money markets have instruments whose term is less than one year. The purpose of the loan in this case is to help a firm survive through a period of short-term negative cash flow, such as meeting this week's payroll. The assumption is that cash collections will soon cause cash flows to be positive again and the loan will be paid back.

The perspective of investors also needs to be considered by entrepreneurs. In order to gain access to funding, entrepreneurs need to know the principles, expectations, and conditions that investors will have. In general:

1. Investors prefer less risk to more risk.
2. Diversified investors are primarily concerned with what is called nondiversifiable, systemic, or market risk.
3. Single-asset or nondiversified investors are concerned with the total risk of the investment, but such investors are relatively rare in the investment world.
4. Investors prefer more return to less.
5. Investors prefer the return to occur sooner rather than later.
6. Investors prefer more liquidity (the ability to turn an investment into cash) to less liquidity.
7. Investors face many different opportunities to invest their money, so raising funds is competitive; the entrepreneur's request for funds must reasonably appear to offer less risk, more return, a faster return, or more liquidity than other requests.
8. No investors are immune to these principles, expectations, and conditions.

WHAT MAKES ENTREPRENEURIAL FINANCE DIFFERENT FROM TRADITIONAL FINANCE?

What potentially makes an early stage company different compared to established, publicly traded corporations is the lack of company history that would allow investors to assess risk, the inability to compare the company with other firms because the industry may be so new, the difficulty of making a profit in the immediate future, and the lack of liquidity. An entrepreneur has to convince investors that despite all these difficulties, investing in the company is in their best interest. As one can imagine, this is quite a tough sell.

LACK OF HISTORICAL DATA TO MEASURE RISK

Traditional finance textbooks always contain an in-depth section on risk and return. A number of Nobel Prizes in Economics have been awarded to researchers in this area. The measures used to monitor risk, such as the standard deviations of stock returns and the stock's beta (a common measure of its riskiness), are extremely helpful in observing and understanding investor behavior with one caveat: historical data such as past stock prices are needed to calculate these risk measures. A recently started firm does not have tradable stock or, if it does, it does not have a long enough history of stock prices to allow statistical calculations. In addition, if a firm is creating a new product or service that has never existed before, then it cannot "borrow" data from the history of firms that have gone the same path. The framework of risk still exists, and investors view risk from this framework, but the means to accurately assess and measure it are not directly available.

TRADITIONAL FINANCIAL CONCEPTS OF RISK AND RETURN

Total risk is sometimes called stand-alone risk. This is conceptually the amount of risk that an investor faces when he holds ownership in only one asset. His fortune rises and falls based on what happens to that one company. If a supplier balks, customers defect, workers strike, or a meteor falls from the sky and hits the building, the investor could lose his entire net worth. An accepted proxy for total risk is the standard deviation of returns to the investment. For a stock, the return, R, would be $(P_1 - P_0)/P_0$. P_1 is the price at the end of a time period; P_0 is the price at the start of a time period, so the return is the percent increase or decrease in price during this period.

Squaring the difference between the return from one period and the period that follows, then dividing the sum of squared differences by the number of periods, results in a statistic called a *variance*.

$$\text{Variance} = \text{sum } (R_i - R_{avg}) \text{ squared}/N$$

where R_i = return in a particular period,
R_{avg} = average or mean return calculated over all available periods, and
N = number of periods of data available.

Taking the square root of the variance results in a statistic called the standard deviation.

$$\text{Standard deviation} = \text{square root of the variance}$$

The standard deviation is a measure of potential volatility from the average return on this stock. The greater this standard deviation value, the more dispersion of returns the stock experiences. In what statisticians would call a normal distribution or bell curve, returns that vary by one deviation or less from the average return on a stock have a 66 percent probability of occurring. Returns that fall two deviations or less from average have a 95 percent probability of occurring, and returns that fall three standard deviations or less from the average have a 99 percent probability of occurring. The implication is that investors who want to be 99 percent sure of what is going to happen to the investment in the coming year would calculate a range that starts at three standard deviations below the historical average return and ends three standard deviations above. If the standard deviation itself is a relatively large number, then this range of possible outcomes would be huge. Likewise, if the standard deviation is a very small number, then the range of possible outcomes known with 99 percent certainty would be somewhat narrow. Therefore, stocks with large standard deviations are riskier than stocks with small standard deviations because the range of possible outcomes is so great that it becomes very difficult to forecast what is likely to happen to the stock in any given time period.

However, the vast majority of investors are not single-asset investors. Most investors have diversified portfolios. Either they own a number of different stocks or they own investments like mutual funds, which are already diversified. From the investor's perspective, diversification causes a substantial amount of the total risk to disappear. If the investor owns stock in a hundred different companies, the concerns about unique incidents such as a labor strike or a meteor smashing one particular company are less significant. As a matter of fact, many of these company-specific situations may actually cancel each other out. For every company with bad labor relations, there may be another one with good relations. For every firm that gets hit by a meteor, the odds are equally likely that some other firm will discover gold under the lawn at corporate headquarters. The portion of total risk that disappears when portfolios are created is called *diversifiable risk.* Since the vast majority of investors are diversified investors, the financial markets value stocks based on the nondiversifiable risk. In other words, the relationship between risk and return is such that the markets price securities to compensate investors only for the nondiversifiable risk that exists in assets, not for the total risk. If an investor is not willing or smart enough to painlessly protect himself by diversification, then financial markets will not show him any mercy. Instead, they price securities on the assumption that everyone else is diversified as well. If an investor is not diversified, then that is his choice and he has to accept the consequences.

Total risk = diversifiable risk + nondiversifiable risk

A widely accepted measure used to proxy the nondiversifiable risk is called *beta.* Betas are usually estimated by regression analysis. Returns on the stock market are calculated for several periods in a row, and returns on a specific stock are calculated for those same time periods. Regression allows the analyst to identify the average change in a company's return given an average size change in the stock market's return. One can think of beta as the line that results from plotting stock market returns on a graph against the returns of the specific stock. This slope would represent how much the return on the specific stock changed given a change in the stock market on average.

$$R_i = A + \text{beta }(R_{mi})$$

where R_i = return on company in period i,
A = constant from regression, and
R_{mi} = return on the stock market in period i. Usually a market proxy such as the New York Stock Exchange Index or Standard and Poor's 500 Index is used to calculate this return.

Beta = change in return on stock/change in return on stock market

For instance, if the beta for a company is two, then when the stock market's return increases, the return on the company is expected to increase by twice that amount. On the downside, if the stock market falls, then the stock would fall twice as fast. The beta of two indicates that the stock is twice as volatile as the stock market. High-risk companies have betas greater than one, low-risk companies have betas of less than one, and average-risk companies have a beta of one. The comparison of an asset's return is made to the most diversified investment that one can have—a portfolio that mirrors the entire stock market. Hence, beta is a measure of nondiversifiable risk, because it is a relative measure compared to the most diversified portfolio available. Conceptually, when averaged over a long enough time period, it should reflect just the nondiversifiable (market-related) risk and none of the diversifiable (company-specific) risk.

An asset's *required rate of return* is a minimum return necessary to compensate an investor for risk. The relationship between nondiversifiable risk and an asset's required rate of return is denoted by a concept called the *security market line*.

$$\text{Required rate of return} = R_f + \text{beta } (R_m - R_f)$$

where R_f = *risk-free rate* such as found with U.S. government treasury notes, and R_m = average return on market portfolio proxy.

Verbally, this says that an investor should demand to earn at least the risk-free rate (which can be proxied by the rate on U.S. government treasury notes). If the entrepreneur wants the investor to accept more risk, then the return should also include a *risk premium* or additional compensation above the risk-free rate. The size of this risk premium is thought to be equal to the beta times the *market risk premium* or the difference between the return on the stock market and the risk-free rate.

$$\text{Market risk premium} = R_m - R_f$$

For instance, if a stock has a beta of two (meaning it is twice as volatile as the stock market), then the investor should demand a risk premium that is twice the size of the market risk premium. Likewise, if a stock's beta is 0.5 (meaning it is only half as volatile as the stock market), then the investor should demand a risk premium that is half the size of the market risk premium.

The beauty of the concepts of traditional finance is that they provide a framework for investors to understand that there are two kinds of risk, and the market will most likely consider only the nondiversifiable risk in estimating an asset's required rate of return. The drawback is that while these concepts provide insight, they are not always easily measured and quantified.

How the Lack of Historical Data and Liquidity Complicates the Practice of Finance in Early Stage Firms

The financial concepts of risk and return as presented above are extremely valuable in understanding the perspective of investors who supply the funds necessary to start and grow early stage firms. For established firms with publicly traded stock, these concepts not only provide insight, but also can be applied to historical data to measure such things as an asset's return, variance, standard deviation, beta, and required rate of return.

For early stage firms that do not have a past history of stock prices and other data, these measurements cannot take place and must be inferred and estimated instead. Further complicating the calculations is the fact that even if prices, returns, and so on could somehow be substituted or borrowed from other similar firms, the relevance would still be highly questionable. First, there is the difficulty of finding truly comparable firms that happen to be publicly traded. Second, the mere fact that an early stage firm is not tradable means that there will be a huge difference in the value and accuracy of the calculations because of the liquidity difference. Conceivably, there can be a difference of as much as 50 percent between a firm that has tradable stock and one that does not.

Therefore, an entrepreneur who tries to use traditional, mathematically based finance techniques for a company that lacks historically measurable data as well as liquidity is like a carpenter who tries to build a house by measuring timber with a micrometer, marking a line with chalk, and then cutting with an ax. The general principles of building a house are the same whether the carpenter uses a laser-guided saw or an ax, but if access to the high-tech saw is a physical impossibility, then general principles and benchmarks must be used instead. For entrepreneurial finance this situation is the same. If historical data are not available, the option of using mathematically sophisticated techniques is not possible; instead, general principles and benchmarks must be used.

An entrepreneur competes for funding from investors who have a wide universe of investment options. While these principles are derived from traditional finance theory, the challenge for the entrepreneur is the application of these principles without the advantage of having direct access to the data and tools that a traditional finance person would have.

USING STAKEHOLDER ANALYSIS TO GUIDE ETHICAL DECISION MAKING

A common challenge faced by all entrepreneurs is identifying and putting into practice the basic ethical standards that will guide their businesses. Ethical issues and challenges arise in all aspects of entrepreneurial financial management. A common framework that helps entrepreneurs navigate ethical issues is based on a stakeholder analysis. Stakeholders are interested parties beyond the owners of a business who have a stake in the decisions made in that business and in the outcomes of those decisions.

The first step in a stakeholder analysis is to identify the relevant stakeholders. There is no standard list because the stakeholders vary from business to business. The list also can vary based on the values of each entrepreneur. Common stakeholders for entrepreneurs include family, partners, investors, employees, customers, suppliers, creditors, and the local community. The list also can include interest groups, trade associations, and unions. Entrepreneurs need to clearly identify their own stakeholders based on personal values and the demands and relationships created by the business.

The second step is to determine the basic ethical principles and values that guide the entrepreneur's interaction with each of these stakeholders. These values may be shaped by generally held beliefs of right and wrong, religious convictions, or a

Table 1.1

Example of Stakeholder Analysis

Stakeholder	Ethical principle or value	Application for financial resource management
Family	Create balance between work demands and family time.	Establish a more moderate financial growth goal to allow for time with family.
Investors (e.g., angel investors, venture capitalists)	Deal with all investors openly and honestly.	Develop a financial reporting system that provides full and accurate historical information as well as realistic forecasts.
Employees	Share financial success with those that helped create it.	Modify financial goals and expense forecasts to allow for programs such as health insurance, profit sharing, stock option plans, phantom stock, ESOP, etc., while still meeting goals of entrepreneur.
Customers	Fair pricing	Establish revenue forecasts that are realistic given this pricing principle.
Suppliers	Prompt payment of money owed.	Establish cash forecasts that are based on an assumption of prompt payment of all invoices submitted by suppliers/vendors.
Banker	Honest disclosure of information.	Assure timely and accurate financial reporting that goes beyond the minimum required by terms of their loans. Also, to assure reasonable financial forecasting that is based on well tested business models.
Community	Company should be source of reliable employment for the community.	Manage cash flow to allow for stable employment even during times of temporary slowdowns.

specific moral code. It is important to develop specific applications of these principles and values as they apply to each stakeholder. For example, an entrepreneur who feels a strong, long-term commitment to his employees will consider their welfare whenever he makes a major decision, such as expanding the business; he may establish a no-layoff policy to ensure that his employees have their employment with his company protected.

The third step is to apply these principles specifically to the financial resource management of the business. In our example, the entrepreneur may insist on careful review of financial forecasts to ensure that any new employees hired during the expansion can be supported financially by his business even under a worst-case scenario. Table 1.1 displays an example of how these three steps might look for a hypothetical business. Note the level of specificity that is achieved by the third column. This specificity fosters the likelihood that the principles will be put into action by the entrepreneur and by his employees. Many entrepreneurs find it helpful to communicate these principles in writing to all employees and even the stakeholders themselves.

Over the long term, the challenge to the entrepreneur is to create a culture based on ethical principles. The culture of a business is created with the very first actions and decisions of its founder. As the business grows, the founder must rely on this culture to guide the actions of employees. No entrepreneur can be in all places at all times.

Entrepreneurs who expect an ethical culture and ethical actions by their workforce must embody these same ethics in every action they take.

SUMMARY

This chapter has presented the basic foundation and model of entrepreneurial financial resource management that will guide the rest of this book. Part I, which begins with Chapter 2, will discuss the process of building a financial forecast. Part II examines various aspects of managing the financial resources of an entrepreneurial venture. Part III presents issues related to financing. Finally, Part IV considers the issues of planning the transition of the entrepreneur out of the business. Also included in this book are a self-assessment instrument to help entrepreneurs begin this critical part of financial planning for the venture and a financial template that will help entrepreneurs create financial forecasts.

DISCUSSION QUESTIONS

1. Why is accounting considered the language of business? Why is it important for the entrepreneur to learn this language?
2. How will you measure your success in your business or entrepreneurial career?
3. What are the six activities that make up entrepreneurial financial management, and why are they important?
4. How is entrepreneurial finance both similar to, and different from, traditional finance?

OPPORTUNITY FOR APPLICATION

1. Interview an entrepreneur to learn how he or she measures success. Is career success defined only in financial terms, or are other yardsticks used to measure success?

REFERENCES

Cornwall, J., and M. Naughton. 2008. *Bringing Your Business to Life.* Ventura, CA: Regal Books.
———. 2003. "Who Is the Good Entrepreneur? An Exploration Within the Catholic Social Tradition." *Journal of Business Ethics* 44 (1): 61–75.
McGrath, R., and I. MacMillan. 1995. "Discovery-Driven Planning." *Harvard Business Review* (July–August): 4–12.

PART I

BUILDING A FINANCIAL FORECAST

2 Setting Financial Goals

In the excitement of starting and growing a business, many entrepreneurs fail to systematically evaluate their own personal goals in relationship to their business ventures. What income do they need? What are their long-term income goals? When do they want to retire? What lifestyle will they want in retirement? How much money will they need to set aside for their children's education? These questions suggest just some of the personal financial goals that need to be integrated into the business plan. Many nonfinancial goals involving family, hobbies, friends, religious commitments, and community groups are important as well. This chapter offers a framework that helps the entrepreneur to integrate a personal assessment with the business planning of the entrepreneurial venture as displayed in Figure 2.1.

WEALTH VERSUS INCOME

It is critical for the entrepreneur to understand that there are two types of financial goals to be considered: income and wealth. By understanding how a business creates income and wealth, the entrepreneur is better able to engineer personal financial goals into the business plan. Simply put, income is the cash that is available from the business to pay the entrepreneur's salary, whereas wealth is the value of the business if sold. Certainly, entrepreneurs may also build wealth through savings from the salary they draw, but for most entrepreneurs their single most valuable asset by far is their business.

Income is fairly simple to understand, as it is the means to meet the day-to-day, month-to-month, and year-to-year monetary needs of the entrepreneur and her family. The entrepreneur should plan not only for short-term income needs but also for long-term needs. It is a myth that bankers are impressed by business plans that show

Figure 2.1 **Model for Entrepreneurial Financial Management**

the entrepreneur taking no income from the business for a long period of time. In fact, to many bankers and other investors, this is a red flag. They have seen too many entrepreneurs who give up on a business that does create enough cash to adequately pay the entrepreneur. Certainly, bankers and investors do not want to find excessive salary being paid to the entrepreneur early on, as they may be funding part or all of this salary through their loans and investments. On the other hand, a business plan that includes a modest, reasonable salary for the entrepreneur is not only acceptable but also desirable for most financial backers.

Stanley and Danko's best-selling book *The Millionaire Next Door* (1996) gives insight into the differences between wealth and income. They point out that many people confuse real wealth with the trappings of wealth. True wealth is the difference between what someone owns less the debts that are owed. Living in a big house or driving an expensive car may give the impression that someone is wealthy. However, many people rely heavily on debt to fund such purchases. If the big house and expensive car are purchased mostly with debt, there is little actual wealth. Stanley and Danko cite an old Texas saying, "Big hat, no cattle," to express the illusion of wealth without the reality.

In their book, Stanley and Danko report the results of their research on millionaires, how they live, and how they created their own wealth. Two-thirds of the millionaires they studied are self-employed, and three out of four of these consider themselves entrepreneurs (the other one-fourth are self-employed professionals, such as physicians or lawyers). Most of the entrepreneurs own a "dull" business rather than a high-tech, high-growth venture; they are contractors, auctioneers, farmers, mobile home park owners, pest controllers, coin and stamp dealers, and office building cleaners. Most live on a fairly modest median taxable income of $131,000; their average wealth is $1.6 million. They live in typical upper-middle-class neighborhoods with an average home value of $320,000, although they average about 6.5 times the wealth of their neighbors. Most reported that they buy inexpensive suits and drive American cars that are at least a couple of years old.

Since most of the wealth of entrepreneurs comes from the value of their business, it is important to understand how businesses are valued. Formal business valuation uses a variety of financial models. Such formal valuation is critical when buying or selling a business. However, many entrepreneurs find it helpful to use a "quick and dirty" method of valuation to monitor progress in building value in their businesses as they grow. Most forms of valuation, whether formal or "quick and dirty," share a common assumption. The real value of a business is its potential to generate profits or, more specifically, cash in the future. A very simple form of "quick and dirty" valuation works as follows:

1. Start with the most recent year-end profits of the business using the measure known as earnings before interest, taxes, depreciation, and amortization (EBIT-DA). EBITDA is used because it tends to reflect the cash profits that are generated by the operations of the business. Interest and taxes are considered unique to the current owners of the business and how the business is legally structured. Depreciation and amortization are ignored because they are noncash items.

2. Add back to EBITDA any unusually high bonuses or other extra compensation beyond a normal salary paid to the owners.
3. Evaluate the growth potential of the business based on recent growth in profits over the past three years.
4. Evaluate any important industry or market trends that might either improve or decrease profits in the next three years.
5. Assign a *profit multiple*, which is a number that is used to multiply the current profits of a business in order to estimate the value of future profits. The profit multiple typically ranges from three to eight times profits, based on the estimate of the expected growth in future profits. A profit multiple of three to four generally indicates that profits are expected to remain steady or may decline, four to five indicates that profits will remain steady or increase modestly, and six and higher suggests that profits are expected to increase significantly.
6. Multiply the profits by the profit multiple to determine the value of the business.
7. Finally, subtract bank debt such as lines of credit or mortgages to determine the estimate of value of the business *to the entrepreneur.*

For example, assume a business had EBITDA profits of $250,000 last year, and the entrepreneur gave herself a bonus of $50,000 over her normal salary that same year. Although the business had strong profit growth over the past several years, there are strong indications that this growth may be difficult to sustain due to changing market conditions. The business has $100,000 in long-term bank debt. The entrepreneur decides that given the positive impact of historical growth in profits in the business, tempered by the less-than-positive outlook in the industry, she will use a mid-range multiple of five times profits. Her calculation would look like this:

EBITDA	$250,000
Plus one-time bonus	50,000
Adjusted EBITDA	$300,000
Times the profit multiple	× 5
Value of business	$1,500,000
Minus business debt	100,000
Quick and dirty estimate of value of business to owner	$1,400,000

Remember that this is not considered a formal valuation. Rather, it is simply a means for the entrepreneur to create an estimate. However, it is not unusual for those seeking to purchase a business to use this method of valuation. Formal valuations can often lead to very different estimates due to factors not addressed in this quick and dirty approach. For example, an entrepreneur estimates the value of his prototyping business at $3 million. However, when he begins negotiations to sell his business, he is delighted that the initial offer is more than twice that figure. Apparently he has created a strong market niche and very loyal customers for which the buyer is willing to pay a premium. In contrast, another entrepreneur who owns a counseling center is greatly disappointed by the offer she receives. She has estimated the value of her business to be $800,000. However, prospective buyers are concerned that most of the profit is tied to the services she provides to patients at the center. The only way that future profits will continue would be if she continues to work as hard as she always has. Since the potential buyers think that she is using the sale to work into retirement, they all make offers that are less than half of what she estimated. Valuation will be discussed more fully in Chapter 15.

Specific goals for wealth can be difficult to plan for, particularly when first starting a business. However, many entrepreneurs will use the wealth that they create from their businesses for long-term needs such as retirement. Therefore, it is important for the entrepreneur to at least estimate when he wants to retire (e.g., at the early age of fifty or the more traditional age of sixty-five) and how much wealth he will need for the lifestyle he wants to maintain during retirement. The self-assessment process can help the entrepreneur begin to think concretely about these types of issues and to then build them into the criteria used to evaluate potential business ventures. However, before moving to the specifics of the self-assessment, it is important to recognize that there are nonfinancial goals that should also be considered.

INTEGRATING NONFINANCIAL GOALS INTO THE BUSINESS

A gifted computer specialist sought assistance from an entrepreneurship professor in getting his cash flow and financing under control.

> He had identified a market niche for a computer application he had been developing with his previous employer. The employer was not interested in the idea, so the entrepreneur gained permission to take the idea and start his own company to develop and market the product. He had methodically refined the concept and done a remarkable job in making the program operational and ready for market. He reported that he was on the verge of breaking through into the market, but was "dealing with some financial distress." If he could raise a little more money, he would be able to make the business profitable. When asked how bad his financial condition was, he matter-of-factly stated that he had funded his start-up primarily through his life savings (i.e., cashed his retirement accounts) and through a second mortgage on his home. He had gotten "a little behind" on his loan repayment and lost his house. This frustrated his wife, who took their children and left him. And, oh yes, he was about to have his car repossessed. But he only needed to raise another $50,000 and he could deliver his product to several customers. He did raise the funds and did become financially successful. However, at what cost? He . . . left behind a trail of damage to his family, friends, creditors, and many others. (Naughton and Cornwall 2001)

Another entrepreneur faced a different problem:

> Cathy Cotton works like a maniac. From 9 a.m. until midnight, Cotton toils away at Meta-Search Inc., her two-year-old . . . technical recruiting company. At midnight an alarm in Cotton's . . . office goes off—her way of reminding herself to quit working. But more often than not, she ignores the clock and keeps going. She typically heads home between 2 a.m. and 4 a.m. (Gruner 1997)

Many entrepreneurs create ventures, such as those in the examples above, that consume all their time and focus. It is understood that many jobs go through periods where long hours are required. This is very common when starting a new business as well. However, the entrepreneur in the second example has a business that is now two years old and she shows no sign of changing her behavior. According to Cornwall and Naughton (2008), there is a growing recognition of the importance of creating a more tempered approach to work and a more balanced life, even during an entrepreneurial start-up. Without addressing the issue of temperance of work and balance in life, entrepreneurs risk damaging their physical and mental health, as well as their relationships with family and friends.

In addition to the financial goals discussed above, entrepreneurs should establish specific nonfinancial goals. Before launching a business, entrepreneurs should consider questions like the following:

- How much time do you want to spend with your family?
- What other interests or hobbies do you want to be able to continue to pursue?
- Do you want to continue your formal education?
- Do you have other aspirations that you want to pursue at some point in your life?

These nonfinancial goals can be even more important than financial goals for some entrepreneurs. This is particularly true for those who are part of the millennial generation. For example, one entrepreneur had a goal to always be at home for dinner with his family when he was in town. Sometimes this meant that he had to go back to work to finish an important project, but he made sure to integrate this commitment into his work. Another entrepreneur was faced with the possibility of an initial public offering for his business. Experts told him that he could expect a large personal return from the offering. However, he realized that taking his business public would mean a great deal of travel that would keep him away from his family. Instead, he chose to find a buyer for his business so he could spend even more time with his children before they grew up. Although the sale resulted in a good financial return, it was a fraction of what he could have received from a public offering. To him, however, the trade-off was well worth it.

The entrepreneur should integrate nonfinancial goals into business planning. Many nonfinancial goals revolve around the ability to dedicate time to family, friends, or other interests. Rapid business growth is one of the major drains on the entrepreneur's time. When planning the business, the entrepreneur may choose to plan for growth that allows some balance in life, rather than planning for the maximum growth the market will allow.

THE IMPORTANCE OF SELF-ASSESSMENT

The process of self-assessment plays an important role for the entrepreneur throughout the life of the business. Aspirations for income and wealth can change over time, so it is important to periodically revisit the process of self-assessment. Lifestyle changes such as getting married or having children require an adjustment to both short-term

Figure 2.2 **Life Cycle of a Business Venture**

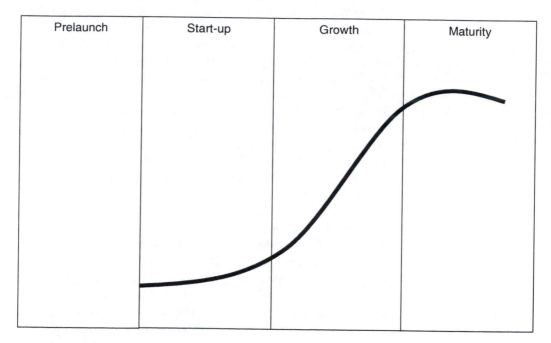

Prelaunch	Start-up	Growth	Maturity

and long-term financial goals. For example, the addition of children to the family means that the entrepreneur needs to plan for added day-to-day expenses, as well as possible long-term costs such as college and weddings.

Changes in lifestyle also can create new nonfinancial goals. For example, an entrepreneur who was single when she started the business marries and eventually has children. She will need to be able to take maternity leave. She may also want to have more time to spend with her children as they grow up. To meet these new nonfinancial goals, she may need to add management staff to take some of the burden from her workload and to cover for her when her new family requires she take time away from her business. She may also decide to temper the growth of her business and forgo opportunities to expand sales or move into new markets.

Changes in aspirations also can occur if ventures either exceed or fall well short of initial expectations, and entrepreneurs need to adjust their expectations accordingly. For example, assume that an entrepreneur had hoped to be able to earn $100,000 a year from his business. But after the business has been in operation for a few years, it becomes clear that this goal is unrealistic: he can earn only $75,000 from the business. The entrepreneur needs to bring his personal financial goals in line with the reality of the true earning power of the venture or choose to exit the venture and pursue a more promising business that can meet the income needs created by his desired lifestyle.

Figure 2.2 displays the distinct phases of growth and development that businesses go through. During each stage, both the entrepreneurial venture and the entrepreneur go through transitions and changes (Churchill 1983). Each stage of development can lead to changes in goals and aspirations.

The first stage is prelaunch, during which the entrepreneur develops the business model and plan and does all the work necessary to open the business, such as securing needed resources, setting up operations, and hiring and training staff. Self-assessment can play a prominent role in the planning of a new venture. In evaluating opportunities and conducting feasibility analyses, the primary criterion is the financial viability of the business idea under consideration. Some entrepreneurs mistakenly assume that breaking even equates to financial feasibility. In reality, to be financially viable the new venture must not only break even, but also meet the financial needs and expectations of the entrepreneur and other investors. Many entrepreneurs fail to factor in their own financial goals during this critical step in evaluating opportunities. Goals like "making a lot of money" or "providing for my family" are not specific enough to integrate into the planning process. Entrepreneurs should take the time to assess their specific expectations of income and wealth from their business venture and integrate those expectations into the feasibility analysis and business planning. It is hard to imagine that someone applying for a management position in a publicly traded company would enter negotiations for the job without a salary and benefit goal in mind. Yet, many entrepreneurs do just that when planning their own ventures.

The second stage is start-up. This is when the venture is launched and begins basic operations. This stage can last until the business is producing well over $1 million in revenue. The entrepreneur is usually very hands-on with the business during this stage, building a customer base and refining the product or service to meet the needs of the market. The start-up of any business can be a time of much excitement and confusion. Many entrepreneurs suddenly identify additional opportunities that were not part of their original plans. There also is a tendency to help cash flow by taking on any orders that come through the door. While this may be necessary, the entrepreneur should have a well-developed plan based on thoughtful self-assessment in order to keep the business focused and headed in the desired direction. Entrepreneurs who stray off-course from their plans in order to reduce their anxiety over cash flow can sometimes lock themselves into a business model that will not let them achieve the personal goals and objectives they hoped to achieve through their businesses. Therefore, any change in direction for a new start-up business should be carefully evaluated.

The third stage is growth. This is when revenues and, hopefully, profits begin to grow quickly. However, the growth phase of a business can be one of the most perilous periods for an entrepreneurial venture. The business may begin to experience many stresses and strains on systems and staff. Flamholtz and Randle, in their book *Growing Pains* (2007), call this the transition from an entrepreneurship to a professionally managed business. During this transition, the entrepreneur's role begins to change. She no longer can use the hands-on, day-to-day management style she used during the start-up. Management and operating systems need to be put in place and upgraded to manage growth effectively. The management team begins to grow and take on ever-increasing responsibilities. One entrepreneur who successfully navigated this transition stated that his "business took on a life of its own." This is a common feeling. Growth is pursued simply because the business can grow. However, the reason that the entrepreneur started the business—that is, her own goals and aspirations—can become blurred and even secondary in importance to the growing body of decision makers. It becomes crucial for the entrepreneur to reinstill her own goals and vision into the business. This may not be as easy as it first appears. However, it is still her company, and she must undertake its leadership based on a strong vision of where the business is headed. This vision should be fundamentally based on the entrepreneur's own goals and aspirations, which may require revisiting the self-assessment process to make sure that any changes in the entrepreneur's goals and aspirations are accurately reflected.

The fourth stage is maturity, which can include the exit of the entrepreneur from the business. Every entrepreneur exits from the business at some point, whether by selling the business, transitioning to the next generation in a family business, going bankrupt, or simply dying. The process of preparing for this departure is called *exit planning*. Most experts recommend beginning the exit planning process at the very beginning of a business venture. They recommend that the entrepreneur be clear on what he wants from the business, how long he wants to be involved in the business, and what he would like to see happen to the business once he leaves. Clearly the exit process, if well executed, relies on careful and thoughtful self-assessment. It is important to note that most ventures do not evolve exactly as planned and that exits do not always happen as the entrepreneur originally intended. However, that does not diminish the importance of such planning. Chapter 16 will examine the exit process in more detail.

THE SELF-ASSESSMENT PROCESS

There are many ways in which entrepreneurs can evaluate their goals and aspirations. In this book, we draw upon self-assessment models developed by Cornwall and Carter (1999) for the individual entrepreneur (Appendix 2.1) and by Cornwall (2006) for those entrepreneurs planning to enter into a new venture as partners (Appendix 2.2).

The first section of the individual self-assessment in Appendix 2.1 helps entrepreneurs begin the process of identifying priorities. In this section, entrepreneurs are asked to identify their financial goals, including both income goals and wealth goals. These goals should be very specific and measurable (being "really rich" is not a measurable goal). These personal financial goals become the basis for setting the financial goals of the entrepreneur's business. For example, an entrepreneur starting a business right out of college may set an income goal of reaching the average salary of college classmates who went into traditional industry jobs by the third year of her business venture, recognizing that in the first two years she will probably make less income due to the demands of start-up. By the fifth year, her goal is to make 50 percent more than her former classmates. Her wealth goals include having enough wealth to retire at fifty so she can pursue her other interests in life and having enough invested to pay her children's college expenses no matter where they want to go to school.

But the self-assessment moves well beyond financial goals. Nonfinancial goals also are included in the questionnaire. As simple as these questions may first appear, they can provoke powerful discernment if approached with honesty and careful thought. One entrepreneur realized after completing his self-assessment that his preoccupation with his company's rapid growth and success had caused him to forget how important his family was to him. Realizing that he had not been able to spend any time with his children for the past year, he decided to build more family time into his business planning in the future. He had reached a point of financial stability, but needed to spend more time addressing his family's stability. Several questions in this section help entrepreneurs define success on their own terms. Success in business, family, and friendship are all parts of a single "equation." And each entrepreneur evaluates success in a different way. The end of this section challenges entrepreneurs to clearly identify the core values that they bring to the business. These are the values that will shape the business ethics of the entrepreneur (see Chapter 1).

The second section of the individual self-assessment questionnaire includes more specific questions regarding personal readiness and personal preferences that can shape how an entrepreneur approaches a new business. These personal preferences and characteristics also should be integrated into the business planning process. For example, entrepreneurs have varying tolerances for risk. All businesses include some degree of financial risk. But entrepreneurs also need to consider nonfinancial risks, such as reputation, career advancement, and additional stress on a family. Some people can tolerate much more risk than others. The level of risk tolerance can be used to determine if a particular venture is the right one for a given entrepreneur to pursue. Such understanding also should be considered in planning how large a venture will become and how rapid a growth plan should be pursued.

Many self-assessments include additional items such as idea generation exercises; thorough evaluations of skills, knowledge, and competencies; personality assessments; and vocational assessments. Although these are important processes to go through in pre-venture planning, they move beyond the scope of setting financial (and nonfinancial) goals for the business. Setting financial goals is the foundation of entrepreneurial financial management.

When entrepreneurs consider entering into a business with other people, all the potential partners need to discuss the types of issues identified in the individual self-assessment. But there are additional issues that should be discussed and understood among the potential partners well before any formal agreement to create a corporation or partnership is pursued. The assessment in Appendix 2.2 can foster an open, honest discussion among the potential partners or shareholders. It addresses goals and aspirations, work ethic, work habits, priorities in life, ability to meet financial obligations the business may face, leadership roles, and ethical values.

It is not unusual for one or more of the potential partners to have a change of heart and decide not to enter into the venture after talking through these issues. That is a good outcome from this assessment. Once people have entered into a corporation or partnership, it can be very expensive and complicated to disentangle the business relationship.

The partnership and shareholder assessment can be used to sort out critical issues that should then be put into legal language by an attorney in a partnership or shareholder agreement. This process should be completed well before any new venture is actually launched.

THE BUSINESS MODEL AND BUSINESS PLAN

Once entrepreneurs have a clear understanding of their financial goals and the business goals needed to achieve their personal goals, these goals should be used to build a *business model* and eventually generate the *business plan* if outside funding is needed for the business. Osterwalder and Pigneur (2010) define a business model as a method used to describe "the rationale of how an organization creates, delivers, and captures value" (p.14). When developing a business model, it is typically done with a visual representation of the various aspects of the venture. Osterwalder and Pigneur (2010) have developed a business model canvas to help the entrepreneur visually represent the key aspects of generating revenue streams through understanding the value proposition offered to the targeted customer segments. The business model canvas also helps identify what it will take in terms of resources, activities, and a network of support to make the organization work toward delivery of the value proposition. Entrepreneurs should always keep their goals in mind when developing a business model to ensure that their ventures can support their pursuits of income and wealth through the business.

The business plan is a comprehensive document describing the intended course that the entrepreneur wants the business to take. It is developed from the business model and used to translate the visual model into a written document that can be used to communicate the details that support the model to outsiders, such as bankers and investors. Figure 2.3 displays a sample outline for a comprehensive business plan. Such an outline is just an example, because each business plan should be tailored for its specific use. For example, business plans used to generate equity financing (see Chapters 12 and 14) should include more detail throughout. Generally, all business plans should include the same comprehensive, fully integrated set of financial forecasts as will be generated by following the process presented in Chapters 3–6.

SUMMARY

This chapter presented a model for financial goal setting. The difference between income and wealth was examined. The importance of thoughtful, thorough personal self-assessment to assist in setting business goals was outlined for each stage of a firm's life cycle. Finally, two models for self-assessment were presented. Chapter 3 explains the basic financial statements used in all business ventures.

DISCUSSION QUESTIONS

1. Discuss the difference between wealth and income. Why is this distinction important for an entrepreneur to understand?
2. What nonfinancial goals are important to you? How can you integrate these goals into your career planning?

OPPORTUNITY FOR APPLICATION

1. Complete the self-assessment in Appendix 2.1 or Appendix 2.2. What did you learn about yourself after completing this questionnaire? How will you integrate what you learned into your business planning?

Figure 2.3 **Business Plan Outline**

I. Executive Summary (one-page summary of the entire plan)
II. The Business Concept
    1. Vision of company
    2. Mission statement description of the business model
    3. Core values
III. Value Proposition and Industry Analysis
    1. Change and "market pain" that created the opportunity
    2. Size and status of the industry (growing, mature, declining)
    3. Trends in the industry and within the specific market
    4. Barriers to entry
IV. Marketing Plan
    1. Target market
       • Description
       • Results of market research and proof of concept
       • Entry strategy
    2. Competitive analysis
    3. Product positioning
    4. Pricing
    5. Promotional plan
    6. Distribution (place)
V. Operating Plan
    1. Mapping out the flow of all aspects of the business
       • Raw materials and supplies
       • Making the product or providing the service
       • Sales process—customer contact from beginning to end
       • Bookkeeping and billing
    2. Team
    3. Advisers
    4. Space requirements and costs
    5. Basic staffing plan as the company grows
VI. Financial Plan
    1. Key financial assumptions
    2. Sources of financing
    3. Financial forecast, including projected financial statements

REFERENCES

Churchill, N. 1983. "Entrepreneurs and Their Enterprises: A Stage Model." In *Frontiers of Entrepreneurship Research*, ed. J.A. Hornaday et al., pp. 1–22. Babson Park, MA: Babson College.

Cornwall, J. 2006. *Partnership and Shareholder Assessment.* Monograph published by the Center for Entrepreneurship, Belmont University, Nashville, TN.

Cornwall, J., and N. Carter. 1999. *University of St. Thomas Entrepreneurial Self-Assessment: Start-Up.* Monograph published by the John M. Morrison Center for Entrepreneurship, University of St. Thomas, St. Paul, MN.

Cornwall, J., and M. Naughton. 2008. *Bringing Your Business to Life.* Ventura, CA: Regal Books.

Flamholtz, E., and Y. Randle. 2007. *Growing Pains.* 4th ed. San Francisco: Jossey-Bass.

Gruner, S. 1997. "Get a Life!" *Inc.*, October.

Naughton, M., and J. Cornwall. 2001. "The Good Entrepreneur and the Role of Virtue." Presented to the 11th International Symposium on Ethics, Business and Society, Barcelona, Spain, July.

Osterwalder, A., and Y. Pigneur. 2010. *Business Model Generation.* Hoboken, NJ: Wiley.

Stanley, T., and W. Danko. 1996. *The Millionaire Next Door.* Atlanta, GA: Longstreet Press.

APPENDIX 2.1. INDIVIDUAL ENTREPRENEURIAL SELF-ASSESSMENT

SECTION I. PERSONAL ASPIRATIONS AND PRIORITIES

- What gets you excited, gives you energy, and motivates you to excel?
- What do you like to do with your time?
- What drains energy from you?
    - In the work you do:
    - In personal relationships:
- How do you measure success in your personal life?
    - Family:
    - Friends and relationships:
    - Personal interests and hobbies:
    - Contributions to community and society:
- What do you consider success in your business and career?
    - Short-term:
    - Long-term:
- What are your specific goals for your personal life?
    - Family:
    - Friends and relationships:
    - Personal interests and hobbies:
    - Contributions to community and society:
- What are your goals for your business and career?
    - Income and lifestyle:
    - Wealth:
    - Free time:
    - Recognition and fame:
    - Impact on community:
    - Other:
- What do you want to be doing:
    - In one year:
    - In five years:
    - In ten years:
    - At retirement:

Core Values

- List the core personal values that you intend to bring to your business (e.g., treating people fairly, giving something back to the community).
- Where does each of these core values come from (religious faith, family, etc.)?
- Why is each of them important to you?

SECTION II. PERSONAL ENTREPRENEURIAL READINESS

- What are the major reasons you want to start a business?
- How many hours are you willing and able to put into your new venture?

- How would you describe your tolerance for uncertainty and risk?
- Do you easily trust other people working with you on a common activity? Why or why not?
- How much financial risk are you willing to take with your new venture (personal assets, personal debt, etc.)?
- Assume you decide not to start your business. A short time later, you see that someone has started the same business and is doing well. How would you feel? Why?
- What are the nonfinancial risks for you in starting a new business?
- How do you react to failure? Give examples.
- How do you react in times of personal stress? How do you deal with stress in your life?
- How much income do you need to support your current lifestyle?
- How long could you survive without a paycheck?
- How much money do you have available to start your business?
- Which of your personal assets would you be willing to borrow against, or sell, to start your business?
- Whose support (nonfinancial) is important for you to have before starting your business (family, spouse, etc.)?

Source: This self-assessment is adapted from J. Cornwall and N. Carter, *University of St. Thomas Entrepreneurial Self-Assessment: Start-Up.* Monograph published by the John M. Morrison Center for Entrepreneurship, University of St. Thomas, St. Paul, MN, 1999. Used with permission.

APPENDIX 2.2. PARTNERSHIP AND SHAREHOLDER ASSESSMENT

1. Each partner or shareholder should complete the following assessment individually.
2. The partners and shareholders should then openly, honestly, and completely discuss what they wrote down and why they responded the way that they did. Use active listening—that is, repeat what you think you hear your partner or shareholder saying to make sure that there is a clear understanding.
3. Do not gloss over differences. In fact, those issues that cause disagreement should be discussed until there is a resolution.
4. The common understanding that comes out of this process should be used to formulate your partnership or shareholder agreement with your attorney before you begin business.

- What is your vision for the business?
- What are your aspirations for the business? Do you want to build an empire, create a small business that you can run with no employees, reach a certain standard of living, etc.?
- What are your specific goals for your business and career?
  Income and lifestyle:
  Wealth:
  Free time:

      Recognition and fame:

      Impact on community:

      Other:

- What do you want to be doing:

      In one year:

      In five years:

      In ten years:

      At retirement:

- What are your work habits and work ethic? Are they compatible enough with your partners' or shareholders' so the contribution feels fair to everyone?
- How much time off do you plan to take each day, each week, each year?
- How much money will you put into the business?
- How much money do you expect to get out of it?
- Who will be the president of the company? What roles will the other shareholders or partners play?
- How will decisions be made?
- What is your credit rating? Can you help to guarantee a loan, if necessary?
- If you get married and your new spouse gets a job offer in another city, would you move away?
- What will you consider to be real success in this business?
- How would you describe your tolerance for uncertainty and risk?
- How much financial risk are you willing to take with your new venture (personal assets, personal debt, etc.)?
- How many hours are you willing and able to put into your new venture?
- What are the nonfinancial risks for you in starting a new business?
- How do you react to failure? Give examples.
- How do you react in times of personal stress? How do you deal with stress in your life?
- How much income do you need to support your current lifestyle?
- How long could you survive without a paycheck?
- How much money do you have available to start your business?
- Which of your personal assets would you be willing to borrow against, or sell, to start your business?
- Whose support (nonfinancial) is important for you to have before starting your business (family, spouse, etc.)?

Core Values

- List the core personal values that you intend to bring to your business (e.g., treating people fairly, giving something back to the community).
- Where does each of these core values come from (religious faith, family, etc.)?
- Why is each of them important to you?
- How would these core values be put into practice day-to-day in your business? For example, how will you treat employees, customers, and suppliers based on your values?

3 Understanding Financial Statements

Chapter 1 described accounting as the language of business. This chapter provides an overview of basic accounting. The entrepreneur should understand the impact of a business decision on both the income statement and the balance sheet prior to making the decision. Chapter 3 is intended as a review for those who have already been exposed to accounting in previous courses. With this review, the reader will be better prepared for the remaining chapters in this book. This chapter may be skipped if the reader feels comfortable enough with the relationship between the income statement, the balance sheet, and the cash flow statement to use the integrated financial statement model presented in Chapter 6.

There are two main types of accounting: financial and managerial. Financial accounting deals mostly with reporting what has happened historically. Users of financial accounting include investors, creditors, potential employees, customers, and government agencies such as the Internal Revenue Service and the Securities and Exchange Commission. Financial accounting reports are prepared using Generally Accepted Accounting Principles (GAAP). This consistency allows readers to make comparisons between companies, knowing that they are accounted for on the same basis.

Managerial accounting relates to accounting information prepared internally to help managers make decisions for the business. Examples include gross profit analysis by product, unit cost analysis, and departmental cost budget to actual analysis, just to name a few. Managerial and financial information are both based on the information generated by recognition of business transactions in the accounting function.

THE ACCOUNTING EQUATION

The basis of all accounting is the following equation:

$$Assets = Liabilities + Owners' Equity$$

Every economic business transaction can be put in this format to assess the impact on the business. Assets are resources owned by an entity. Assets include cash,

Box 3.1
Separating the Personal From the Business

It is important that the entrepreneur keeps personal transactions separate from her company's transactions. There are several important reasons for this. One, the entrepreneur sends a message to employees that the assets of the business are not for personal use, including her personal use. Two, by following the policies and operating procedures of the business herself, the entrepreneur models the behavior she expects from her employees. Another important reason is that it is against the tax code to run personal transactions through the business and claim them as business deductions.

accounts receivable (amounts owed by customers), prepaid expenses, inventory, land, equipment, patents, copyrights, and so on. Liabilities are amounts owed to others. Liabilities include accounts payable (amounts owed to suppliers), wages payable, taxes payable, notes payable, bank loans, and so on. Owners' equity represents the ownership rights of the investors. It is the owners' claims to assets after all liabilities have been satisfied. In other words, if the company assets were used to satisfy the liabilities, the remaining balance of the assets would belong to the owners. Owners' equity also is known as stockholders' equity, net assets, and book value of the company.

Owners' equity consists of two primary components: the investment in the business by the owners and the retained earnings of the business. Retained earnings represent the earnings of the business (prior years' earnings plus the current year's income) that have been retained for use in the business rather than disbursed to stockholders as dividends or to owners as withdrawals.

AN EXAMPLE

The accounting process results in recording the transactions of a company for a period of time as they affect the accounting equation. Periodically, be it monthly, quarterly, or yearly, a company will summarize these transactions and issue the financial statements. Working through an example is the easiest way to understand the accounting equation and the interrelationship of the financial statements. In this example, "The Company" is the name of a new merchandising business that buys inventory and then sells it to customers. Table 3.1 displays a more detailed version of the basic accounting equation.

Dennis Becker, the entrepreneur, sells shares of stock in The Company to investors for $100,000. This means The Company now has $100,000 in cash and the owners have shares of stock. This transaction would increase the asset Cash while at the same time increasing Common Stock, a part of owners' equity (see Table 3.2).

Table 3.1

Accounting Transactions

	Assets					=	Liabilities			+	Owners' Equity			
Cash	+ Accounts receivable	+ Inventory	+ Equipment	− Accum. deprec.		=	Notes payable	+ Accounts payable	+ Wages payable	+	+ Common stock	+ Retained earnings	+ Revenues	− Expenses
						=				+				
						=				+				

Table 3.2

Accounting Transactions

	Assets					=	Liabilities			+	Owners' Equity			
Cash	+ Accounts receivable	+ Inventory	+ Equipment	− Accum. deprec.		=	Notes payable	+ Accounts payable	+ Wages payable	+	+ Common stock	+ Retained earnings	+ Revenues	− Expenses
100,000						=				+	+ 100,000	—		—
Balance 100,000	—	—	—	—		=	—	—	—	+	+ 100,000	—	—	—

$$\text{Assets} = \text{Liabilities} + \text{Owners' equity}$$
$$\$100,000 = \$0 + \$100,000$$

The entrepreneur's company then buys a piece of equipment for $36,000 in cash. This transaction reduces the asset Cash but increases the asset Equipment. After this transaction, assets still equal $100,000, but there are two categories of assets, Cash and Equipment (Table 3.3).

$$\text{Assets} = \text{Liabilities} + \text{Owners' equity}$$
$$\$64,000 + \$36,000 = \$0 + \$100,000$$

Now the entrepreneur decides The Company needs to borrow money from his local bank. The loan is for $15,000 and the entrepreneur signs a note agreeing to pay back the principal to the bank at a future date with annual interest of 8 percent. The impact of this transaction is to increase the asset Cash and to increase the liability Notes Payable (Table 3.4).

$$\text{Assets} = \text{Liabilities} + \text{Owners' equity}$$
$$\$79,000 + \$36,000 = \$15,000 + \$100,000$$

The Company purchases inventory to be resold to customers; $40,000 of inventory is purchased on account. "On account" means the inventory will be paid for in the future. The impact of this transaction is to increase the asset Inventory and increase the liability Accounts Payable (Table 3.5).

$$\text{Assets} = \text{Liabilities} + \text{Owners' equity}$$
$$\$79,000 + \$40,000 + \$36,000 = \$15,000 + \$40,000 + \$100,000$$

The Company is now ready to open for business. During the first month, $10,000 of the inventory previously purchased is sold for $35,000 on account. In this case "on account" means that the sale was on credit. The customer will be paying at a later date. However, accrual accounting under GAAP says the sale should be recorded in the same period that the customer receives the goods or services. Therefore, the sale is recorded with an increase to accounts receivable instead of cash. Since the customer has the inventory, a second entry is required to reduce inventory for its cost, $10,000, and to show the expense or "cost of goods sold" of $10,000 (Table 3.6).

$$\text{Assets} = \text{Liabilities} + \text{Owners' equity}$$
$$\$79,000 + \$35,000 + \$30,000 + \$36,000 = \$15,000 + \$40,000 + \$100,000 + \$35,000 - \$10,000$$

After this transaction, assets increased by a net $25,000 while equity increased by a net $25,000. Revenues increase equity because they increase income. Expenses decrease equity because they decrease income. The minus sign in front of the expenses means that as expenses increase, equity decreases.

Table 3.3

Accounting Transactions

	Assets					=	Liabilities			+	Owners' Equity			
Cash	Accounts receivable	Inventory	Equipment	Accum. deprec.			Notes payable	Accounts payable	Wages payable		Common stock	Retained earnings	Revenues	Expenses
100,000					=					+	100,000	—		—
(36,000)			36,000		=					+				
Balance 64,000	—	—	36,000	—	=		—	—	—	+	100,000	—	—	—

Table 3.4

Accounting Transactions

	Assets					=	Liabilities			+	Owners' Equity			
Cash	Accounts receivable	Inventory	Equipment	Accum. deprec.			Notes payable	Accounts payable	Wages payable		Common stock	Retained earnings	Revenues	Expenses
100,000					=					+	100,000	—		—
(36,000)			36,000		=					+				
15,000					=		15,000			+				
Balance 79,000	—	—	36,000	—	=		15,000	—	—	+	100,000	—	—	—

Table 3.5

Accounting Transactions

	Assets					=	Liabilities			+	Owners' Equity			
	+	+	+	+	−	=	+	+	+	+	+	+	+	−
	Cash	Accounts receivable	Inventory	Equipment	Accum. deprec.	=	Notes payable	Accounts payable	Wages payable		Common stock	Retained earnings	Revenues	Expenses
	100,000					=				+	100,000	—		
	(36,000)			36,000		=				+				
	15,000					=	15,000			+				
			40,000			=		40,000		+				
Balance	79,000	—	40,000	36,000	—	=	15,000	40,000	—	+	100,000	—	—	—

Table 3.6

Accounting Transactions

	Assets					=	Liabilities			+	Owners' Equity			
	+	+	+	+	−	=	+	+	+	+	+	+	+	−
	Cash	Accounts receivable	Inventory	Equipment	Accum. deprec.	=	Notes payable	Accounts payable	Wages payable		Common stock	Retained earnings	Revenues	Expenses
	100,000					=				+	100,000	—		
	(36,000)			36,000		=				+				
	15,000					=	15,000			+				
			40,000			=		40,000		+				
		35,000	(10,000)			=				+			35,000	(10,000)
Balance	79,000	35,000	30,000	36,000	—	=	15,000	40,000	—	+	100,000	—	35,000	(10,000)

The next transaction involves the payment of $10,000 for rent for the month. Rent is a cost of running a business. Costs of running a business are called expenses. Because the rent is for the current month, it is recorded as an expense in the current month. Paying rent reduces the asset Cash and reduces equity because expenses have increased (Table 3.7).

Assets   = Liabilities   + Owners' equity

$69,000 + $35,000 + $30,000 + $36,000 = $15,000 + $40,000 + $100,000 + $35,000 − $20,000

The Company receives a bill for utilities (heat and lights) for $2,000, which it will pay the following month. Under accrual accounting, the expense is recognized when it is incurred even though it will not be paid until the following month. The impact on the equation is to increase the liability Accounts Payable and to increase expenses, which reduce equity (Table 3.8).

Assets   = Liabilities   + Owners' equity

$69,000 + $35,000+$30,000 + $36,000 = $15,000 + $42,000 + $100,000 + $35,000 − $22,000

The Company receives a check in the mail for $10,000 as partial payment of the account receivable owed by its customer. The asset Cash increases by $10,000 while the asset Accounts Receivable decreases by $10,000 (Table 3.9).

Assets   = Liabilities   + Owners' equity

$79,000 + $25,000 + $30,000 + $36,000 = $15,000 + $42,000 + $100,000 + $35,000 − $22,000

The Company makes a $20,000 partial payment to the supplier of the inventory. The asset Cash goes down by $20,000. The liability Accounts Payable also decreases by $20,000 (Table 3.10).

Assets   = Liabilities   + Owners' equity

$59,000 + $25,000 + $30,000 + $36,000 = $15,000 + $22,000 + $100,000 + $35,000 − $22,000

At the end of the month, The Company owes its employee $5,000 in wages, which it will pay at the beginning of the next month. The Company must record the cost of those services as an expense and will record a liability called Wages Payable to show that it owes the employee for work performed in the current month (Table 3.11).

Assets   = Liabilities   + Owners' equity

$59,000 + $25,000 + $30,000 +   = $15,000 + $22,000 +   + $100,000 +

$36,000 $5,000 $35,000 − $27,000

The Company now needs to record depreciation on the equipment. Depreciation expense represents the allocation of the cost of a piece of equipment to expense over its useful life. Through recognition of depreciation expense, the income statement reflects the cost of using equipment in the business. The process of recording depreciation expense is not meant to reflect the equipment at market value. Most companies use

Table 3.7

Accounting Transactions

	Assets						Liabilities			Owners' Equity			
	Cash	+ Accounts receivable	+ Inventory	+ Equipment	− Accum. deprec.	=	Notes payable	+ Accounts payable	+ Wages payable	+ Common stock	+ Retained earnings	+ Revenues	− Expenses
	100,000					=				100,000	—		
	(36,000)			36,000		=							
	15,000					=	15,000						
		35,000	40,000			=		40,000				35,000	(10,000)
			(10,000)			=							(10,000)
	(10,000)					=							
Balance	69,000	35,000	30,000	36,000	—	=	15,000	40,000	—	+ 100,000	—	35,000	(20,000)

Table 3.8

Accounting Transactions

	Assets						Liabilities			Owners' Equity			
	Cash	+ Accounts receivable	+ Inventory	+ Equipment	− Accum. deprec.	=	Notes payable	+ Accounts payable	+ Wages payable	+ Common stock	+ Retained earnings	+ Revenues	− Expenses
	100,000					=				100,000	—		
	(36,000)			36,000		=							
	15,000					=	15,000						
		35,000	40,000			=		40,000				35,000	(10,000)
			(10,000)			=							(10,000)
	(10,000)					=		2,000					(2,000)
Balance	69,000	35,000	30,000	36,000	—	=	15,000	42,000	—	+ 100,000	—	35,000	(22,000)

Table 3.9

Accounting Transactions

	Assets					=	Liabilities			Owners' Equity			
	Cash	Accounts receivable	Inventory	Equipment	Accum. deprec.	=	Notes payable	Accounts payable	Wages payable	Common stock	Retained earnings	Revenues	Expenses
	100,000					=				100,000	—		—
	(36,000)			36,000		=							
	15,000					=	15,000						
			40,000			=		40,000					
		35,000	(10,000)			=						35,000	(10,000)
	(10,000)					=							(10,000)
						=		2,000					(2,000)
	10,000	(10,000)				=							
Balance	79,000	25,000	30,000	36,000	—	=	15,000	42,000	—	100,000	—	35,000	(22,000)

Table 3.10

Accounting Transactions

	Assets					=	Liabilities			Owners' Equity			
	Cash	Accounts receivable	Inventory	Equipment	Accum. deprec.	=	Notes payable	Accounts payable	Wages payable	Common stock	Retained earnings	Revenues	Expenses
	100,000					=				100,000	—		—
	(36,000)			36,000		=							
	15,000					=	15,000						
			40,000			=		40,000					
		35,000	(10,000)			=						35,000	(10,000)
	(10,000)					=							(10,000)
						=		2,000					(2,000)
	10,000	(10,000)				=							
	(20,000)					=		(20,000)					
Balance	59,000	25,000	30,000	36,000	—	=	15,000	22,000	—	100,000	—	35,000	(22,000)

Table 3.11

Accounting Transactions

	Assets				=	Liabilities			+	Owners' Equity			
Cash	Accounts receivable	Inventory	Equipment	Accum. deprec.	=	Notes payable	Accounts payable	Wages payable	+	Common stock	Retained earnings	Revenues	Expenses
100,000					=				+	100,000	—		—
(36,000)			36,000		=				+				
15,000					=	15,000			+				
	35,000	40,000			=		40,000		+			35,000	
		(10,000)			=				+				(10,000)
(10,000)					=				+				(10,000)
					=		2,000		+				(2,000)
10,000	(10,000)				=				+				
(20,000)					=		(20,000)		+				
					=			5,000	+				(5,000)
Balance 59,000	25,000	30,000	36,000	—	=	15,000	22,000	5,000	+	100,000	—	35,000	(27,000)

Table 3.12

Accounting Transactions

	Assets				=	Liabilities			+	Owners' Equity			
Cash	Accounts receivable	Inventory	Equipment	Accum. deprec.	=	Notes payable	Accounts payable	Wages payable	+	Common stock	Retained earnings	Revenues	Expenses
100,000					=				+	100,000	—		—
(36,000)			36,000		=				+				
15,000					=	15,000			+				
	35,000	40,000			=		40,000		+			35,000	
		(10,000)			=				+				(10,000)
(10,000)					=				+				(10,000)
					=		2,000		+				(2,000)
10,000	(10,000)				=				+				
(20,000)					=		(20,000)		+				
					=			5,000	+				(5,000)
				(1,000)	=				+				(1,000)
Balance 59,000	25,000	30,000	36,000	(1,000)	=	15,000	22,000	5,000	+	100,000	—	35,000	(28,000)

the straight-line method to record depreciation in their financial statements. Under straight-line depreciation, the cost of the equipment less its trade-in value (if any) is divided by the number of months the company expects to use it. The Company plans to use this piece of equipment for 36 months and does not expect it to have any trade-in value at the end of the 36 months. Therefore, it will record $1,000 of depreciation every month ($36,000/36 months = $1,000). Depreciation is recorded by setting up a contra-asset account (an account that reduces assets) called Accumulated Depreciation. This account will accumulate all depreciation until the piece of equipment is sold or discarded. The other account impacted will be Depreciation Expense. Depreciation expense reduces income, reflecting the fact that the company had to use this equipment to run its operations (Table 3.12).

Assets	= Liabilities	+ Owners' equity
$59,000 + $25,000 + $30,000 +	= $15,000 + $22,000 +	+ $100,000 + $35,000 –
$36,000 – $1,000	$5,000	$28,000

Finally, the interest paid on the Note Payable needs to be recorded. The interest for one month is determined using the interest formula:

$$\text{Interest} = \text{Principal} \times \text{Rate} \times \text{Time}$$

In this case, the interest for one month would be $15,000 \times 0.08 \times 1/12$, or $100. Cash would decrease by $100 and Interest Expense would increase by $100. The increase in expense results in a decrease to owners' equity (Table 3.13).

Assets	= Liabilities	+ Owners' equity
($58,900 + $25,000 + $30,000 +	= $15,000 + $22,000 +	+ ($100,000 +
$36,000 – $1,000)	$5,000	$35,000 – $28,100)

A typical company records many more transactions in any given month. The intent of the above example is to show how transactions impact the accounting equation. Some transactions impact only the balance sheet, while others impact the income statement and the balance sheet. Entrepreneurs need to understand the impact their decisions have on the financial statements. For an in-depth treatment of accounting transactions, the reader should review any introductory accounting textbook.

BASIC FINANCIAL STATEMENTS

The next step in the accounting cycle is to prepare the financial statements. A company has four basic financial statements. The *income statement* tells how a company has performed—that is, its income or loss for a period of time. The *balance sheet* reports what a company owns and owes at a given point in time. It also is known as a statement of financial position. The *statement of changes in owners' equity* summarizes any investments by owners and earnings of the company, less any distributions made to owners, for a period of time. The *statement of cash flows* reports how the company generated and used cash for a period of time.

Table 3.13

Accounting Transactions

	Assets						Liabilities				Owners' Equity		
Cash	Accounts receivable	Inventory	Equipment	Accum. deprec.	=	Notes payable	Accounts payable	Wages payable	+	Common stock	Retained earnings	Revenues	Expenses
100,000					=				+	100,000	—		
(36,000)			36,000		=				+				
15,000					=	15,000			+				
		40,000			=		40,000		+				
	35,000	(10,000)			=				+			35,000	(10,000)
(10,000)					=				+				(10,000)
10,000	(10,000)				=				+				
					=		2,000		+				(2,000)
(20,000)					=		(20,000)		+				
					=			5,000	+				(5,000)
				(1,000)	=				+				(1,000)
(100)					=				+				(100)
Balance 58,900	25,000	30,000	36,000	(1,000)	=	15,000	22,000	5,000	+	100,000	—	35,000	(28,100)

Exhibit 3.1

The Company: Income Statement (month ended April 30, 2002)

	(in dollars)	(in percent)
Sales	35,000	100.0
Cost of goods sold	10,000	28.6
Gross profit	25,000	71.4
Operating expenses		
Rent expense	10,000	28.6
Utilities expense	2,000	5.7
Wages expense	5,000	14.3
Depreciation expense	1,000	2.8
Total operating expenses	18,000	51.4
Earnings before interest and taxes (EBIT)	7,000	20.0
Interest expense	100	0.3
Earnings before taxes	6,900	19.7

INCOME STATEMENT

The first statement to be prepared is the income statement. The income statement is a scorecard for a *period* of time. Prepared according to GAAP, as discussed at the beginning of this chapter, it answers basic questions about the performance of the business. Did the company make money? What were the financial results of its operations for the most recent time period?

There are only two categories on the income statement: revenues and expenses. Revenues are created when the entity sells a product or provides services and receives cash or creates a receivable in return. There are many labels for revenues, including sales, net sales, net revenues, and fees.

Expenses are outflows of cash or using up of assets or incurring a liability for services or goods received. They may be recognized with the revenues that relate to the expense (e.g., cost of goods sold). Expenses also may be recognized in the period they are incurred (e.g., rent, administrative salaries). Finally, expenses may be recognized to reflect an allocation of cost to the period (e.g., depreciation). The income statement for The Company example is displayed in Exhibit 3.1.

Gross profit is the difference between sales and the cost of the goods sold. Usually expressed as a percentage of sales, it serves as an important metric to measure whether a company is generating enough profit margin to cover operating expenses and provide income. However, it is not a metric used by companies that provide services. Operating expenses may be classified into selling, general and administrative, research and development, and other. Internally, a company may classify them as direct or indirect, variable or fixed. In the income statement above, each expense is listed individually instead of being grouped into categories. Gross profit less operating expenses is often referred to as Earnings Before Interest and Taxes (EBIT). It is usually considered a key measurement of management's ability to utilize a firm's assets to generate income.

Interest expense or interest income is usually shown as a separate line item. Most users want to know this amount because it is a contractual obligation. EBIT less interest equals EBT or earnings before taxes. This book will not address the topic of income tax expense. How taxes are calculated and recorded depends on how the company has been organized (e.g., sole proprietorship, partnership, limited liability corporation, subchapter S). Entrepreneurs should consult a legal and tax adviser about the optimum method of organization for their personal circumstances. Another measurement of income is Earnings before Interest, Taxes, Depreciation, and Amortization (EBITDA). The Company's EBITDA is $8,000 ($7,000 of EBIT plus $1,000 of depreciation). EBITDA often is used by entrepreneurs and bankers as a quick measure of cash flow.

The percentages provide a type of vertical analysis of the income statement. The Company was able to generate 71.4 cents of gross profit for every dollar of sales. Out of the 71.4 cents, 51.4 cents was used to cover operating expenses, leaving 20 cents of every dollar of sales in EBIT. Companies can then compare their EBIT to last year, the budget, or the industry average to determine if they are operating efficiently or as planned. See Chapter 7 for an in-depth discussion of financial statement analysis.

BALANCE SHEET

The second statement is the balance sheet, which is displayed in Exhibit 3.2. This statement records the assets, liabilities, and equity of the company at a point in time. It usually is prepared monthly but at a minimum is done annually.

A balance sheet classifies assets and liabilities as either current or long-term. Current assets are cash or assets that can be turned into cash or used up within one year of the balance sheet date. Current liabilities are liabilities that must be paid within one year of the balance sheet date. Working capital refers to the difference between current assets and current liabilities. Management issues concerning current assets and liabilities relate to seasonal cycles, which dictate a need for planning cash inflows and outflows, investing excess cash, and borrowing cash when needed. Liquidity is having enough cash on hand to meet cash flow needs.

Assets

Cash is the liquid monetary asset a company has on hand or in checking and savings accounts. Cash equivalents are short-term investments that mature within ninety days or less, e.g., certificates of deposit (CDs) or Treasury bills (T-bills).

If the company has excess cash, the entrepreneur may choose to invest it in debt (bonds) or equity (stocks) securities. These investments are often called marketable securities. They result in interest and/or dividend income.

Accounts receivable represents sales to customers on credit. Under accrual accounting, a sale is recognized when the product or service is delivered to the customer. The timing of the receipt of cash impacts the cash flow statement, but not the income statement. GAAP requires accounts receivable to be recorded at net realizable value,

Exhibit 3.2

The Company: Balance Sheet (April 30, 2012)

Assets
    Current assets
        Cash $58,900
        Accounts receivable   25,000
        Inventory   30,000
        Total current assets $113,900

    Fixed assets
        Equipment   36,000
        Less: accumulated depreciation   (1,000)
        Net fixed assets   35,000

    Total assets $148,900

Liabilities
Current liabilities
        Notes payable $15,000
        Accounts payable   22,000
        Wages payable   5,000
        Total current liabilities   42,000

Stockholders' equity
        Common stock   100,000
        Retained earnings   6,900
        Total stockholders' equity   106,900

Total liabilities and stockholders' equity $148,900

which is the amount expected to be collected. Therefore, an estimate of what is uncollectible needs to be made at the time the sale is made. This estimate results in the creation of a contra-asset account called allowance for bad debts. The company records an expense for the amount it estimates will not be collected in the future. The net effect is that the income statement reflects both the sales and the bad debt expense related to the sales that will not be collected, in the same period. When a receivable is written off in the future because it has been determined to be uncollectible, the asset and the allowance are both reduced and net income is not affected.

Inventory is merchandise held by a company to be sold to its customers. It is typically the most significant asset for merchandising or manufacturing firms. Inventories for a manufacturing company consist of raw materials, work in process (WIP), and finished goods. Inventories are recorded as an asset until sold. Upon a sale, the inventory account is reduced and the expense account called cost of goods sold (or cost of sales) is increased. A company has a choice of methods to record cost of goods sold and ending inventory under GAAP. The three most common methods are FIFO (First-in, First-out), LIFO (Last-in, First-out), and Average Cost. FIFO and LIFO describe how costs flow from inventory to cost of goods sold, *not* how the physical product moves. FIFO assumes that the oldest costs in inventory are moved to cost of goods sold first; the result is that ending inventory consists of the most recent costs. LIFO assumes that the newest costs in inventory are the first ones moved to cost of goods sold, resulting in the oldest costs remaining on the balance sheet. In times of inflation, as the cost of new inventory purchases is increasing, LIFO increases cost of goods sold, thereby reducing taxable income. Companies choose the LIFO method because by reducing income, they reduce their income tax expense and increase cash flow. In the average cost method, the average cost of all the purchases is used to determine the cost of goods sold. The entrepreneur should work with a tax accountant to determine which method is the most appropriate for the business.

Noncurrent assets are assets that are not expected to be turned into cash within a year or have a useful life longer than one year. For most entrepreneurs, these assets consist of land, buildings, equipment, furniture, and fixtures. Tangible or physical assets with lives longer than one year are used by the company in the production or sale of inventory or in providing goods and services. They are recorded on the balance sheet at their acquisition cost, which includes the invoice price, freight, sales tax, assembly, and installation. These costs are also referred to as capital expenditures. A capital expenditure means that a physical asset is recorded (capitalized) on the balance sheet if it has a life longer than one year. However, the dollar value also is considered. A relatively small expenditure usually is expensed on the income statement and not capitalized in order to minimize cumbersome record keeping. Most companies have a capitalization policy, which says to capitalize all expenditures over a certain dollar amount if they have a life longer than one year. The entrepreneur should work with the accountant to develop this policy.

Depreciation is a systematic method of allocating the original cost of a long-term asset to expense over the asset's expected life. It does *not* necessarily indicate a decline in market value. Land is never depreciated because it has an infinite life. The two methods commonly used to depreciate an asset are straight-line depreciation and an accelerated method called the modified accelerated cost recovery system (MACRS). Most companies use the straight-line method for their financial statements because of its simplicity and its result in a constant level of depreciation expense. However, the IRS allows companies to use accelerated methods for tax purposes. This allows a company to expense a greater amount of depreciation in the early years, thus saving on income taxes and cash flow, and a lesser amount in later years. A company may use one method for its financial statements and a different method on its tax return.

Straight-line depreciation is calculated as follows:

$$\frac{\text{Historical cost} - \text{Salvage value}}{\text{Years of use}} = \text{Annual depreciation expense}$$

In our previous example of The Company, this calculation resulted in an annual depreciation charge of $12,000, or $1,000 per month:

$$\frac{\$36,000 - \$0}{3 \text{ years}} = \$12,000 \text{ annually, or } \$1,000 \text{ per month}$$

A company may finance a capital expenditure by leasing a building or piece of equipment. There are two types of leases, operating and capital. An operating lease has no attributes of ownership and is not reflected on the lessee's balance sheet. The lease payment is shown as an operating expense. Under a capital lease, the lessee assumes the benefits and risks of ownership. Buildings and equipment purchased under a capital lease are reflected on the balance sheet as an asset with an offsetting liability. An accountant or leasing company can determine whether a lease is a capital or operating lease. Leasing is a financing tool. A company may choose to lease a piece of equipment rather than buy it for three reasons. Leasing reduces the risk of obsolescence, gives the company more flexibility, and helps with cash flow.

Intangible assets represent the company's right to something. Examples are patents, copyrights, and trademarks. Goodwill is also an intangible asset. Goodwill is recorded only when one company purchases another company for more than its fair market value (i.e., paying more than the fair market value of its assets less its liabilities). Intangible assets are amortized (written off to expense) except for goodwill, which is reduced only if it is impaired.

Liabilities

Liabilities—the claims of creditors to the assets of a company—usually arise due to an expense or the purchase of an asset. Current liabilities are those that are due within one year of the balance sheet date. An entrepreneur may have several types of current liabilities. A working capital loan is short-term credit obtained to finance the buildup of accounts receivable or inventory in a seasonal business. Once the inventory is sold and accounts receivable are collected, the loan is repaid. A revolving line of credit is a predetermined, maximum amount of credit that is flexible in the timing and amount of borrowing.

Current liabilities also include obligations where the exact amount owed will not be known until a later date. An example is warranty expense. Under GAAP, a company needs to accrue an estimate of what the warranty may cost in the future if it warranties its products or services. The warranty expense and the related liability are recorded when the sale is recognized, just as with bad debt expense. When warranty work is done, the liability and the asset impacted to service the warranty are reduced; there is no impact on net income.

Current maturities of long-term debt represent the principal payment due on the debt within the next year. Current maturities usually occur because funds borrowed on a long-term basis are often repaid in monthly installments. On all debt, interest must be accrued and recognized in the period it is incurred, whether or not it is paid. The interest rate charged will be based on the lender's rating of the risk associated with the loan and the current prime rate. The prime rate is the interest rate established by lenders for their "most creditworthy" borrowers.

Accounts payable are amounts owed to suppliers for goods and services. Chapter 10 will discuss trade debt as a financing tool. Accounts payable are based on an invoice that has been received. Accruals are obligations a business has incurred but for which no formal invoice has been received, such as wages, payroll taxes, sales taxes, and property taxes.

Unearned revenues, also called deferred revenues, occur when customers pay for products or services in advance. These are recorded as liabilities because the company has the cash up front but has done nothing to earn the payment. Instead, the company owes the customer the product or service in the future. Examples are magazine subscription payments received by a publisher or season ticket payments received by a sports team. Collecting cash up front is a method of improving cash flow by using the cash collected to fund costs incurred prior to a sale.

Long-term liabilities are those obligations that are not due within the current year. They may include borrowing from banks or the issuance of bonds. See Chapter 10 for a discussion of debt financing strategies.

Owners' Equity

Owners' equity represents the claim of the entity's owners to the assets on the balance sheet. In a corporation, it is called stockholders' equity. If the corporation is dissolved, stockholders' liability is limited to the amount they have invested in the stock. Equity consists of two main categories, contributed capital and retained earnings. Contributed capital is the original investment in the company by the owners. In a corporation, the investment by the owners is usually called common stock. In a partnership or sole proprietorship, this investment is called capital.

Retained earnings, as discussed earlier, represent the net income of the company since its inception, which has not been disbursed back to the owners in the form of dividends or withdrawals. Retained earnings *do not represent a cash account.*

$$\text{Beginning R/E} + \text{Net Income} - \text{Dividends (or withdrawals)} = \text{Ending R/E}$$

The Statement of Changes in Owners' (Stockholders') Equity (not shown) reconciles the change in the common stock or capital account and retained earnings account from the beginning of the year to the end of the year.

STATEMENT OF CASH FLOWS

The last of the basic financial statements is the statement of cash flows. This statement tracks the sources and uses of cash in the company. Chapter 8 discusses cash flow management and the statement of cash flows in detail.

THE LIMITATIONS OF BUSINESS FINANCIAL STATEMENTS

Financial statements have limitations. For one thing, not all assets of a company are included (e.g., employees or brand names). The research and development costs leading to a patent or trademark also are not reflected as an asset but are expensed as they are incurred. Most assets are reflected at historical cost—that is, their purchase price. The balance sheet usually does not reflect current market value (except in the case of marketable securities). Historical cost is an objective measurement but is less useful. There are many estimates reflected in the financial statements that impact both the income statement and the balance sheet. These estimates include the lives used for depreciation, the collectibility of accounts receivable, the salability of inventory, and the amount of warranty liability outstanding. These estimates are only as good as the methods used to calculate them and the assumptions used by management in the calculations. The numbers reflected in financial statements also are affected by the choice of accounting methods (e.g., FIFO, LIFO, or average cost), which can impact both the income statement and the balance sheet.

SUMMARY

Accounting is the language of business; therefore, a working knowledge of this language is key to understanding entrepreneurial finance. This chapter discussed the basic workings of the accounting equation and how this equation impacts financial statements and their interrelationships. Chapters 4 and 5 will examine the process of forecasting revenues and expenses. Chapter 6 in this section will present an integrated spreadsheet model that can be used to create financial forecasts for new ventures. The remainder of this book will build on the basic understanding of accounting presented in this chapter.

DISCUSSION QUESTIONS

1. Discuss the importance to entrepreneurs of understanding their financial statements.
2. How does net income affect the balance sheet?
3. What does an income statement communicate about a business?
4. What does a balance sheet communicate about a business?
5. How would you define assets? Liabilities? Owners' Equity?
6. What is the definition of revenue? An expense?

OPPORTUNITIES FOR APPLICATION

1. Practice Makes Perfect Inc. was started on July 1 of the current year. Practice Makes Perfect provides piano lessons for students of all abilities. You are the founder, president, office manager, etc. You have not yet hired an accountant but your bank is asking for an income statement and balance sheet for the first month of operation. Using the following information, put each transaction into the equation format given in Table 3.14. Then, prepare a simple income statement and a balance sheet to present to the bank.

   Transactions:
   a. You started your company with $100,000 that you raised by selling stock in Practice Makes Perfect Inc. to your family and friends.
   b. Knowing that you would need additional funds, you presented your business plan to the bank and were able to get a $50,000 loan at 10 percent.

Table 3.14

Accounting Transactions

Assets					=	Liabilities			+	Owners' Equity			
Cash	+ Accounts receivable	+ Inventory	+ Equipment	− Accum. deprec.	=	Notes payable	+ Accounts payable	+ Wages payable	+	Common stock	+ Retained earnings	+ Revenues	− Expenses

c. You purchased three pianos for $16,000 each, paying cash. You believe these pianos will last five years before you replace them. At the end of the five years, you think you can sell each piano for $1,000.

d. You spent $2,000 on supplies, which you charged on account.

e. The newspaper bills you $500 for the advertisement you ran. You plan on paying the bill next month.

f. Rent for the space you have leased is $1,000 a month, which you paid.

g. The first month you bill students $2,000 for lessons.

h. You pay your two part-time piano teachers $500 each at the end of the month.

i. One of your students paid the $200 invoice you sent earlier in the month.

j. You write the check for the interest owed for the month.

k. You adjust the supplies account for $300 of sheet music that you gave to students.

l. You record one month of depreciation on the pianos.

2. Make a list of the assets and liabilities you would want to keep track of in a company you owned. What types of revenues would you have? What types of expenses would you want to track?

3. Look on the Internet for the financial statements of a publicly held company. (If you own stock in a company, look for the financial statements in the last annual report you received.) OR ask your employer if you can look at a set of the company's financial statements.

a. Create the accounting equation for the balance sheet. Does it balance?

b. What is the company's EBIT?

c. Identify an asset or a liability you are not familiar with and look it up in an accounting or finance resource.

4 | Revenue Forecasting

This chapter examines the second major component in the model for entrepreneurial financial management (Figure 4.1) used in this book: revenue forecasting. Meeting the financial goals discussed in Chapter 2, specifically the profit goals, requires that a venture achieve a certain level of revenues. Sound financial management requires entrepreneurs to develop a model of revenue forecasting that helps establish the validity of the venture's ability to realize these revenue levels.

COMMON FORECASTING MISTAKES

Before examining how reliable and accurate revenue forecasts are developed, it is important to identify three very common mistakes found in unreliable and inaccurate revenue forecasts. All three mistakes can be found in business plans ranging from the simplest small business start-up plan to the most elaborately developed business plans seeking millions of dollars in funding from venture capitalists.

1. THE LINEAR FORECAST MISTAKE

The most basic mistake in revenue forecasting is to assume a simple linear growth in revenues. This is a common mistake of entrepreneurs who have a strong technical knowledge base that has led them to start their businesses. These entrepreneurs tend to have strong process knowledge about how a product is made or a service is provided. For example, assume an entrepreneur is creating a plan to open a software company to develop and produce a software application that his current employer is not interested in developing. He has spent countless hours perfecting the software and

Figure 4.1 **Model for Entrepreneurial Financial Management**

Setting financial goals → **Revenue forecasting** → Expense forecasting → Monitoring performance

its applications. When it comes time to pursue the funding he needs to put the software into full production and bring it to the marketplace, he develops his forecasted income statement. First he estimates the expenses, which he knows in detail from his previous job at another software company. Then he estimates revenues. He assumes that he will sell five units in the first month, ten in the second month, fifteen in the third, and so on. He has no support for this revenue growth model. He simply assumes that sales will grow by five units a month because the number seems reasonable to him. He then develops an income statement based on that assumption. Entrepreneurs who start their businesses because they have a strong passion for a specific idea also commonly suffer from the linear forecasting mistake.

There are many risks with using the oversimplified assumption underlying a linear revenue forecast. Sales may grow much slower than assumed, and the entrepreneur may run out of funds before he breaks even. On the other hand, sales may grow much faster than he assumed, and he may run out of product, thus risking angry customers. An even greater, yet hidden risk is that the entrepreneur has no knowledge of what will generate sales. He assumes that if he builds a good product the customers will find it and buy it. Very few new ventures have ever had the luxury of a product that "sells itself." Most successful businesses result from a thorough knowledge of the customers and what they want from the product.

2. THE HOCKEY STICK FORECAST MISTAKE

A mistake that is very similar to the linear forecast, but even riskier, is the hockey stick revenue forecast. In this case, the entrepreneur assumes that her sales will begin slowly and then suddenly increase dramatically for no documented reason other than her blind faith in her new business. Bankers and others who work with new businesses are very wary of such forecasts, as they are based on nothing more than the optimism of the entrepreneur.

3. THE 20/80 VERSUS 80/20 MISTAKE

Even entrepreneurs who take the time to develop more sophisticated revenue forecasts than the two methods discussed thus far may make the third type of mistake. The 20/80 versus 80/20 mistake in forecasting refers to the allocation of time spent in creating the two main sections of the income statement, forecasting revenues and forecasting expenses. Commonly, as little as 20 percent of time spent on developing the forecast is dedicated to developing the revenue portion of the forecast, while as much as 80 percent is spent on detailing the expenses. Accurately developed expense forecasts are vitally important. However, the information used to develop expense forecasts is relatively straightforward to identify and research (Chapter 5 examines expense forecasting in more detail). This information may be very familiar to the entrepreneur if she has worked in the industry before starting her own venture.

Revenue forecasts are not as easy to build. Unfortunately, rather than spend the time necessary to develop accurate revenue forecasts, entrepreneurs often establish revenue forecasts that seem to make sense based on a few simple assumptions. For example, an entrepreneur may establish an income statement forecast that shows steady growth in revenues but allows for the seasonal variability she knows will occur each year. Although she gathered enough information to support the seasonal variation of the forecast, she has no specific justification for either the level of sales or the growth in sales underlying the revenue model. She completed some research on revenues but not enough to generate confidence in the numbers. Clearly, the point is not that the entrepreneur should spend *less* time on the expense forecast—in fact, she should not. On the contrary, she should be spending much *more* time on the revenue forecast, using the methods presented in the following sections of this chapter. Avoiding mistakes in income statement forecasting may require that entrepreneurs spend *four times* as much time on revenue forecasts as on expense forecasts. The increased time spent on revenue forecasts is dedicated to developing and testing the business model, and developing a marketing plan containing accurate, detailed market data, as outlined in the next section. These data are then used to create a sophisticated, robust revenue forecast.

THE LINK BETWEEN THE MARKETING PLAN AND REVENUE FORECASTS

Investors, bankers, and other people who regularly evaluate business plans follow a similar and consistent pattern. Their first step is to evaluate the executive summary to determine if the plan is one they want to read about in more depth. This decision may be based on a variety of factors, including the nature of the business, the management team, the industry, and revenue and profit potential. If the executive summary catches their attention, the focus then shifts to the marketing plan. After careful review of the marketing plan, they immediately move to examine the revenue forecasts in the financial pro-formas (i.e., forecasted financial statements). What they look for is a consistent story between the marketing plan and the forecasted revenues. The marketing plan and the revenue forecast should be telling the same story—the marketing plan in a narrative format and the revenue forecast in numbers, the language of business. Experience has shown these experts that a strong link between these two parts of a business plan reduces the types of risk outlined above.

The link between the marketing plan and revenue forecast can be understood by examining the basic formula of revenues:

$$\text{Revenues} = \text{Price} \times \text{Quantity}$$

A marketing plan describes what is known as the marketing mix—product positioning, pricing, promotion, and distribution (place), also known as the 4Ps of marketing. These four components of the marketing mix correspond directly to the equation for revenues. Both the revenue equation and the marketing mix address the issue of pricing. The marketing plan should offer clear support, rationale, and justification for the pricing used in the revenue forecast. Quantity should be explained and supported by the rest of the marketing mix. Product positioning explains who the customers are, how many customers are in the target market, and why customers will choose the product over those offered by the competition. Promotion explains how the business will communicate with customers to

Figure 4.2 **Backbone of an Effective Business Plan**

motive them to buy the product. Distribution (place) explains how the business will get the product to the customers in the most efficient, convenient manner possible.

A revenue forecast based on a sound marketing plan reduces the risk that the business venture will fail to meet projected revenues by offering evidence from sound research that clearly supports the marketing strategy being pursued by the entrepreneur. The link between the marketing plan and the revenue forecast, as illustrated in Figure 4.2, creates what is known as the backbone of the business plan.

The marketing mix is supported by three underlying pillars that support the conclusions of the marketing plan and its link to the revenue forecast. These are generally included in a business plan as support for the marketing strategies chosen for the venture.

1. INDUSTRY AND MARKET TRENDS

Market and industry trends can lend support to the financial projections in a business plan. If the industry and/or local markets that a business operates in are forecasted to have significant future growth, this can help justify growth projections for a specific business within that industry or market. Conversely, if an industry or market is forecast to experience a downturn, it will be difficult to argue that a new venture could operate contrary to those trends. Data on industry and market trends are available from a variety of public domain sources. Also, entrepreneurs can gather data on a specific market by networking with potential customers, suppliers, and others familiar with that local market environment. Business plan readers, such as bankers and investors, often will seek independent research to confirm the industry and market trends cited in the marketing plan.

2. MARKET RESEARCH

A marketing plan should clearly demonstrate that the entrepreneur understands the needs, wants, and buying behaviors of his potential customers. Many entrepreneurs assume that their customers will think the way they do. However, this is often not the case. For example, an optometrist who was planning to set up a series of privately owned retail eyeglass outlets was committed to providing the absolute highest quality. He was convinced that quality was all that mattered. However, the customers in his market were equally concerned with price and were looking for retail outlets that offered "value" (i.e., good quality for a reasonable price). The optometrist failed to understand how his potential customers thought and behaved, and consequently his business closed before he could even open his second store. Effective market research is critical to understanding the thought process and behavior of potential customers.

Entrepreneurs rarely have the funds to support a sophisticated market study, such as those conducted by large corporations. However, useful and reasonably accurate market research is possible on even the smallest budget. Entrepreneurs can gain important insight into how their potential customers think by getting out and talking to them. The conversation should be approached with an open mind and without any leading questions. By networking with just a few potential customers, the entrepreneur can begin to discern consistent patterns that should help him create a venture that will succeed in attracting the customers necessary to reach his financial goals.

3. COMPETITIVE ANALYSIS

Accurate revenue forecasting requires a thorough understanding of the competitive environment. This knowledge helps the entrepreneur develop a clear picture of the potential market share, which is the proportion of a given market that buys a company's products or services. Market research has helped the entrepreneur gain a better understanding of customer preferences. Competitive analysis compares that understanding with the product or service offerings of each business within a given market. A competitive analysis is generally constructed as follows:

- Generate an inventory of all competitors that do business in the market. Include current competitors, potential competitors (that is, companies that are planning to enter the market), and any businesses that offer a close substitute product or service that can easily be chosen by the customer as an alternative (e.g., a bus service can serve as a substitute for a taxicab company).
- Estimate the market share for each competitor. This can be calculated by estimating the sales for each competitor, adding the sales of all competitors to estimate the size of the market, and then dividing each competitor's sales by the total market sales to get the percentage of market share for each company. If sales cannot be estimated, a surrogate (such as number of customers) can be substituted for sales.
- Use the data gathered through market research to identify features that customers like and do not like about the competitors' products and services. If possible, the entrepreneur should visit competitors to understand how a customer experiences interacting with these companies and to determine how each performs in terms of the key products and services it delivers. Finally, the entrepreneur should talk to customers to determine how they rate the competitors on the important traits and features.
- Create a *competitive analysis grid.* List the businesses that will be in most direct competition with the new venture being planned along the left side of the grid. Across the top are the customer decision criteria (key customer needs and preferences) *in order of importance to the customer.* Rate or describe each competitor for each customer decision criterion within the grid. It is important to be honest in the evaluation. Avoid the temptation to belittle or underrate the competition. Figure 4.3 displays a sample competitive grid.
- Identify the competitive strategies to be pursued given this analysis. Through this analysis, the entrepreneur should be able to create an estimate of potential market share. This estimate then can be used to forecast revenues. Also, it is important

Figure 4.3 **Sample Competitive Grid**

	Cleanliness of facilities	Hours of operation	Selection	Price
Joe Inc.	Generally clean in public areas, but back rooms usually messy	8:00 a.m.–6:00 p.m.	Most commonly purchased products available	$5–$20
Jane Co.	Consistently clean and orderly throughout all facilities	8:00 a.m.–8:00 p.m.	All commonly purchased available and some specialty items in stock	$12–$30
Sally & Jim's Shop	Public areas somewhat messy and disorganized and back areas very messy	9:00 a.m.–4:00 p.m.	Many common items not in stock—usually have to special order	$3–$15
Dr. C's Place (the new business being planned)	Plan to be spotless throughout	7:00 a.m.–9:00 p.m.	All common items plus most many specialty items not found at competitors' stores	$5–$35

to estimate how long it might take to build up to that market share based on the perception of customer loyalty and on how well the competition is meeting the needs and wants of the customers.

CREATING SCENARIOS

Once the revenue forecasts are supported and validated through the marketing plan, the entrepreneur should create multiple scenarios. Most bankers and investors want to see a presentation of best-case, worst-case, and most-likely-case scenarios. To accomplish this, the assumptions that were used to develop the marketing plan and any additional ones used in creating the revenue plan should be listed. The entrepreneur should then rate the probability and importance of each assumption and choose the three to five assumptions that are critical to the success or failure of the venture. That is, which assumptions are most likely to keep the entrepreneur awake at night worrying? Typically, one or more of these will be assumptions related to the revenue forecast. The others are usually tied to the largest expense variables with the most uncertainty (Chapter 5 examines expense forecasting in more detail).

The first scenario should be based on what the entrepreneur believes is likely to occur. This should be treated as the *best-case scenario*. Entrepreneurs tend to be overly optimistic when planning their ventures. It is human nature to do so. The excitement of launching the new venture leads to a rosy outlook. In addition, no matter how carefully the entrepreneur plans the new business, there are events and factors that simply cannot be foreseen. Therefore, using the entrepreneur's estimate for the key assumptions will be treated as the best-case scenario to offset the typically optimistic outlook of the entrepreneur and the uncertainty that is part of any new venture.

The second scenario to develop is the *most-likely scenario*. The entrepreneur takes the three to five critical assumptions and adjusts them all downward to reflect a less than ideal set of circumstances. With these new values, the entrepreneur will reforecast the financial outlook for the business. This is the main scenario from which the business plan will be derived. It is the scenario that will be used to develop the financial statements in the plan that will be presented to bankers and investors.

The *worst-case scenario* is developed by pushing all the critical assumptions to the extreme. It is often a scenario of failure. Certainly the entrepreneur is not planning to fail, but this scenario creates an understanding of what failure would look like. How much debt would still be owed? How much cash, if any, would be available to the owners of the business to repay their initial investment? These are not easy questions to think about, but they are important nonetheless. Bankers and investors will want to understand this scenario. The entrepreneur should use it to develop a plan that has the greatest chance of avoiding this worst-case scenario. It may lead the entrepreneur to grow more cautiously, take on more or less outside money, take greater care in managing cash flow (Chapter 8), and/or be more prudent in spending (the topic of Chapter 11).

For example, an entrepreneur makes an assumption that he can add two new customers each month during the first two years. This growth assumes that he gets an equal share of new customers entering the market. This situation is what he considers most likely to occur, so to be cautious this will be used to model the best-case scenario. The most-likely scenario may be based on adding only one new customer in each month of the first year and two per month in the second year. The worst-case scenario is that the entrepreneur will be able to attract only a small fraction of new customers, which he assumes would create a growth rate of two new customers each year. He then creates three different scenarios of revenue growth that reflect each of these cases. He will eventually create three sets of financial statement projections that are based on these three cases.

THE LINK BETWEEN THE REVENUE FORECAST AND THE CASH FLOW FORECAST

When forecasting revenues, it is important to identify the cash flow associated with those revenues. Although revenues are important, it is the actual receipt of cash or cash flow from those revenues that is critical to the entrepreneur. If credit is not extended to customers, then the sales projections will equal the cash receipts projections. However, if credit is extended (i.e., accounts receivable are recorded when the sale is made, but cash is collected at a later time), then the cash collections will lag the recognition of sales on the income statement. This is called accrual accounting. Sales and expenses are recorded when the business delivers the product or service or benefits from the expenses incurred, but the cash does not exchange hands until a later time. Chapter 8 discusses cash flow in more detail. There are three key steps in transforming revenue forecasts to cash flow forecasts.

First, the entrepreneur needs to determine whether she will be extending credit to customers. The competitive analysis discussed above should include gaining an understanding of the standards for payment within the industry. In some industries, such as most manufacturing businesses, extension of credit to customers is expected. The entrepreneur has no real choice but to extend credit to her customers. In other businesses, credit may be optional. For example, some health care providers, such as medical clinics, extend credit to clients while others expect payment at the time of service. In this case, credit can be used as a competitive feature offered to customers, but it is important in the competitive analysis to determine if credit is actually something the customers want. Other businesses operate on a cash basis with payment received at the time of the sale. Most retail operations operate in this manner. In today's electronic age, credit card sales are like cash. However, there is a cost to accepting credit cards that can range from 2 to 7 percent of the sale.

Second, if credit is extended, the entrepreneur should estimate the percentage of the sales that will be on credit and the percentage that will be cash. Many businesses that extend credit have a portion of sales that are immediate cash collections due to the preferences or past bad credit history of certain customers.

Third, the entrepreneur will need to determine how long it will take to collect credit sales. Average times for collection of accounts receivable are available for most industries through industry associations or publications such as Robert Morris Associates. An assumption also will need to be made on what percentage of accounts receivable are never collected. Industry averages for this percentage also are available. The financial statement template included in Chapter 6 incorporates those assumptions when calculating the cash flow projections.

A cash flow forecast is a key component of a business plan. The entrepreneur will want to demonstrate to a potential lender or investor that she understands the future cash needs of her company.

THE IMPACT OF BUSINESS TYPE ON REVENUES

This section will examine how revenue forecasting will differ between manufacturing firms and service firms and how commission-based selling and seasonal sales affect forecasting models. The examples used in this section involve small businesses that are already in operation. For start-ups, these data can be estimated using industry data that are often readily available through industry trade associations or economic development agencies. Other entrepreneurs can use their experience gained by working in the industry to create these estimates.

MANUFACTURING FIRMS

Revenues in manufacturing firms are limited by their production capacity, which is the maximum number of units that can be produced with a given number of machines, employees, and raw materials available. An assembly line can run for only twenty-four hours per day and make only so many units per hour; moreover, it can run only as long as there are enough raw materials to feed the assembly line and employees to run the machines. In addition, downtime must be factored into any estimate to allow for needed service and maintenance of the assembly equipment. Therefore, if an owner is unwilling to buy the equipment for a second line and is even resistant to opening up a second or third shift on the same line, then there are natural limits to the number of units and, therefore, the amount of revenue that can physically be produced. It would not make sense to extrapolate sales unit projections from a past trend that result in a number that is greater than the amount that the firm can physically produce.

For example, an assembly line can produce fifty units per hour assuming normal downtime. Currently, there is only one shift of workers, and the owner does not want to use space in her warehouse to set up a second assembly line. What is the maximum number of sales possible per month if she were to add a second shift one month and a third shift the next, assuming each shift operates eight hours?

	Month 1	Month 2	Month 3
First shift	8×50	8×50	8×50
Second shift		8×50	8×50
Third shift			8×50
Maximum number of sales	400 units	800 units	1,200 units

The number of units sold in this example represents the maximum number of units that can be produced. There likely will be a time lag between when these units are produced and when they are actually sold. In addition, if sales are made to customers on trade credit, there can be further time lag before the firm receives payment for the units sold. In the meantime, the firm will have to pay suppliers for raw materials and employees for their labor. Hence, a period of rising production and sales will probably correspond to a period of net cash outflows until the dollar revenue climbs above the current cost of production.

SERVICE FIRMS

For service firms such as law firms, accounting practices, and lawn care, the firm's capacity to provide the service has to be established in order to calculate accurate forecasts. Service firms bill in different ways, such as hourly and per job completed. These billing methods also should be factored into any forecast.

Billing by the Hour

For service firms that require a specialized skill, such as law firms and auto repair shops, the skill may be something that by its nature is not easily transferred. This trait limits the capacity for expansion of revenues. Therefore, these types of businesses have certain general characteristics in common:

1. Typically, specialized services can be billed by the hour or by the job, based on how many hours a typical job should take. Per job fees become very close substitutes for per hour fees in this framework.
2. There are approximately 2,000 work hours in one year, which equates to approximately 160 work hours in one month.
3. No employee can physically be 100 percent involved in billable time. Depending on the industry and whether the employee is expected to perform sales or administrative duties, the utilization ratio (the percentage of time spent in billable work) could be as low as 40 percent or as high as 80 percent. Factors such as travel time or ongoing required training will lead to lower utilization ratios.

For example, the owner of a high-end personal training firm wants to hire one associate per month during the growth phase of the business. Associates can work at 70 percent utilization. The owner can work only at 20 percent utilization due to administrative work that he must complete. Each new associate has to be trained, so they average only 35 percent utilization for the first month. The service is billed at $100 per hour. Assume that there are 160 work hours per month.

Revenue per employee = 160 hours per month × utilization × $100 per hour

	Month 1	Month 2	Month 3
Owner	160 × 0.20 × 100	160 × 0.20 × 100	160 × 0.20 × 100
Associate 1	160 × 0.35 × 100	160 × 0.70 × 100	160 × 0.70 × 100
Associate 2		160 × 0.35 × 100	160 × 0.70 × 100
Associate 3			160 × 0.35 × 100
Total revenue	$8,800	$20,000	$31,200

Thus, these figures provide a month-by-month revenue forecast based on the firm's ability to deliver the service. As was discussed in the previous section, revenue is not necessarily the same thing as cash flow. In this example, for instance, if customers are granted a thirty-day deferral before payment is due, then each of the above monthly revenue numbers would be collected in the next month (i.e., $8,800 would be collected in month 2, not month 1, and so on). On the expense side, the associates would have to be paid their monthly salary almost immediately, even though the revenue they generate would not be collected until the next month.

Billing by the Job

Using a methodology similar to the hourly example, the owner of a business that bills by the job must still understand that since there are only so many hours in a day, there is a limit to the number of jobs that can be generated per employee.

For example, suppose an information technology (IT) firm has one owner who is planning to add associates to meet forecasted revenue growth. When an employee is trained and at full productivity, the typical IT software installation takes about twenty-five hours. For a new employee it takes twice as long. Each job is priced at $2,000.

The owner wants to hire one associate per month, and the productivity measures are the same as in the previous example (employee utilization rate is 70 percent at full efficiency and the owner is at 20 percent).

$$\text{Revenue per employee} = \$2{,}000 \text{ per job} \times \text{number of jobs per month}$$
$$\text{Number of jobs per month} = 160 \text{ hours per month} \times \text{utilization/number of hours per job}$$

	Month 1	Month 2	Month 3
Owner	$2{,}000 \times 160 \times 0.2/25$	$2{,}000 \times 160 \times 0.2/25$	$2{,}000 \times 160 \times 0.2/25$
Associate 1	$2{,}000 \times 160 \times 0.7/50$	$2{,}000 \times 160 \times 0.7/25$	$2{,}000 \times 160 \times 0.7/25$
Associate 2		$2{,}000 \times 160 \times 0.7/50$	$2{,}000 \times 160 \times 0.7/25$
Associate 3			$2{,}000 \times 160 \times 0.7/50$
Total revenue	$7,040	$16,000	$24,960

These sales numbers are on a prorated basis since some job installations are started in one month but completed in the next. Also, just as in the hourly billing example, the revenue amounts are booked in their respective months but are actually received in the following month if thirty-day payment deferral is extended to customers.

RECURRING REVENUE FIRMS

Some businesses provide a service that is used by the customer repeatedly. Wire-based and wireless services such as digital messaging, cell phones, cable, and Internet access are some examples. A typical recurring revenue firm requires that a customer sign a contract for a particular term of service. Depending on the nature of the service, the customers may be able to physically disconnect from the service during the contract period. In other words, a customer who has signed a one-year contract may not stay with the company for the full year. It also could be the case that rigorous collection activities might not be economically justified to enforce the customer contract because (1) there is no asset to be repossessed or (2) the dollar amount of monthly revenue is less than the cost of enforcement. Therefore, an entrepreneur cannot automatically forecast and base plans on the assumption that each customer represents a full contract's worth of revenue and cash flow.

Because customers can potentially disconnect no matter what a contract says, a measurement tool is needed to assist in monitoring the customer behavior and to help forecast revenues. This measurement is called the disconnect rate. The disconnect rate is the inverse of the average customer's economic life.

$$\text{Disconnect rate} = (1/\text{avg. customer life in months})$$

For instance, if the disconnect rate is 10 percent, it means that the average customer disconnects after ten months' worth of service. If the disconnect rate = 10 percent = (1/customer life in months), so customer life must = (1/disconnect rate) = (1/0.10), which = 10 months. Put another way, if a company loses 10 percent of its previous month's customers each month, then after ten months the company has essentially replaced all its customers with new ones.

Likewise, if the disconnect rate is 5 percent, then losing 5 percent of the previous month's customers means that the company replaces all its customers over twenty months, which is the average customer life. If the disconnect rate = 5 percent or 0.05 = (1/customer life in months), then customer life = (1/0.05) = 20 months.

It might be more accurate to keep track of every single customer in order to project and monitor revenue, but if the business in question is a very high-volume business, then that method might not be feasible. All that is needed to create an estimate of the disconnect rate is the gross number of customers this month, the gross number of customers on service last month, and the number of new customers added this month.

Disconnect rate = [(number of customers this month – number of new customers – number of customers last month)/number of customers last month]

Because customers may be able to unilaterally disconnect (i.e., without notifying the company) from the service by not paying their invoice, the number of customers that a company *truly* has in a particular month would have to be estimated by dividing the actual revenue collected in that month by the monthly average price charged per customer. Because of the potential for customers to simply stop paying for a service, there can be a time lag before the company's customer information system can recognize that it has lost a customer. This could cause the firm to overestimate its actual number of customers at any one time and therefore overestimate its revenue projections.

For example, sales revenue last month for Real Cheap TV Cable Company Inc. (RCTV) was $10,000. The price RCTV charges for service is $10 per month. Revenue for this month is $11,000. The sales division told the company that it added 150 new customers this month.

Estimated number customers last month	= ($10,000/$10)	= 1,000
Estimated number customers this month	= ($11,000/$10)	= 1,100
New customers		= 150
Disconnect rate	= [(1,100 – 150 – 1,000)/1,000]	= 0.05 or 5 percent

This is what RCTV has learned:

- Fifty customers disconnected last month (1,100 – 150 – 1,000)
- 5 percent is the disconnect rate
- The average customer is disconnecting after twenty months
  (1 / disconnect rate) = average customer life
  (1 / 0.05) = 20 months

Given the understanding of the disconnect rate, it can now be applied to forecasting revenue. For example, RCTV had 1,000 paying customers last month at a monthly service fee of $10. The sales force believes that it can add 150 new customers each month based on the number of salespeople and its commission structure. RCTV believes that the disconnect rate is 5 percent (or that the average customer life is twenty months).

Number of customers

Month 1	Month 2	Month 3
$(1,000 + 150) \times (1 - 0.05)$	$(1,093 + 150) \times (1 - 0.05)$	$(1,181 + 150) \times (1 - 0.05)$

Revenue per month

Month 1	Month 2	Month 3
$1,093 \times \$10$	$1,181 \times \$10$	$1,264 \times \$10$
\$10,930	\$11,810	\$12,640

   Recurring revenue firms frequently have cash flow challenges due to fixed costs that must be paid up-front to establish service for a new customer. Once a customer is established, the marginal cost of providing the service or product decreases. There-fore, a high disconnect rate (or short customer life) means that the firm is constantly paying that start-up cost. The company would be making a larger profit at the same level of revenue if customer turnover rate were reduced.

COMMISSION-BASED SELLING FIRMS

   A similarity between commission-based selling and service industries is that sales revenue is partially a function of the number of employees. The difference in this case is that the employees are salespeople rather than consultants or service providers.
   A typical arrangement is that a salesperson is required to sell a set number of units or dollars called the base, which the company considers a minimum level of acceptable performance. If the salesperson exceeds this base, then she is eligible for a commission. In some firms, salespeople work entirely on commission, but this is dependent on the industry norm and the potential supply of employable salespeople.
   Given the typical situation, a sales forecast can be crudely established by multiply-ing the number of units for the base by the number of salespeople. The base should be determined as the number of units necessary to justify the fixed cost of a sales employee. It also can be set at the number of units that are considered acceptable for sales professionals in that industry. Hopefully, the industry standard is greater than what is necessary to cover the fixed costs, and the standard amount of commission that is paid per unit is less than the profit margin on each unit. Otherwise, a company would be selling each unit at a net loss.
   For example, the Harmon Company plans to hire one new salesperson per month during the first five months of the start-up year. The base level of sales is 100 units per month per salesperson. It takes three months for salespeople to be fully effective (i.e., they sell 33 units in the first month, 66 in the second, and they start selling their full quota of 100 in the third). The price per unit is $50.

	Month 1	Month 2	Month 3	Month 4	Month 5
Salesperson 1	33 × 50	66 × 50	100 × 50	100 × 50	100 × 50
Salesperson 2		33 × 50	66 × 50	100 × 50	100 × 50
Salesperson 3			33 × 50	66 × 50	100 × 50
Salesperson 4				33 × 50	66 × 50
Salesperson 5					33 × 50
Revenue	$1,650	$4,950	$9,950	$14,950	$19,950

Of course, if a salesperson cannot meet the minimum base number of sales, then the actual sales would be less than the projection. Similarly, if a salesperson were productive enough to earn commissions, then these projections would be underestimated. Unless the method of sales can be changed or expanded, such as through the Internet or retail stores, then the amount of sales will primarily be a function of the number of salespeople.

CYCLICAL OR SEASONAL SALES FIRMS

Some businesses, whether service, manufacturing, or commission-based, have a seasonal customer base. Some classic examples are snowmobile manufacturers, tax preparers, and ski resorts. The key element is not to count on a sustainable level of revenue (and certainly not growth) during months that a firm physically cannot have any customers.

For example, Sammy's Ski Jumping School can operate only in the months of December, January, and February. The price for instruction is $100 per day, and only five students can be taught per day. Because of holidays and bad weather conditions, the school typically is open only twelve days in December, eighteen days in January, and seventeen days in February. What is the maximum amount of revenue per month?

	November	December	January	February	March	April
	0	5 × 12 × 100	5 × 18 × 100	5 × 17 × 100	0	0
Sales	$0	$6,000	$9,000	$8,500	$0	$0

Seasonal firms have to be especially careful with cash flow management, especially if they have expenses that must be paid throughout the year.

QUANTITATIVE FORECASTING TECHNIQUES

Established businesses often use sophisticated statistical forecasting techniques such as regression analysis, exponential smoothing, and moving averages. However, these methods are almost impossible for a start-up firm to use, since the entrepreneur does not have the historical data needed for them. Regression, which can be performed on an Excel spreadsheet using an available download, is an extremely useful tool to quantify the relationships between sales (the dependent variable) and factors (the independent variables) that a manager may have some control over, such as pricing and level of advertising spending, as well as factors that a manager cannot control, such as the population of an area and the state of the economy. For an entrepreneur, this would be very valuable information. However, a regression cannot be performed unless the firm has been in business for a sufficient length of time to collect the necessary amount of data for statistical significance. For instance, managers cannot mathematically approximate the effect of price changes on the quantity sold unless the business has been in operation long enough to have undergone at least one price change. However, entrepreneurs can use the principles of (1) linking the marketing plan to the revenue forecast by identifying industry and market trends, (2) market research, and (3) competitive analysis to create estimates that can serve as substitutes for historical data. The following is an example of how to use a quantitative approach to apply these principles to forecast sales revenue.

American One-Way Inc. has been an electronic messaging company for several years. It has recently begun exploring a new handheld, wireless device that has even more full computing and Internet-access power than the fastest desktop computer. This device would require an all-new system of transmitting satellites because it uses a totally different technology than a cell phone or other Internet-connecting device. Therefore, American One-Way intends to create an all-new venture with a different brand and organization to reduce customer confusion and to raise capital. An estimate of expenses suggests that the price of the service has to be at least $120 per year in order to cover costs and earn an adequate profit, but that over five years it can be phased down to $100. Since no such device has ever been offered in the market before, the forecasting process must start from scratch (see Table 4.1).

First, the marketing department consults the U.S. census Website to find the population of the counties in which the company intends to build the necessary towers and offer the service. The population of these counties has been growing at 5 percent a year.

Second, since this is a communications device, the marketers look at the history of paging, cell phones, and hybrid devices like the iPhone and iPad and find that, given enough time, communications devices eventually achieve a penetration rate of 32 percent. This means that at the most mature phase of its life, 32 percent of the population will own the newest version of a handheld device. However, it takes roughly five years for this level of acceptance to occur. Given no other data, the marketers assume that market penetration of this new product might follow a similar pattern.

Third, a competitive analysis suggests that for the first two years American One-Way's new venture will be the only one offering this new device. However, after two years, competitors will probably have their own satellites, and American One-Way's market share will fall to 80 percent in the third year, 60 percent in the fourth, and 55 percent in the fifth.

For American One-Way Inc., forecasting revenue for a particular year would first require estimating the population of the geographic market areas such as counties and multiplying this figure by the estimated penetration rate to get the estimated total potential market for the new product. Next, the total potential market is multiplied by market share to get the theoretical number of American One-Way's customers. The final step is to multiply the number of customers by the price to get the estimated sales revenue.

Table 4.1

American One-Way's Competitive Analysis

Population	Year 1	Year 2	Year 3	Year 4	Year 5
5,010,000 =	5,010,000 × (1.05) = 5,260,500	5,260500 × (1.05) = 5,523,525	5,523,525 × (1.05) = 5,799,701	5,799,701 × (1.05) = 6,089,686	6,089,686 × (1.05) = 6,394,171
Penetration rate	5%	10%	20%	27%	32%
Total potential market =	5,260,500 × 0.05 = 263,025	5,523,525 × 0.10 = 552,353	5,799,701 × 0.20 = 1,159,940	6,089,686 × 0.27 = 1,644,215	6,394,171 × 0.32 = 2,046,135
One-way market share percentage	100%	100%	80%	60%	55%
One-way customers =	263,025 × 1 = 263,025	552,353 × 1 = 552,353	1,159,940 × 0.80 = 927,952	1,644,215 × 0.60 = 986,529	2,046,135 × 0.55 = 1,125,374
Pricing	$120	$120	$115	$110	$100
One-way revenue forecast =	263,025 × 120 = $31,563,000	552,353 × 120 = $66,282,360	927,952 × 115 = $106,714,480	986,529 × 110 = $108,518,190	1,125,374 × 100 = $112,537,400

In this particular case it is demonstrated that a quantitative approach can be used despite the absence of direct historical data for this product. A potential strength of this approach is that one can actually see (and therefore evaluate) the assumptions that are necessary to achieve particular sales levels. For instance, the actual level of sales achieved by any company is a function of macro factors, such as the number of people living in a geographic area and the rate of acceptance of a new product. It is also a function of factors specific to the company, such as the firm's market share and the price that the company charges.

THE IMPORTANCE OF REVENUE FORECASTING

The consequences of missing revenue targets can be devastating for an entrepreneurial venture. Any number of decisions might be based on the revenue assumptions in the entrepreneur's business plan. Banks may lend money based on revenue forecasts. If the targets are not met, the business might become a problem loan for the bank. One commercial real estate company faced such a crisis. Its bank loans were based on growth that matched its historical rate of 20 percent. However, due to a variety of unforeseen factors, such as a hurricane and the pullout of a major employer in town, office vacancies rose and the company's revenues declined slightly. This caused the key financial ratios to fall below the acceptable range that a bank can accept from its customers (see Chapter 13). Even though the company still had positive cash flow, the bank was forced to call in its loans to the company. Fortunately, the company found alternative funding.

Inventory assumptions are also based on revenue forecasts. A small company that manufactured mittens and scarves had projected a significant increase in sales due to positive negotiations under way with a major retailer. The company had to commit to raw material purchases nine months in advance of the ultimate sale to customers at its retail outlets. Based on the positive forecast, the company placed a large order for raw materials in January. It would take possession of the materials by April so that manufacturing could take place from April through August, when the orders were to be shipped. By late July, however, it became clear that the large order from the retailer that the company had planned for was not going to occur due to a projected softening of the economy. Retailers were cutting back on new product orders. The company was left with a large amount of finished and partially finished inventory that was likely to go unsold. The company ultimately had to liquidate its assets in bankruptcy (see Chapter 16).

Revenue forecasts also are used to make commitments to increased staffing and additional space. A Website consulting business rented a large new office and hired several high-priced staff members, many with six months of severance guaranteed in their contracts (a standard practice at the time). Unfortunately, these commitments were made only two months before the dot-com stock crash. After the crash, many of the company's major customers went out of business as their stock values became worthless. Soon, the entrepreneurs in this firm were faced with major commitments to staff and space that they could not meet with their significantly reduced cash flow. Only through drastic measures and an infusion of money from a family member was this business able to stay open.

Investors, from angel investors to venture capitalists (see Chapters 12 through 14), make their investments based on expectations created by forecasts. An entrepreneur who had developed a process for converting farm waste into energy faced a crisis due to unmet expectations of his investors. Although the business was doing fairly well, it was nowhere near to meeting the 100 percent per year growth forecast in his business plan. He had taken a significant amount of venture capital. The venture capital firm decided that the business could meet the projected growth, but not with its current management. As was allowed in the investment agreement, the venture capital firm removed the entrepreneur from his management role and brought in outside executives to run the company.

The examples given here clearly demonstrate the impact of missed revenue forecasts. Revenue forecasts are vitally important because so many decisions rest on the assumption that these numbers are accurate. Therefore, basic guidelines should be followed when making revenue forecasts:

1. Conduct enough market research to ensure the quality of the assumptions behind the revenue forecasts.
2. Validate assumptions with more than one source of data. Do not ignore conflicting data. They are a sign that further research may be required.
3. Base the plans for the business on conservative as opposed to optimistic assumptions. It is much easier to adjust to higher-than-expected revenues than to deal with the consequences of missed revenue targets.

SUMMARY

This chapter presented an overview of revenue forecasting for entrepreneurial ventures. The critical linkage between the marketing plan and accurate revenue forecasts was examined. The importance of taking into account the relevant features of the business, including type of business and sales patterns, was also discussed. Quantitative techniques can help a start-up venture reach a fairly accurate forecast, although they are not as accurate as when used in businesses with historic data. Missed revenue forecasts can be devastating to an entrepreneurial venture. The next chapter will examine the second major category of forecasting: expenses.

DISCUSSION QUESTIONS

1. What are the linear forecast and hockey stick forecast mistakes, and why would they be common among inexperienced entrepreneurs?
2. Given how crucial sales revenue is to the survival of a business, why is there a natural tendency for an entrepreneur to make the 20/80 versus 80/20 mistake?
3. What are the three main parts of the marketing plan, and why is linking the marketing plan to the revenue forecast so important?
4. What is the value of creating scenarios?

5. What is the difference between revenue and cash flow, and why is the distinction so important?
6. How should entrepreneurs take into account the productive capacity of their facilities when making a revenue forecast?
7. In what type of businesses do customers gained in the past have the most impact on revenue today? Why?
8. How do the following factors relate to revenue forecasting: population, penetration rate, market share, and price?
9. Why are sophisticated statistical techniques difficult to perform in an entrepreneurial environment?
10. What would be the potential risk of not directly linking the marketing plan and the financial forecast?

OPPORTUNITIES FOR APPLICATION

1. Mortinson Manufacturing plans to open one assembly line per month for the next seven months. Each assembly line is capable of manufacturing 14,250 toys per day. When at full capacity seven months from now, what will be the maximum total revenue that Mortinson Manufacturing could achieve if the toys could be sold for thirty-five cents apiece?
2. The Andersonian Consulting Company currently has five employees. The best-case situation is for the employees to be at 70 percent utilization. At 160 hours per month and a billing rate of $55 per hour, what is the maximum revenue that can be achieved?
3. Assume that a lawn service company collected $127,000 last month and that it charges a typical customer $100 per month for its service. This month the revenue is $134,000 and the sales department claims to have added 300 new customers.
   a. How many customers did the company actually have and collect payments from last month?
   b. How many paying customers does the company have this month?
   c. How many customers probably disconnected from the company's service in the past month?
   d. What is the disconnect rate?
4. The Extron Company sells a home electronics convergence device for $1,050 each. The company uses commission-based selling and the quota per salesperson is 40 units per month. If Extron has three employees who are new and are only expected to hit 50 percent of quota, two employees who can hit 75 percent of quota, and five experienced people who can consistently reach 100 percent, then what is this month's anticipated level of revenue?
5. The Wankel Publishing Company is planning to start a new magazine devoted to girls' high school basketball. The company has the following information. According to census data, one of the states where it wishes to introduce the magazine has a population of 1 million girls aged thirteen to eighteen years. A national study found that 42 percent of high school girls compete in sports,

and the High School League Annual Report suggests that 20 percent of high school girl athletes play basketball. Wankel Publishing has found, through past experience in specialty magazines, that it can have monopoly status in a market for at most three years (100 percent market share). Under a best-case scenario, it plans to have 4 percent market penetration in year 1, 8 percent in year 2, and 12 percent in year 3.

  a. What will be the peak number of subscribers in the best-case scenario over the next three years?

  b. What will be the number of subscribers over the next three years under a worst-case scenario? Assume that the worst-case scenario has a penetration rate of 1 percent in year 1, 2 percent in year 2, and 3 percent in year 3.

  c. If the most likely case scenario is one-half of the best-case scenario penetration rates, calculate the number of subscribers for years 1, 2, and 3.

6. Micki Manufacturing's market study suggests that 1.2 million novelty dolls can be sold per year through carnivals and county fairs. If an assembly line at maximum capacity can produce 15,000 dolls a month per shift, can the company meet its sales goal for the year if it runs only two shifts?

7. The recently started law firm of Dewey, Cheetum, and Howe has three partners. Between "rain-making" work to get business and administrative duties, the partners believe that the average utilization rate is only 40 percent at best. At a billing rate of $200 per hour and a forty-hour work week, what is the maximum revenue per week?

8. How many new sales are necessary per month in order for a firm to average a constant 1,200 customers if the disconnect rate is 4.5 percent?

9. If you need to pay an average of $4,000 per month in order to attract auto sales employees, then what must be the per employee monthly quota to achieve commission, given the following information?

  a. Cars sell for approximately $24,000.

  b. The manufacturer charges your dealership $21,000 per car on average.

  c. Your dealership needs about $2,275 per car in gross profit to cover fixed costs and generate an adequate return to the investors.

  d. What is left over after the gross profit can be used to pay the commission to the salesperson.

10. If your product sells for $200 per unit, the population of your area is 10 million people, and the penetration rate for the product is 50 percent, what market share would your firm need to achieve a sales goal of $1 million?

5 Expense Forecasting

Once profitability goals have been established and the revenue forecasts determined, the final component of the income statement, expenses, should be forecast. This chapter presents several methods for expense forecasting. The key to understanding expenses is to understand the possible behavior of the costs; that is, how will a particular cost react or adjust as changes occur in the level of activity in the business? With an understanding of how costs behave, the entrepreneur will be better able to predict what will happen under various operating circumstances and within different types of businesses.

DEFINING COSTS

Expenses are the costs of being in business and providing a product or service to a customer. In a business that sells products, expenses are generally classified as cost of goods sold, selling, general and administrative, and other.

Cost of goods sold represents the cost of the product to the seller. In a manufacturing firm, this includes the cost of the raw materials, direct labor costs, and overhead costs to run the manufacturing plant, such as rent, utilities, and production supervision. In a merchandising firm, the cost of goods sold represents the cost of the product to the entrepreneur when it was purchased. A company selling services would not incur cost of goods sold.

Selling expenses represent costs related to selling the product or service. They may include advertising, salaries and benefits, commissions, travel and entertainment, retail store operations costs, marketing, and so on.

Figure 5.1 **Model for Entrepreneurial Financial Management**

Setting financial goals → Revenue forecasting → **Expense forecasting** → Monitoring performance

72

General and administrative expenses include the entrepreneur's salary, office personnel salaries and benefits, office supplies, insurance, accounting and legal fees, depreciation on office equipment, and any other costs incurred in running a business.

Other expenses are costs incurred outside of those discussed here. Typically, interest expense (or interest income) and any losses (or gains) incurred on the sale of equipment would be included here.

Capital expenditures also represent a cost for companies. Capital expenditures include the purchase of a piece of equipment or a building. As discussed in Chapter 3, these types of purchases are not expensed immediately but are allocated to expense over their useful lives. Therefore, depreciation expense reduces income on an accrual basis but does not impact monthly cash expenses. The entrepreneur must identify and budget for these capital costs as they can have a huge impact on cash flow in the month of purchase. How capital expenditures are funded also will impact cash flow and the income statement.

The accurate forecasting of expenses is critical to the establishment of reliable budgets and as input for various business decisions that must be made during the start-up and growth of a business venture. Without accurate expense forecasting and a good understanding of how costs behave, an entrepreneur may be unable to manage the business financially as events unfold. Simply constructing a budget is never enough for an entrepreneurial venture because there are too many unknowns and unforeseen events that make a budget an inaccurate barometer of the financial performance of an emerging business. The entrepreneur needs to understand the behavior of costs so that, as events change, midcourse adjustments can be made to any budget or forecast that has been created. For example, an entrepreneur makes an assumption about the number of employees and amount of materials needed for a project under bid. After winning the project and beginning the work, the entrepreneur realizes that due to outside events, another employee and higher-priced materials are needed. What will these changes mean for profits on this project? Will there be enough cash to finish the project? What can be done, if anything, to ensure that profit targets are met and cash is not depleted? An understanding of cost behavior can help the entrepreneur answer these questions and make sound decisions as the new business develops.

COST BEHAVIOR

Typically, costs can be defined as variable, fixed, or mixed, depending on how they react to changes in output.

VARIABLE COSTS

Variable costs change in direct proportion to the level of activity of the business. Activities that change variable costs can be very specific or can be as general as the number of units being produced. For example, sales commission expense is directly related to the level of sales. Direct materials costs change directly in relationship to units produced. For an airline operating a flight, the variable cost of meals is tied to

Table 5.1

Examples of Activity Bases for Variable Costs

Type of expense	Activity base
Sales commissions	Sales
Materials cost	Units produced
Health insurance expense	Number of employees covered
Wages expense	Number of hours worked
Payroll tax expense	Dollars of wages paid

the number of passengers. The cost of fuel depends on the length of the trip. With variable costs, the total cost changes with the change in activity while the cost per unit remains the same. For the airline, the longer the trip, the higher the total cost of the fuel. However, the cost per mile will stay the same. Table 5.1 displays some examples of expenses and the activity base that might be used to estimate those expenses.

A small manufacturer of snowshoes can serve as an example of variable cost behavior. Assume that the cost of materials for each pair of snowshoes is $20. The total variable cost at different levels of activity, in this case the production of snowshoes, would then be as follows:

Number of units produced (pairs)	Materials cost per unit	Total materials cost
5,000	$20	$100,000
7,500	20	150,000
10,000	20	200,000

The cost of materials per pair of snowshoes does not change. However, the total cost changes with the change in level of production. At 5,000 pairs, the total materials cost is $100,000. When production doubles to 10,000 pairs, the total cost also doubles to $200,000. When determining variable costs, entrepreneurs should make certain that the actual activity base that drives the cost has been identified. In this example, the total cost of materials does not vary with the number sold but rather with the number produced. Figure 5.2 displays a graph of the behavior of variable cost of materials in this example.

Figure 5.2 **Variable Cost Behavior**

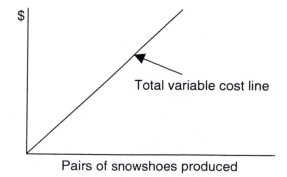

Pairs of snowshoes produced

Figure 5.3 **Fixed Cost Behavior**

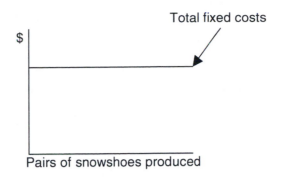

FIXED COSTS

The second basic type of costs, called *fixed*, remains constant in total dollar amount within a relevant range of activity. That is, these costs do not change with a given activity such as sales or units produced. Figure 5.3 displays the behavior of fixed costs for the snowshoe company.

An example of a fixed cost is rent on a manufacturing plant. No matter what the production level, the amount of rent stays the same. Even though the total amount of fixed cost does not change, the cost per unit decreases as the activity level increases. In the case of rent, the more units produced, the lower the cost of rent per unit, since the amount of rent does not change but is now spread over more units. At some point the company may outgrow its facilities and need to acquire additional space, causing rent to increase, but until that happens the cost of rent is fixed.

As stated in the definition, fixed costs remain the same within the *relevant range* of activity. As an example, consider the fixed cost of a production supervisor. Ten production workers can be hired before another supervisor will need to be hired. At the point when another supervisor is needed, production has moved out of the relevant range for that cost. The relevant range for a fixed cost is the range of activity over which the graph of the cost is flat. In this example, the relevant range is ten production workers for each supervisor; that is, the cost of supervision is fixed within this range.

Returning to the snowshoe example, assume that the company rents manufacturing space at $5,000 per month. The cost of the space is $5,000 whether it manufactures 5,000 pairs of snowshoes or 10,000 pairs. Therefore, the cost per pair can vary from $1.00 ($5,000/5,000) to $.50 ($5,000/10,000), while the total cost remains the same at $5,000 per month. However, if production jumped up to 15,000 pairs, the company might have to rent additional space. The 15,000 pairs are said to be "outside the relevant range"; that is, the fixed costs are fixed only up to a certain range of production.

One category of fixed costs is termed *committed fixed costs*. Two key traits of committed fixed costs are that they are long-term in nature and are difficult to cut back to zero without impacting profitability or long-term goals. Generally, committed fixed costs include investments in facilities, equipment, and basic infrastructure. The resulting expenses include depreciation of buildings and equipment, real estate taxes, and insurance. Because a committed fixed cost is by definition difficult to cut, an entrepreneur needs to be careful when adding such a long-term obligation for the business. Many companies have built a new office building only to experience a downturn in sales, thereby causing the failure of the business due to its inability to pay for the new committed fixed cost.

A second category of fixed costs is *discretionary fixed costs*. The key trait of a discretionary fixed cost is that it is usually annual in nature and can be cut back for short periods of time without too much impact on the company. An example would be a company-sponsored wellness program.

Management strategy and the culture of the business often determine whether a cost is committed or discretionary. For example, if plant workers are considered to be discretionary costs, they will be laid off more quickly than if they are considered committed costs. Why would employees be considered committed costs? The entrepreneur may have created a culture in the business in which employee layoffs are avoided at almost any cost; commitment to employees is considered a cornerstone of the company culture. Treating plant worker costs as committed can also be economic in nature. The cost of hiring, training, and getting new workers to be fully productive can be greater than keeping employees through a business downturn.

MIXED COSTS

Many costs do not behave simply as fixed or variable costs. Such costs are termed *mixed costs*, as they have both a fixed component and a variable component. Business cell phone expense is a good example of a mixed cost. There is a basic cost, i.e., a monthly charge that must be paid just to have telephone service available. However, there is an additional, variable portion of telephone expense that is based on the actual service used, such as text and data messaging. Sales staff salaries also might be mixed. The company may pay each salesperson a base salary along with a commission that is based on the number of units sold. When forecasting a mixed cost, the estimate should include the fixed portion plus the variable component based on the appropriate activity base.

In summary, it is critical to identify the type of cost behavior—variable, fixed, or mixed—for each expense in a forecast. The activity base for the variable costs and the relevant range for the fixed costs should then be determined. Too often, start-up businesses will miss profitability estimates because the entrepreneurs made the simple assumption when making forecasts that all costs are variable with sales. Also, many entrepreneurs fail to realize that variable costs may vary with a variety of activities, not just sales. Cost behaviors should be documented and included in the assumptions for the forecast used in making financial projections (see Chapter 6). For costs directly related to sales, managers should document the percentage relationship between that cost and sales. For indirect costs, managers should document the total dollars of cost. Exhibit 5.1 shows how a merchandising company might set up an income statement.

Exhibit 5.1

Example: Merchandising Company

			Assumptions used
Sales	$100,000	100.0%	
Cost of goods sold	65,000	65.0	65 percent of sales
Gross profit	35,000	35.0	35 percent of sales
Sales salaries	15,000	15.0	No. of salespeople × monthly base
Sales commissions	1,500	1.5	1.5 percent of sales
Store rent	3,500	3.5	monthly rent
Total selling expenses	20,000	20.0	
Office rent	2,500	2.5	monthly rent
Office salaries	12,000	12.0	No. of people × monthly pay
Depreciation	500	0.5	cost of equipment/months of life
Total general and administrative	15,000	15.0	
EBIT	500	0.5	

The cost of goods sold and the selling expenses are considered direct costs, and of these, only the cost of goods sold and sales commissions are variable. The general and administrative expense is considered indirect and in this case is fixed since the dollars will not vary with sales.

BREAKEVEN ANALYSIS

Breakeven analysis is a way to look at costs and revenues to assess the likelihood of profitability. Basically, it is the calculation of the minimum number of units of product or service that a firm must produce and sell in order to cover all its variable and fixed expenses. Beyond this level of sales the firm starts to make a profit.

It should be noted that breakeven quantity is *not* an optimum; it is a minimum. If a firm's marketing projection suggests that it cannot sell at least the breakeven level of production, then the firm should abandon this endeavor before any money has been wasted. If a firm's marketing projection suggests that more than this minimum amount can be produced and sold, then further analysis should be conducted to determine whether the level of profit that is anticipated is acceptable.

Breakeven analysis can sometimes be thought of as a "back-of-the-envelope" type of calculation to assess possible feasibility before a significant amount of time and energy has been invested in a business. It is a critical step in the opportunity assessment stage of a proposed new venture.

As an example, suppose a firm makes standard-sized signs for businesses. The entrepreneur can buy the sign material for $50 and hire part-time workers to paint it for $20 per sign. Therefore, the variable cost per sign is $70. The firm rents a warehouse to house the operation at a cost of $1,000 per month and pays an accounting firm $500 a month to handle the company's books, so the fixed costs add up to $1,500 a month. The signs can be sold for $100 each. Profit on a before-tax basis would be as follows:

$$\text{Profit} = (P \times Q) - (V \times Q) - F$$

where P = price per unit, $100
          Q = quantity produced and sold
          V = variable cost per unit, $70
          F = fixed cost, $1,500.

Therefore, we can solve for the minimum number of units by setting the profit equal to zero and solving for Q:

$$Q = F/(P - V)$$
$$Q = 1500/(100 - 70) \text{ or } 50 \text{ units}$$

   If the firm makes and sells less than fifty units, the level of profit would be negative. At fifty units, the level of profit is exactly zero; at more than fifty units, the profit becomes positive and increases with each additional unit produced and sold. In this example, the difference between price and variable cost ($100 – $70) is $30 per unit. Therefore, the firm has to make fifty units just to cover the fixed costs of $1,500, which the firm would be paying whether or not any units were produced. The term *contribution margin* is used to describe the difference between price and variable cost. It is the amount contributed to covering fixed costs.

EXPENSE FORECASTING: THE IMPACT OF BUSINESS TYPE ON EXPENSES

MANUFACTURING FIRMS

   The expenses of a manufacturer typically include the following costs: raw materials, direct labor, overhead, and administration and selling or distribution expenses. Different products require different proportions of expenditures. Some manufacturing schemes are so automated that direct labor is a very small part of total expenses. Other manufacturers require a very labor-intensive technology where direct labor is the largest component. Manufacturing firms also provide some of the best examples of fixed versus variable costs. Direct labor and raw material costs are variable, meaning that they vary with the level of production. Expenses such as accounting, secretarial help, and managers are usually fixed expenses, as is the cost of leasing equipment or a building. As discussed earlier in the chapter, fixed expenses such as these do not vary with the level of production, at least in the short term. To demonstrate the general expense characteristics of a manufacturing firm, the assembly line example used in Chapter 4 for revenue forecasting will be used here.
   Assume an assembly line can produce fifty units per hour. The plan is to open up a second shift in the second month and a third shift in the following month. The product requires $25 per unit in materials to make. Each assembly line requires one employee who is paid $20 per hour and works twenty days per month. The owner is also the manager and accountant and collects a salary of $4,000 per month. Benefits

amount to $200 per employee per month. The Social Security tax contribution for the company is 7.65 percent. The final product sells for $100 per unit. What are the monthly expenses and resulting net cash flow?

	Month 1	Month 2	Month 3
Owner salary	$4,000	$4,000	$4,000
Employee 1	3,200	3,200	3,200
Employee 2		3,200	3,200
Employee 3			3,200
Benefits ($200 per employee)	400	600	800
Social Security (7.65 percent)	551	796	1,040
Materials	200,000	400,000	600,000
Total expenses	$208,151	$411,796	$615,440
Revenue	$800,000	$1,600,000	$2,400,000
Net cash flow before taxes	$591,849	$1,188,204	$1,784,560

In this example, labor expense is only a very small portion of the total expense. Because cash flow is being measured, depreciation expense on equipment is not included in this example. If net income were being measured, depreciation expense would be included, resulting in income lower than cash flow.

In nonmanufacturing firms, certain expense attributes may exist that someone from a manufacturing background may not anticipate. The following discussion will highlight some of these attributes.

SERVICE FIRMS

Firms that provide a service, such as consulting companies, law firms, accounting firms, and lawn care companies, typically have employee salary or wages as one of their most significant (if not *the* most significant) expenses. Typically, this expense behaves like a fixed cost. For instance, a fairly standard practice is to pay an employee a fixed salary plus a periodic (yearly) bonus. A wise way to handle the bonus is to calculate it based on some measure of year-end profit. That way the firm does not have to commit itself to paying bonuses when experiencing a loss.

In Chapter 4, the revenue characteristics of a service firm were discussed; that same example will serve to illustrate the related expenses. A fitness training company has one associate and one owner. The plan is to hire one associate per month during the growth phase. The owner is collecting a base salary of $4,000 per month. Associates can be hired for $4,500 per month with a bonus at the end of the year *if* the firm makes a profit. Benefits are $200 per month per employee and the employer must contribute 7.65 percent of an employee's salary for Social Security. Associates are paid their base salary even though their utilization is not at peak efficiency until they have worked for two months or more. Office rental is $2,000 per month and computer lease and phone costs are $100 per month per employee. What are the monthly expenses and resulting cash flow?

	Month 1	Month 2	Month 3
Owner salary	$4,000	$4,000	$4,000
Associate 1	4,500	4,500	4,500
Associate 2		4,500	4,500
Associate 3			4,500
Benefits ($200 per employee)	400	600	800
Social Security (7.65 percent)	650	995	1,339
Office rent	2,000	2,000	2,000
Computer and telephone	200	300	400
Total expenses	$11,750	$16,895	$22,039
Revenue	$8,800	$20,000	$31,200
Net cash flow before taxes	($2,950)	$3,105	$9,161

In this example, expenses related to the number of employees are the most significant. Also, since salaries have to be paid even when an employee is too new to be fully productive in producing revenue, the firm experiences a negative net cash flow in the first month before enough employees are generating sufficient revenue to "carry" the new employee cost.

RECURRING REVENUE FIRMS

Recurring revenue firms, such as wireless communications and cable services, frequently have relatively large expenses at the front end of service and then somewhat lower recurring expenses as the service is provided. For instance, a fixed wireless or cable company typically requires an employee to install an electronic device at a job site, which can be an expensive endeavor. In addition, a salesperson may have to be compensated with a commission. Once the service is operating, however, the monthly cost and effort to provide it could be quite low.

Here are the estimated expenses for Real Cheap TV Inc. from Chapter 4. The company pays $23 in labor costs in order to hook up a new device. The salesperson, who is hired as a subcontractor, gets a commission equal to three months' revenue for each new customer. In order to maintain growth in revenues, 150 new customers must be added each month to make up for the 5 percent disconnect rate. Monthly revenue is $10 per customer and the firm starts out with 1,000 current customers. The monthly cost of providing the service is $1 per customer per month for airtime. Finally, salary for the owner is $4,000 per month with benefits of $200 and a Social Security tax contribution of 7.65 percent. Office rental is $2,000. What are the monthly expenses and the resulting cash flow?

	Month 1	Month 2	Month 3
Hook-up cost (150 × $23)	$3,450	$3,450	$3,450
Commission (3 months revenue for each new customer)	4,500	4,500	4,500
Airtime cost (# old customers + 150 new) × (1 minus 5% disconnect) × ($1/month)	1,093	1,181	1,265
Owner's salary	4,000	4,000	4,000
Benefits	200	200	200
Social Security (7.65 percent)	306	306	306
Total expenses	$13,549	$13,637	$13,721
Revenue	$10,930	$11,810	$12,640
Cash flow before taxes	($2,619)	($1,827)	($1,081)

Clearly, having a lot of new customers creates a large amount of one-time expenses. Therefore, when a firm is in a period of trying to grow its customer base, it often winds up experiencing negative cash flow. New growth means new customers, and new customers may mean large up-front expenditures. Therefore, this type of business model may result in losses when the company aggressively pursues sales growth; ironically, the firm will be more likely to experience profits when sales growth is stopped or at least slowed. However, this does not mean that firing all the salespeople is the answer for achieving long-term profits because 5 percent of the customers disconnect each month. Eventually, all the revenue will disappear unless disconnected customers are continually replaced with new customers.

COMMISSION-BASED SALES FIRMS

The commission-based selling model typically requires that salespeople take part or all of their compensation in the form of a sales commission. The expense of paying a commission can be forecasted simply by multiplying the number of units forecasted to be sold by the commission per unit. A key element is to set a commission structure that attracts people into the sales profession and, at the same time, is not so generous that the firm ends up operating at a loss just to pay the commission.

We will use the same commission-based company example from Chapter 4 to analyze the expense side of a commission-based company. The Harmon Company plans to hire one new salesperson per month during the first five months of the start-up year. The base level of sales expected from each salesperson is 100 units per month. It takes three months for a salesperson to be fully effective (i.e., sell 33 units in the first month, 66 in the second, and 100 in the third). The price per unit is $500, and salespeople are paid a commission equal to $50 per unit. The wholesale cost per unit is $100. The owner is to be paid $4,000 per month, the benefit package costs $200 per employee, and the employer's Social Security contribution will cost 7.65 percent of the gross payroll. Office rent is $2,000 per month. Telephone and computer leasing costs are $100 per month per employee. What are the monthly expenses and resulting cash flow?

Table 5.2

The Harmon Company's Commission-Based Payroll Example

	Month 1	Month 2	Month 3	Month 4	Month 5
Salesperson 1	33 × 50	66 × 50	100 × 50	100 × 50	100 × 50
Salesperson 2		33 × 50	66 × 50	100 × 50	100 × 50
Salesperson 3			33 × 50	66 × 50	100 × 50
Salesperson 4				33 × 50	66 × 50
Salesperson 5					33 × 50
Commissions	1,650	4,950	9,950	14,950	19,950
Owner salary	4,000	4,000	4,000	4,000	4,000
Social Security (7.65%)	432	685	1,067	1,450	1,832
Benefits (200/empl)	400	600	800	1,000	1,200
Telephone/computer	200	300	400	500	600
Office rent	2,000	2,000	2,000	2,000	2,000
Wholesale cost	3,300	9,900	19,900	29,900	39,900
Total expenses	$11,982	$22,435	$38,117	$53,800	$69,482
Revenue	$16,500	$49,500	$99,500	$149,500	$199,500
Net cash flow	$4,518	$27,065	$61,383	$95,700	$130,018

Table 5.2 shows that the salespeople were officially made employees of the firm. As a result, benefits had to be paid for each new salesperson added and Social Security taxes had to be calculated and paid on the salesperson's commissions. Notice the difference from the Real Cheap TV example, in which a commission was paid to a salesperson for each new customer and the salesperson was considered a subcontractor. The salesperson for RCTV was *not* an employee but a separate business that performed the sales function in exchange for a fee. Out of that fee, the salesperson was responsible for paying Social Security taxes, insurance, and so on. Hence, benefits and Social Security taxes were not paid for by RCTV, which demonstrates a possible advantage of outsourcing some of the functions of the firm rather than hiring employees to do everything in-house. Subcontracting out functions such as sales, accounting, human resources, and payroll will not always be the most efficient way to handle a particular business function, but frequently it can be effective in reducing the amount of time and attention that an entrepreneur has to spend on paperwork and legal responsibilities.

CYCLICAL OR SEASONAL FIRMS

It is important for businesses that have only a seasonal demand for their product or service not to count on a sustainable level of revenue (and certainly not growth) during months that they cannot maintain customers.

Sammy's Ski Jumping School, for example (from Chapter 4), can operate only in the months of December, January, and February. Because there is only one ski jump in the entire state, the number of students that can be taught is limited. Only five students can be taught per day at a fee of $100 per student, and because of holidays and lift times, the school is open only twelve days in December, eighteen days in January, and seventeen days in February. The ski resort that has the ski jump has agreed to make Sammy the official ski jumping instructor. In return, however, the resort demands an annual fee of $4,800 to reserve the ski jump, payable at the rate of $400 per month. Sammy works as a construction worker during the spring, summer, and fall months. What are the monthly expenses and the resulting cash flow?

	Nov.	Dec.	Jan.	Feb.	March	April
Fee to resort	400	400	400	400	400	400
Revenue	0	6,000	9,000	8,500	0	0
Net cash flow	(400)	5,600	8,600	8,100	(400)	(400)

The key point to consider in this situation is that somehow the entrepreneur must be prepared to survive during the times of the year when revenue is not coming in. In this case, Sammy runs this business only during the peak winter months and has alternative employment to meet his living expenses for the rest of the year.

REDUCING EXPENSES THROUGH BOOTSTRAPPING

For many entrepreneurs, simply understanding cost behavior and using accurate forecasting techniques are not enough to achieve profitability and positive cash flow. Because of limited resources or a desire to keep control of their business, these entrepreneurs might need to find ways to "sharpen the pencil" and bring expenses down below their initial forecasts. At first this may seem an impossible task. However, there is a variety of techniques and tools that can help achieve the same outcomes while greatly reducing marketing, employee, and overhead costs. This process is known as *bootstrapping* (Cornwall 2009). Chapter 11 will examine bootstrapping management techniques in detail and provide examples of a variety of tools and techniques that can reduce expenditures in all categories.

SUMMARY

Forecasting expenses requires an understanding of how costs behave—that is, as variable, fixed, or mixed costs. Expense behaviors also differ by type of business and type of sales cycle. Bootstrapping is a means of managing expenses by creatively reducing costs without reducing the impact of the activity. Chapter 6 will integrate the financial model built in the first five chapters into a spreadsheet format that can be used to forecast financial statements for new and growing ventures.

DISCUSSION QUESTIONS

1. What are the three different types of costs, and how do they differ?
2. What would be the relationship between sales revenue and profit when a firm operates with a very high degree of fixed expenses and very little variable costs?
3. How are profit and revenue related in a business where almost all the expenses are variable?

4. Why should an entrepreneur need to know what the operation's breakeven point is if the goal is to make a profit?

5. How are the expenses and the resulting cash flow likely to differ for a service company such as a law firm compared with a service company with recurring revenue that has an up-front hook-up expense and can provide the service almost for free?

6. What is the key challenge for a seasonal firm in terms of revenues versus expenses?

7. What is bootstrapping, and why is it important to a start-up firm?

8. Given a long enough time frame, can expenses always be fixed?

9. Having all sales employees working on a totally commission-based compensation plan has certain advantages for the firm. What difficulties would an entrepreneur face in trying to implement such a plan?

10. What is the difference between expenses and cash flow?

11. Why do recurring revenue and commission-based firms frequently experience losses during periods of rapid sales growth?

OPPORTUNITIES FOR APPLICATION

1. If a product can be sold for $1,000 per unit, the variable cost per unit is $550, and fixed costs are $2 million, how many units must be produced and sold before the firm can break even?

2. If an employee has a salary of $50,000 per year, benefits cost the company $7,200 per employee per year, and the employer's share of the Social Security tax is 7.65 percent, what is the direct cost per year for this employee?

3. A salesperson in a recurring revenue firm is paid the equivalent of 2.5 months' sales revenue for each new customer added. The charge for the service is $120 per month, and providing the service costs the company $50 per month per customer. It costs $25 to initially hook up each new customer. What would be the effect on this month's expenses if the salesperson added fifty-five new customers this month?

4. An assembly line can produce 120 units per hour and the material cost is $15 per unit. A single employee, who is paid $22 per hour, can operate the assembly line. The employee works an eight-hour day and there are twenty workdays in a month. The company's contribution to Social Security is 7.65 percent of employee pay, and benefits cost the company about $565 per month per employee. Maintenance on the assembly line costs $1,000 per month. What is the total cost of producing the product for one month?

5. Facility rent is $2,200 per month, accounting services cost $2,600 per month, insurance is $1,100 per month, and utilities such as phone and electricity cost $550 per month. The manager is paid $89,000 per year, gets benefits worth $6,500 per year, and the Social Security contribution is 7.65 percent. Given this information, what is the amount of annual fixed expense that this company has to pay?

6. Given the information in problem 5, if the profit contribution after variable expenses is $125 per unit, is the firm making a profit if it produces and sells 1,000 units per year?
7. If a product has variable costs of $50 per unit, fixed costs of $100,000, and revenue of $65 per unit, would it be possible for this firm to achieve a 22 percent rate of return on an investment of $2.5 million at a sales level of 2,000 units?
8. If a firm's total material cost increases by $150,000 when the level of production increases by 6,500 units, what is the variable cost on a per unit basis?
9. Categorize the various expenses and examine the cost behaviors of a business you now operate or plan to start in the near future.

REFERENCE

Cornwall, J. 2009. *Bootstrapping*. Englewood Cliffs, NJ: Pearson/Prentice-Hall.

6 Integrated Financial Model

The previous chapters have presented a model of financial forecasting for entrepreneurial ventures. Chapter 6, which completes the first section of this book, integrates all the forecasts, assumptions, goals, and objectives into a working spreadsheet model. A spreadsheet tool such as this allows the entrepreneur to adjust plans, create multiple "what-if" scenarios, and develop the beginnings of a system for the financial management of the entrepreneurial venture. By creating an inventory of assumptions and milestones, the entrepreneur is able to track and make adjustments in the forecasts as the situation changes. Once completed, the financial statements that flow out of the spreadsheet can be integrated into a business plan or funding document.

THE ENTREPRENEUR'S ASPIRATIONS RECONSIDERED

As discussed in Chapter 2, any financial modeling of a new business venture should begin with the aspirations of the founders. Although an entrepreneur may have various aspirations, clearly identifying the *financial* aspirations is the first step in building a financial model (see Figure 6.1). Both the income and wealth needs of the entrepreneur should be considered. Generally speaking, the income needs of the entrepreneur should be built into the model as a fundamental assumption. Although many entrepreneurs plan to take a low salary in the early stages of a new venture, a clear set of income expectations for the entrepreneur over the first three years of the business should be established. Entrepreneurs who go into a venture with the thought that they will get by on whatever extra cash is created by the business are often disillusioned within a short time. The plan for the entrepreneur's income from the business should be as deliberate and explicit as the plan to pay rent and employee payroll. Of course, if the business does not go according to plan, it is the owner's paychecks that are the first to be deferred. However, that does not mean that the plan should not attempt to account for a reasonable salary for the owner in the forecasts and budgets.

Integrating into the plan the creation of wealth for the owner, while less precise than planning for income, is no less important. As discussed in Chapter 2, wealth for the entrepreneur is ultimately created through the ability of the business to generate a

Figure 6.1 **Model for Entrepreneurial Financial Management**

profit. While Chapter 15 presents a detailed discussion of valuation for a going concern, the "quick and dirty" method of valuation can help set profit targets in the forecasting stage of a new venture. Using the methods described in Chapter 2, a profit target can be established for the forecasting model. An important consideration is the ultimate timing of when the entrepreneur would like to take the wealth "out of the business," typically through some form of exit from the venture (Chapter 16 discusses such transitions in detail). This process is called *realization of wealth*. For example, if the entrepreneur wants to realize the wealth from a business within five years, the forecasting model should show clear and steady progress toward the profitability levels necessary to achieve this goal. Another entrepreneur might have a longer time frame in which the realization of wealth is tied to retirement in twenty years. For that entrepreneur, the pressure to build necessary profits might not be as great in the short term. The challenge for the second entrepreneur is to build a venture that can sustain profitability over a long period. This is no small accomplishment in itself and requires a different approach to forecasting, with less concern for engineering high profitability into the new venture quickly.

Once the entrepreneur establishes the wealth and income goals for the business that will serve as the foundation of financial planning, the actual spreadsheet modeling can begin. The next section discusses how the format of the income statement can help the entrepreneur better understand the business.

CONTRIBUTION FORMAT INCOME STATEMENT

A useful tool for assessing company performance and pinpointing potential problems is the style of income statement that is generated by the templates supplied with this textbook. (The specific instructions for these templates can be found in Appendix 6.1 on page 96.) This style is called the *contribution format*. It shows the contribution from sales, also called *operating margin*, before considering the indirect costs related to general and administrative expenses. With this style, entrepreneurs can locate the major sources of profit and, conversely, where that profit is most likely to disappear. The top of the income statement starts with the revenue, followed by the expenses that most professionals would consider direct expenses. The difference between revenues and direct expenses results in operating margin, which represents the amount available to cover indirect expenses. The balance left after indirect expenses are covered is called *Earnings Before Interest and Taxes* (EBIT).

EARNINGS BEFORE INTEREST AND TAXES

EBIT represents the income earned by the company before considering interest and income taxes. Interest is a result of the decision the entrepreneur made about how the business would be financed. The templates in this chapter allow the input of an interest rate for both long- and short-term borrowings.

The templates do not attempt to provide a tax calculation because that depends on the entrepreneur's decision about how to organize the business. However, the entrepreneur needs to keep in mind the cash flow implications related to income taxes. A good rule of thumb measure is to assume that up to 35 percent of any income generated will be needed to pay income taxes if the business is organized as a corporation and 15 percent to 35 percent (depending on the owner's tax bracket) if it is organized as a sole proprietorship or partnership. Therefore, when evaluating cash flows generated by the business, the entrepreneur must take taxes into consideration as a cash outflow.

At each subtotal stage the entrepreneur sees the level of profit that still exists and, as a result, can start to see which types of expenses have the most significant impact on reducing profit. For most firms, direct operating expenses are the most significant expense. Materials costs and labor costs associated with providing a product typically make up most expenses for a manufacturing firm. In a service business, the salaries of those employees providing the service are usually the largest single expense. For others, administrative or financing costs could have the greatest effect. The main point, however, is that the operating margin allows a businessperson to see where to focus attention for continued profitability or the most likely location of a problem if the firm is not profitable.

INVENTORY OF ASSUMPTIONS

A crucial part of planning in general and raising funds from investors in particular is to list and justify the key assumptions that the entrepreneur is making about how business will be conducted. The forecasting template included with this book includes an assumption section that allows the entrepreneur to begin to determine the kind of information that must be uncovered or assumed for the future.

Items about which assumptions would need to be made and justified might include the following:

1. The level of sales in units.
2. The selling price per unit.
3. The cost of goods sold per unit or per dollar of revenue.
4. The credit terms, if any, that the firm will offer its customers. Will all sales be made in cash, or will customers be allowed a month or two before payment is due?
5. The relationship between inventory and future sales.
6. The salaries, rent, utilities, telephone, transportation, and insurance costs that are directly related to delivering sales.
7. The administrative expenses of the business, such as managers' salaries, accounting, insurance, and so on.
8. The amount of equipment that must be purchased and how long it will last.
9. The relationship between accounts payable and expenses. Will all expenses be paid immediately or can some of them be delayed for a month or two?

10. The financing currently available to the firm. How much is borrowed funds and how much is investment by owners?
11. The interest rate the firm is expecting to pay on its debt.

Chapter 5 discusses how to make and justify the assumptions that deal with costs. The most important of all these assumptions will, of course, be the ones made about sales. To arrive at these, an entrepreneur must first answer the following two questions.

1. Will there be product development time, and if so, how many months will it take before the product can actually be sold to the public? During this time the firm would be operating without any revenue. To determine the length of the development period, information could be gathered from engineers, potential employees who are expected to be involved with development, or industry experts.
2. Once the product can be offered for sale, how many units can reasonably be expected to sell in the first month, the second month, and so forth? Chapter 4 provides the foundation to answer this question.

SOCIAL VENTURES

Nonprofit social ventures are organized not to make a profit but to deliver a needed service in the community. Nonprofit ventures utilize a different type of income statement than for-profit ventures. The income statement shows the total revenue and support that the organization has received. The expenses are organized into *program costs*, the costs to deliver the programs to the community it serves, and *general and administrative costs*, i.e., those costs incurred to support the programs. Often, a nonprofit income statement also will break out fund-raising costs into a separate category.

The difference between a nonprofit's revenue or support and its total expenses is not called operating income or loss but instead is called a change in net assets.

The balance sheet is organized into assets and liabilities, but instead of the category called stockholders' equity or owners' equity, the difference between assets and liabilities is called net assets. The financial statement model for social service ventures reflects these differences from the for-profit models.

The cash flow statement is much the same as that for a for-profit venture and just as important, since a nonprofit venture often relies on the donations and grants of others versus revenues that it generates.

Not all social ventures are set up as nonprofits. If the social venture is a sustainable model that is based on revenue flows from a product or service, then use the product or service template as applicable. The nonprofit template is only for ventures that seek nonprofit status with the Internal Revenue Service (IRS).

DETERMINING THE AMOUNT OF FUNDS NEEDED

A detrimental mistake for a new venture is to fail to raise enough money, running out before the next funding stage. Therefore, knowing beforehand the amount of funds necessary for a company to reach its next goal or stage of development is crucial. If the necessary amount cannot be raised, then management needs to decide whether to abandon the endeavor or whether it is both possible and still feasible to change the strategy and mode of operation in order to operate within the funding constraint.

When putting together a funding request, it is easy to add up the cost of equipment that must be purchased and the typical monthly expenses of salaries, office rent, and so on that must be paid during the initial phase of the business. What is less obvious, but just as important, is the amount of financing that is necessary to deal with working capital needs. *Working capital* is a term that refers to the current assets of a firm, such as accounts receivable and inventory. For example, inventory must typically be purchased in advance of sales. Frequently, deposits must be made for some purchases before delivery if the firm does not have a credit history with a vendor. Working capital also is needed when sales to customers are made with trade credit. The accounting effect would be to increase the level of accounts receivable as sales are booked, which by itself can cause a huge differential between net income as recorded on the income statement and the actual cash flow generated by the firm. During periods of no sales, and especially during periods of very rapidly growing sales, huge cash outflows can be caused by the need for working capital. If only direct expenditures such as equipment purchases and directly observable expenses are accounted for, and not working capital needs, the firm will run out of cash and go bankrupt long before the next round of financing becomes available. The potential of an entrepreneur's idea becomes totally irrelevant once a firm finds itself unable to pay employees, purchase raw materials, or pay rent.

One of the benefits of using a model that requires assumptions by month is that it reflects what happens in a start-up as business grows or what happens in a seasonal business. Cash flow can fluctuate tremendously in either situation, and that is where a business can be successful and run out of cash because the credit line requested from the bank did not take into account the monthly fluctuations in the cash needs of the company.

Using the Forecasting Template to Determine the Amount of Funds Needed

The template included in the chapter appendix can be used to determine the total amount of financing needed by the firm to get through a particular stage of development. It includes the following steps.

For the initial development stage:

Step 1. Enter all the assumptions in the assumption section except for those concerning long-term debt and investment by owners.

Step 2. Repeat step 1 for all the months or years that correspond to this particular financing stage.

Step 3. Allow the model to recalculate and balance itself automatically on the short-term loan line.

Step 4. Go to the month of the forecasted period where the number on the short-term loan line is largest. This number is the minimum amount of financing necessary to allow the firm to survive during this development stage.

The logic of this is that because the short-term loan line has to represent the amount of funding needed to make the balance sheet balance, it therefore represents the total amount of financing needed when no values are entered for other financing sources.

For any succeeding financing stage:

Step 1.   Enter all the assumptions in the assumption section, including the amounts of long-term debt and investment by owners supplied during the previous stage.

Step 2.   Repeat step 1 for all the months or years that correspond to this particular financing stage.

Step 3.   Allow the model to recalculate and balance itself automatically on the short-term loan line.

Step 4.   Go to the month of the forecasted period where the number on the short-term loan line is largest. This number now represents the minimum amount of additional financing necessary to allow the firm to survive during this stage.

Note that the dollar amounts from the short-term loan line represent the total minimum amount of financing needed to survive that stage of the business. If investors require an itemized list of where the funds will be used, the amount specifically needed for working capital needs can be determined by subtracting the known expenditures in the assumption section, such as equipment to be purchased, salaries of employees, rent, utilities, and so on from the total financing needed. The balance represents the amount of funds that were "burned up" during this phase for working capital purposes.

TIME OUT OF CASH

A measurement that can be used for assessing progress and that is sometimes asked for by potential investors is the firm's *time out of cash*. Raising money frequently requires a lead time of months, especially when a firm has to go through the investment banking process. The time out of cash is a measure of how long the current amount of cash will theoretically last. This is an especially important piece of information during the development stage when revenue is zero or close to zero. Knowing time out of cash is crucial to determining whether a firm will survive until the next round of financing. Operating cash flow from the current month's statement of cash flow is sometimes called the firm's *burn rate* because it represents the amount of cash used that month just for running the business. When compared to the amount of cash that the business currently has on hand, the burn rate can give an entrepreneur a sense of the urgency faced by the firm similar to time out of cash.

Time Out of Cash = Cash/Operating Cash Outflow per Month

Time out of cash represents the number of months that the firm's current cash balance would last if the firm were to continue operating in its current manner. Cash on hand is found on the balance sheet, and operating cash flow is found on the statement of cash flows. This calculation is only an approximation, however, and it is relevant only if operating cash flow is negative. If the firm were actually generating positive cash flow from its operations, it could theoretically be self-sustaining and would never need additional financing to survive.

For example, Standard Start-Up Inc. is a recently started venture. It has $225,000 in cash from its last round of financing. Its statement of cash flows in the most recent month showed that operating cash flow was a negative $12,555, because the firm currently has operating expenses and working capital needs that exceed revenue by this amount.

$$\text{Time Out of Cash} = \$225,000/\$12,555 = 17.9$$

The calculation shows that Standard Start-Up Inc. will run out of cash in approximately eighteen months unless its revenues start to exceed expenses.

ASSESSMENT OF RISK SENSITIVITY

When making financial models for a new venture, it is important to look at more than one set of possible assumptions. That is, the entrepreneur should examine multiple scenarios of demand, pricing, and costs in order to understand the possible situations the business may face. The scenarios that the entrepreneur should look at include the most-likely case, the best case, and the worst case. The most-likely case scenario would include the assumptions that are deemed most realistic and, therefore, most likely to occur. The best-case scenario would include the most optimistic assumptions. The purpose of the best-case scenario is to give the investor some sense of the upside potential given the anticipated investment. The worst-case scenario, logically, would be a set of assumptions representing the situation where everything that could go wrong does go wrong. The projection from this set of assumptions would reflect the downside risk of the investment. It provides the entrepreneur the opportunity to think about the unthinkable and, therefore, develop alternative strategies before things go wrong. Both the best-case and the worst-case scenarios have small probabilities of occurrence, but the point of creating these scenarios is to help the entrepreneur assess the range of potential outcomes in order to prepare the organization for the possible risks.

Assessment of various scenarios is known as a *what-if analysis.* Performing this analyis in advance constitutes a critical management tool. For example, assume an entrepreneur has made financial forecasts using a certain set of assumptions about demand and pricing of the product. If demand is not as strong as initially forecast, the entrepreneur may decide to lower prices to attract new customers. By reducing prices, however, the entrepreneur may push the point of cash flow breakeven well into the future. If the implications of this decision are not fully understood, the entrepreneur may have inadvertently created a new financial model that uses up available working capital before enough cash comes in to pay the ongoing bills. If this situation is anticipated in advance through a what-if analysis, then the entrepreneur would be aware that costs must be cut to keep the business operating successfully with the lower prices.

This type of analysis can also be used when certain large contracts are pending. The entrepreneur can examine multiple scenarios assuming different contracts and timing of contracts to see the impact on profits and cash flow, which can help the entrepreneur understand the impact of a new large customer on a business. What additional overhead will be required? How much working capital will be needed to support the timing of cash flow from the new customer? These are critical questions that need to be answered before the entrepreneur even considers committing to the new customer.

INTEGRATING FINANCIAL FORECASTS INTO BUSINESS PLAN OR FUNDING DOCUMENT

Once the financial forecasting is completed, the forecasted statements need to be used in conjunction with a well-developed business model, built into a formal business plan if one is developed (see Chapter 2), and integrated into other funding documents. Most often, the plan should include at least two years of month-by-month forecasts, with annual or quarterly statements for the next one to two years of operation. Figure 6.2 displays an example of statements generated by the template in Appendix 6.1 as they would appear in a business plan for a service company. The templates produce monthly statements for three years.

A business plan typically includes a most-likely case scenario and a worst-case scenario of assumptions and the accompanying financial statements, particularly if bank financing is being pursued. The most-likely case scenario is what the entrepreneur expects to happen during the time horizon of the business plan. The worst-case scenario usually addresses the instance where a few key assumptions, such as demand for the product or service or pricing for raw materials, prove to be inaccurate. Sometimes worst-case scenarios represent a much slower growth than is anticipated in the most-likely case scenario. The inclusion of two scenarios means that a business plan will need to include two full sets of financial statements, one for each of the possible scenarios.

Bankers, investors, and other professionals who read many business plans look for consistency between the text of the business plan and the numbers in the financial statement forecasts. Specifically, the marketing plan should be consistent with the revenue forecasts and assumptions, and the operating plan should be consistent with the expense forecasts and assumptions. Also, any growth discussed in the plan, typically contained in the marketing plan and industry analysis sections, should be consistent with the trends in the financial statements over time.

SUMMARY

This chapter has presented an integrated spreadsheet model that allows the entrepreneur to place all forecasts, assumptions, goals, and objectives into a single spreadsheet.

Figure 6.2
Income Statement, Year 1
Accrual Basis

	Month 1	Month 2	Month 3	Month 4	Month 5	Month 6	Month 7	Month 8	Month 9	Month 10	Month 11	Month 12	TOTAL
REVENUES													
Cash Sales	-	-	-	-	-	-	-	-	-	-	-	-	-
Charge Sales	8,800	20,000	31,200	36,800	36,800	36,800	36,800	36,800	36,800	36,800	36,800	36,800	391,200
TOTAL SALES	8,800	20,000	31,200	36,800	36,800	36,800	36,800	36,800	36,800	36,800	36,800	36,800	391,200
DIRECT EXPENSES													
Direct Costs	1,320	3,000	4,680	5,520	5,520	5,520	5,520	5,520	5,520	5,520	5,520	5,520	58,680
Salaries	4,500	9,000	13,500	13,500	13,500	13,500	13,500	13,500	13,500	13,500	13,500	13,500	148,500
Benefits	704	1,409	2,113	2,113	2,113	2,113	2,113	2,113	2,113	2,113	2,113	2,113	23,240
Rent	2,000	2,000	2,000	2,000	2,000	2,000	2,000	2,000	2,000	2,000	2,000	2,000	24,000
Utilities	-	-	-	-	-	-	-	-	-	-	-	-	-
Telephone	200	200	200	200	200	200	200	200	200	200	200	200	2,400
Transportation	-	-	-	-	-	-	-	-	-	-	-	-	-
Insurance	-	-	-	-	-	-	-	-	-	-	-	-	-
Bad debt expense	-	-	-	-	-	-	-	-	-	-	-	-	-
TOTAL DIRECT EXPENSES	8,724	15,609	22,493	23,333	23,333	23,333	23,333	23,333	23,333	23,333	23,333	23,333	256,820
OPERATING MARGIN	76	4,392	8,707	13,467	13,467	13,467	13,467	13,467	13,467	13,467	13,467	13,467	134,380
General & Admin. Expenses													
Salaries	4,000	4,000	4,000	4,000	4,000	4,000	4,000	4,000	4,000	4,000	4,000	4,000	48,000
Benefits	626	626	626	626	626	626	626	626	626	626	626	626	7,512
Rent	-	-	-	-	-	-	-	-	-	-	-	-	-
Utilities	-	-	-	-	-	-	-	-	-	-	-	-	-
Telephone	-	-	-	-	-	-	-	-	-	-	-	-	-
Transportation	-	-	-	-	-	-	-	-	-	-	-	-	-
Insurance	-	-	-	-	-	-	-	-	-	-	-	-	-
Legal & Accounting	-	-	-	-	-	-	-	-	-	-	-	-	-
Marketing	-	-	-	-	-	-	-	-	-	-	-	-	-
Office supplies	-	-	-	-	-	-	-	-	-	-	-	-	-
Equipment leases	-	-	-	-	-	-	-	-	-	-	-	-	-
Depreciation-Building	-	-	-	-	-	-	-	-	-	-	-	-	-
Depreciation-Equipment	100	100	100	100	100	100	100	100	100	100	100	100	1,200
TOTAL G&A	4,726	4,726	4,726	4,726	4,726	4,726	4,726	4,726	4,726	4,726	4,726	4,726	56,712
EBIT	(4,650)	(335)	3,981	8,741	8,741	8,741	8,741	8,741	8,741	8,741	8,741	8,741	77,668
Interest Expense		65	122	158	143	100	56	12	0	0	0	0	656
NET INCOME BEFORE TAXES	(4,650)	(399)	3,859	8,583	8,598	8,642	8,685	8,729	8,741	8,741	8,741	8,741	77,012
Cash	1,000	1,000	1,000	1,000	1,000	1,000	1,000	7,459	16,288	25,129	33,971	42,812	
Accounts Receivable	8,800	20,000	31,200	36,800	36,800	36,800	36,800	36,800	36,800	36,800	36,800	36,800	
Total Current Assets	9,800	21,000	32,200	37,800	37,800	37,800	37,800	44,259	53,088	61,929	70,771	79,612	
Land	-	-	-	-	-	-	-	-	-	-	-	-	
Building	-	-	-	-	-	-	-	-	-	-	-	-	
Equipment	3,600	3,600	3,600	3,600	3,600	3,600	3,600	3,600	3,600	3,600	3,600	3,600	
LESS Accum. Depreciation	(100)	(200)	(300)	(400)	(500)	(600)	(700)	(800)	(900)	(1,000)	(1,100)	(1,200)	
Net Fixed Assets	3,500	3,400	3,300	3,200	3,100	3,000	2,900	2,800	2,700	2,600	2,500	2,400	
TOTAL ASSETS	13,300	24,400	35,500	41,000	40,900	40,800	40,700	47,059	55,788	64,529	73,271	82,012	

	1	2	3	4	5	6	7	8	9	10	11	12	Total
LIABILITIES													
Accounts payable	-	-	-	-	-	-	-	-	-	-	-	-	-
Short-term loan inc. interest	12,950	24,450	31,690	28,608	19,909	11,168	2,382	12	0	0	0	0	0
Interest on long-term	-	-	-	-	-	-	-	-	-	-	-	-	-
TOTAL CURRENT	12,950	24,450	31,690	28,608	19,909	11,168	2,382	12	0	0	0	0	0
Long-term loans	-	-	-	-	-	-	-	-	-	-	-	-	-
Total liabilities	12,950	24,450	31,690	28,608	19,909	11,168	2,382	12	0	0	0	0	0
OWNERS' EQUITY													
Investment by owner	5,000	5,000	5,000	5,000	5,000	5,000	5,000	5,000	5,000	5,000	5,000	5,000	5,000
Retained earnings (loss)	(4,650)	(5,050)	(1,190)	7,392	15,591	24,632	33,318	42,047	50,788	59,529	68,271	77,012	77,012
Net equity	350	(50)	3,810	12,392	20,591	29,632	38,318	47,047	55,788	64,529	73,271	82,012	82,012
TOTAL LIAB AND OWNERS' EQUITY	13,300	24,400	35,500	41,000	40,900	40,800	40,700	47,059	55,788	64,529	73,271	82,012	82,012
Receipts													
Cash sales	-	-	-	-	-	-	-	-	-	-	-	-	-
Accounts Receivable collections	-	8,800	20,000	31,200	36,800	36,800	36,800	36,800	36,800	36,800	36,800	36,800	354,400
Total receipts	-	8,800	20,000	31,200	36,300	36,800	36,800	36,800	36,800	36,800	36,800	36,800	354,400
Disbursements													
Direct expenses except bad debt	8,724	15,609	22,493	23,333	23,333	23,333	23,333	23,333	23,333	23,333	23,333	23,333	256,820
G&A except depreciation	4,626	4,626	4,626	4,626	4,626	4,626	4,626	4,626	4,626	4,626	4,626	4,626	55,512
Interest on long-term	-	-	-	-	-	-	-	-	-	-	-	-	-
Total disbursements	13,350	20,235	27,119	27,959	27,959	27,959	27,959	27,959	27,959	27,959	27,959	27,959	312,332
Net cash flow from operations	(13,350)	(11,435)	(7,119)	3,241	8,841	8,841	8,841	8,841	8,841	8,841	8,841	8,841	42,068
Cash flow from investing activities													
Purchase of Land	-	-	-	-	-	-	-	-	-	-	-	-	-
Purchase of Building	-	-	-	-	-	-	-	-	-	-	-	-	-
Purchase of Equipment	(3,600)	-	-	-	-	-	-	-	-	-	-	-	(3,600)
Net cash flow from investing activities	(3,600)	-	-	-	-	-	-	-	-	-	-	-	(3,600)
Cash flow from financing activities													
Investment by owners	5,000	-	-	-	-	-	-	-	-	-	-	-	5,000
Long-term loan additions (payments)	-	-	-	-	-	-	-	-	-	-	-	-	-
Net cash flow from long-term financing activities	5,000	-	-	-	-	-	-	-	-	-	-	-	5,000
Net cash increase (decrease)	(11,950)	(11,435)	(7,119)	3,241	8,841	8,841	8,841	8,841	8,841	8,841	8,841	8,841	43,468
Short-term loan increase (decrease)	12,950	11,435	7,119	(3,241)	(8,841)	(8,841)	(8,841)	(2,382)	(12)	(0)	(0)	(0)	(656)
Beginning cash	-	1,000	1,000	1,000	1,000	1,000	1,000	1,000	7,459	16,288	25,129	33,971	33,971
Ending cash	1,000	1,000	1,000	1,000	1,000	1,000	1,000	7,459	16,288	25,129	33,971	42,812	42,812

From this spreadsheet, forecasted financial statements can be created to serve both the entrepreneur and potential outside funders. Parts II and III of this book discuss the management of a venture's financial resources once it is operating. Monitoring the financial performance, managing the scarce resources, including cash, of a new venture, and using external sources of funding will be examined in Chapters 7–14.

APPENDIX 6.1. INSTRUCTIONS FOR USING THE INTEGRATED FINANCIAL STATEMENTS TEMPLATE

There are three versions of the Integrated Financial Statements Template Spreadsheet. The first version is for businesses that have inventory. Examples of this type of business include retail, distribution, resellers, and manufacturing. The second version is for businesses with no inventory. Examples include service, consulting, health care, software, and engineering. The third version is for nonprofits, which are part of a new field of entrepreneurship called *social entrepreneurship*. This book contains all three versions of the spreadsheet template. The Excel spreadsheets also can be found online at Dr. Cornwall's blog, *The Entrepreneurial Mind* (www.drjeffcornwall.com). There are hard links to all three versions of the template at this site in the side column in the block labeled "Financial Analysis Spreadsheets." These templates, which are free to download, can be used multiple times to test different possible ventures under consideration or to explore multiple assumptions and scenarios for a single business.

The proper development of assumptions is key to getting the most out of these spreadsheets. Each assumption should be carefully documented and any changes in assumptions should be noted. The financial statement assumptions should come out of the business plan assumptions, with all assumptions being consistent and clearly tied together.

The use of the templates requires only a very basic understanding of the use of computer spreadsheets. No programming is required. Simply enter data in the proper cells as instructed. If unusual errors occur when entering data, it may be the result of entering a space in the assumptions worksheet instead of a zero. In troubleshooting this problem, make sure that zeros are entered into any "empty" cell.

There are four worksheets for each version of the template. One is for the assumptions, and the remaining three are the actual financial statements for three years. Yellow cells indicate data to be entered. Blue cells indicate model calculations. The worksheets will provide financial statements for three years when completed.

PRODUCT MODEL [FOR A BUSINESS THAT SELLS INVENTORY]

- Assumptions Worksheet, Year 1 (see Figure 6.A1)

Sales

Step 1. Assumptions for sales should be derived directly from the marketing plan. Assumptions can be entered using two different approaches:

Figure 6A.1
Year One

Lightly shaded cells are input cells
Darkly shaded cells will calculate. No input is required.

FINANCIAL STATEMENT ASSUMPTIONS	Month 1	Month 2	Month 3	Month 4	Month 5	Month 6	Month 7	Month 8	Month 9	Month 10	Month 11	Month 12
Units sold	-	-	-	-	-	-	-	-	-	-	-	-
Selling price per unit	-	-	-	-	-	-	-	-	-	-	-	-
% sales in cash	0%	0%	0%	0%	0%	0%	0%	0%	0%	0%	0%	0%
% sales on account	100%	100%	100%	100%	100%	100%	100%	100%	100%	100%	100%	100%

Accounts Receivable Collections

	Month 1	Month 2	Month 3	Month 4	Month 5	Month 6	Month 7	Month 8	Month 9	Month 10	Month 11	Month 12
% collected in month of sale	0%	0%	0%	0%	0%	0%	0%	0%	0%	0%	0%	0%
% collected in month following	0%	0%	0%	0%	0%	0%	0%	0%	0%	0%	0%	0%
% collected in second month following	0%	0%	0%	0%	0%	0%	0%	0%	0%	0%	0%	0%
% collected in third month following	0%	0%	0%	0%	0%	0%	0%	0%	0%	0%	0%	0%
% not collected (bad debt expense)	0%	0%	0%	0%	0%	0%	0%	0%	0%	0%	0%	0%

Cost of Goods Sold - enter % of sales by month

Enter amount for each month directly on the income statement worksheet or create your own worksheet to link to the income statement.

Direct Expenses
General and Administrative Costs

Enter amount for each month directly on the income statement worksheet or create your own worksheet to link to the income statement.

Payroll Taxes

FICA	0.062
Medicare	0.0145
Unemp	0.01
Other Benefits	0.07
TOTAL	0.1565

Enter % - Required coverage = 0%
Minimum coverage = 7%
Competitive coverage = 10%+

INTEREST (annual rate in %)

	Month 1	Month 2	Month 3	Month 4	Month 5	Month 6	Month 7	Month 8	Month 9	Month 10	Month 11	Month 12
Short-term-added to loan	0%	0%	0%	0%	0%	0%	0%	0%	0%	0%	0%	0%
Long-term-paid month following	0%	0%	0%	0%	0%	0%	0%	0%	0%	0%	0%	0%

Balance Sheet Assumptions

	Month 1	Month 2	Month 3	Month 4	Month 5	Month 6	Month 7	Month 8	Month 9	Month 10	Month 11	Month 12
Minimum cash	-	-	-	-	-	-	-	-	-	-	-	-
Inventory: 1-5 months supply of inventory	-	-	-	-	-	-	-	-	-	-	-	-
Land purchase	-	-	-	-	-	-	-	-	-	-	-	-
Building purchase	-	-	-	-	-	-	-	-	-	-	-	-
Equipment purchases	-	-	-	-	-	-	-	-	-	-	-	-
Life in months-Building	-	-	-	-	-	-	-	-	-	-	-	-
Life in months-Equipment	-	-	-	-	-	-	-	-	-	-	-	-

Accounts payable

	Month 1	Month 2	Month 3	Month 4	Month 5	Month 6	Month 7	Month 8	Month 9	Month 10	Month 11	Month 12
% of current month's expenses paid next month Balance paid in current month	100%	100%	100%	100%	100%	100%	100%	100%	100%	100%	100%	100%
Current month's inventory purchases	-	-	-	-	-	-	-	-	-	-	-	-

	Month 1	Month 2	Month 3	Month 4	Month 5	Month 6	Month 7	Month 8	Month 9	Month 10	Month 11	Month 12
Long-term loan additions (payments)	-	-	-	-	-	-	-	-	-	-	-	-
Investments by owners	-	-	-	-	-	-	-	-	-	-	-	-

1. Enter the number of units sold by month, and
2. Enter the average sales price per unit by month

or enter -budgeted sales as a single amount:

1. Enter 1 in the units sold cell, and
2. Enter the actual dollar amount of budgeted sales in the selling price cell

Step 2. Enter the percentage of sales that is expected to be collected in cash. This can range from 0 percent to 100 percent, based on the nature of the business. For example, a retail business may make all sales for cash and have no sales on credit. A wholesaler may send out invoices for all of its sales, thus making 100 percent of its sales on credit. After entering the percentage of cash sales, the spreadsheet will automatically enter the balance of sales as credit sales (accounts receivable). Sales paid for with bank credit cards (Visa, MasterCard, etc.) are considered cash sales.

Step 3. If credit is extended to customers, the next assumption needed is how quickly the business will collect these receivables. This assumption is entered into the spreadsheet as follows:

1. Percent collected in the month of sale
2. Percent collected in the next 31–60 days
3. Percent collected in the next 61–90 days
4. Percent collected in the next 91–120 days
5. Percent never collected (bad debt)—this amount will show up on the income statement as bad debt expense

An entrepreneur can obtain estimates for these percentages from other businesses in the same industry, from industry trade associations, or from published financial data available in many libraries or the Internet. This assumption should be entered for each month in the spreadsheet (however, the amount may be kept the same for each month). *The total of the percentages entered must equal 100 percent!*

Expenses

- Cost of goods sold: Enter the cost of the products being sold as a percentage of the selling price. Enter the percentage into the spreadsheet for each month (the percentage can be the same if that is appropriate, or it can change if the cost changes over time due to factors such as volume discounts or inflation).
- Direct operating expenses: These are the expenses directly related to the selling and distribution of the product. They do not include general and administrative expenses. Enter the salaries, rent, utilities, telephone, transportation, insurance, and any other expenses directly related to delivering sales into the income statement worksheet within the spreadsheet. Several cells have

been left blank to allow users to enter expenses pertinent to their particular business.

The model assumes the following percentages of salaries for benefits: 6.2 percent for FICA, 1.45 percent for Medicare, and 1 percent for unemployment. A cost percentage for health-care benefits will need to be entered directly into the assumptions page. If no health-care or dental benefits will be offered to employees, enter 0 percent. If a minimal amount of health-care benefits will be provided (e.g., very basic health insurance, but no dental, and employees pay part of the cost), a reasonable assumption is to enter 10 percent. If more comprehensive and competitive coverage is planned, it is reasonable to enter 12 percent or higher. The total percentage shown multiplied by salaries will be used to calculate benefits expense on the spreadsheet.

- General and administrative expenses: These are the expenses of running a business that are not directly tied to delivering sales. These could also be considered indirect costs. Examples include salaries for managers, information services, general office staff, rent for office space, utilities, supplies, marketing, accounting, legal, services contracted for outside, equipment lease payments (monthly rentals), and depreciation related to equipment or buildings purchased. There are additional blank cells where other general and administrative expenses pertinent to a business may be inserted.

Figures for all these categories are entered by month directly into the income statement worksheets except for benefits and depreciation, which are calculated based on assumptions entered on the assumptions worksheet.

Interest

The model assumes that interest on short-term debt is added to the short-term loan. The amount of borrowing against the short-term line is calculated based on all the other assumptions entered into the worksheets. The interest on any long-term debt is assumed to be paid the month following the borrowing.

A rate for short-term debt *must be entered* even if the assumption is that no debt will be used (the rate can fluctuate from month to month—it is usually based on the prime rate plus a factor of 1 to 5 percent depending on the risk of the business venture as determined by the lender).

Enter a rate for long-term debt (i.e., loans to finance fixed assets). This rate is usually fixed.

Balance Sheet Assumptions

- Cash: Enter the minimum amount of cash to be kept on hand at month end.
- Inventory: Enter the number of months of future sales at cost that are intended to be kept on hand in inventory.
- Land: If land will be purchased, enter the amount paid for the land in the month of purchase. Enter it only once.

- Building and equipment: If a building or equipment is going to be purchased, enter the dollar amount of the estimated purchase price in the appropriate cell. Also enter the number of months that the building or equipment is expected to be used. This model assumes a minimum life of 36 months. Life should be entered in multiples of 12 months. Enter the amount only in the month that the asset is planned to be purchased. If capital assets of differing lives will be purchased, enter each purchase in a separate month.
- Accounts payable: Enter the percent of the current month's expenses that are anticipated to be paid the following month. The model will assume the remainder is paid in the current month. At a minimum, assume all payroll and benefits will be paid in the current month. Some businesses try to manage cash by postponing payments, while others try to pay current bills in the current month. The ethical issues involved in delaying payments are discussed in Chapter 1.

    The model will calculate the current month's inventory purchases, which are assumed to be paid in the following month.

- Long-term debt: Enter the amount borrowed on long-term notes (any borrowings that mature more than one year out). Also enter any payments if applicable (be sure to enter payments as a negative value).
- Investments by owners: Enter the amount of any cash investments in the business that the owners plan to make.

Years 2 and 3

Repeat the process above for each of the next two years on the assumption worksheet. Because inventory is based on future sales projections, enter information for the months 37–42 for sales and cost of sales.

- Financial Statement Worksheet (see Figure 6.A2)

There is a worksheet for each of the three years. Each worksheet takes the assumptions entered and provides an income statement, balance sheet, and statement of cash flows using the direct method. Some additional data will need to be entered into the financial statement worksheets. Lightly-shaded cells in the worksheet indicate data to be entered, while the darkly-shaded cells indicate model calculations that are derived from the assumptions entered in the assumption worksheet.

Income Statement

- Sales: The actual dollar amount and category (cash vs. charge) are automatically calculated by the worksheet based on the assumptions entered in the assumption worksheet. No new data are entered here.
- Cost of goods sold: The worksheet will calculate this figure based on the percentage entered in the assumption worksheet. No new data are entered here.

- Gross profit: This represents the profit the business has made on sales after deducting the cost of the product but before any direct operating or general and administrative expenses.

Direct Operating Expenses

- Salaries: These assumptions need to tie to the staffing portion of the business plan. Enter the gross dollar amount of payroll for non-administrative personnel by month. As new staff members are added due to growth, this number should increase to reflect the new staff hired. Benefits will be calculated based on the assumptions already entered in the assumption worksheet.
- Rent, utilities, telephone, transportation, and insurance directly related to delivering sales should be entered by month. Enter either a dollar amount or a formula that is based on a percentage of sales.
- Bad debt expense: This expense is calculated based on the assumptions entered in the assumption worksheet, so no new data are entered here.
- Additional expenses: There are extra rows to add other expenses on the income statement worksheet. Be sure to document any assumptions behind these expenses.

Operating Margin

Operating margin represents the difference between gross profit and direct operating expenses. This gives the entrepreneur a picture of the profitability of the business model. In order for a business to be viable, this margin must be high enough to cover the indirect costs of the business and generate the profit required by the entrepreneur.

General and Administrative Expenses

- Salaries: Enter the total gross salary by month for employees not directly related to production or sales. Again, be sure to tie to staffing plan assumptions in the business plan. Enter amount by month directly on the income statement worksheet. Benefits will be calculated based on the assumptions entered previously in the assumption worksheet.
- For rent, utilities, telephone, transportation, insurance, and supplies for general and administrative activities, enter an amount by month directly on the income statement worksheet.
- Legal, accounting, and marketing represent services that have been contracted for with outside vendors. Enter an amount by month. In some companies, marketing might be considered a direct expense. In those cases, it should be entered under direct operating expenses instead.
- Equipment leases: The amount for rented equipment that will go back to the vendor at the end of the lease term is entered directly on the worksheet.

Figure 6.A2
Income Statement - Year 1
Accrual Basis

	Month 1	Month 2	Month 3	Month 4	Month 5	Month 6	Month 7	Month 8	Month 9	Month 10	Month 11
REVENUES											
Cash sales											
Charge sales											
TOTAL SALES											
COST OF GOODS SOLD											
GROSS PROFIT											
Direct Expenses											
Salaries											
Benefits											
Rent											
Utilities											
Telephone											
Transportation											
Insurance											
Bad debt expense											
TOTAL DIRECT EXPENSES											
OPERATING MARGIN											
General & Admin. Expenses											
Salaries											
Benefits											
Rent											
Utilities											
Telephone											
Transportation											
Insurance											
Legal & Accounting											
Marketing											
Office supplies											
Equipment leases											
Depreciation-Building											
Depreciation-Equipment											
TOTAL G&A											
EBIT											
Interest Expense											
NET INCOME BEFORE TAXES											

	Balance	Month 1	Month 2	Month 3	Month 4	Month 5	Month 6	Month 7	Month 8	Month 9	Month 10	Month 11
BALANCE SHEET - Year 1												
Cash		FALSE	FALSE	FALSE	FALSE	FALSE	FALSE	FALSE	FALSE	FALSE	FALSE	FALSE
Accounts Receivable												
Inventory												
Total Current Assets												
Land												
Building												
Equipment												
LESS Accum. Depreciation												
Net Fixed Assets												
TOTAL ASSETS												

LIABILITIES

	Month 1	Month 2	Month 3	Month 4	Month 5	Month 6	Month 7	Month 8	Month 9	Month 10	Month 11
Accounts payable											
Short-term loan inc. interest											
Interest on long-term											
TOTAL CURRENT											
Long-term loans											
Total liabilities											
OWNERS' EQUITY											
Investment by owner											
Retained earnings (loss)											
Net equity											
TOTAL LIAB AND OWNERS											

CASH FLOW - Year 1

	Month 1	Month 2	Month 3	Month 4	Month 5	Month 6	Month 7	Month 8	Month 9	Month 10	Month 11
Cash flow from operations											
Receipts											
Cash sales											
Accounts Receivable collections											
Total receipts											
Disbursements											
Prior month's inventory purchases											
Direct expenses except bad debt											
G&A except depreciation											
Interest on long-term debt											
Total disbursements											
Net cash flow from operations											
Cash flow from investing activities											
Purchase of Land											
Purchase of Building											
Purchase of Equipment											
Net cash flow from investing activities											
Cash flow from financing activities											
Investment by owners											
Long-term loan additions (payments)											
Net cash flow from long-term financing activities											
Net cash increase (decrease)											
Short-term loan increase (decrease)											
Beginning cash											
Ending cash											

Again, extra lines are provided for additional expense categories reflecting any other expenses specific to the business under consideration in this plan.

- Depreciation: This will be automatically calculated based on the assumptions in the assumption worksheet. No data are entered here.
- Earnings before interest and taxes (EBIT): This number reflects the operating margin less general and administrative expenses.
- Interest: This is calculated automatically based on the interest rates entered in the assumption worksheet. No data are entered here.
- Earnings before taxes (EBT): This may also be referred to as income before taxes. Taxes are not considered in this model due to the many variables related to the legal form of business organization chosen by the entrepreneur.

Balance Sheet [No data should be entered into the balance sheet]

Assets. All assets are calculated automatically based on assumptions entered on the assumptions worksheet.

Liabilities

- Accounts payable: This represents the current month's inventory purchases and direct and general and administrative expenses (except depreciation and bad debt expense) not paid in the current month. It is calculated based on the assumptions worksheet.
- Short-term loan including interest: The short-term loan is the balancing figure to all of the assumptions. The model will automatically borrow short-term funds if cash is depleted. Any cash shortfall in the model will be reconciled with this account. It represents how much will be owed at the end of each month plus the current month's interest.
- Long-term loan interest: This is the interest due on the balance of long-term debt at the end of the previous month. The model assumes it will be paid the following month.
- Long-term loans: This represents the balance in long-term debt based on assumptions entered.
- Owners' equity: This includes any cash investments by the owners based on amounts entered in the assumptions page.
- Retained earnings (deficit): This is calculated by the model. It represents income (loss) since inception of the company.

Cash Flow Statement [No data should be entered]

This statement shows the activity in cash by month with a total for the year. It looks at cash flow from operating the business, cash flow from investments made in land, buildings, and equipment, and cash flow from financing decisions. The model borrows or pays down the short-term loan based on what is needed to maintain cash on hand at the minimum balance set on the assumptions page.

SERVICE MODEL [FOR A BUSINESS THAT SELLS SERVICES]

- Assumptions Worksheet, Year 1 (see Figure 6.A3)

Sales

Step 1. Assumptions for sales should be derived directly from the marketing plan. Assumptions can be entered using two different approaches:

1. Enter the number of units of service sold by month, and
2. Enter the average sales price per unit by month

or enter budgeted sales as a single amount:

1. Enter 1 in the units sold cell
2. Enter the actual dollar amount of budgeted sales in the selling price cell

Step 2. Enter the percentage of sales that is expected to be collected in cash. This can range from 0 percent to 100 percent, based on the nature of the business. For example, a retail service business such as a dry cleaner may make all sales for cash and have no sales on credit. A consulting business may send out invoices for all its sales, thus making 100 percent of its sales on credit. A medical clinic may have a combination, with 20 percent paid in cash and 80 percent on credit to insurance companies. After the percentage of cash sales is entered, the spreadsheet will automatically enter the balance of sales as credit sales (accounts receivable). Sales paid for with bank credit cards (VISA, MasterCard, etc.) are considered cash sales.

Step 3. If credit is extended to customers, the next assumption needed is how quickly the business will collect these receivables. This assumption is entered into the spreadsheet as follows:

1. Percent collected in the month of sale
2. Percent collected in the next 31–60 days
3. Percent collected in the next 61–90 days
4. Percent collected in the next 91–120 days
5. Percent never collected (bad debt)—This amount will show up on the income statement as bad debt expense

An entrepreneur can obtain estimates for these percentages from other businesses in the same industry, from industry trade associations, or from published financial data available in many libraries or the Internet. This assumption should be entered for each month in the spreadsheet (however, the amount may be kept the same for each month). *The total of the percentages entered must equal 100 percent!*

Figure 6A.3

☐ Lightly shaded cells are input cells
▨ Darkly shaded cells will calculate. No input is required.

FINANCIAL STATEMENT ASSUMPTIONS

	Month 1	Month 2	Month 3	Month 4	Month 5	Month 6	Month 7	Month 8	Month 9	Month 10	Month 11	Month 12
Units sold	-	-	-	-	-	-	-	-	-	-	-	-
Selling price per unit												
Percent sales in cash												
Percent sales on account	100%	100%	100%	100%	100%	100%	100%	100%	100%	100%	100%	100%

Accounts Receivable Collections

	Month 1	Month 2	Month 3	Month 4	Month 5	Month 6	Month 7	Month 8	Month 9	Month 10	Month 11	Month 12
Percent collected in month of sale	0%	0%	0%	0%	0%	0%	0%	0%	0%	0%	0%	0%
Percent collected in month following	0%	0%	0%	0%	0%	0%	0%	0%	0%	0%	0%	0%
Percent collected in second month following	0%	0%	0%	0%	0%	0%	0%	0%	0%	0%	0%	0%
Percent collected in third month following	0%	0%	0%	0%	0%	0%	0%	0%	0%	0%	0%	0%
Percent not collected (bad debt expense)	0%	0%	0%	0%	0%	0%	0%	0%	0%	0%	0%	0%

Direct costs as a percent of sales by month

	Month 1	Month 2	Month 3	Month 4	Month 5	Month 6	Month 7	Month 8	Month 9	Month 10	Month 11	Month 12
	0%	0%	0%	0%	0%	0%	0%	0%	0%	0%	0%	0%

All other direct costs — Enter amount for each month directly on the income statement worksheet or create your own worksheet to link to the income statement.

General and Administrative Costs — Enter amount for each month directly on the income statement worksheet or create your own worksheet to link to the income statement.

Payroll Taxes

FICA	0.062
Medicare	0.0145
Unemp	0.01
Other Benefits	0.07
TOTAL	0.1565

Enter % - Required coverage = 0%
Minimum coverage = 7%
Competitive coverage = 10%+

INTEREST (annual rate in %)
Short-term-added to loan
Long-term-paid month following

Balance Sheet Assumptions

	Month 1	Month 2	Month 3	Month 4	Month 5	Month 6	Month 7	Month 8	Month 9	Month 10	Month 11	Month 12
Minimum cash												
Land purchase	-	-	-	-	-	-	-	-	-	-	-	-
Building purchase	-	-	-	-	-	-	-	-	-	-	-	-
Equipment purchases	-	-	-	-	-	-	-	-	-	-	-	-
Life in months-Building	-	-	-	-	-	-	-	-	-	-	-	-
Life in months-Equipment	-	-	-	-	-	-	-	-	-	-	-	-

Accounts payable

% of current month's expenses paid in following month	100%	100%	100%	100%	100%	100%	100%	100%	100%	100%	100%	100%
Balance paid in current month	-	-	-	-	-	-	-	-	-	-	-	-

Long-term loan additions (payments) | - | - | - | - | - | - | - | - | - | - | - | - |
Investments by owners | - | - | - | - | - | - | - | - | - | - | - | - |

Expenses

- Direct costs: These are the material or supply costs directly related to the service the business is delivering—for example, printing, paper, or supplies. Enter this as a percentage of sales by month.
- Other direct operating expenses: These are the expenses directly related to the delivery of the service. They do not include general and administrative expenses. Enter the salaries, rent, utilities, telephone, transportation, insurance, and any other expenses directly related to delivering sales into the income statement worksheet within the spreadsheet. Several cells have been left blank to allow users to enter expenses pertinent to their particular business.

  The model assumes the following percentages of salaries for benefits: 6.2 percent for FICA, 1.45 percent for Medicare, and 1 percent for unemployment. A cost percentage for health-care benefits will need to be entered directly into the assumptions page. If no health-care or dental benefits will be offered to employees, enter 0 percent. If a minimal amount of health-care benefits will be provided (e.g., very basic health insurance, but no dental, and employees pay part of the cost), a reasonable assumption is to enter 10 percent. If more comprehensive and competitive coverage is planned, it is reasonable to enter 12 percent or higher. The total percentage shown multiplied by salaries will be used to calculate benefits expense on the spreadsheet.
- General and administrative expenses: These are the expenses of running a business that are not directly tied to delivering sales. These would be considered indirect costs. Examples include salaries for managers, information services, general office staff, rent for office space, utilities, supplies, marketing, accounting, legal, services contracted for outside, equipment lease payments (monthly rentals), and depreciation related to equipment purchased. There are additional blank cells where other categories of general and administrative expenses pertinent to a business may be inserted.

All these categories are entered by month directly into the income statement worksheets except for benefits and depreciation, which are calculated based on assumptions entered on the assumptions worksheet.

Interest

The model assumes that interest on short-term debt is added to the short-term loan. The amount of borrowing against the short-term line is calculated based on all the other assumptions entered into the worksheets. The interest on any long-term debt is assumed to be paid the month following the borrowing.

A rate for short-term debt *must be entered* even if the assumption is that no debt will be used (the rate can fluctuate from month to month—it is usually based on the prime rate plus a factor of 1 to 5 percent depending on the risk of the business venture as determined by the lender).

Enter a rate for long-term debt (i.e., loans to finance fixed assets). This rate is usually fixed.

Balance Sheet Assumptions

- Cash: Enter the minimum amount of cash to be kept on hand at month end.
- Land: If land will be purchased, enter the amount paid for the land in the month of purchase. Enter it only once.
- Building and equipment: If a building or equipment is going to be purchased, enter the dollar amount of the estimated purchase price in the appropriate cell. Also enter the number of months that the building or equipment will be expected to be used. This model assumes a minimum life of 36 months. Life should be entered in multiples of 12 months. Enter the amount only in the month that the asset is expected to be purchased. If capital assets of differing lives will be purchased, enter each purchase in separate months.
- Accounts payable: Enter the percentage of the current month's expenses that is expected to be paid the following month. The model will assume the remainder is paid in the current month. At a minimum, assume all payroll and benefits will be paid in the current month. Some businesses try to manage cash by postponing payments, while others try to pay current bills in the current month. The ethical issues involved in delaying payments are discussed in Chapter 1.
- Long-term debt: Enter the amount borrowed on long-term notes (any borrowings that mature more than a year out). Also enter any payments if applicable (be sure to enter payments as a negative value).
- Investments by owners: Enter the amount of any cash investments in the business that the owners plan to make.

Years 2 and 3

Repeat the process above for each of the next two years on the assumption worksheet.

- Financial Statement Worksheet (see Figure 6.A4 on pages 109–110)

There is a worksheet for each of the three years. Each worksheet takes the assumptions entered and provides an income statement, balance sheet, and statement of cash flows using the direct method. Some additional data will need to be entered into the financial statement worksheets. Lightly-shaded cells in the worksheet indicate data to be entered, while the darkly-shaded cells indicate model calculations that are derived from the assumptions entered in the assumption worksheet.

Income Statement

- Sales: The actual dollar amount and category (cash vs. charge) are automatically calculated by the worksheet based on the assumptions entered in the assumption worksheet. No new data are entered here.

Figure 6.A4
Income Statement - Year 1
Accrual Basis

	Month 1	Month 2	Month 3	Month 4	Month 5	Month 6	Month 7	Month 8	Month 9	Month 10	Month 11
REVENUES											
Cash sales											
Charge sales											
TOTAL SALES											
DIRECT EXPENSES											
Direct Costs											
Salaries											
Benefits											
Rent											
Utilities											
Telephone											
Transportation											
Insurance											
Bad debt expense											
TOTAL DIRECT EXPENSES											
OPERATING MARGIN											
General & Admin. Expenses											
Salaries											
Benefits											
Rent											
Utilities											
Telephone											
Transportation											
Insurance											
Legal & Accounting											
Marketing											
Office supplies											
Equipment leases											
Depreciation-Building											
Depreciation-Equipment											
TOTAL G&A											
EBIT											
Interest Expense											
NET INCOME BEFORE TAXES											

BALANCE SHEET - Year 1	Balance	Month 1	Month 2	Month 3	Month 4	Month 5	Month 6	Month 7	Month 8	Month 9	Month 10	Month 11
Cash												
Accounts Receivable												
Total Current Assets												
Land												
Building												
Equipment												
LESS Accum. Depreciation												
Net Fixed Assets												
TOTAL ASSETS												

LIABILITIES
Accounts payable
Short-term loan inc. interest
Interest on long-term
TOTAL CURRENT

Long-term loans

Total liabilities

OWNERS' EQUITY
Investment by owner
Retained earnings (loss)
Net equity

TOTAL LIAB AND OWNERS

CASH FLOW - Year 1

	Month 1	Month 2	Month 3	Month 4	Month 5	Month 6	Month 7	Month 8	Month 9	Month 10	Month 11
Cash flow from operations											
Receipts											
Cash sales											
Accounts Receivable collections											
Total receipts											
Disbursements											
Direct expenses except bad debt											
G&A except depreciation											
Interest on long-term											
Total disbursements											
Net cash flow from operations											
Cash flow from investing activities											
Purchase of Land											
Purchase of Building											
Purchase of Equipment											
Net cash flow from investing activities											
Cash flow from financing activities											
Investment by owners											
Long-term loan additions (payments)											
Net cash flow from long-term financing activities											
Net cash increase (decrease)											
Short-term loan increase (decrease)											
Beginning cash											
Ending cash											

Direct Operating Expenses

- Direct costs: The worksheet will calculate this based on the percentage entered on the assumptions worksheet.
- Salaries: These assumptions need to tie to the staffing portion of the business plan. Enter the gross dollar amount of payroll for non-administrative personnel by month. As new staff members are added due to growth, this number should increase to reflect the new staff hired. Benefits will be calculated based on the assumptions already entered in the assumption worksheet.
- Rent, utilities, telephone, transportation, and insurance directly related to delivering sales should be entered by month. Enter either a dollar amount or a formula that is based on a percentage of sales.
- Bad debt expense: This expense is calculated based on the assumptions entered in the assumption worksheet, so no new data are entered here.
- Additional expenses: There are extra rows to add other expenses on the income statement worksheet. Be sure to document any assumptions behind these expenses.

Operating Margin

Operating margin represents profit made on sales after deducting the direct costs of delivering the service, but before any general and administrative costs of running the business. In order for a business to be viable, this margin must be high enough to cover the indirect costs of the business and generate the profit required by the entrepreneur.

General and Administrative Expenses

- Salaries: Enter the total gross salary by month for employees not directly related to sales. Again, be sure to tie to staffing plan assumptions in the business plan. Enter the amount by month directly on the income statement worksheet. Benefits will be calculated based on the assumptions entered previously in the assumption worksheet.
- For rent, utilities, telephone, transportation, insurance, and supplies for general and administrative activities, enter an amount by month directly on the income statement worksheet.
- Legal, accounting, and marketing represent services that are contracted for with outside vendors. Enter an amount by month. In some companies, marketing might be considered a direct expense. In those cases, it should be entered under direct operating expenses instead.
- Equipment leases: The amount for rented equipment that will go back to the vendor at the end of the lease term is entered directly on the worksheet.

Again, extra lines are provided for additional expense categories reflecting any other expenses specific to the business under consideration in this plan.

- Depreciation: This will be automatically calculated based on the assumptions in the assumption worksheet. No data are entered here.

- Earnings before interest and taxes (EBIT): This number reflects the operating margin less general and administrative expenses.
- Interest: This is calculated automatically based on the interest rates entered in the assumption worksheet. No data are entered here.
- Earnings before taxes (EBT): This also may be referred to as income before taxes. Taxes are not considered in this model due to the many variables related to the legal form of business organization chosen by the entrepreneur.

Balance Sheet *[No data should be entered into the balance sheet]*

Assets. All assets are calculated automatically based on assumptions entered on the assumptions worksheet.

Liabilities

- Accounts payable: This represents the current month's direct and general and administrative expenses (except depreciation and bad debt expense) not paid in the current month. It is calculated based on the assumptions worksheet.
- Short-term loan including interest: The short-term loan is the balancing figure to all of the assumptions. The model will automatically borrow short-term funds if cash is depleted. Any cash shortfall in the model will be reconciled with this account. It represents how much will be owed at the end of each month plus the current month's interest.
- Long-term loan interest: This is the interest due on the balance of long-term debt at the end of the previous month. The model assumes it will be paid the following month.
- Long-term loans: This represents the balance in long-term debt based on assumptions entered.
- Owners' equity: This includes any cash investments by the owners based on amounts entered in the assumptions page.
- Retained earnings (deficit): This is calculated by the model. It represents income (loss) since inception of the company.

Cash Flow Statement *[No data should be entered]*

This statement shows the activity in cash by month with a total for the year. It looks at cash flow from operating the business, cash flow from investments made in land, buildings, and equipment, and cash flow from financing decisions. The model borrows or pays down the short-term loan based on what is needed to maintain cash on hand at the minimum balance set on the assumptions page.

SOCIAL VENTURE MODEL [FOR A NONPROFIT BUSINESS]

- Assumptions Worksheet, Year 1 (see Figure 6.A5)

Figure 6.A5

Lightly shaded cells are input cells
Darkly shaded cells will calculate. No input is required.

113

FINANCIAL STATEMENT ASSUMPTIONS

	Month 1	Month 2	Month 3	Month 4	Month 5	Month 6	Month 7	Month 8	Month 9	Month 10	Month 11	Month 12
Units sold	-	-	-	-	-	-	-	-	-	-	-	-
Selling price per unit	-	-	-	-	-	-	-	-	-	-	-	-
% sales in cash	100%	100%	100%	100%	100%	100%	100%	100%	100%	100%	100%	100%
% sales on account	0%	0%	0%	0%	0%	0%	0%	0%	0%	0%	0%	0%

Accounts Receivable Collections

	Month 1	Month 2	Month 3	Month 4	Month 5	Month 6	Month 7	Month 8	Month 9	Month 10	Month 11	Month 12
% collected in month of sale	0%	0%	0%	0%	0%	0%	0%	0%	0%	0%	0%	0%
% collected in month following	0%	0%	0%	0%	0%	0%	0%	0%	0%	0%	0%	0%
% collected in second month following	0%	0%	0%	0%	0%	0%	0%	0%	0%	0%	0%	0%
% collected in third month following	0%	0%	0%	0%	0%	0%	0%	0%	0%	0%	0%	0%
% not collected (bad debt expense)	0%	0%	0%	0%	0%	0%	0%	0%	0%	0%	0%	0%

	Month 1	Month 2	Month 3	Month 4	Month 5	Month 6	Month 7	Month 8	Month 9	Month 10	Month 11	Month 12
Program costs as a % of sales by month	0%	0%	0%	0%	0%	0%	0%	0%	0%	0%	0%	0%

All other program costs — Enter amount for each month directly on the income statement worksheet or create your own worksheet to link to the income statement

General and Administrative Costs — Enter amount for each month directly on the income statement worksheet or create your own worksheet to link to the income statement

Payroll Taxes

FICA	0.062
Medicare	0.0145
Unemp	0.01
Other Benefits	0.07
TOTAL	0.1565	Calculated as a % of salaries

Enter % - Required coverage = 0%
Minimum coverage = 7%
Competitive coverage = 10%+

INTEREST EXPENSE (annual rate in %)

	Month 1	Month 2	Month 3	Month 4	Month 5	Month 6	Month 7	Month 8	Month 9	Month 10	Month 11	Month 12
Short-term-added to loan	0%	0%	0%	0%	0%	0%	0%	0%	0%	0%	0%	0%
Long-term-paid month following	0%	0%	0%	0%	0%	0%	0%	0%	0%	0%	0%	0%

Balance Sheet Assumptions

	Month 1	Month 2	Month 3	Month 4	Month 5	Month 6	Month 7	Month 8	Month 9	Month 10	Month 11	Month 12
Minimum cash	-	-	-	-	-	-	-	-	-	-	-	-
Land purchase	-	-	-	-	-	-	-	-	-	-	-	-
Building purchase	-	-	-	-	-	-	-	-	-	-	-	-
Equipment purchases	-	-	-	-	-	-	-	-	-	-	-	-
Life in months-Building	-	-	-	-	-	-	-	-	-	-	-	-
Life in months-Equipment	-	-	-	-	-	-	-	-	-	-	-	-

Accounts payable

	Month 1	Month 2	Month 3	Month 4	Month 5	Month 6	Month 7	Month 8	Month 9	Month 10	Month 11	Month 12
% of current month's expenses paid in following month	0%	0%	0%	0%	0%	0%	0%	0%	0%	0%	0%	0%
Balance paid in current month	100%	100%	100%	100%	100%	100%	100%	100%	100%	100%	100%	100%

Long-term loan additions (payments)

Month 1	Month 2	Month 3	Month 4	Month 5	Month 6	Month 7	Month 8	Month 9	Month 10	Month 11	Month 12
-	-	-	-	-	-	-	-	-	-	-	-

Sales

Step 1. Many nonprofits have sources of revenues in addition to donations and grants. For example, a nonprofit museum may charge an entrance fee for every visitor. The museum may have a snack shop and a gift shop that generate revenues, and it may rent out its space for weddings and other social events. Many hospitals and private schools are nonprofits. They have charges and fees for those who use their services. Assumptions for fees or sales should be derived directly from the marketing plan. Assumptions can be entered using two different approaches:

1. Enter the number of units of service sold by month, and
2. Enter the average sales price per unit by month

or enter budgeted fees or sales as a single amount:

1. Enter 1 in the units sold cell
2. Enter the actual dollar amount of budgeted sales in the selling price cell

If the venture does not have fees or sales but relies only on donations or grants, these sources of revenue should be entered directly on the income statement worksheet of the template.

Step 2. Enter the percentage of sales that is expected to be collected in cash. This can range from 0 percent to 100 percent, based on the nature of the nonprofit. For example, all fees may be due upon the delivery of the program services and no credit given. Grants, however, may be awarded but the cash not received for several months. After entering the percentage of fees collected in cash, the spreadsheet will automatically enter the balance of fees as accounts receivable. Sales paid for with bank credit cards (Visa, MasterCard, etc.) are considered cash sales.

Step 3. If credit is extended to customers, the next assumption needed is how quickly the business will collect these receivables. This assumption is entered into the spreadsheet as follows:

1. Percent collected in the month of sale
2. Percent collected in the next 31–60 days
3. Percent collected in the next 61–90 days
4. Percent collected in the next 91–120 days
5. Percent never collected (bad debt)—This amount will show up on the income statement as bad debt expense

An entrepreneur can obtain estimates for these percentages from other nonprofits or from nonprofit associations. This assumption should be entered for each month in the spreadsheet (however, the amount may be kept the same for each month). *The total of the percentages entered must equal 100 percent!*

Expenses

- Direct program costs: These are the expenses, other than payroll costs, directly related to delivering the programs or services offered by the venture. They do not include general and administrative expenses.
- Salaries and other program delivery costs: Enter the salaries, rent, utilities, telephone, transportation, insurance, and any other expenses directly related to delivering programs into the income statement worksheet within the spreadsheet. Several cells have been left blank to allow users to enter expenses pertinent to their particular business.

  The model assumes the following percentages of salaries for benefits: 6.2 percent for FICA, 1.45 percent for Medicare, and 1 percent for unemployment. A cost percentage for health-care benefits will need to be entered directly into the assumptions page. If no health-care or dental benefits will be offered to employees, enter 0 percent. If a minimal amount of health-care benefits will be provided (e.g., very basic health insurance, but no dental, and employees pay part of the cost), a reasonable assumption is to enter 10 percent. If more comprehensive and competitive coverage is planned, it is reasonable to enter 12 percent or higher. The total percentage shown multiplied by salaries will be used to calculate benefits expense on the spreadsheet.

- General and administrative expenses: These are the expenses of running a business that are not directly tied to delivering the programs of the nonprofit. These would be considered indirect costs. Examples include salaries for managers, information services, general office staff, rent for office space, utilities, supplies, marketing, accounting, legal, services contracted for outside, equipment lease payments (monthly rentals), and depreciation related to equipment purchased. There are additional blank cells where other categories of general and administrative expenses pertinent to a business may be inserted.

  All these categories are entered by month directly into the income statement worksheets except for benefits and depreciation, which are calculated based on assumptions entered on the assumptions worksheet.

Interest

The model assumes that interest on short-term debt is added to the short-term loan. The amount of borrowing against the short-term line is calculated based on all the other assumptions entered into the worksheets. The interest on any long-term debt is assumed to be paid the month following the borrowing.

A rate for short-term debt *must be entered* even if the assumption is that no debt will be used (the rate can fluctuate from month to month—it is usually based on the prime rate plus a factor of 1 to 5 percent depending on the risk of the business venture as determined by the lender).

Enter a rate for long-term debt (i.e., loans to finance fixed assets). This rate is usually fixed.

Figure 6.A6
Income Statement - Year 1
Accrual Basis

	Month 1	Month 2	Month 3	Month 4	Month 5	Month 6	Month 7	Month 8	Month 9	Month 10
REVENUE AND SUPPORT										
Direct Fees-Cash										
Direct Fees-Charge										
Grants										
Donations										
In-Kind Donations										
Other										
TOTAL REVENUE AND SUPPORT										
Program Expenses										
Direct Program Costs										
Salaries										
Payroll Taxes/Benefits										
Rent										
Professional fees/consultants										
Insurance-W/C										
Program Supplies										
Marketing/Advertising										
Repairs and Maintenance										
Telephone										
Other Utilities										
Equipment Service Contracts										
Web Site										
In-Kind Donations										
Travel Costs										
Bad Debt Expense										
Other										
Other										
Total Program Expenses										
General and Administrative Expenses										
Payroll Taxes/Benefits										
Rent										
Accounting/Legal Fees										
Insurance-Casualty										
Insurance-D&O										
Fundraising Expense										
Gifts/Charitable Donations										
Travel										
Licenses/Permits										
Office Supplies										
Payroll Service										
Consultants										
Repairs and Maintenance										
Subscriptions										
Telephone										
Other Utilities										
Miscellaneous										
Depreciation-Building										
Depreciation-Equipment										
Total General and Administrative Expenses										
Total Operating Expenses										
Interest Expense										
Change in Net Assets										

BALANCE SHEET - Year 1

Balance	Month 1	Month 2	Month 3	Month 4	Month 5	Month 6	Month 7	Month 8	Month 9	Month 10
Cash										
Accounts Receivable										
Total Current Assets										
Land										
Building										
Equipment										
-LESS Accum. Depreciation										
Net Fixed Assets										
TOTAL ASSETS										
LIABILITIES										
Accounts payable										
Short-term loan inc. interest										
Interest on long-term										
TOTAL CURRENT										
Long-term loans										
Total liabilities										
NET ASSETS										
Unrestricted										
Change in Net Assets										
Total Net Assets										
Total Liabilities and Net Assets										

CASH FLOW - Year 1

	Month 1	Month 2	Month 3	Month 4	Month 5	Month 6	Month 7	Month 8	Month 9	Month 10
Cash flow from operations										
Receipts										
Cash fees										
Accounts Receivable collections										
Grants										
Donations										
Other										
Total Receipts										
Disbursements										
Program expenses except bad debt										
G&A except depreciation & donations in kind										
Interest on long-term debt										
Total disbursements										
Cash flow from operations										
Cash flow from investing activities										
Purchase of land										
Purchase of building										
Purchase of equipment										
Net cash flow from investing activities										
Cash flow from financing activities										
Long-term loan additions (payments)										
Net cash flow from long-term financing activities										
Net cash increase (decrease)										
Short-term loan increase (decrease)										
Beginning cash										
Ending cash										

Balance Sheet Assumptions

- Cash: Enter the minimum amount of cash to be kept on hand at month's end.
- Land: If land will be purchased, enter the amount paid for the land in the month of purchase. Enter it only once.
- Building and equipment: If a building or equipment is going to be purchased, enter the dollar amount of the estimated purchase price in the appropriate cell. Also enter the number of months that the building or equipment will be expected to be used. This model assumes a minimum life of 36 months. Life should be entered in multiples of 12 months. Enter the amount only in the month that the asset is expected to be purchased. If capital assets of differing lives will be purchased, enter each purchase in separate months.
- Accounts payable: Enter the percentage of the current month's expenses that is expected to be paid the following month. The model will assume the remainder is paid in the current month. At a minimum, assume all payroll and benefits will be paid in the current month. Some businesses try to manage cash by postponing payments, while others try to pay current bills in the current month. The ethical issues involved delaying payments are discussed in Chapter 1.
- Long-term debt: Enter the amount borrowed on long-term notes (any borrowings that mature more than a year out). Also enter any payments if applicable (be sure to enter payments as a negative value).
- Investments by owners: Enter the amount of any cash investments in the business that the owners plan to make.

Years 2 and 3

Repeat the process above for each of the next two years on the assumption worksheet.

- Financial Statement Worksheet (see Figure 6.A6 on pages 116–117)

There is a worksheet for each of the three years. Each worksheet takes the assumptions entered and provides an income statement, balance sheet, and statement of cash flows using the direct method. Some additional data will need to be entered into the financial statement worksheets. Lightly-shaded cells in the worksheet indicate data to be entered, while the darkly-shaded cells indicate model calculations that are derived from the assumptions entered in the assumption worksheet.

Income Statement: Revenue and Support

Fees. The actual dollar amount and category (cash vs. charge) are automatically calculated by the worksheet based on the assumptions entered in the assumption worksheet. In the museum example, these fees would include revenues from the gift store and snack bar and charges for the use of the facilities. If the museum also receives donations and grants, these revenues will be entered directly in the income statement. In-kind donations are donations of tangible goods instead of cash.

Program Expenses

- Direct program costs: The worksheet will calculate these based on the percentage entered on the assumptions worksheet.
- Salaries: These assumptions need to tie to the staffing portion of the business plan. Enter the gross dollar amount of payroll for non-program personnel by month. As new staff members are added due to growth, this number should increase to reflect the new staff hired. Benefits will be calculated based on the assumptions already entered in the assumption worksheet.
- Rent, utilities, telephone, transportation, and insurance directly related to delivering the programs of the venture should be entered by month. Enter either a dollar amount or a formula that is based on a percentage of sales, if applicable.
    Enter the value of the in-kind donations received as in-kind donations expense. This reflects the cost incurred in delivering programs or services even though there is no cash outflow.
- Bad debt expense: This expense is calculated based on the assumptions entered in the assumption worksheet, so no new data are entered here.
- Additional expenses: There are extra rows to add other expenses on the income statement worksheet. Be sure to document any assumptions behind these expenses.

General and Administrative Expenses

- Salaries: Enter the total gross salary by month for employees not directly responsible for delivering the venture's programs and services. Again, be sure to tie to staffing plan assumptions in the business plan. Enter the amount by month directly on the income statement worksheet. Benefits will be calculated based on the assumptions entered previously in the assumption worksheet.
- For rent, utilities, telephone, transportation, insurance, and supplies for general and administrative activities, enter an amount by month directly on the income statement worksheet.
- Legal, accounting, and marketing represent services that are contracted for with outside vendors. Enter an amount by month.
- Fund-raising expenses can be a significant cost and should be budgeted carefully and realistically because they represent cash outflow before cash inflows will be received.
- Equipment leases: The amount for rented equipment that will go back to the vendor at the end of the lease term is entered directly on the worksheet.

Again, extra lines are provided for additional expense categories reflecting any other expenses specific to the business under consideration in this plan.

- Depreciation: This will be automatically calculated based on the assumptions in the assumption worksheet. No data are entered here.
- Interest: This is calculated automatically based on the interest rates entered in the assumption worksheet. No data are entered here.
- Change in net assets: This represents the excess of revenue and support over total operating expenses. This number is comparable to the net income of a for-profit venture.

Balance Sheet *[No data should be entered into the balance sheet]*

Assets. All assets are calculated automatically based on assumptions entered on the assumptions worksheet.

Liabilities

- Accounts payable: This represents the current month's program and general and administrative expenses (except depreciation and bad debt expense) not paid in the current month. It is calculated based on the assumptions worksheet.
- Short-term loan including interest: The short-term loan is the balancing figure to all of the assumptions. The model will automatically borrow short-term funds if cash is depleted. Any cash shortfall in the model will be reconciled with this account. It represents how much will be owed at the end of each month plus the current month's interest.
- Long-term loan interest: This is the interest due on the balance of long-term debt at the end of the previous month. The model assumes it will be paid the following month.
- Long-term loans: This represents the balance in long-term debt based on assumptions entered.
- Net assets: Unrestricted net assets represent the total change in net assets since the inception of the company, other than the current year. Change in net assets represents the net assets generated in the current year. In a for-profit company, net assets would be referred to as retained earnings.

Cash Flow Statement *[No data should be entered]*

This statement shows the activity in cash by month with a total for the year. It looks at cash flow from operating the business, cash flow from investments made in land, buildings, and equipment, and cash flow from financing decisions. The model borrows or pays down the short-term loan based on what is needed to maintain cash on hand at the minimum balance set on the assumptions page.

PART II

MANAGING THE FINANCIAL RESOURCES OF A VENTURE

7 Monitoring Financial Performance

Part I of this book presented a model and techniques that can assist an entrepreneur in planning the finances of a new venture. Once a business has actually started and is beginning to generate revenues, a whole new set of financial challenges emerges. In addition to the tools for monitoring financial performance examined in this chapter, cash flow management (discussed in Chapter 8) is critical to the survival of a new business. Part III of this text examines the process of securing the funding needed to support a growing business.

But first, this chapter examines how the entrepreneur can gain control of "the numbers" for utilization in decision making. Successful financial management requires a systematic approach. The integrated financial template presented in Chapter 6 clearly demonstrated the importance of identifying and documenting key assumptions that drive financial forecasts. Developing a system for tracking and monitoring these assumptions is the first step in effective financial management in an entrepreneurial business. The model in Part I of this book assumes that the entrepreneur has established long-term personal financial goals for income and wealth that drive the financial goals of the business. The second major step in effective financial management is to establish clear milestones that can track progress toward these long-term goals.

Effective financial management requires an understanding of how to use numbers to manage and make decisions. However, this assumes that the entrepreneur understands what numbers are actually needed for the business and that those numbers are made available by the staff and the accounting systems. Finally, entrepreneurs need to learn how to work effectively with accountants. As discussed in Chapter 1, this can be a challenge, as accountants and entrepreneurs often speak in different languages.

TRACKING ASSUMPTIONS

All financial forecasts and projections are based on a number of assumptions. Demand for the product or service, pricing, staffing requirements, the cost of materials, rents, and so on all have to be estimated, and these estimates are based on assumptions. In Chapter 6, many assumptions were listed in the preparation of the financial statement templates. Certainly, all these assumptions should be carefully documented and listed within the business plan, but there can be any number of additional key assumptions behind the basic assumptions listed in the template.

For example, Carlos Lopez, an entrepreneur, has made the assumption that sales of his product will grow by ten units per month. This assumption is based on a thorough marketing plan that clearly supports this revenue model. However, behind this critical assumption he has explicitly made several additional assumptions. He has assumed that his two salespeople can each make thirty sales calls per month to prospective customers. Of these sixty sales calls, one in ten (in this case, six) will result in a proposal being written up and submitted to the prospective customer. One-third of these six proposals submitted to prospective customers results in an order. This example would yield two orders. The average size of each order is ten units, and each customer will order the average each month, which means these two new customers will order twenty units. Each month, one current customer will stop ordering from the company, which results in the loss of ten units sold to that customer. Table 7.1 displays the additional assumptions behind the assumption of ten new units sold each month. At this point, Lopez has no data for these assumptions. However, even when data become available as the business begins to grow, the assumptions should continue to be tracked, as they are key to the basic revenue growth assumptions in the financial forecast he is relying on to mange his business.

This example illustrates the importance of identifying, listing, and tracking all additional key assumptions that underlie the basic assumptions in the financial forecasts. It should be noted that revenue assumptions are usually the most complex in terms of underlying assumptions. All these additional assumptions should be added to the business plan. At some point, some of the assumptions, such as many of the cost assumptions, will become known facts. These can then be removed from the assumption list, because they will no longer need to be monitored. But even with data, many assumptions will remain uncertain, subject to volatility, and worthy of close scrutiny as the business expands.

Once a comprehensive list of assumptions has been created, the entrepreneur should develop measurements for each assumption. Collectively, these measures create what is known as a *performance dashboard* to monitor the progress of the business (Eckerson 2005). The performance dashboard is the set of financial measures that are specific to the assumptions of a given business, which when examined together offer a view of where the business is headed. It provides the entrepreneur and key management with a consistent set of financial measures that can be consistently monitored and used to manage the business effectively.

In the example above, each sales person develops and maintains a sales log, which allows for data to be gathered that can be used to measure all the key assumptions. The second column in Table 7.1 displays how the data can be gathered to allow for measurements of these assumptions. The sales log will document all sales calls and a complete history of the results of those calls, including proposals made, orders placed, and so forth. A dashboard made up of these performance measures becomes a tool to ensure that the key drivers of the performance of the business are meeting goals.

A key step in this process is making sure that someone in the business is responsible for tracking, summarizing, and interpreting the data gathered for key assumptions.

Table 7.1

Sample List of Assumptions

Assumption	Measurement technique
Thirty sales calls per sales person per month.	Sales staff will keep a log of sales calls with the name of the contact, the date of first contact, proposals submitted to customer, and orders placed by this customer each month.
One in ten sales calls results in proposal to customer.	Sales staff will enter proposals made to each prospective client in the sales activity log.
One third of proposals results in an order.	When a customer places an order, this will be noted in the sales log.
Each order averages 10 units.	The size of each order will be noted in the sales log.
Customers make an average of one order per month.	The date of each order is noted in the sales log.
An average of one customer will stop ordering each month.	If a customer does not make an order in a given month, the sales staff will contact to see if this client intends to make any future orders.

People must report the data that go into the dashboard in a clear, usable format for the entrepreneur and the management team. In this example, the entrepreneur has decided to take on this responsibility. Each month all of the sales logs maintained by the sales force will be reviewed to get the information needed from the raw data about the assumptions used in the business plan. If, for example, the sales logs indicate that the sales staff is making on average only twenty sales calls per month, but that all the other assumptions seem to be fairly accurate, that information can help the entrepreneur understand specifically why sales are not growing as planned. If sales personnel are not making 30 calls, the entrepreneur would need to determine if this was due to their lack of effort or due to unrealistic assumptions. Whatever the cause, the entrepreneur is better able to take corrective action quickly to ensure that the projections in the business plan can be realized.

ESTABLISHING MILESTONES

Financial forecasts, as discussed in Part I of this book, should be based on profit goals that are derived, at a minimum, from the income and wealth goals of the entrepreneur. The profit goals are usually longer-term in nature. For example, Sally Burton, an entrepreneur, has determined that her income goal from her business is to earn twice the salary that she can earn in the market as an employee in an existing business. She sets this goal to compensate for the risk she is taking and to build wealth through this business. Burton realistically assumes that it will take her three years to build the business to the point where she can draw this level of salary. In building the financial forecast, she decides that she should be able to earn 50 percent of her current salary in the first year of the business, match her current salary in the second year, and reach the goal of twice her current salary in the third year. Thus, she has established specific *milestones* to help her monitor the overall progress of the business.

Milestones can be based on time, as in this example, or on sales growth. Sally Burton could have set milestones such as earning the equivalent of her current salary when the business reaches $500,000 in annual sales and earning twice her salary when the business grows to $1 million in sales. Finally, milestones may be tied to certain events in the company's development. For example, Burton could set a milestone of earning her current salary when the first office is fully operational and earning twice her current salary by the time her second office, located in another part of town, is open and fully operational. Whatever milestone is chosen should make sense for a given business.

Setting milestones keeps the entrepreneur's focus on what is critically important in the growth of a business. It keeps the business plan on target for the aspirations and intentions that the entrepreneur had when first starting the new venture. Milestones not only provide a clear focus during the often chaotic growth that businesses can experience as revenues begin to build, but also allow for adjustments in plans as the business grows. Assume that Sally Burton had tied salary milestones to opening new offices. Once her business begins to grow, she realizes that her profit assumptions were overly optimistic. It would take three offices to reach her salary goal. With this information, she can adjust her plan to focus on growing to three offices rather than two, still allowing her original personal goal to be realized through the business.

USING NUMBERS TO MANAGE

Monitoring the financial performance of an entrepreneurial business can take many forms; however, all methods for monitoring financial performance use some standard to compare and evaluate actual financial performance. Current year results can be compared with the results of the previous year, a budget, a competitor, the industry, or the entrepreneur's own expectations.

Performance metrics are different for almost every company. Ottenheimer (1999) recommends that entrepreneurial ventures identify the activities that, when taken together, are critical for building sales and profitability. It also is important to identify measures for both short-term and long-term performance and to include some that measure cash flow. Ottenheimer recommends using only five to eight key measures, because there is a risk that the management team may lose focus if too many activities are measured. These key measures should be discussed and developed with the accountants, both internal and external, to ensure that they understand the unique needs of the business and can help identify useful metrics. The key set of metrics may include daily, weekly, monthly, quarterly, and annual measures. These should become part of the performance dashboard of the business.

Most companies use several standard metrics, all of which fall into two basic categories: financial statement analysis and ratio analysis. This section provides an overview of the various performance metrics, including cash flow, using data from a medical products business. Given the importance of cash flow to entrepreneurial ventures, Chapter 8 will be devoted to covering this important topic in detail.

Exhibit 7.1

Medical Products Inc.: Income Statement (for the years ended December 31)
($000)

	2011		2010	
Net sales	$10,979	100.0%	$9,013	100.0%
Cost of goods sold	5,440	49.5%	4,644	51.5%
Gross profit	5,539	50.5%	4,369	48.5%
Operating expenses				
Research and development	1,053	9.6%	914	10.1%
Selling expense	1,200	10.9%	1,000	11.1%
General and administrative expense	2,825	25.7%	2,358	26.2%
Total operating expenses	5,078	46.3%	4,272	47.4%
Operating income (EBIT)	461	4.2%	97	1.1%
Other income (expense)				
Interest expense	(146)	−1.3%	(95)	−1.0%
Interest income	50	0.4%	38	0.4%
Total other income (expense)	(96)	−0.9%	(57)	−0.6%
Net income before taxes	365	3.3%	40	0.5%
Income taxes	(124)	−1.1%	(14)	−0.2%
Net income	$241	2.2%	$26	0.3%

FINANCIAL STATEMENT ANALYSIS

Vertical analysis is a useful analytical technique for evaluating the income statement. In vertical analysis, items on the income statement are expressed as a percentage of total sales, which can be used to track the relationship of key expenses to sales. This technique is used to spot trends or changes in the relationship between expenses and sales in the business. At a minimum, it allows for examination of the trends in sales, gross profit, expenses, and operating margin on a monthly basis, comparing them with the current month's budget or historical figures from previous periods.

In the example displayed in Exhibit 7.1, the gross profit percentage for Medical Products Inc. has increased by two percentage points compared to a year ago. This means it is generating 50.5 cents of gross profit for every $1 of sales compared with 48.5 cents a year ago. If one of the goals of the company has been to increase gross profit, this is a positive trend. If, however, a new competitor is coming into the market, the company may need to decrease selling prices, which will decrease the gross profit margin. Research and development expense increased in total dollars but declined as a percentage of sales. This means that for every $1 of sales in 2011, the company spent 9.6 cents compared with 10.1 cents a year ago. Again, this decrease in the percentage to sales could be a positive or a negative. It may indicate a drop in the company's commitment to new product development, or it may be the result of

Exhibit 7.2

Medical Products Inc.: Income Statement (for the years ended December 31)
($000)

	2011	2010	Increase (decrease)	Increase (decrease)
Net sales	$10,979	$9,013	$1,966	21.8%
Cost of goods sold	5,440	4,644	796	17.1
Gross profit	5,539	4,369	1,170	26.8
Operating expenses				
Research and development	1,053	914	139	15.2
Selling expense	1,200	1,000	200	20.0
General and administrative expense	2,825	2,358	467	19.8
Total operating expenses	5,078	4,272	806	18.9
Operating income (EBIT)	461	97	364	375.3
Other income (expense)				
Interest expense	(146)	(95)	(51)	53.7
Interest income	50	38	12	31.6
Total other income (expense)	(96)	(57)	(39)	68.4
Net income before taxes	365	40	325	812.5
Income taxes	(124)	(13)	(111)	853.8
Net income	$241	$27	$214	692.6

a significant sales increase. Income from operations as measured by earnings before interest and taxes (EBIT) is 4.2 cents of every $1 sold compared with 1.1 cents a year ago. In general, this indicates that the company is getting more of its sales dollars to the bottom line.

Financial statements also can be analyzed by comparing this year's results with last year's, thus analyzing the percentage increase or decrease (Exhibit 7.2). To calculate the percentage increase or decrease from month to month or year to year, the entrepreneur takes the difference between the two years and divides by the starting point. For example, taking sales from 2011, subtracting sales for 2010, and dividing the difference by the sales for 2010 will calculate the percentage change for Medical Products Inc.

$$\text{Medical Products' sales increase for 2011} = \frac{\$10,979,000 - -\$9,013,000}{\$9,013,000} =$$
$$0.218 \text{ or } 21.8 \text{ percent}$$

Sales for Medical Products Inc. increased $1,966,000, or 21.8 percent. Cost of goods sold increased $796,000, or 17.1 percent. Because sales increased faster than cost of goods sold, gross profit as a percent of sales increased, as mentioned, from 48.5 percent to 50.5 percent. There could be several reasons why sales increased faster than the cost of goods sold. Selling prices might have gone up compared with a year ago. The mix of the products sold might have changed. The cost of manufacturing the products might have declined. Selling expenses in 2011 increased $200,000 or 20 percent compared with 2010. Even though sales increased 21.8 percent, selling expenses did not increase to the same degree, allowing the company to increase profits compared with a year ago.

Several issues should be considered when examining percentage changes in financial statements. First, it cannot be stated definitively that all increases are good or all decreases are bad. It depends on the facts of the situation. If gross profit percent keeps increasing because the entrepreneur keeps raising selling prices, the company may price itself out of the market. If administrative expenses increase at the same rate as sales, the business may be building an infrastructure (overhead) that cannot be supported in a downturn. If investment in research and development is declining as a percent of sales, the company may not be investing in innovations to generate future sales. Therefore, when looking at trend analysis, it is imperative to compare the results to the budget, the previous year, and competitors or industry averages in order to ensure a complete understanding of the trends. Each of these comparisons can provide information that will allow the entrepreneur to understand current performance and to make future operating decisions.

RATIO ANALYSIS

Another set of tools for evaluating financial performance is ratio analysis. A variety of ratios can be calculated, but most fall into one of four categories: liquidity ratios, activity ratios, profitability ratios, and solvency and coverage ratios. Liquidity ratios are used to measure a company's short-term ability to pay maturing obligations. Activity ratios are used to measure how effectively a company is managing the assets under its control. Profitability ratios measure the degree of success or failure of a company for a given period of time. Solvency and coverage ratios measure the degree of protection for long-term creditors and investors.

There is no right or wrong answer in ratio analysis. It is never advisable to simply calculate a ratio for one time period and, based on that, draw a conclusion. Indeed, it is often said that the interpretation of financial ratios is more an art than a science. Ratios should be calculated over time to determine trends. Ratios also should be compared with ratios from past periods, ratios of competitors, and industry ratios. Information on competitors or an industry may be difficult to obtain. However, information is available from the Internet, trade journals, local chambers of commerce, trade shows, and conferences.

Exhibits 7.2 and 7.3 will be used to calculate sample ratios using the results for Medical Products Inc.

The first category of ratios is liquidity ratios. A basic measure of liquidity is the working capital of a company. Working capital equals current assets minus current liabilities. Current assets are cash and other assets that will be turned into cash or used up by the business within one year. Current liabilities are obligations of the business that are due within one year. Working capital is the lifeblood of the company. If the

Exhibit 7.3

Medical Products Inc.: Balance Sheet (December 31)
($000)

	2011	2010
Assets		
Current assets		
Cash and cash equivalents	$799.0	$706.0
Accounts receivable, less allowance for doubtful		
accounts of $15,000 and $12,000, respectively	1,572.4	1,176.0
Inventories	1,427.0	1,310.0
Prepaid expenses	49.0	73.0
Total current assets	3,847.4	3,265.0
Property and equipment		
Equipment	2,814.0	2,402.0
Office furniture, fixtures, and computers	682.0	673.0
Capitalized leases	692.0	366.0
	4,188.0	3,441.0
Less accumulated depreciation	(2,854.0)	(2,750.0)
Net property and equipment	1,334.0	691.0
Total assets	$5,181.4	$3,956.0
Liabilities and shareholders' equity		
Current liabilities		
Note payable to bank	$1,551.0	$1,252.0
Accounts payable	437.0	383.0
Accrued expenses	668.0	334.0
Current installment of capitalized lease obligations	58.0	22.0
Income taxes payable	124.1	13.6
Total current liabilities	2,838.1	2,004.6
Long-term liabilities		
Capitalized lease obligations, less current installments	215.0	47.0
Total liabilities	3,053.1	2,051.6
Shareholders' equity		
Common stock, $.01 per value, 4,112,000 shares		
issued and outstanding	41.0	41.0
Additional paid-in capital	1,677.0	1,677.0
Retained earnings	410.3	186.4
Total shareholders' equity	2,128.3	1,904.4
Total liabilities and shareholders' equity	$5,181.4	$3,956.0

company has enough current assets that can be converted to cash in time to meet its current liabilities, it will not need to borrow long-term funds. Two ratios are used to measure liquidity, the current ratio and the quick ratio.

The current ratio is expressed as follows:

$$\text{Current Ratio} = \text{Current Assets/Current Liabilities}$$

The current ratio for Medical Products Inc. is calculated as follows:

2011	2010
$\dfrac{\$3,847,400}{\$2,838,100} = 1.36$	$\dfrac{\$3,265,000}{\$2,004,600} = 1.63$

This analysis shows that the company had $1.36 of current assets for every $1 of current liabilities in 2011, while in 2010 it had $1.63 of current assets for every $1 of current liabilities. To determine if the current ratio is good, it must be compared with some benchmark. Again, the ratio can be compared to last year, the industry standard, or a competitor. The current ratio may be too high if the company's current assets include past due accounts receivable or obsolete inventory. It also could be too high if the company is not using accounts payable as a means of financing short-term purchases. The current ratio might be too low if the company is not generating sufficient cash flow from operations to meet upcoming payments.

The quick ratio can be defined in several ways, but usually the numerator consists of all current assets listed on the balance sheet before inventories. These assets generally include cash, accounts receivable, and short-term investments, if the company has any. The denominator is current liabilities. The quick ratio is expressed as follows:

$$\text{Quick ratio} = \frac{(\text{Cash} + \text{Accounts Receivable} + \text{Short-term Investments})}{\text{Current Liabilities}}$$

The quick ratio also is called the acid test ratio because it measures the ability of a company to meet the current liabilities over the next thirty to ninety days versus the next year with the current ratio.

The quick ratio for Medical Products Inc. is calculated as follows:

2011	2010
$\dfrac{\$799,000 + \$1,572,400}{\$2,838,100} = .84$	$\dfrac{\$706,000 + \$1,176,000}{\$2,004,600} = .94$

This analysis shows that Medical Products Inc. had 84 cents of quick assets for every $1 of current liabilities in 2011 and 94 cents for every $1 in 2010. Is this good or bad? It depends. The company does not quite have enough quick assets to cover all liabilities due within a year. This may not be a problem unless all the liabilities are due within thirty to ninety days and the receivables cannot be collected within that same time period or the company does not have availability on its line of credit.

Can liquidity ratios be too high? Yes. Is excess cash sitting around and not getting used? Are receivables high because they are not getting collected? Are there excess inventories not getting sold? Is the company not taking advantage of trade credit? If the liquidity ratios appear high, the entrepreneur may want to examine the makeup of current assets by looking at activity ratios or by evaluating supplier relationships.

Activity ratios reveal how well assets are being managed. Two key ratios are accounts receivable turnover and inventory turnover. Accounts receivable turnover is calculated by dividing net sales for a period by the average accounts receivable during that period. This ratio measures how fast sales are being collected.

$$\text{Accounts Receivable Turnover} = \text{Sales/Average Accounts Receivable}$$

Average accounts receivable (calculated using a simple average of the current period balance and the previous period balance in this account) are used because sales are over a period of time, while the accounts receivable balance on the balance sheet is at a point in time. A turnover of twelve would indicate that accounts receivable are being collected every thirty days, or twelve times a year.

The number of days sales remaining in accounts receivable is another ratio that can be used for this purpose. It is calculated by dividing 360 days by the accounts receivable turnover ratio. This ratio is often expressed as days sales outstanding (DSO). A DSO of thirty indicates that thirty days of sales are outstanding, or that accounts receivable are being collected every thirty days. If credit terms to customers are net thirty, a DSO of thirty or turnover of twelve times is good. If credit terms are net fifteen, the company might be having a problem collecting its accounts receivable in a timely manner. Accounts receivable turnover for Medical Products Inc. is as follows:

<table>
<tr><td align="center">2011</td><td align="center">2010</td></tr>
<tr>
<td align="center">$\dfrac{\$10,979,000}{(\$1,572,400 + \$1,176,000) / 2} = 8.0$</td>
<td align="center">$\dfrac{\$9,013,000}{\$1,100,000*} = 8.2$</td>
</tr>
</table>

*Average for 2010 and 2009

The DSO in this example is as follows:

<table>
<tr><td align="center">2011</td><td align="center">2010</td></tr>
<tr><td align="center">360 / 8.0 = 45</td><td align="center">360 / 8.2 = 43.9</td></tr>
</table>

What can be concluded about Medical Products Inc. from these two ratios? The company is collecting its accounts receivable about eight times a year, down slightly from 8.2 times in 2010. On average, it has 45 days worth of sales outstanding, which is up about one day from 2010. Is this good or bad? If the terms it offers its customers are net forty-five days, this is good. If the terms are net thirty days, then Medical Products Inc. might want to see how it can speed up collections. As will be seen in Chapter 8, any time customers are slow to pay, they are using the entrepreneur's cash. If there is not enough cash, the entrepreneur may have to borrow from the bank until customers pay the money they owe. Any time money is borrowed, income decreases due to interest expense. The more interest paid, the less cash available. It can become a vicious circle.

Inventory turnover measures how fast the inventory is being sold. It is calculated by taking the cost of goods sold from the income statement and dividing it by the average inventory on the balance sheet. (A company providing a service instead of selling goods would not calculate this ratio.)

$$\text{Inventory Turnover} = \text{Cost of Goods Sold/Average Inventory}$$

A turnover of twelve would indicate that the company is selling and restocking its inventory every thirty days. Inventory turnover for Medical Products Inc. would be calculated as follows:

<u>2011</u>   <u>2010</u>

$$\frac{\$5,440,000}{(\$1,427,000 + \$1,310,000) / 2} = 4.0 \qquad \frac{\$4,644,000}{\$1,295,000^*} = 3.6$$

*Average for 2010 and 2009

Medical Products Inc. is turning over or selling its inventory four times a year or once every three months. This rate is faster than in 2010. Is this good or bad? Again, it depends. If it takes Medical Products Inc. longer than three months to replace its inventory, it might run out. However, if it takes the company only three weeks to replace its inventory, it might have too much. The more inventory on hand that is not moving, the more cash that is tied up in inventory.

Control of inventory is essential for an entrepreneur. Having enough of the right inventory on hand when a customer walks in the door must be balanced with having too much inventory. Sometimes, inventory is old because the entrepreneur is loath to mark it down or sell it at a loss. However, inventory that is sitting around is not generating a return and may actually be costing more than if it is sold at a loss. It takes up space, has to be moved, and must be insured. The business may also be paying interest on a line of credit that could have been paid down with the proceeds of a liquidation sale.

When measuring profitability ratios, it is important to first define what numerical measures will indicate profitability for the company. One of the most common measures is return on sales. This ratio expresses how much profit is generated by every dollar of sales.

$$\text{Return on Sales} = \text{Net Income/Sales}$$

Exhibit 7.1 shows that Medical Products Inc.'s return on sales is 2.2 percent for 2011. As discussed earlier in this chapter, this means that for every dollar sold in 2011,

Medical Products earned 2.2 cents, while in 2010 the company only earned 0.3 cents for every dollar of sales.

<table>
<tr><td align="center">__2011__</td><td></td><td align="center">__2010__</td></tr>
<tr><td align="center">$$\frac{\$240,900}{\$10,979,000}$$</td><td align="center">$= 2.2\%$</td><td align="center">$$\frac{\$26,400}{\$9,013,000} = 0.3\%$$</td></tr>
</table>

However, because net income is influenced by capital structure and tax implications, a better measure of return on sales might be EBIT/sales.

<table>
<tr><td align="center">__2011__</td><td></td><td align="center">__2010__</td></tr>
<tr><td align="center">$$\frac{\$461,000}{\$10,979,000}$$</td><td align="center">$= 4.2\%$</td><td align="center">$$\frac{\$97,000}{\$9,013,000} = 1.1\%$$</td></tr>
</table>

Using EBIT indicates the return the company is generating from its ongoing operations before taking into account interest costs and taxes.

What return on sales does not measure is the level of assets necessary to support those sales. This is measured by calculating asset turnover:

$$\text{Asset Turnover} = \text{Sales/Average Assets}$$

Medical Products Inc.'s asset turnover is calculated as follows:

<table>
<tr><td align="center">__2011__</td><td></td><td align="center">__2010__</td></tr>
<tr><td align="center">$$\frac{\$10,979,000}{(\$5,181,400 + \$3,956,000) \, / \, 2}$$</td><td align="center">$= 2.4$</td><td align="center">$$\frac{\$9,013,000}{\$3,825,000^*} = 2.3$$</td></tr>
</table>

*Average for 2010 and 2009

If these two ratios are combined into one calculation, the result is the formula for return on assets (ROA), which can be measured as follows:

$$\text{Return on Assets} = \text{EBIT/Average Assets}$$

For Medical Products Inc., return on assets is calculated as follows:

<table>
<tr><td align="center">__2011__</td><td></td><td align="center">__2010__</td></tr>
<tr><td align="center">$$\frac{\$461,000}{(\$5,181,400 + \$3,956,000) \, / \, 2}$$</td><td align="center">$= 10.1\%$</td><td align="center">$$\frac{\$97,000}{\$3,825,000} = 2.5\%$$</td></tr>
</table>

The return on assets ratio indicates that Medical Products Inc. generated 10.1 cents for every $1 invested in assets in 2011, or about a dime for every dollar. This result was obviously better than in 2010 when the return was 2.5 cents for every $1 invested in assets.

By looking at the two parts of the return on assets equation, it is possible to determine what is driving the business, a type of analysis called the *duPont Model*. In the 1930s E.I. duPont de Nemours & Co. developed this model, which is an expansion of the basic ROA model:

$$\frac{\text{EBIT}}{\text{Sales}} \times \frac{\text{Sales}}{\text{Avg. Assets}} = \frac{\text{EBIT}}{\text{Avg. Assets}}$$

The significance of the duPont model is that it leads management to consider utilization of assets, including keeping investment in assets as low as feasible, as well as the income generated by sales. If the asset level is too high, the company may be borrowing money to pay for the assets before enough cash is generated internally. In turn, this increases interest expense, which reduces net income.

For Medical Products Inc. the 2011 ratio would appear as follows:

$$\frac{\$\ 461,000}{\$10,979,000} \times \frac{\$10,979,000}{(\$5,181,400 + \$3,956,000) / 2}$$

$$4.2 \qquad \times \qquad 2.4 \qquad = 10.1\%$$

For 2010 the ratio would be as follows:

$$\frac{\$\ 97,000}{\$9,013,000} \times \frac{\$9,013,000}{\$3,825,000}$$

$$1.1\% \quad \times \quad 2.3 \quad = 2.5\%$$

The lower ROA in 2010 was due less to asset turnover than to the lack of return on the sales generated. The owners and management may not be satisfied with the 2011 return and may wish to increase it. With the duPont equation, they can evaluate the impact of increasing the profit margin versus trying to increase sales without adding additional assets versus reducing assets without harming sales, and so on. For example, in 2011, just reducing average assets by $200,000 would improve asset turnover to 2.5, which would improve return on assets to 10.5 percent. Such an analysis gives entrepreneurs an objective evaluation of the return they are receiving from the investments they have made in their businesses. The duPont ratio also can be calculated using net income instead of EBIT.

Many lenders will look at solvency and coverage ratios in evaluating whether to extend long-term credit to a company. One solvency ratio is debt to equity, a ratio that measures the relationship between the amount financed by the creditors of the company and by the owners. If this ratio is greater than 1, then the creditors have a greater claim against the assets than do the owners. Again, there is no one right number for this ratio, but lenders may use it to evaluate the riskiness of making a loan (see Chapter 13).

$$\text{Debt to Equity} = \text{Total Liabilities/Owners' Equity}$$

<u>2011</u>

<u>2010</u>

$$\frac{\$3,053,100}{\$2,128,300} = 1.4$$

$$\frac{\$2,051,600}{\$1,904,400} = 1.1$$

For Medical Products Inc., this ratio indicates that in 2011 the creditors had a claim that was 1.4 times what the owners had. This is an increase compared to 1.1 in 2010. Is this good or bad? Again, it depends. If the company borrowed money to expand or to purchase equipment to increase its efficiency, it might be good. However, if the ratio increased only due to borrowing additional money to fund negative cash flow, then the increase would not be positive.

A similar ratio is the debt ratio, which measures the level of assets against which creditors have a claim. A debt ratio greater than 50 percent means that the creditors have a claim against more of the assets than the owners do. A lender will usually use only one of the two ratios.

$$\text{Debt Ratio} = \text{Total Liabilities/Total Assets}$$

For Medical Products Inc., the debt ratio is as follows:

<u>2011</u>

<u>2010</u>

$$\frac{\$3,053,100}{\$5,181,400} = 58.9\%$$

$$\frac{\$2,051,600}{\$3,956,000} = 51.9\%$$

Creditors had a claim against almost 60 percent of Medical Products Inc.'s assets in 2011 compared with just over 50 percent in 2010. Again, management would have to determine why the company's liabilities had increased faster than its assets in order to evaluate whether this result is good or bad.

Another ratio most lenders use is interest coverage or times interest earned. Times interest earned measures how many times income before interest and taxes (EBIT) exceeds interest expense. Lenders use this metric to measure the level of risk that they will not be paid their interest (see Chapter 13).

$$\text{Times Interest Earned} = \text{EBIT/Interest Expense}$$

The higher the number, the more likely the lender will be paid. Sometimes a lender will require the company to maintain a minimum number in order to meet debt covenants, usually at least 2.0 and sometimes much higher.

For Medical Products Inc., the ratios are as follows:

2011   2010

$$\frac{\$461,000}{\$146,000} = 3.2 \qquad\qquad \frac{\$97,000}{\$95,000} = 1.0$$

Although Medical Products Inc. has increased its debt and therefore increased interest expense, income also has increased, resulting in higher interest coverage than a year ago.

WORKING WITH ACCOUNTANTS

Entrepreneurs typically work with two types of accountants, internal and external. The first are the staff accountants and bookkeepers. Professional accountants are trained to follow certain procedures in keeping a company's financial records. Their technical training can create the kind of language barriers between the entrepreneur and accountants described in Chapter 1. Overcoming these barriers requires that both parties take action. The entrepreneur needs to learn the language of accounting in order to manage the business effectively. He also should become familiar with the policies and procedures used by accounting and bookkeeping staff that is guided by their professional training and ethics. In turn, the staff accountants and bookkeepers need to know the business and what the different departments and functional areas do for the business so they can effectively tailor their work to fit the needs of the company.

It is important for the entrepreneur to understand the functions that the internal accounting staff can perform. Many businesses start with a *bookkeeper.* A bookkeeper's primary responsibility is to keep accurate financial records, which will serve as the basis for the preparation of the company's financial statements and tax returns. Almost all businesses use computer-based accounting software to enter and record financial transactions. The bookkeeper also provides basic accounts payable and accounts receivable management. As a business grows, it might need the services of a *controller.* In addition to the types of activities that a bookkeeper performs, the controller can generate custom financial reports weekly or monthly, thus providing better data for decision making. The controller also can manage the day-to-day cash flow in most businesses. Some businesses eventually need a chief financial officer (CFO) who can structure complex financing, generate complex financial projections, and manage the relationship with bankers and other sources of financing while also performing all the usual duties of a controller.

External accountants are used to generate business tax returns and, for some companies, to perform a review or an annual audit. In the book *The Entrepreneur's Guide to Business Law*, Bagley and Dauchy (2007) provide a useful guide to hiring and working with attorneys that also applies to hiring and working with outside accountants. When hiring an accounting firm, the entrepreneur should collect referrals from other professionals and entrepreneurs and choose two or three to interview. During the interview, the accounting firm's culture and even the personality of its staff should be carefully evaluated to ensure a good fit. This includes making sure that the accounting firm staff will be compatible with the internal accounting staff, as they will need to work together very closely. It can be beneficial to hire an accounting firm that understands the industry in which the business operates, since such specific knowledge can make the firm's work more efficient and more effective. The entrepreneur must clearly understand the accounting firm's billing policies and be clear about whatever cost constraints may be in the budget for outside accounting services. Some accounting firms are too expensive for small businesses. However, lower cost does not necessarily mean inferior service. Many accounting firms are well equipped to handle the needs of small businesses efficiently without sacrificing quality.

After an accounting firm is chosen, there are ways to assure a good working relationship. Entrepreneurs should prepare for meetings with their accountants in advance. The accounting firm and the entrepreneur should reach an understanding as to what tasks can be performed by the internal accounting staff in order to keep the cost of external accounting services to a minimum. External accountants should be kept apprised of any significant developments in the company, because such events may have an impact on the tax or audit situation of the business. It is beneficial to give the outside accounting firm permission to challenge decisions and assumptions made by the entrepreneur. An outside perspective from someone knowledgeable about the business can be invaluable to a growing venture.

Summary

This chapter examined how the entrepreneur can actually gain control of "the numbers" for utilization in decision making. To achieve this goal, a system for tracking and monitoring key assumptions should be developed in every company. The entrepreneur should establish clear milestones that can track progress toward long-term goals. Furthermore, every owner or manager has different needs for information; the key is to identify what a specific business needs to assess and then find a way to get that information. Important information required by the entrepreneur may be different from what the bank needs or what the accountants normally prepare. It is up to the entrepreneur to work closely with the accountant, using accounting language, to develop the reports required. This process assumes that the entrepreneur understands which numbers are actually needed to follow the activity of the business and that those numbers can be generated through the accounting systems and staff. This chapter also discussed the importance of recruiting and working with accountants who know the business and get along well with the internal staff. Chapter 8 will explore the process of managing daily cash flow in an entrepreneurial venture.

Discussion Questions

1. Why are lenders interested in a company's liquidity and solvency ratios?
2. What is DSO, and why is it important to an entrepreneur?
3. Why should an entrepreneur monitor inventory turnover? What might a low turnover indicate? A high turnover?
4. How do you plan to accomplish the accounting for your business? What steps will you take to make sure your accountant understands your business and you understand your financial statements?

5. What other types of metrics could an entrepreneur use?
6. How would you determine what should be measured?

OPPORTUNITIES FOR APPLICATION

1. Using the financial statements you generated in Chapter 6, calculate the following if appropriate:

   Current ratio
   Quick ratio
   DSO
   Inventory turnover
   Debt ratio
   Debt to equity
   Times interest earned
   Return on assets using the duPont ratio

   What areas do you think a lender would be concerned about? What areas are you concerned about?
2. Using the financial statements you obtained in Chapter 3, repeat the process in problem 1.
3. What other metrics would be important to measure for your company?
4. Interview a small CPA firm. Ask how it approaches a new client. How does it get to know the business? What types of services does it offer? How does it bill a company?
5. Interview some accounting students at your school. Ask them if they plan to work with entrepreneurs. Ask how they would approach working in a new business. Ask them why they decided to major in accounting.
6. Contact a local bank or small business administration (SBA) office and ask for an interview with a loan officer. Is there a minimum set of reporting requirements from companies the bank or SBA office does business with? What are the biggest issues involved in dealing with small businesses? What does the loan officer look for in the numbers when evaluating a small business? What does the officer look for outside of the numbers?

REFERENCES

Bagley, C., and C. Dauchy. 2007. *The Entrepreneur's Guide to Business Law.* 3d ed. New York: South-Western.

Eckerson, W. 2005. *Performance Dashboards: Measuring, Monitoring and Managing Your Business.* Hoboken, NJ: Wiley.

Fraser, J. 1998. "Hire Finance." *Inc.* (January): 87.

McGrath, R., and I. MacMillan. 1995. "Discovery-Driven Planning." *Harvard Business Review* (July–August): 4–12.

Ottenheimer, J. 1999. "How Are We Doing?" *Journal of Accountancy* (February): 35–37.

8 Day-to-Day Cash Flow Management and Forecasting

Most experts agree that effective cash flow management is one of the most important areas of financial management for entrepreneurial ventures. With the tightening of credit for smaller businesses that followed the Recession of 2008, cash flow management has become an even higher priority for start-up and growing ventures. Lines of credit to fund working capital and other forms of debt have become much more difficult to secure (see Chapter 13).

The National Federation of Independent Business (NFIB) Education Foundation did a survey of small business owners about cash flow. The survey found that one out of five small business owners experienced "continuing" cash flow problems. Fifty percent of the businesses suffered from cash flow problems, but not on a continuous basis. Only one in three owners said they "never" experienced cash flow difficulties. The primary reason cited for cash flow problems was the difficulty in collecting monies owed, the second was seasonality of sales, and the third was unexpected variations in sales (Dennis 2001).

The inability to manage cash can destroy an otherwise promising venture. The entrepreneur should consider both the technical and emotional side of cash flow management. An entrepreneur also should know the answers to several important questions when developing a business model and a business plan. Why is cash flow management important? Why is cash flow different from net income? How is cash flow measured? This chapter will examine each of these technical questions in detail and also explore the emotional burden of cash flow problems on an entrepreneur.

WHY IS CASH FLOW DIFFERENT FROM NET INCOME?

Generally Accepted Accounting Principles (GAAP) require companies to recognize revenues when earned and expenses when incurred regardless of when cash exchanges hands. This means that net income is reported on an accrual basis on the income statement. Accrual accounting means that revenues and expenses are recognized when the activities associated with them occur rather than when cash is received or expended. The statement of cash flows is used to reconcile net income on an accrual basis to the change in cash since the last balance sheet date. To an entrepreneur, the statement of cash flows is second in importance only to the income statement. Yet many entrepreneurs do not receive this statement from their accountants on a regular basis, and many who do have no understanding of its importance for managing their businesses.

Several examples show the differences that arise due to the practice of accrual accounting compared with actual cash flow in the business. Depreciation is an example of an expense on the income statement that does not use up cash; the cash is used when the equipment is purchased. Sales are recognized on the income statement when the product or service is delivered; however, the cash might not show up until the following month or even later. Employees who work through the end of the month may not receive the paycheck for those hours until the following month. The income statement recognizes the wages expense in the month worked, not the month paid.

WHY IS AN ACCRUAL-BASED INCOME STATEMENT IMPORTANT?

If the entrepreneur only looks at income on a cash basis, there is no sense of how the business is really doing on a month-to-month basis. One month may look great because $20,000 in accounts receivable were collected but actual sales in the month may have only been $5,000. The results for the month could look great but, in reality, sales are on the decline and expenses need to be reviewed. If a major investment in inventory is made in anticipation of future sales, monthly results may reflect a cash loss while the business was actually profitable and in a good position to meet sales needs in the upcoming months.

Both statements are needed to monitor the success of the business. The accrual income statement matches the sales with the costs incurred to generate those sales in the period the sales occurred. The cash flow statement keeps the entrepreneur apprised of how much cash is being generated by the operations of the business and serves as a warning when cash outflows outweigh the inflows.

HOW IS CASH FLOW MEASURED?

The statement of cash flows contains three parts that represent the three major functions an entrepreneur must manage in order to gain optimal cash flow:

1. *Cash flow from operating activities.* This is the cash inflow and outflow from the company's day-to-day operations. Cash inflows include cash sales to customers, collection of customer accounts receivable, customers' down payments, and interest received on investments. Cash outflows occur as a result of payments for wages, office supplies, inventory, advertising costs, travel, and so on.
2. *Cash flow from investing activities.* This is the cash inflow and outflow related to purchasing or selling property, plant, and equipment, or investments in marketable securities or other nonoperating assets. Examples include cash receipts from the sale of land, equipment, buildings, or marketable securities.

Cash outflows include payments for equipment, buildings, or land or for the purchase of another company or stock as an investment.

3. *Cash flow from financing activities.* Cash flow from financing activities relates to the cash flow from debt holders and shareholders. Cash receipts come from borrowings or the sale of company stock. Cash payments include repayment of debt, dividends, or withdrawals by the owner.

Although entrepreneurs do not usually receive the statement of cash flows, they should ask to have it included with regular financial statements and should understand what it is telling them. Understanding cash flow helps entrepreneurs make appropriate business decisions. Entrepreneurs also need to monitor cash flow projections regularly to avoid an unexpected phone call from the bank telling them they are overdrawn and at the end of their line of credit.

There are two methods of presenting cash flow statements, differing mainly in the presentation of the operating cash flows. The indirect method starts with net income on an accrual basis and adjusts it to show what net income would have been on a cash basis. The advantage of this method is that it directly ties net income to cash flow, allowing the entrepreneur to see why the company may be showing a profit but using up cash or vice versa. However, this method is not as user-friendly as the direct method. The direct method actually spells out where the operating cash came from (e.g., collections from customers) and where it went (e.g., payment for inventory). Most software packages generate a cash flow statement using the indirect method. However, an accountant should be able to generate the cash flow statement using the direct method.

To illustrate the cash flow statement, we will return to the example of The Company from Chapter 3. The transactions that occurred within the cash account will be examined first. Then each of these transactions will be placed into the cash flow statement using the direct method.

The transactions that involve the cash account and how they will be entered into the cash flow statement are summarized as follows (Table 8.1):

A. This represents the entrepreneur's initial investment in the business. This $100,000 would show up under financing activities, since it was a means of financing the new company.

B. The company then used $36,000 of the cash to buy a piece of equipment. This represents an investment in the company in that the equipment will enable the company to carry out its business. Therefore, this is an investing activity and since it is a cash outflow, it shows up as a negative.

C. The $15,000 borrowed from the bank is another type of financing activity. It is another source of funds to finance the company's business operation. When The Company repays the loan, it will show up as a negative amount and represent a cash outflow.

D. The payment for rent represents an operating activity. Rent is a cost of operating a business.

E. The collection of $10,000 from a customer who purchased merchandise for $35,000 on account represents a cash inflow. This is also an operating activity.

Table 8.1

Accounting Transactions Example From Chapter 3

	Assets					=	Liabilities			+	Owners' Equity			
	Cash	+ Accounts receivable	+ Inventory	+ Equipment	− Accum. deprec.	=	Notes payable	+ Accounts payable	+ Wages payable	+	Common stock	+ Retained earnings	+ Revenues	− Expenses
A.	100,000					=				+	100,000	—		
B.	(36,000)			36,000		=								
C.	15,000					=	15,000							
		35,000	40,000			=		40,000					35,000	(10,000)
D.	(10,000)		(10,000)			=								(10,000)
E.						=		2,000						(2,000)
F.	10,000	(10,000)				=		(20,000)	5,000					
	(20,000)					=								(5,000)
G.	(100)				(1,000)	=								(1,000)
														(100)
Balance	58,900	25,000	30,000	36,000	(1,000)	=	15,000	22,000	5,000		100,000	—	35,000	(28,100)

Although the income statement shows sales on an accrual basis of $35,000, the cash flow is only $10,000 because that is all that was collected in the current month.

F. $20,000 represents the amount of cash paid for the inventory that was purchased earlier. The total cost of the inventory was $40,000, but only $20,000 has been paid so far. Again, this is an operating activity because it is part of the business's day-to-day operations. The balance remains in accounts payable. The income statement reflects an expense of just $10,000 because that is the only portion of the inventory sold. The remainder is an asset on the balance sheet waiting to be sold in the future.

G. The last cash payment for the month is the $100 for interest paid on the note. This is an operating activity. If a business borrows money, it must pay interest, which shows up as an expense on the income statement.

Exhibit 8.1 is the statement of cash flows for The Company based on these transactions:

INTERPRETING A STATEMENT OF CASH FLOWS: DIRECT METHOD

Exhibit 8.2 displays a cash flow statement for the company used in Chapter 7, Medical Products Inc. This statement has been prepared using the direct method.

Medical Products Inc. generated $354,000 in cash flow from operating activities in 2011 compared with $438,000 in 2010. This means that the company is generating positive cash flow from its day-to-day activities. Why did operating cash flow decrease in 2011? Two reasons stand out. First, the company spent $5,503,000 for inventory in 2011 compared with $4,500,000 the previous year. Is this good or bad? It depends. If the company is growing—that is, if sales are increasing—it is probably good. However, if inventory turnover (see Chapter 7) is decreasing, it may mean inventories are building up or are obsolete. Payments for operating expenses have also increased, from $4,000,000 in 2010 to $4,616,000 in 2011. To evaluate whether this is good or bad requires an examination of where the money was spent and whether the growth of the company justified it. Cash flow from operating activities will often be negative during the start-up phase of a company. However, if this phase continues too long or at least beyond what the entrepreneur expected, the cash already raised will be used up and other sources of cash must be found.

Cash flows from investing activities are usually negative because the company is continuously investing in new equipment or systems. Cash flow related to the acquisition of another company also would be shown here. Medical Products Inc. purchased $747,000 of property and equipment in 2011 compared with $525,000 in 2010. Later in the book we will discuss ways to make this investment without upfront cash outflow.

Cash flows from financing activities describe where the cash is raised. Medical Products Inc. used capital leases to fund some of its equipment purchases and also borrowed money from the bank. The payments it made on these capital leases are netted out of the total shown. The company also paid out dividends to its owners.

Exhibit 8.1

The Company: Statement of Cash Flows (month ended April 30, 2012)

	(in dollars)
Cash flow from operating activities	
Collections from customers	10,000
Payment for inventory	(20,000)
Payment for operating expenses	(10,000)
Payment of interest	(100)
Net cash flow from operating activities	(20,100)
Cash flow from investing activities	
Purchase of equipment	(36,000)
Cash flow from financing activities	
Issuance of common stock	100,000
Proceeds from note payable	15,000
Net cash flow from financing activities	115,000
Net cash increase (decrease)	58,900
Beginning cash	0
Ending cash	58,900

The net change in cash for Medical Products Inc. for 2011 was an increase of $93,000, which when added to the cash at the beginning of the year, $706,000 (found on the balance sheet for the year ended 2010), results in cash at the end of the year of $799,000. (This number also is found on the balance sheet for the year ended 2011.)

The cash flow statement explains where the cash came into the business and where it flowed out. Thus the entrepreneur can start to determine what needs to be done to improve cash flow or invest the cash that is coming in more profitably. The cash flow statement in Exhibit 8.1 shows the results for one year. The template in Chapter 6 projects cash flow month by month for up to three years.

STATEMENT OF CASH FLOWS: INDIRECT METHOD

Comparing the cash flow statement prepared under the direct method (Exhibit 8.2) and the cash flow statement prepared under the indirect method (Exhibit 8.3) for Medical Products Inc. reveals that the major difference is the presentation of the cash flow from operating activities. The indirect method starts with net income (on an accrual basis) and reconciles it to cash flow, in effect, net income on a cash basis. Depreciation is added back since it is an expense for which no cash exchanges hands, as discussed earlier in the chapter. The cash outflow for equipment, buildings, and so on happens when they are purchased.

The $396,400 change in accounts receivable indicates a reduction in cash flow. This is because the company sold more on credit than it collected in the current year. Under accrual accounting, all sales are recorded when delivered; in this case, more sales were recorded than were collected in the same year. Therefore, an increase in the balance of the accounts receivable account represents a reduction in cash flow.

Exhibit 8.2

Medical Products Inc.: Statement of Cash Flows, Direct Method
(for the years ended December 31) ($000)

	2011	2010
Cash flows from operating activities		
Collections from customers	10,582	9,000
Interest received	50	38
Payments for inventories	(5,503)	(4,500)
Payments for operating expenses	(4,616)	(4,000)
Payments for taxes	(13)	(5)
Payments for interest	(146)	(95)
Net cash provided by operating activities	354	438
Cash flows from investing activities		
Purchases of property and equipment	(747)	(525)
Net cash used in investing activities	(747)	(525)
Cash flows from financing activities		
Net change in capital lease obligations	204	10
Borrowings on note payable to bank	299	100
Dividends paid	(17)	(15)
Net cash provided by financing activities	486	95
Net increase (decrease) in cash and cash equivalents	93	8
Cash and cash equivalents, beginning of year	706	698
Cash and cash equivalents, end of year	799	706

Accounts receivable 12/31/10	$1,176,000
Sales during 2011	10,979,000
Less: Accounts receivable 12/31/11	$1,572,400
Cash collections	$10,582,600

Cash collections were $396,400 less than sales. Therefore, when starting with net income and working to convert it to cash flow, $396,400 needs to be backed out, as seen in Exhibit 8.3. In 2010, the company actually collected more in accounts receivable than it sold. In other words, the collections from the prior year's receivables plus the current year receivables exceeded the sales for the current year. So, in 2010, $177,600 was added to net income to determine cash flow from sales. Inventories work the same way. In 2011, the company purchased $117,000 more in inventory than it sold. Since the cost of goods sold shown on the income statement only reflects what was sold, the cash outflow related to inventories is higher than the cost of goods sold. In effect, when current assets increase during the year, cash flow is decreased. When current assets decrease during the year, cash flow is increased.

Changes in current liabilities work the opposite way. As current liabilities increase, cash flow is increased; in effect, the company is using someone else's money. In other words, the company has recorded more expenses (which reduce net income) than it

Exhibit 8.3

Medical Products Inc.: Statement of Cash Flows, Indirect Method
(for the years ended December 31) ($000)

	2011	2010
Cash flows from operating activities		
Net income	241	26
Adjustments to reconcile net income to net cash provided by operating activities		
Depreciation	104	100
Changes in operating assets and liabilities		
Accounts receivable	(396)	178
Inventories	(117)	(125)
Prepaid expenses	24	(10)
Accounts payable	54	40
Accrued expenses	334	224
Income taxes payable	110	5
Net cash provided by operating activities	354	438
Cash flows from investing activities		
Purchases of property and equipment	(747)	(525)
Net cash used in investing activities	(747)	(525)
Cash flows from financing activities		
Net change in capital lease obligations	204	10
Borrowings on note payable to bank	299	100
Dividends paid	(17)	(15)
Net cash provided by financing activities	486	95
Net increase (decrease) in cash and cash equivalents	93	8
Cash and cash equivalents, beginning of year	706	698
Cash and cash equivalents, end of year	799	706

has paid out. If current liabilities decrease between years, the company has paid out more in the current year than it has recorded as expense.

Entrepreneurs do not necessarily need to know how to prepare the cash flow statement. However, they do need to know how to read it and how to ask for the information they need in a format they can use to make decisions. EBITDA (Earnings Before Interest, Taxes, Depreciation, and Amortization) is often used as a quick measure of cash flow. For many companies, depreciation expense is the largest difference between income on an accrual basis and cash flow from operating activities. For Medical Products Inc., EBITDA can be calculated as follows:

	2011	2010
EBIT	$461,000	$ 97,000
Depreciation expense	104,000	100,000
EBITDA	$565,000	$197,000

Although EBITDA does not equal cash flow from operating activities, it does give the amount of cash the operation is generating before considering the cyclical changes in accounts receivable, inventory, accounts payable, and other working capital balances.

INVESTORS' AND CREDITORS' USE OF THE CASH FLOW STATEMENT

Investors' and creditors' primary concern when evaluating a company is often whether a company is generating cash from operations. If cash is being generated simply by selling off investments and long-term assets or by borrowing in order to meet cash requirements, this situation will raise significant concerns, particularly with bankers. Investors and creditors also want to know where the company is spending its cash. They want to know how the company is coming up with cash if it is not generating it from its operating activities. They want to know why net income is different from operating cash flow.

Negative operating cash flow cannot be sustained over the long term without forcing a company to sell off assets or try to raise additional cash. Investors and creditors become nervous about engaging in a relationship with a business if its operating cash flow is negative, unless it is a start-up company or a company going through expansion. Long-term negative operating cash flows can be evidence of impending bankruptcy. Investors and creditors will examine what other sources of cash the company is using. They will examine how much debt the company is adding and when the money has to be paid back. Investors may be concerned if their investment is being diluted because the company has to sell more stock to raise cash. If the company is selling off pieces of its operating units in order to raise cash, this will raise concerns about what the company will do when it runs out of assets to sell. Usually a company does not sell off significant assets unless it is reorganizing or is unable to raise cash from other sources.

When forming a relationship with bankers and investors, it is important for the entrepreneur to establish the amount of cash needed to fund the business from the very beginning. If an entrepreneur has to go back to ask for more cash, lenders and investors become concerned that there may be something seriously wrong with the company. Why does the business need more cash? What was not foreseen in the assumptions behind the original projections? If the business cannot come up with cash when it is needed, the company may be forced to liquidate even if it is profitable!

Even as a business moves out of the early period of negative cash flow experienced by most start-ups, it is important to keep in mind that periods of negative cash flow can recur as a business grows. This is particularly true during periods of rapid growth, when the company needs money to buy inventory, hire employees, expand faculties, fund growing accounts receivable, and buy new equipment. Many entrepreneurs are surprised that cash flow management challenges are not just a one-time event during start-up. The graph in Figure 8.1 shows how a typical entrepreneurial venture can experience negative cash flow both during start-up and during growth, even with profits remaining positive after the initial start-up period. These trends, which can often be

Figure 8.1   **Example of the Cash Flow Cycle Over the Life Cycle of a Business**

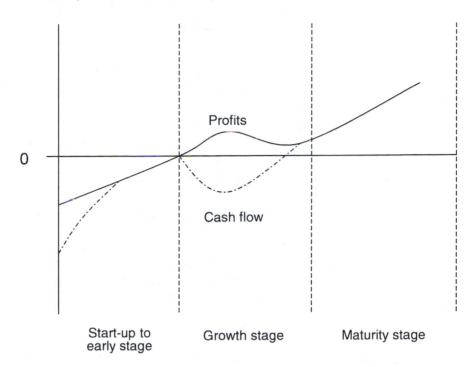

predicted during forecasting, can be used to communicate with bankers and investors well in advance about future cash needs as the business grows. When the business reaches a second period of negative cash flow due to the demands of preparing for growth, the sources of funding will not be surprised, understanding this phase as a planned part of the business's needs.

EFFECTIVE CASH MANAGEMENT

As cited in the NFIB survey, the primary reason that entrepreneurs give for cash flow problems is the difficulty in collecting receivables. This would indicate the need to carefully manage the credit extended to customers. Explicit credit policies should be established for any business and should include payment terms and possibly cash discounts for timely payment. The credit terms tell the customer when payment is expected, such as "balance due in full within 30 days of invoice." Credit policies need to be tight enough to maintain cash flow without losing good customers. In situations where a project requires large cash outlays up front, it is not unreasonable for a business to consider asking the customer for an up-front deposit. Needless to say, timely and accurate billing of work performed is also important.

Seasonality of sales is the second reason given for cash flow problems. Diversifying the offering of products and services can help. For example, many ski resorts have converted parts of their land to golf courses. This not only keeps rooms filled more months out of the year, but it also generates cash flow from an entirely new product. Some vendors are willing to modify payment plans for a seasonal business, particularly if this is a common issue for many of their customers. Such modifications include negotiating dating (extended payment terms) or cash discounts.

The third most common reason cited for cash shortages is unexpected variation in sales. This is often related to the entrepreneur's inability to develop an accurate sales forecast. As discussed in Chapter 4, accurate revenue forecasting requires thorough, careful consideration of all assumptions underlying sales. A cash forecast should always include at least two scenarios: most-likely case and worst-case. With the worst-case scenario, the entrepreneur can be proactive about how to fund any cash shortfall, rather than getting caught by surprise.

Other issues beyond the three cited by entrepreneurs in the NFIB survey also affect cash management on a day-to-day basis. Policies on how payments are made to suppliers affect cash flow. A company might choose to pay vendors on a sixty-day cycle. This is good for cash flow, but it can cause problems if the vendor holds shipments because invoices are not paid promptly. Large expenditures up-front for customer projects or capital projects might also use up cash in the short term, resulting in a cash shortage. Payments to suppliers can be delayed, but it is critical to call the vendor in advance and negotiate longer terms. Most vendors are willing to work with a good customer if they understand the issue and are kept informed. Just withholding payment or refusing to take vendors' phone calls can badly damage a business's reputation and reduce future cooperation from suppliers.

Ineffective inventory management is another major cash flow problem. Inventory on hand should be reviewed on a regular schedule. If it is obsolete and just sitting around, it is using cash. Even if the excess inventory has to be sold at a loss, the sale will result in more cash flow into the business. Dead inventory, which will likely go unsold unless offered at a deep discount, is a sunk cost that takes up space and hurts cash flow. Inventory purchasing policies are another tool for cash management. Many companies will order extra inventory in order to reduce the price per item. However, this again uses cash. If the business holds those inventories for a while, the actual costs may be higher than what has been paid. What are these additional costs? If the company has borrowed money from the bank, then interest is being paid due to the purchase of this excess inventory. If space is being rented to store inventory, the extra inventory requires the payment of additional rent. If the inventory is getting in the way of production workers due to ineffective storage or lack of space, it may be causing inefficiencies in production. If the inventory sits around too long, it may be damaged or even become obsolete.

During extremely difficult cash flow periods, it may be possible to delay the payment of commissions or bonuses. Employees may agree if they understand the issues and are warned in advance; however, this should be a last resort and done only with their knowledge. Banks may be willing to offer flexibility on delaying or reducing interest payments until cash flow improves. However, it is *never* advisable to delay payroll tax payments. Although this may be a temptation, as these payments are usually due right after payroll is paid when cash might be especially tight, the government does not hesitate to close down companies that fall behind in their payroll taxes. The employer is the legal liaison between the employee and the government in that it collects this money on behalf of the employee. It is *not* the company's cash and should never be treated as such.

One early-stage entrepreneur in the video rental business fell behind on all his bills, including his payroll taxes. As the tax notices came from the government, he just put them in a drawer and ignored them. Then came the notice that the authorities would lock the doors if he did not pay in a certain number of days. A consultant brought in to help turn the business around attempted to negotiate time for payment. However, because the situation had gone on so long, the only thing that saved the video store operator was an emergency influx of cash from his brother. The payroll taxes themselves were not the biggest expense. The Internal Revenue Service charges huge penalties and interest on late payments. These are difficult to negotiate away. Another business, a restaurant, actually had government authorities show up during the breakfast hour, take the cash from the register, and shut down the business for failure to pay taxes.

In Chapter 7 we discussed developing metrics to monitor a company's performance. One overall metric that also should be utilized by entrepreneurs is the relationship of operating cash flows to sales. This metric tells how much cash is being generating for every $1 of sales. The formula is as follows:

Operating Cash Flow/Sales

In the example of Medical Products Inc., the results were as follows:

<table>
<tr><td>2011</td><td>2010</td></tr>
<tr><td>$\dfrac{354,000}{10,979,000} = .032$</td><td>$\dfrac{438,000}{9,013,000} = .049$</td></tr>
</table>

In 2011 Medical Products Inc. generated 3.2 cents in cash flow for every $1 of sales. This figure was down from 4.9 cents per $1 of sales the year before. As with other metrics discussed thus far, there is no wrong or right answer to this metric. More important are the trends, the entrepreneur's expectations, and the business's cash situation.

Another measurement that helps the entrepreneur plan is a calculation of the cash conversion cycle. Simply stated, the cash conversion cycle measures the length of time it takes between incurring a cash expenditure (e.g., purchasing inventory) and the receipt of cash from the sale of the goods. The shorter the conversion cycle, the more liquid the firm. This measurement can be calculated as follows:

Number of days inventory on hand
+ Days in accounts receivable (DSO)
− Days in payables

Days in Cash Conversion Cycle

In Chapter 7, inventory turnover for Medical Products Inc. was calculated at 4.0 times in 2011. To convert this to days inventory on hand, the number of days in a year, 360, is divided by the turnover: 360/4.0 = 90 days. DSO for 2011 was 45. Days in payables can be calculated in several ways. Days in payables represent how long it is taking to pay for the inventory sold (cost of goods sold) and some operating expenses. Because the accounts payable for companies that sell inventory consist mostly of inventory purchases, a good measure involves taking cost of goods sold/average accounts payable to get accounts payable turnover. For Medical Products Inc., this turnover in 2011 was

$$\frac{\$5,440,000}{(\$437,000 + 383,000) / 2} = 13.3 \text{ times}$$

To convert this to days in payables, 360 is divided by 13.3, which equals 27 days in payables. For Medical Products Inc., the cash conversion cycle equals the following:

Average DSO	45
Days inventory on hand	91
Total days in operating cycle	136
Less: days in payables	−27
Cash conversion cycle	109

The company's operating cycle means that it takes 136 days from the time raw materials are purchased and converted into inventory until the inventory is sold and cash from the sale is collected. Suppliers provide twenty-seven days of credit, but the remaining 109 days must come from working capital. The shorter this cycle, the higher the liquidity and the greater the cash flow.

THE EMOTIONAL SIDE OF CASH FLOW MANAGEMENT

The NFIB survey cited at the beginning of this chapter found that two-thirds of entrepreneurs reported at least some problems with cash flow in their businesses. Cash flow management can cause a great deal of stress for an entrepreneur. Cash is expected to be tight during start-up, but the stress can become emotionally wearing when the expected cash shortfall goes on longer than planned. Some entrepreneurs find that although they can overcome the start-up cash shortage, the problems only arise again and can become even worse during periods of rapid growth. Cash flow once more becomes negative as the business adds new staff and overhead and as accounts receivables balloon while revenues expand. Some cash flow problems are short-term and may simply be part of the transition that every business must endure as it grows.

Other cash flow problems, however, are more systemic, requiring a complete rethinking of the business model. The business plan that was the original guide for the new venture might need to be abandoned in order to keep the business afloat. When the business plan shifts to survival, growth and expansion are put on hold and staffing is cut back. Systemic cash flow problems might arise from overly ambitious plans or

---

Box 8.1
Entrepreneurs and the Emotional Side of Cash Flow

"I remember waking up, night after night, at 3:00 a.m. I kept going through spreadsheets in my head. . . . How could I move cash around to make payroll? What could I cut to end this mess? All I wanted was enough relief from the constant worry to get one good night's rest."

"It was the worst day of my life. It had become clear that we had to cut about 10 percent of our expenses. In our business, all I could cut was people, so I spent a day and a half going from office to office, letting people go. Thirty people all together had to be laid off. They cried, they yelled at me, they asked me how I could do this to them. Some of them were pretty nice, though. They seemed to understand what I was going through."

"The hardest part was coming home and telling my wife that we weren't going to get paid again. We had spent all of our savings and cashed into our retirement funds, so we were barely able to make ends meet. She handled it real well, but I felt like I had failed her and failed our family."

"I felt completely paralyzed. I didn't know what to do next."

Source: Anonymous entrepreneurs.

---

market changes. No matter what the cause, the psyche of the entrepreneur can certainly be challenged. Systemic cash flow problems often cut to the core of the entrepreneur's ego, leading to self-doubt and a crisis of self-confidence. The stress of cash flow can challenge the entrepreneur's relationships with partners, family members, and other business contacts. Box 8.1 displays several quotes from entrepreneurs regarding the emotional strains created by cash flow crises in their businesses.

SUMMARY

This chapter discussed the technical aspects of cash flow management. Effective cash flow management requires careful monitoring, effective planning and forecasting, and judicious day-to-day policies. The entrepreneur also faces the emotional side of cash flow management, which can create great stress and strained relationships if not effectively handled. Part III will discuss the various methods of generating funding for an entrepreneurial venture, which also can be critical in developing methods for effective long-term cash management.

DISCUSSION QUESTIONS

1. Why is cash flow different than net income?
2. Why is it important to track both net income and cash flow?

3. What does EBITDA measure?
4. How would you increase cash flow if your bank would not loan you any more money and you had a payroll due at the end of the week?
5. Why is it not a good idea to delay payroll tax payments to the government?
6. What does the cash conversion cycle measure? Why is it important?
7. Can you ever have too much cash?

OPPORTUNITIES FOR APPLICATION

Using the statements you prepared in Chapter 6, answer the following questions.

1. What month will you have borrowed the most cash?
2. How long is your cash conversion cycle?
3. What is EBITDA for your company for the first year?
4. How long does it take you to achieve positive operating cash flow?
5. Find a recent article on cash flow in a business magazine or on the Internet. What recommendations are made to improve cash flow?
6. Interview a local entrepreneur. How does the entrepreneur manage cash? Has the company ever run out of cash? What did the entrepreneur do?

REFERENCE

Dennis, W., Jr., ed. 2001. *The Cash Flow Problem.* NFIB Education Foundation Series, 1 (3).

Part III

Sources of Financing

9 Financing Over the Life of a Venture

Each stage in the growth of a business, from start-up to growth and expansion and finally to the point of exit, presents new and unique financial challenges to the entrepreneur. Financing comes from a variety of sources, which will change over the life of the business. This chapter examines the complex, dynamic puzzle of providing the right amount of funding for an entrepreneurial venture during the early stages of the business. Before examining the various options for financing, the chapter will address common misconceptions that many people have regarding financing entrepreneurial ventures.

COMMON MISCONCEPTIONS ABOUT ENTREPRENEURIAL FINANCING

To be successful at raising the money a business needs, the business owner must be knowledgeable and realistic. Yet, many entrepreneurs share the following five misconceptions about financing entrepreneurial businesses.

1. *Venture capitalists fund most businesses.* Actually, one recent study found that only 38 out 100,000 new businesses reported receiving venture capital funding (Reynolds et al. 2003). In other words, 99.962 percent of all new businesses had funding from sources other than venture capital. Although firms backed by venture capital can grow quickly and gain significant attention in the media, they are a very small percentage of all entrepreneurial firms. We will discuss what venture capital firms are and how they operate later in this chapter.

2. *Banks lend to start-ups.* Generally bankers do not lend money to start-up businesses. To understand why, it is important to understand how bankers make lending decisions. Much of the money they keep on deposit is in demand deposits, such as checking accounts, which need to be available when people need or want their funds. When you write a check to pay your rent, you want to know that the money is in the bank available for your landlord to put into his account in his bank. Therefore, bankers tend to be conservative when lending money. They need to know that loans will be paid back, because the money for those loans comes

from customers who trust that their bankers will keep it safe and secure. Bankers tend to loan only to established businesses that have a proven ability to repay the loan based on their profitability and strong cash flow. Bankers also like to see that the owners can personally pay back the loan if the business fails and that there is collateral to back the loans.

3. *SBA lends money directly to entrepreneurs.* Many entrepreneurs mistakenly contact the Small Business Administration (SBA) for loans because they have heard about the SBA loan programs. The fact is that the SBA does not loan money directly to small businesses. What it actually does is provide federal guarantees of loans to small businesses issued through commercial banks (U.S. Small Business Administration 2008). This guarantee is similar to a parent's cosigning a car loan for a college-age child. Without the parent's signature guaranteeing that the loan will get repaid, the college student would find it difficult to get a conventional car loan. In a similar way, banks are more willing to fund small businesses that might be a credit risk if the loan is guaranteed by the SBA.

4. *Entrepreneurs tend to rely on a single source of funding.* Most new ventures end up with an array of financing. The financing need—for example, working capital, equipment, or buildings—will dictate which type of financing works best. It is rare to find an entrepreneur who raises one big pot of money from one single source to meet all of the business's needs. Working capital may come from a bank, equipment may be financed by a leasing company, and a building may get backed through money from an investor. It is usually best for the entrepreneur to meet each need as it occurs, finding the type of financing that is best suited for that need.

5. *Government grants are a good source of money for small businesses.* Although some governmental programs have been established to provide grants for new ventures, they are very specialized and often quite complex. Most government grants are set up to assist a specific disadvantaged segment of the population or a small business trying to develop a new high-tech product. In general, government grants are not a source of funding for most new businesses.

THE DIVERSE NATURE OF BUSINESS FINANCING

Since venture capital, banks, and government grants are not likely sources of funding for start-ups, where does the typical entrepreneur find the money needed to support the business? The answer to this question depends on three major factors: (1) the nature of the business model, (2) the aspirations of the entrepreneur, and (3) the stage of development of the business venture.

THE NATURE OF THE BUSINESS MODEL

New businesses generally fall into one of three categories. The first is what is commonly called a *lifestyle business*. As of 2009, there were 15.3 million self-employed people in the United States, which is a decline of more than 4 million from 2006 (U.S. Census Bureau 2006; Hipple 2010). This is a typical decline as seen in previous recessions.

The self-employed work in a wide array of industries and businesses, including construction, Internet-based services, retail businesses, and various types of consulting. A growing number of the self-employed have consciously chosen to work independently to better support their chosen lifestyles. For example, a growing number of women choose to work from home as self-employed entrepreneurs so they can both raise their children and run a small business (Fairlie 2004). Lifestyle businesses can grow out of hobbies, past work experience, or educational training. Most lifestyle businesses have little or no need for outside funding. Generally there are few operating expenses, as many of these ventures are run out of the entrepreneur's home and use resources the entrepreneur already has available, such as computers, cell phones, and automobiles.

The second general category includes *small businesses* that have employees and a slow to moderate potential for growth. While these businesses are small in size, they have become large in number and are now a major force in the U.S. economy. The U.S. Census Bureau reported that in 2008 there were 6.5 million small businesses with twenty or fewer employees in the United States (U.S. Census Bureau 2012). Small businesses now account for more than 50 percent of all jobs in the U.S. economy and more than 50 percent of the gross domestic product (GDP), which is a measure of the size of the total economy. These small businesses are engaged in manufacturing, retailing, distribution, and various services. Most serve specific groups of customers within specific market locations, which limit the company's capacity to grow. Although small businesses use different types of financing at different stages, generally most of their financing comes from the entrepreneur, friends and family members, and loans from banks and other sources once the business becomes established. Beginning in 2008, the number of businesses closing exceeded the number of business being started for the first time in many years. Additionally, the number of bankruptcies among small businesses tripled from 2006 to 2009.

The third general category of entrepreneurial businesses includes those known as *high-growth, high-potential ventures.* As the name implies, these ventures have the potential to grow to a very large size in a short period of time. Many high-potential businesses develop high-tech applications or are health-care-related, including breakthrough medical devices or new pharmaceuticals. Still others promise the ability for rapid national expansion of an innovative retail, restaurant, or service business concept. Often this type of high-potential business will use a franchising model to allow for rapid growth in many locations. By their very nature, most high-potential businesses need access to large amounts of money to get launched and to support their rapid growth. Since they tend to be rather risky with high failure rates, the most common source of funding tends to be equity investors, such as angel investors and venture capitalists, who seek out the high returns that these businesses offer and who can tolerate their high rates of failure.

ASPIRATIONS OF THE ENTREPRENEUR

Chapter 2 of this book highlighted the importance of integrating an entrepreneur's aspirations with the plans for a new venture. The entrepreneur's aspirations are the second factor that influences the level and type of financing an entrepreneurial venture needs to support its start-up and growth. Understanding entrepreneurs' aspirations begins with understanding how they view success for their venture. As discussed in Chapter 1, the meaning of success varies considerably among entrepreneurs and includes many non-financial criteria. Although financial outcomes may not be the primary aspirations that drive an entrepreneur to start the business, they are an important consideration. There are two financial needs that must be satisfied. The first is the business owner's income needs. These can vary widely from person to person since they are driven by lifestyle, family, geographic location, and so forth. Before starting a business, an entrepreneur should have a very clear understanding of day-to-day financial needs based on a detailed personal budget. The second financial need is wealth needs. Wealth needs, which also vary widely from person to person, are driven by retirement plans, educational needs of children, lifestyle, and so forth. It is essential to keep in mind the difference between wealth and income as discussed in Chapter 2.

To fully understand what is needed from the business, entrepreneurs must integrate their nonfinancial and financial needs. For example, one entrepreneur may have a very strong commitment to his family. Having time to coach his children's sports teams and take frequent family vacations is important, so he deliberately decides to limit the size and growth of his business in order to balance time between his business and family. Another entrepreneur may have the goal to retire to a wealthy lifestyle at a very young age, so her business model will need to have the potential for high growth and significant value that can be realized through the sale of her business. The first entrepreneur may need very little outside financing for his business, while the second will probably need significant outside investment to achieve her ambitious business goals.

THE STAGE OF DEVELOPMENT OF THE BUSINESS VENTURE

The third factor that determines the best type of financing for a business is its stage of development. As described in Chapter 2, a business goes through distinct stages of growth: prelaunch, start-up, growth, and finally transition (also known as the maturity stage). Each stage in the life of a business lends itself to a different combination of financing sources.

FITTING THE PIECES OF THE FINANCING PUZZLE TOGETHER

None of the three factors discussed above alone determines what type of financing is best for a given business. But when taken together, these factors can help solve the financing puzzle for a specific venture. The business model and the entrepreneur's aspirations shape the basic nature of the business and its potential for growth; the stage of its development adds to this mix the dynamic nature of a venture over time. More specifically, the type of financing typically found at each stage differs between small businesses with modest growth potential and high-growth, high-potential ventures. The next two sections examine the most common combinations of these factors in detail.

Financing Small Businesses with Modest Growth Potential

Financing for the early stages of a business is known as *seed financing.* Small businesses with modest growth potential and/or modest growth goals established by the entrepreneur tend to have limited access to financing. Most of the financing for this type of entrepreneurial venture comes from the entrepreneur's own resources. The entrepreneur may also draw upon resources provided by friends and family members. Financing from the entrepreneur, family members, and friends will be discussed in more detail in Chapter 10. Entrepreneurs starting small ventures need to rely on careful cash management and the array of techniques known as bootstrapping to stretch their limited resources (Cornwall 2009). Entrepreneurs who bootstrap may start their businesses out of their own homes to save on rent, buy used equipment and furniture, and engage in hands-on marketing techniques that save money but still have the desired impact. A summary of common bootstrapping strategies is presented in Chapter 11.

Charles Hagood and Mike Brown, cofounders of the manufacturing engineering company called The Access Group, are a good example of entrepreneurs who successfully used bootstrapping techniques when starting their business.

> During their initial start-up, they decided to save as much of their precious self-funded working capital as possible. They decided to work out of Mike's basement and garage, with PCs set up on folding tables they had purchased at Sam's Club. Charles joked that "Mike's Chihuahua became our Vice President of Security," as he announced the arrival of each UPS truck, mail delivery or visitor to their "corporate headquarters." Hagood added, "We were broke but were having a blast. We were never worried that we'd make it. The question was when." (Cornwall 2006)

As the business begins to expand and enters the growth stage, the entrepreneur may seek additional financing to fund the need for permanent space, additional equipment, or significant working capital. Although bootstrapping and the personal resources of the entrepreneur, friends, and family may still be used, the business's needs may be beyond what they are able to provide. The entrepreneur might then seek additional equity financing from local angel investors. Equity financing from outside investors is explored in greater detail in Chapter 12.

As the business gains a track record of financial performance, often later in the start-up stage or early in the growth stage, it will reach a point when the business is considered "bankable." Banks and other sources of debt financing will be more willing to extend credit once a business has a proven record of positive cash flow that can easily support the repayment of a requested loan. Debt financing is the topic of Chapter 13.

Figure 9.1 summarizes the sources of financing for a small business with modest growth. Note that this is a generalized model of financing for a small business. The specific experiences of any given business may vary depending on the specific circumstances of the entrepreneur and of the business. For example, an entrepreneur with significant experience as a successful business owner may gain access to equity and debt financing much earlier in the life of the business. Or, if the entrepreneur does not have a good history of financial responsibility, outside debt or equity financing may take longer or may never be an option. However, this model presents the most

Figure 9.1   **Financing a Small Business with Modest Growth**

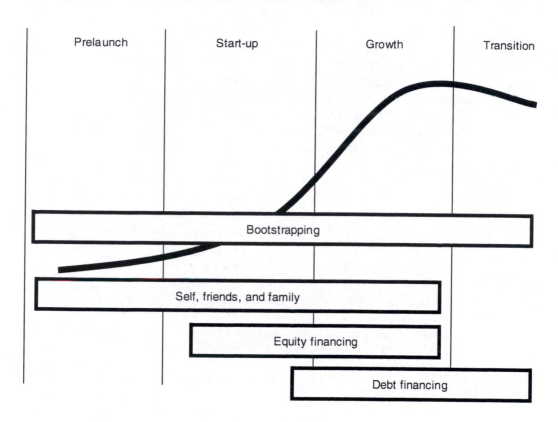

common rule of thumb for what financing is most likely to be available to a small venture with limited growth over its life cycle.

FINANCING HIGH-GROWTH, HIGH-POTENTIAL VENTURES

Just like businesses with limited growth, high-potential business ventures often engage in various bootstrapping techniques and rely on some self-financing by the founding entrepreneurs. However, these sources of funding are generally not enough, since these ventures require access to large amounts of funding to support significant expenses:

- Working capital to support employees needed to launch and manage the start-up of the venture, often including many high-salary professionals and executives.
- Capital to develop intellectual property and build working prototypes.
- Working capital to fund large commitments to inventories and accounts receivable.
- Large start-up expenses for fixed assets, such as equipment and buildings.

Therefore, entrepreneurs starting high-potential businesses may need to seek outside seed financing, which most often will come from angel investors with very high net

Figure 9.2 **Financing a High-Growth, High-Potential Venture**

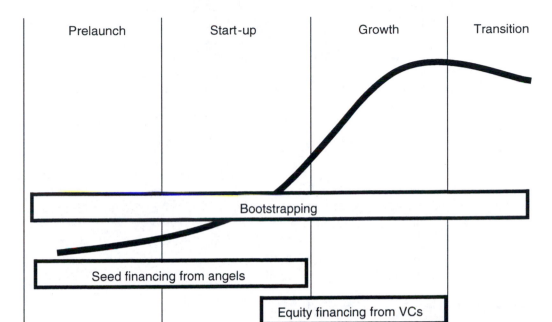

worth. It should be noted that these types of funding sources have become much more difficult to secure since the beginning of the Recession of 2008.

Once a high-growth, high-potential business begins to market its product and possibly even sell its first units, it will usually need additional funding. Such businesses will often need outside financing for the first several years due to their rapid growth and high capital needs. Later rounds of financing typically come from institutional equity investors known as venture capitalists. Each round is named in succession, starting with *Series A financing*, then *Series B financing*, and so forth as needed for future growth and expansion. While the angel investor may typically put several hundred thousand dollars or even a million into the business at its inception, the venture capitalist may put $5 million to $50 million into the firm as it begins to accelerate into its rapid growth. Chapter 14 will discuss high-growth financing in entrepreneurial ventures in greater detail. The business might also have enough cash flow at this point in its growth to obtain debt financing through banks or other institutions. Figure 9.2 displays a summary of the typical financing of a high-growth, high-potential venture over its life cycle.

SUMMARY

This chapter has presented an overview of the financing strategies used in small entrepreneurial ventures with modest growth potential and those commonly seen in high-growth, high-potential ventures. Financing can come through self-financing, debt financing, and equity financing. The type of financing used for a venture depends on the nature of its business model, the financial and nonfinancial aspirations of the entrepreneur, and the stage of the business in its life cycle. The types of financing appropriate for the different stages in the business life cycle differ between a small business with modest growth and a high-growth, high-potential business venture. The remaining chapters in this section will examine each source of financing in more detail.

Discussion Questions

1. What are some of the common misconceptions about financing an entrepreneurial venture? Why do you think these misconceptions are so prevalent?
2. Discuss the three major factors that affect where an entrepreneur is likely to find financing.
3. How does financing differ for a small business with modest growth versus a high-growth, high-potential venture? What accounts for these differences in financing strategies?

Opportunities for Application

1. Interview an entrepreneur to determine what financing was used at each stage of the business from start-up to the present. Make sure to ask why each type of financing was used, addressing the factors discussed in this chapter.
2. Develop a financing plan for the start-up and growth stages of a business you have started or plan to start. Be sure to consider why each type of financing should be used, addressing the factors discussed in this chapter.

References

Cornwall, J. 2009. *Bootstrapping.* Englewood Cliffs, NJ: Pearson/Prentice-Hall.
———. 2006. "TAG." Case presented at the United States Association for Small Business and Entrepreneurship Annual Conference, Tucson, AZ.
Fairlie, R.W. 2004. "Self-Employed Business Ownership in the United States: 1979–2003." *Small Business Research Summary* 243 (December). http://www.sba.gov/advo/research/rs243tot.pdf.
Hipple, S. 2010. "Self-employment in the United States." *Monthly Labor Review* (September). http://www.bls.gov/opub/mlr/2010/09/art2full.pdf.
Reynolds, P.D., S.M. Camp, W.D. Bygrave, A. Autio, and M. Hay. 2003. *The Global Entrepreneurship Monitor 2003 Report.* Babson Park, MA, and London: Babson College and London Business School.
U.S. Census Bureau. 2006. "Business with No Paid Employees Increase to 19.5 Million." Press release, July 27. http://www.census.gov/Press-Release/www/releases/archives/economic_census/007172.html.
———. 2012. "Nonemployer Establishments and Receipts by Industry: 2000 to 2008." Report. Washington, DC. http://www.census.gov/compendia/statab/2012/tables/12s0758.pdf.
U.S. Small Business Administration. 2008. "Financial Assistance." http://www.sba.gov/services/financialassistance/index.html.

10 Start-Up Financing from the Entrepreneur, Friends, and Family

A common myth is that entrepreneurial ventures usually start with money from outside sources such as banks and investors. Some potentially viable business opportunities never get off the ground because the entrepreneurs behind them mistakenly postpone start-up while waiting for outside funding that never materializes. The reality is that most entrepreneurial ventures rely on funding from the founders. And the most common source of outside finding is the entrepreneur's family and friends. This chapter examines how entrepreneurs approach these sources of funding and the inherent potential pitfalls (Figure 10.1).

Self-Financing

Recent studies suggest that self-financing is the primary source of financing start-up ventures. A survey of women entrepreneurs conducted in 2011 by Wobwire.com found that 95 percent of women fund their start-ups with their own money. A study conducted by Wells Fargo found that approximately three out of every four entrepreneurs surveyed started their businesses with money from their personal finances. While this method may seem like a barrier to starting a business, the entrepreneurs only needed capital of about $10,000 to launch their businesses (Wells Fargo 2006). These findings are consistent with previous surveys that found that start-ups generally began with $7,000 to $10,000 and that self-financing was used by 70 to 85 percent of all start-ups. A survey by the U.S. Census Bureau actually found that one in five businesses in the United States started with no funding at all.

When self-financing, the entrepreneur may draw upon any number of potential sources of personal funds, including the following:

1. *Personal cash.* Entrepreneurs who have some personal net worth may draw upon their personal assets to support a new venture. These funds may be invested directly into the business in the form of equity. Personal cash assets might come from cash in bank accounts or investments that can be liquidated. Common uses of personal cash invested in the business include buying equipment, inventory, and other start-up expenses. Per-

Figure 10.1 **Most Common Sources of Financing**

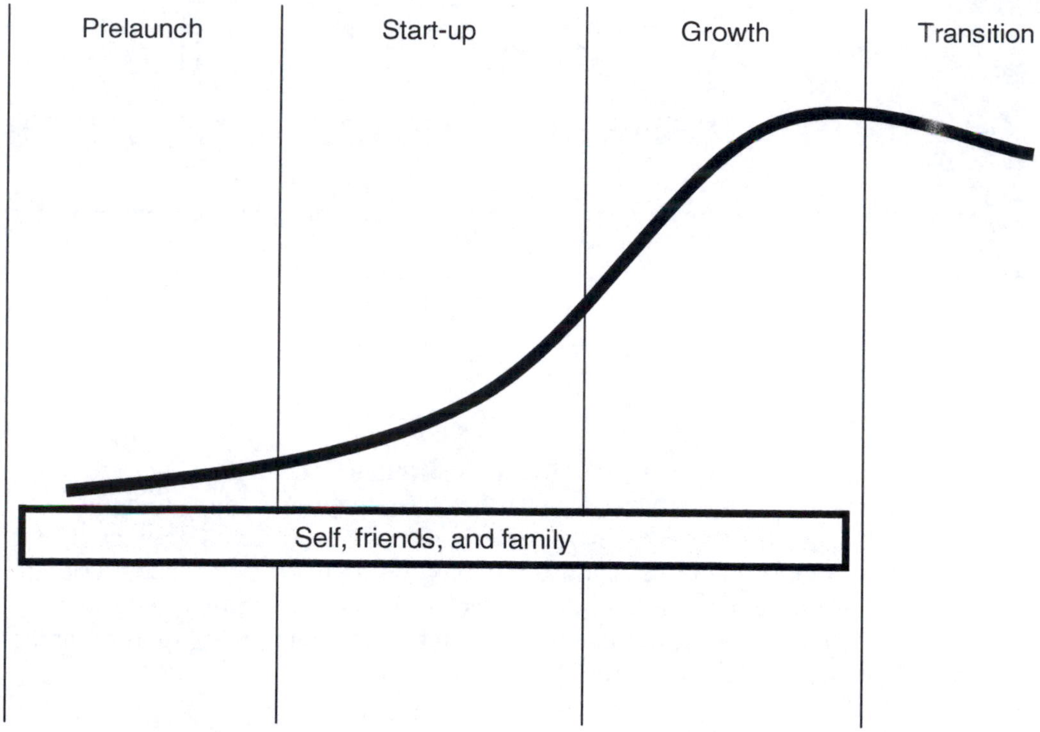

| Prelaunch | Start-up | Growth | Transition |

Self, friends, and family

sonal cash may also be used as a back-up source of cash for personal needs for those times when a business is not able to pay the entrepreneur a salary. A common rule of thumb is to have enough cash saved to cover at least six months of basic personal living expenses before starting a business. It takes time for any business to reach breakeven and then to be able to provide consistent cash flow to pay the founding entrepreneurs. Many entrepreneurs are forced to give up on a new business simply because they cannot afford to give the business enough time to reach this point.

2. *Other personal assets.* Often a business grows out of a part-time endeavor, personal interest, or hobby. In such cases, the entrepreneur already will have purchased tools and equipment that can be used in the business. For example, when Kurt Nelson and Tyler Seymour started their video production company Just Kidding Productions, they brought with them equipment that they had purchased as students studying video production at Belmont University. This equipment became an asset of the business and was treated as part of their equity contribution as shareholders of the business. Other common assets that are brought into a business include computers, cell phones, and office furniture.

3. *Unsecured personal credit.* A new venture is not likely to be able to secure credit financing. Many entrepreneurs will use personal credit cards or unsecured personal lines of credit to help finance a business start-up. When personal credit is used for the business, it is essential to track personal versus business transactions very carefully in order to ensure clean record keeping. If an entrepreneur plans to use a personal credit

card for the start-up, it is preferable to get a separate credit card for the business trans-actions. Some credit card companies explicitly prohibit the use of personal credit cards for business purposes. Entrepreneurs should read carefully the terms of use in the credit card contract for any personal credit card being considered for use in the business.

4. *Second mortgage on property.* For entrepreneurs who have built up equity in real estate, securing a second mortgage on a home or other property may be a way to fund a business start-up through a bank loan. It is important to understand that this will be treated as a personal loan by the bank. The entrepreneur will be personally liable for repayment of the loan independent of the success or failure of the business.

5. *Pledging other personal assets.* The entrepreneur also may be able to obtain a loan for the business by pledging personal assets that are easily liquidated and have verifiable market value, such as publicly traded stock or government bonds. Again, this loan will likely be considered a personal loan by the bank and not a direct loan to the business.

6. *Working a second job.* During the start-up of a new business, many entrepreneurs continue to work their "day job" to support their personal expenses. If the new venture requires the entrepreneur to work during daytime hours, the entrepreneur may pick up an evening job. If the business hours of the new venture are flexible, the entrepreneur may be able to keep a daytime job to make ends meet. A significant challenge is deciding when to phase out of the second job and rely fully on the proceeds of the new venture for personal income. In a perfect world, this would be an easy, painless transition. However, in reality the entrepreneur often is faced with a difficult, potentially risky decision of when to leap into a full-time, exclusive commitment to the new business.

ADVANTAGES AND DISADVANTAGES OF SELF-FINANCING

Self-financing may be the sole source of funding for a new venture or it may be used in conjunction with external sources. There are several advantages to relying solely on self-financing to launch a new business. First, it is fairly easy to obtain funds this way since the resources are under the entrepreneur's control. However, the ease of self-financing can lead to rather impulsive decisions to start the new venture and commit personal resources without full consideration of the risks involved. When outsiders are approached about funding a business, they will ask challenging questions that can expose flaws or holes in the entrepreneur's business plan. When self-financing, the entrepreneur should seek advice from people who can play this same role. The entrepreneur should fully understand the implications. Can she afford to lose any money invested in the business? Will she be able to repay any debt that is personally secured? Will there be any career implications from a failure? These are not easy questions to answer, but outside investors will have thought through these same types of questions when considering an investment. It does not mean that entrepreneurs must plan to fail or make an assumption that failure is likely. But even if failure is not probable, they should enter a business with full understanding of its implications for their personal finances.

The second advantage of self-financing is that it avoids the need to bring other partners or investors into the business. Many entrepreneurs start a business, in part, because they desire to be independent. Once an entrepreneur adds partners, complexity is added to the business. Major decisions are no longer just the entrepreneur's to make.

Other owners now have legal and ethical rights in the business that might constrain or slow down major decision making. The Partnership and Shareholder Assessment found in Appendix 2.2 of Chapter 2 summarizes the myriad issues that can face business partners. The entrepreneur should consider these issues carefully before deciding to approach possible partners or outside investors. If the decision is made to bring in other partners, an honest and thoughtful discussion should be conducted using the Partnership and Shareholder Assessment as a guide. It is this complexity that leads many entrepreneurs to prefer going it alone as the sole owner of the business.

A third advantage of self-financing is that the entrepreneur can better align the business to meet personal aspirations. Partners and investors may have different aspirations for the venture that must be taken into account. For example, the entrepreneur may be willing to trade off growth potential in other markets for a much simpler business, operating in a single market that allows more time for family and other interests. Adding partners, particularly outside investors, may add pressure to grow the business to meet their expected returns on investments in the business. This pressure may conflict with the aspirations of the entrepreneur.

A fourth advantage is that self-financing reduces the dilution effect of adding other owners. Adding partners or shareholders means that any profits or gains from the venture must be shared by all owners. If the business is self-funded, the profits and gains are not shared with others and the returns to the entrepreneur are not diluted.

A final advantage is that self-financing makes the future exit from a business relatively simple. An entrepreneur may choose to exit a business for a variety of reasons (Chapter 16 examines the exit process in more detail). There may be an opportunity to sell the business for a reasonable price to an interested buyer. As discussed in Chapter 2, the entrepreneur might decide that the current business is no longer meeting his aspirations. Another opportunity may have arisen that better meets his goals. Whatever the reason, when the entrepreneur is the sole owner of the business and has no business debt, the decision to exit is his decision alone. In addition, if the exit is created by the failure of the business, it becomes an easier issue to face. Additional partners in the business can complicate the process of exiting due to a business failure. As a sole owner, the entrepreneur can develop an orderly exit plan that meets personal needs and preferences.

There are, however, several disadvantages to relying solely on self-financing to launch a new venture. First, relying only on the resources that the entrepreneur can bring to the new business may limit its size and scope. Some ventures require significant funding to launch, particularly those that are capital-intensive or that require a long time to break even due to high fixed costs. The following requirements of some businesses can make self-financing difficult or even impossible in some situations:

- Large equipment budget for start-up, such as a manufacturing venture or certain technology businesses.
- Large initial investment needed to build specialized facilities, such as restaurants, manufacturing facilities, or health-care facilities.
- High level of staffing required at start-up.
- Significant inventories needed for the launch of the venture.

Table 10.1

Advantages and Disadvantages of Self-Financing

Advantages	Disadvantages
Relative ease of securing funding	May limit size and scope of start-up
Avoid complexity created by adding partners	May limit ability to grow
Better alignment with entrepreneur's aspirations	Increases exposure to personal risk from business failure
No dilution of profits or gains Eventual exit process is often simpler	Entrepreneur may lack all necessary experience, contacts, skills, and/or knowledge

Second, using self-financing may also limit the entrepreneur's ability to grow the business to its fullest potential. Although starting the venture may be possible with limited funding, many businesses require the largest amount of investment capital during growth and expansion. For example, an entrepreneur may be able to patent and develop a prototype for a new medical device using personal savings. However, to scale up production and build the organization to manufacture and distribute the medical device requires levels of funding far beyond the personal resources available to commit to the business. In another example, an entrepreneur may be able to fund a single location for a new restaurant. But once the decision is made to roll the restaurant out into several new markets, personal assets are no longer adequate to fund the growth.

Third, by relying only on their own funding for new ventures, entrepreneurs increase their personal exposure to risk. Adding more partners spreads out the risk among several people. For example, a new Web 2.0 venture requires $100,000 to launch and reach breakeven. Funding this venture alone puts the entrepreneur at risk for losing the entire $100,000. But if the entrepreneur has three other partners who all contribute an equal investment to launch the venture, each risks losing only $25,000 if the business fails.

Finally, adding other shareholders brings additional experience, contacts, skills, and knowledge to the venture. For example, a health-care venture launched by one of the authors of this book drew upon the unique health-care experience of two of the partners and the experience in launching and growing a venture that the author brought as a successful entrepreneur. The partners with health-care experience lacked the business experience to be successful, and the author lacked the health-care background to even attempt such a launch. Together, however, they created a successful business. Table 10.1 summarizes the advantages and disadvantages of self-financing.

FRIENDS AND FAMILY FINANCING

Beyond the entrepreneur's own sources of money for a new business, investments and loans from family and friends are the most readily available source of funding. Self-funding from the entrepreneur combined with money invested by friends and family accounts for 85 to 90 percent of all start-up financing for new businesses. Even high-growth, high-potential ventures rely on these sources for about 80 percent of all start-up capital (Kauffman Foundation of Kansas City 2003). However, given the loss of wealth that occurred in the United States as a result of the Recession of 2008 and the collapse of real estate values that was part of the economic downturn, it has become more difficult to raise as much funding from friends and family. They have less wealth to invest, and most have become much more cautious with their investments.

Because the funding comes from family members and friends, this can lead to short-cuts in proper and important business practices. These shortcuts often result in serious family conflicts and broken friendships if the business does not meet expectations in performance or fails. Experts agree that entrepreneurs need to treat any investments or loans from friends or family as a formal business transaction. This section will examine the proper steps to ensure that business transactions with family members or friends of the start-up entrepreneur follow standard business practices.

In some instances it is the entrepreneur who rushes an infusion of cash from friends and family into the business. There are two common reasons that an entrepreneur might rush the deal. First, entrepreneurs typically are full of exuberance and boundless optimism about their new business. Just like the old saying "love is blind," the enthusiastic entrepreneur may be blind to significant risks that face any new venture. He paints too rosy a picture of the potential outcomes of the business, ignoring potential stumbling blocks or risks. He does not deliberately withhold information or try to deceive, but rather his enthusiasm removes objectivity regarding the realities of the business.

Desperation to get the business launched can also lead an entrepreneur to rush through the process of securing funding from family and friends. For example, an entrepreneur who was trying to get a new medical product to market failed in several attempts to convince professional investors to back his idea. He needed part of the initial funding to get a patent to protect the intellectual property associated with the product. The remaining funds would allow him to build a prototype that could demonstrate its performance capabilities. Seeing no other option, he approached family members and friends to raise the funding he believed he needed to reach these two critical milestones. Once these milestones were reached, he was hopeful that he could get the professionals to invest much larger sums to take his business to the point of producing and selling the product. The entrepreneur was worried that other companies might obtain a patent before he could submit his, or beat him to market with an alternative product, if he was delayed much longer. In his presentation to family and friends, he pressured them to make quick decisions, assuring them that his business had an excellent chance of becoming successful. Using guilt and loyalty, he was able to get the money. Unfortunately, although he was able to develop a prototype and a provisional patent, no professional investors were interested in funding his business further due to significant market risks and a lack of confidence in his ability to manage the business. This failure ruined several longtime friendships and created significant rifts with family members who had invested in the business.

Entrepreneurs can take several steps to improve the chances that investments by family members and friends will not end disastrously, even if the business fails. While there is never complete certainty that these steps will be successful, just as no new business venture is ever completely assured of success, treating investments by family and friends as true business relationships offers the best hope of keeping the peace.

DETERMINE TRUE MOTIVATIONS

Family and friends can have many reasons behind their willingness to invest in an entrepreneur's new business. Some family and friends invest in a business out of altruism. They care about the entrepreneur as a family member or friend and want to help her pursue a dream. They may offer the money with no expectations that it will ever get paid back or create any kind of return. Other family members and friends may offer money out of a feeling of obligation. Finally, it is sad, but true, that some family and friends are motivated by greed. They see the entrepreneur as an easy vehicle to wealth, especially given the amount of wealth that was lost since 2008. However, most experts consistently agree that whether the motivation is kindness, loyalty, or greed, friends and family should never offer money to entrepreneurs as an outright gift. Accounting for the money as a business transaction will avoid misunderstandings or changes of heart after the investment has been made.

The entrepreneur must take the time to fully understand the motivation behind any investment from friends and family. It is the entrepreneur's responsibility to set realistic expectations among all family and friend investors no matter what their motivations. Part of this responsibility is setting up these investments or loans as true "arm's length" transactions; that is, the transactions should be treated as if the money was coming from total strangers. Borrowed money should be treated as a formal loan, with the terms of the loan clearly stated and fully understood by both parties. If the money is treated as an equity investment, the transaction should include formal and complete documentation developed by a qualified business attorney.

USE A FORMAL BUSINESS PLAN

One of the primary uses of a formal business plan is to communicate details of the business to those considering investment. Any family member or friend contemplating financial support to an entrepreneur should be provided with a complete business plan (see Chapter 2). The entrepreneur should give the potential funders time to review the plan. A formal presentation should be made to allow for questions and answers about the business and its prospects. This should not be a sales pitch. Rather, it should be an honest, realistic presentation of the potential gains and the possible risks of the venture. Since the aspirations of the entrepreneur are the foundation of the business plan, they should be made explicit. If the entrepreneur has no immediate plans to exit the venture, for example through a sale of the business, the potential funders need to understand that their money may be tied up in the business for a long time.

The discussion of the plan may result in some modifications, including those addressing the financial goals and objectives of the business. For example, family and friends may want to see a clear plan to pay back their initial funding. The entrepreneur should be open to suggestions and, if mutually agreed upon, should provide potential family and friend funders with a revised plan that reflects these changes.

A critical goal of reviewing and discussing the business plan is to make everyone fully aware of all the risks involved in the business. This is the key to setting realistic expectations and it can be a significant challenge. For example, an entrepreneur named Tim sought investment from a group of friends he knew in college to take a patented invention to market. They pooled their money to provide him with the $250,000 he needed. Tim provided them with a business plan and carefully explained all the risks and hurdles that faced the venture as he tried to get it to launch. All that his friends seemed to focus on, however, was the significant returns their investments would generate if the venture worked as planned. It did not. One of the key risks identified in the plan was the ability to obtain a contract with a major retailer to distribute and sell the product. Even with his best efforts, Tim was unable to gain the interest of a single retailer—all believed that the item was too expensive and not significantly better than products they already carried. His friends were furious, accusing him of tricking them into investing. Not only did Tim fail in his dream to launch his business, he also lost a group of friends.

PROVIDE ACCURATE, OBJECTIVE, AND FULL INFORMATION ABOUT THE BUSINESS

The business plan is not the end of information provided to funders—it is only the beginning. Once the business is launched, the entrepreneur should provide regular reports to funders. Many family and friends may say they really do not want this type of information. However, it is in everyone's best interest for the entrepreneur to continue to provide regular quarterly or even monthly reports on progress, achievements, and significant problems, preferably in both written and oral forms. If necessary, the entrepreneur should also provide additional updates that address specific issues related to either good *or* bad news.

KEEP BOUNDARIES

Experts also stress the importance of keeping boundaries when financing comes from family members and friends: business should be kept as business, family as family, and friendship as friendship. Family gatherings and social outings with friends are neither the time nor the place to talk about the business. Although they may seem the most convenient time to do so, talking business on social occasions breaks down the barriers that should be maintained between the business relationship and the personal relationship. The entrepreneur should set up meetings that are specifically designated as opportunities to talk about the business. If family or friends try to engage in business talk in social settings, the entrepreneur should politely defer such talk to another time and place set aside for that purpose.

TAX PLANNING

The most common legal structures used for entrepreneurial ventures are what are known as *pass-through entities*. The pass-through entity generally pays no corporate tax on income. Any profits *pass through* to the shareholders or partners who own the business. This type of structure is used to avoid double taxation for the entrepreneur on any income generated by the business. Without this tax structure, income would be taxed at both the corporate level and to the individual owners as the profits are distributed. Here is a simple example assuming a flat tax rate of 30 percent for personal income and 40 percent for corporate profits (this example assumes that all profits after corporate taxes are paid are distributed to the ownership):

Without a pass-through entity:	
Corporate profits	$500,000
Corporate income tax (40% of $500,000)	$200,000
Individual taxes on balance (30% of $300,000)	$90,000
Total taxes	$290,000

With a pass-through entity:	
Corporate profits	$500,000
Corporate income tax	n.a.
Individual taxes (30% of $500,000)	$150,000
Total taxes	$150,000

The advantage of using a pass-through entity from a tax perspective is clear—a savings of $140,000 in taxes in the above example. The most common legal forms of businesses that are pass-through entities are partnerships, limited liability corporations (LLC), limited liability partnerships (LLP), and subchapter S corporations (S-corp).

It is important to keep in mind a critical difference between a pass-through entity and a traditional corporation. In a traditional corporation, the owners and shareholders pay taxes only when any profits are actually distributed to them. In the example above, if the non-pass-through entity did not pay out profits as dividends to the shareholders, they would incur no personal income tax liability. Only the corporate income tax of $200,000 would be due. With a pass-through entity, the shareholders and owners incur a liability for the profits of the business even if those profits are not distributed to them. In the example, if the entrepreneur decided not to distribute the $500,000 profits to the owners, they would all still owe personal taxes on the profits based on their percentage ownership of the business. So if there were, in our example, three equal shareholders, each would personally owe one-third or $50,000 of the $150,000 owed in taxes.

This point should be made very clear to all family members and friends who are considering an equity investment in a business set up as a pass-through entity. Everyone should agree in advance how cash will be distributed from the business to share the profits and to cover any individual tax liability that shareholders incur due to their ownership. Even if the entrepreneur plans to keep some of the profits in the business to fund growth, it is advisable to distribute enough cash to the shareholders to at least cover any income taxes they will incur due to their ownership in the business. In such cases, a good rule of thumb is the 1/3–1/3–1/3 approach to profits. The first one-third of profits should always be set aside to cover the personal income tax obligation that will be incurred by the owners. This can be distributed quarterly to the shareholders based on their percentage of ownership. Distributing it quarterly helps to account for unusual monthly fluctuations and will provide the funds for any shareholders who have to pay estimated income taxes quarterly. The second third can be left in the business for such uses as funding cash flow related to growth (for example, paying for new employees or additional inventory), for buying assets, or for paying down debt. The final third can be either paid to the shareholders to provide them with a return on their investments in the business or added to the third left in the business, depending on the wishes of the owners.

The entrepreneur should strongly recommend that friends or family investing in the business consult with tax professionals in order to fully understand any possible tax issues that may arise due to the investment. It is advisable to encourage them to use a tax professional who is not working with the business entity, thus ensuring that they get independent, objective advice.

STRUCTURE OF FUNDS INVESTED

Small business expert Cliff Ennico recommends that, whenever possible, money secured from family members or friends should be structured either as a loan or as nonvoting stock (Ennico 2002). If the funds are structured as a loan, the entrepreneur should use a formal loan agreement that defines the interest rate and payment terms. Of course, a clear advantage of securing funding from family and friends is that the terms of agreement can be flexible (Score and Circle Lending 2006). For example, it might be agreed upon in advance that payments can be delayed if cash flow becomes tight. However, interest should always continue to accrue during this time, and careful records should be kept of interest and principle owed on any business loan. Even if payments are delayed, eventually all interest accrued and all principle owed must be repaid. Interest rates should be no less than the Internal Revenue Service (IRS) standard interest rates. These rates are adjusted over time to reflect market rates. Current IRS standard interest rates can be found at the IRS Web site, http://www.irs.gov/ (enter "interest rate" into its search feature). The published IRS interest rate is the minimum interest rate to use in any business loan.

If the funding is going to be structured as an equity investment rather than as a loan, the family member or friend would become one of the entrepreneur's partners or shareholders. Shareholders and partners have legal rights even as nonvoting shareholders. These rights should be clearly understood by both the entrepreneur and the family member or friend. In a corporation, for example, the shareholders who have voting rights can vote to elect members to the board of directors and must approve certain major decisions about the business, such as a sale of the business.

SUMMARY

Most funding for entrepreneurial start-ups comes from the entrepreneurs, their family members, and/or their friends. While it is probably inevitable that entrepreneurs will need to fund at least part of the start-up, they must consider both the advantages and disadvantages when deciding how much of the start-up to fund. Entrepreneurs considering funding from family members and friends should keep in mind that many family weddings, birthdays, and holidays have been ruined by lost investments in failed business deals. Entrepreneurs should take several key steps to ensure that family relationships and friendships are not destroyed by poorly executed business relationships. A carefully devised business plan should be the cornerstone of any business dealings with family and friends. Care should be taken to create open, honest communication channels about business matters and clear boundaries between personal relationships and business relationships. Finally, family members and friends should understand tax issues and the impact of the capital structure of the business and the type of funding they provide. The next chapter will explore how entrepreneurs can use bootstrapping to minimize the amount of external funding they will need for the business as it is launched and as it grows.

DISCUSSION QUESTIONS

1. What are the various sources that an entrepreneur may draw upon to self-fund a business venture? Reflect on your willingness to use these sources to fund a business that you might launch in the future. Or, if you already have started a business, examine why you chose or did not choose each of these sources.
2. Discuss the advantages of self-funding a business. Be sure to reflect on how these apply to you in your business plans.
3. Why do entrepreneurs typically look to family members and friends for funding?
4. Discuss the steps that can be taken to ensure that funding from family members and friends will be treated as a business relationship.
5. Explain how profits and taxes are treated in a pass-through entity.

OPPORTUNITIES FOR APPLICATION

1. Interview an entrepreneur to determine how much self-funding was used in the start-up of the business. Explore the emotional aspects of using the entrepreneur's own money to launch the venture.
2. Talk to family members and friends about their willingness to invest in a business that you have started or are thinking about starting. Try to determine what motivates them. Discuss how such funding might be formalized to ensure that it remains a true business relationship.

REFERENCES

Ennico, Cliff. 2002. "Accepting Money From Friends & Family: 4 Ways to Get Your Cash Without Wreaking Havoc on Your Personal Relationships." Entrepreneur.com, May 6. http://www.entrepreneur.com/money/financing/loansfromfriendsandfamily/article51542.html.

Kauffman Foundation of Kansas City. 2003. National Dialogue on Entrepreneurship and *E-News*, Monday, October 13. http://www.publicforuminstitute.org/nde/news/2003/enews-03-10-13.htm.

Score and Circle Lending. 2006. *Financing Your Small Business: How to Borrow Money from People You Know.* 2d ed. http://www.entrepreneurship.org/uploadedfiles/Documents/Financing_Small_Bus.pdf.

U.S. Census Bureau. 2007. "Survey of Business Owners." http://www.census.gov/econ/sbo/methodology.html (accessed December 27, 2011).

Wells Fargo. 2006. "How Much Money Does It Take to Start a Small Business?" News release, August 15. http://www.wellsfargo.com/press/20060815_Money?year=2006.

Wobwire.com. 2011, "Start-up Capital. Posted on April 27, 2011 http://www.wobwire.com/Share_Your_Woman_Owned_Business_Story_Survey_results_credit_2_7_11.html (accessed December 27, 2011).

11 Bootstrapping

One of the first things that most entrepreneurs focus on is raising external funding to support the launch of their businesses. There are numerous sources of external funding that can be used to capitalize a business. As discussed in the previous chapter, entrepreneurs seek money from sources as varied as family members, friends, and venture capitalists with their untold billions of investment dollars looking for the next Microsoft. The various means of securing external debt and equity financing will be discussed in Chapters 12 to 14. However, before pursuing *external* funds, the entrepreneur should consider how the business could be managed in a way that reduces the external funding required. One way to is to learn how to manage the cash flow of the business, discussed in Chapter 8. Another way is by using what is commonly known as *bootstrapping*. Many successful companies were started and built with bootstrapping techniques. Logo Athletic, for example, was started in 1971 with only $250. By 1994 it had grown to over $230 million in revenues. The founder of Yankee Candle started his business with $20 that he borrowed from a friend. Within seven years Yankee Candle grew to over $30 million in revenues. This chapter will summarize a variety of bootstrapping techniques that can help an entrepreneur achieve success without needing to raise a large amount of start-up capital.

WHY BOOTSTRAP?

Bootstrapping is defined as the "process of finding creative ways to exploit opportunities to launch and grow businesses with the limited resources available for most start-up ventures" (Cornwall 2009). The most common reason entrepreneurs bootstrap is they do not have access to funding. Many young entrepreneurs bootstrap for this reason. Since they have not spent many years receiving high salaries in the business world, they have not been able to save money that can be invested in their own start-ups. Bootstrapping is also commonly used by entrepreneurs in places that do not normally attract investment monies, such as the inner city or poor rural areas.

As will be discussed in Chapters 12–14, securing debt and equity funding can be difficult for many new ventures. This becomes even more of a challenge during difficult economic times when the future is less certain and wealth constricts, as has been experienced since the Recession of 2008 began.

However, places like Austin, Texas, Boston, and Silicon Valley—known as communities that are favorable for aggressive start-ups backed by huge sums of venture capital—are beginning to see more and more bootstrapped businesses created and thriving. Among technology start-ups, a form of bootstrapping termed *lean start-ups* have become more common (Ries 2011). Rather than follow the traditional path for technology start-ups of raising large amounts of venture capital from the beginning stages of the business, a lean start-up creates a rapid series of prototypes designed to test market assumptions and use customer feedback to evolve the business model more quickly and efficiently. This approach is closely linked to the approach to developing a business model discussed in Chapter 6. The lean start-up approach postpones the need for capital to scale the business until the market has affirmed the value proposition of the business model, which generally lessons the amount of funding needed and offers investors a stronger proof of concept based on real customer data. In some start-ups, taking a lean approach has eliminated the need to raise money from outside investors as wasted expenses are greatly reduced and the flow of revenues from customers is greatly accelerated.

But the reasons that entrepreneurs choose to bootstrap are more diverse than one might first assume.

Many entrepreneurs bootstrap because they want to keep 100 percent of the ownership in their own hands. Entrepreneurs desire to keep control of their business for a variety of reasons (Bhide 1992). Entrepreneurs who secure financing through outside investors, known as equity financing, give up a percentage of ownership in the business in exchange for cash that can then be used to start or grow the business. People who invest cash in a business, in exchange for equity, become shareholders or partners with the entrepreneur. However, equity financing may decrease the amount of income the entrepreneur will receive from the business and the wealth that the entrepreneur can accumulate in the business. *Dilution* is the term for this reduction in income and wealth available due to the use of equity financing. Any cash that is available to the entrepreneur due to profits or the sale of the business must now be shared with the new owners that have invested in the business. Thus, the amount available to the entrepreneur has been diluted over more shareholders or partners. The intent of equity financing is that the business will grow larger than it could have otherwise thanks to the extra cash received from investors. But there is growing evidence that this is not always the case.

As an example of the impact of raising external funds, assume an entrepreneur wants to build a business that creates $1 million in wealth. To achieve this goal, the entrepreneur decides to sell stock in the business and is able to raise $500,000 by doing so. The investors receive 50 percent of the stock in the company in return. To achieve the goal of creating $1 million in wealth, the entrepreneur must build a business worth $2 million, because the equity investors now own half of the company due to dilution.

$2 million in total value × 50% ownership = $1 million diluted value to the entrepreneur

Now assume a second entrepreneur has the same financial goal, $1 million in wealth. To reach this goal, this entrepreneur decides to raise the $500,000 by borrowing the money (debt). Just as the value of a home to the owner is worth the market value less any mortgage owed, so too does debt reduce the value of a business to its owner. The entrepreneur who borrowed the funds will need to build the business to a value of $1.5 million to realize the goal of building a business that creates $1 million in wealth. Thus, debt financing can have a similar effect as using equity.

$1.5 million total value – $0.5 million owed to the bank = $1 million net value to the entrepreneur

A third entrepreneur with the same goal of gaining $1 million in wealth decides to use bootstrapping techniques to build a business without using debt *or* equity. To achieve the $1 million goal, the entrepreneur will only need to build a business worth $1 million. And if the business becomes worth $1.5 million or $2 million, the entire value belongs to the entrepreneur. The value is neither diluted by other shareholders nor reduced by paying off loans.

If an entrepreneur is able to build a similar business using less equity and/or debt financing or even by using no outside financing at all, the impact on wealth and income for that entrepreneur can be significant. Rather than beginning the entrepreneurial process by raising as much money as possible, bootstrapping provides a variety of management techniques that reduces the amount of necessary funding. Thus, these techniques become an *internal* source of funding for the business. Every dollar saved by using these internal sources reduces the need of external funding by that same dollar.

Even though some new ventures may fit the criteria for external debt or equity investment, the entrepreneur may choose to minimize the use of outside funding or delay its use for as long as possible (Ebben and Johnson 2006), a proceeding commonly known as "extending the runway" (Berkus 2006). Although the entrepreneur is not able to completely eliminate the dilution effect, postponing outside funding means that more value is created in the business due to its larger size and established cash flow. This puts the entrepreneur in a stronger bargaining position with outside funders. It also gives the entrepreneur more time to set the vision and culture of the business without having to navigate and integrate the potentially varied aspirations of outside funders.

There are also many reasons why entrepreneurs continue to bootstrap well beyond the start-up period of the business. Using bootstrapping to reduce the need for debt financing reduces the risk the business faces during difficult economic times when sales may become soft, inflation heats up, or interest rates climb. Many entrepreneurs find that bootstrapping techniques used during start-up actually create a more effective way to run the business even as it grows. Finally, for some entrepreneurs, bootstrapping is an ethical practice in which they are able to be better stewards of the resources given to them by the various stakeholders of the venture (Cornwall and Naughton 2008). Figure 11.1 shows that bootstrapping is used by entrepreneurs throughout the life of their venture.

The next sections will summarize some of the common bootstrapping techniques used by entrepreneurs. These techniques will be organized around the four rules of bootstrapping (Cornwall 2009):

Figure 11.1 **Bootstrapping Throughout the Life of a Venture**

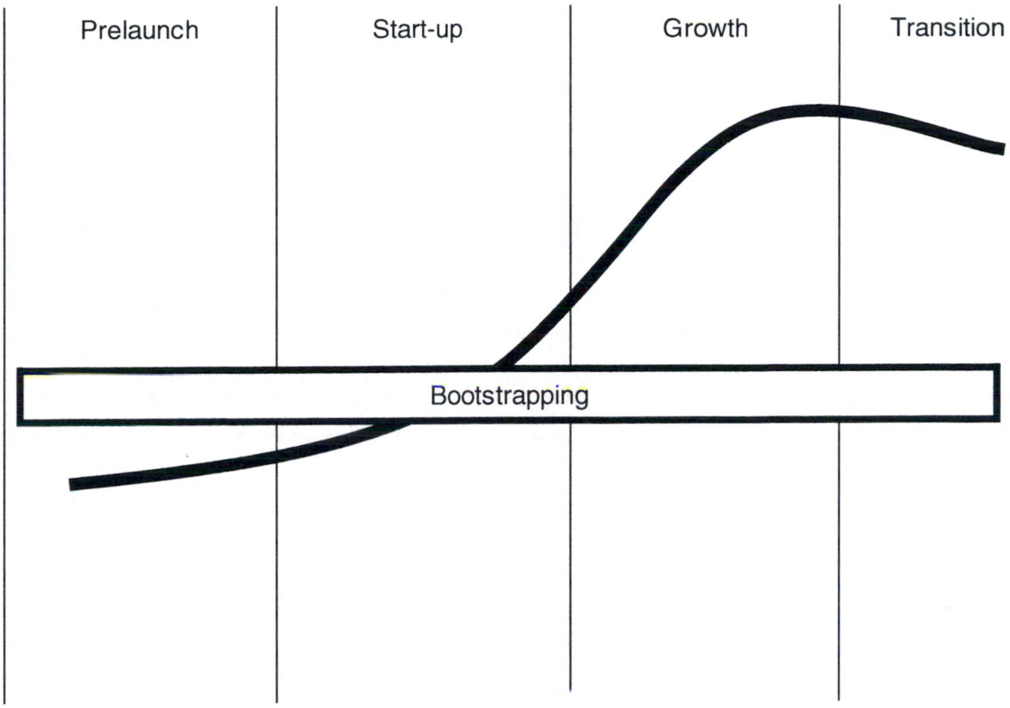

Rule 1: Overhead matters.
Rule 2: Employee expenses are usually the highest single recurring cost.
Rule 3: Minimize operating costs.
Rule 4: Marketing matters, but know your customers and how they make decisions.

BOOTSTRAPPING ADMINISTRATIVE OVERHEAD

> When Allen Shatto started his consulting firm in 1988, renting office space was out of the question. He worked from his house in Bel Air, Maryland. When he could no longer shoulder the workload, he hired four engineers and a scientist, who worked from their houses. . . . Shatto added an "adjunct staff" of 15 freelancers who worked out of their homes. (Finegan 1995)

Overhead includes expenses that are not directly related to making product or providing a service. The functions represented in overhead are required by most businesses if they are to operate effectively. Although the importance of administrative staff and systems grows as a business grows, the costs associated with these functions can create a significant financial burden for a new or growing venture. Administrative overhead includes expenses such as bookkeeping, accounts receivable, accounts payable, sales and marketing, human resources, information systems, and the general management of the business. An entrepreneur trying to grow a business through bootstrapping quickly learns that these are expenses that must be carefully managed.

It is not uncommon for entrepreneurs to successfully raise a large amount of external funding only to commit to large amounts of expenses that are tied to administrative overhead and not to producing goods or providing services. For example, a new venture was started in the 1990s with millions of dollars of external funds to manufacture a new, high-end motorcycle. Before a single motorcycle was produced, the entrepreneurs had committed to a large, highly paid administrative team and built a state-of-the-art office complex, next to a state-of-the-art manufacturing facility, to house this team of administrators. The company ran out of cash before any significant sales could be generated, due in large part to the overhead expenses that had been created. The business was forced into bankruptcy.

Chapter 5 discussed the concept of breakeven. In the preceding example, the fixed overhead costs were so high that the breakeven became impossible to attain before the business ran out of cash. Bootstrapping overhead can lower the point of breakeven effectively and thus reduce the amount of cash required to start a business. This section will examine common methods for reducing overhead expenses without necessarily sacrificing the company's ability to perform the administrative functions it needs to operate.

SPACE

The start-up locations of many businesses have become legend. Hewlett Packard and Apple Computer are two businesses that were literally started in the owners' garages. Other businesses have been started in bedrooms, basements, dining rooms, kitchens, and barns. All these entrepreneurs were able to eliminate a major overhead expense item, rent for space, until the business could afford to pay for it through operating profits. New businesses today can create "virtual offices" through copy centers and mail service centers that rent conference rooms and even offices as needed. Coffee shops and other businesses actually encourage this type of use to boost their own sales.

Other entrepreneurs are able to get free space from companies that have unused space, particularly if these larger companies have an interest in seeing the new business succeed. For example, a large mental health clinic allowed psychologists just starting in practice to use space in the facility with the hope that as the psychologists became successful they would refer patients to the clinic for its specialized programs. Other entrepreneurs may barter their services in exchange for temporary space. Once a business can afford to move into its own space, locating in areas with high vacancy rates can save money through lower rents.

FURNISHINGS AND OFFICE EQUIPMENT

Many entrepreneurs find that forgoing brand-new furnishings and equipment can reduce overhead expenses. Certain dealers specialize in high-quality used furnishings; some also refurbish their merchandise. Even more cash can be saved by buying at auctions or from businesses that are closing or moving and willing to sell furnishings at a drastic discount.

The digital economy comes with the potential to use up a significant amount of the entrepreneur's scarce financial resources. Even with falling prices, computers, copiers, printers, and other office machines come with hefty price tags. The entrepreneur needs to understand clearly what equipment is really needed and when it is needed. Instead of purchasing all the equipment that might be useful, entrepreneurs can use copy centers, which offer highly sophisticated equipment that can be used as needed. One information technology consultant observed that well over 50 percent of computers and other equipment sits idle at any one time in the small businesses in which she consults.

Telephone costs are a hidden expense that entrepreneurs do not always plan for accurately in their forecasts. Although phone systems can be quite expensive, the entrepreneur can easily install many smaller systems. Each additional line the company carries is a new fixed cost, so phone line usage should be monitored during the day to make sure that the business has enough, but not too many, phone lines. Cell phones need not be standard equipment for every employee who works off-site.

ADMINISTRATIVE SALARIES

In small companies, administrative staff must be able to perform a variety of functions. Many entrepreneurs serve as their own bookkeeper, receptionist, salesperson, and janitor. New staff must be able to assume a broad range of responsibilities. Some functions, such as payroll, can be outsourced for less money than when done in-house, even when there are only a few employees.

BOOTSTRAPPING EMPLOYEE EXPENSES

Employee expenses are often the largest single expense category in new and growing ventures. Although the temptation is to hire people early enough so that they are in place when they are actually needed, this is a luxury that many start-ups cannot afford due to cash flow constraints. A basic principle is to insist on periods of "stretching," in which new hiring is delayed as long as possible and current employees carry an added workload until the business's cash flow can support additional staff. It is important to make sure that newly hired staff members understand the way growing businesses need to operate. Spreading tasks among several employees, with each working a few extra hours, can reduce the impact of stretching on individual employees. Entrepreneurs need to be informed about state and federal employment laws and pay all overtime owed. Hourly employees should never be asked to work "off the clock." Clear milestones should be established when new staff will be hired, and those promises should be kept. When new staff is brought on, it is advisable to offer extra time off to the employees who have been carrying the extra workload. Another bootstrapping principle is that it is usually cheaper to develop management talent within the company rather than hire from the outside.

INDEPENDENT CONTRACTORS

Many small companies use independent contractors to keep employee expenses low. Independent contractors do not have to be covered under workers' compensation insurance or employee benefits, and the company does not have to pay the employer portion of Social Security and Medicare taxes. However, in recent years the Internal Revenue Service and the courts have established strict guidelines on independent contractors. The status of independent contractor versus employee is guided not by a specific law, but by a series of court cases. There is no simple checklist, but rather a growing list of criteria that determine independent contractor status. Therefore, a certified public accountant or an attorney should be consulted to ensure that a business is in compliance with the current interpretation of this area of employment law.

EMPLOYEE LEASING AND TEMPORARY EMPLOYEES

Entrepreneurs can reduce employment costs by subcontracting with firms that provide employees for short-term needs through employee lease or temporary employment contracts. This avoids the problems that can arise by hiring permanent employees for what are really only short-term workload needs. Using such firms also can lower administrative overhead, as they perform all the human resources functions for these employees. It is now possible to bring in executive-level employees through such arrangements. Small companies can gain the expertise of a part-time, temporary CEO or controller to navigate through a specific, complex issue or a particularly difficult time in the company's growth.

STUDENT INTERNS

A growing number of businesses are taking advantage of a relatively underutilized workforce—students. Students in high school may wish to obtain more significant work experience that they can get through traditional teenage job categories. University students are eager to work in internships in business so they can list such work experience on their résumés. Finding internship experience has become even more of a pressing goal for university students since unemployment spiked during the Recession of 2008 and the number of entry level jobs constricted. Small businesses are beginning to take advantage of this pool of workers, which in the past was used mainly by large corporations. Student interns are willing to work for relatively low pay in exchange for the experience that can be gained by such work, and most are seeking part-time rather than full-time positions.

EQUITY COMPENSATION

Entrepreneurs are able to offer lower salaries by offering various equity compensation programs to key employees. Many employees are willing to work for less salary now with the hope of earning much more through sharing in future profits or in the proceeds of a business sale or taking a business public. Employees who join the company near the time of the start-up may be issued actual stock in the company. *Stock options* are another vehicle for employee equity compensation. With stock options, employees have the right to purchase a set number of shares of stock in the company at a predetermined price (usually at a slight discount of the value of the shares when the stock is issued). If the company becomes highly profitable, the employees can purchase the stock (known as exercising an option) and receive the benefits of those profits. Or, if the business is sold, the employees can purchase the stock at the discounted price and immediately sell it as the business is sold. *Phantom stock* (also called Mirror stock) is a type of bonus compensation for employees in which the employees do not actually receive stock or the promise of stock through options. Instead, the employees are given a written promise of a bonus whenever profits are distributed to owners or a lump sum if the company is ever sold. The bonus amount is based on what the employees would have received if they had actually owned stock.

NONMONETARY BENEFITS

Small companies can offer nonmonetary benefits that are not available in a larger company. Many employees are willing to work for a little less salary in exchange for these nonmonetary benefits. Small companies can offer flexibility on hours or even workdays because the companies usually have not developed a large number of formalized policies. Small businesses often have a very positive work environment with a strong team or even family feeling. Employees also may see excellent professional growth potential, because a growing company offers the opportunity for rapid advancement. Finally, participating in a start-up can be as fun and exciting for employees as it is for the entrepreneur.

BOOTSTRAPPING OPERATING EXPENSES

> Buschman had little money, but he was clever with machinery. Keeping his regular job—and using $500 in overtime pay—he scrounged in junkyards for materials to construct a little factory in his basement. "There's a feeling you need tons of money and bank financing and all kinds of crapola to start a business. . . . If I needed a tow motor, I'd find something at a junkyard, change the engine and transmission, and rebuild it."
> (Caggiano and Finegan 1995)

Several bootstrapping techniques are available for businesses that manufacture products. At the beginning, it may be possible to outsource production until there is enough cash flow to support bringing production in-house. Once production is brought in-house, it is possible to realize significant savings by buying equipment through auctions, from business closings, from other businesses that have outgrown their smaller machinery, and even from salvage companies or junkyards. For example, a start-up box manufacturing company was able to find all the machinery it needed for its first two years of operation by buying equipment that another company was ready to send to salvage. Once it had been painted and basic maintenance performed, the equipment was in good enough condition to operate reliably for several more years.

The cost of buying, transporting, and restoring this equipment was less than 20 percent of the cost of buying comparable new equipment. In addition, the company that sold the machinery allowed payment over two years with no interest.

Manufacturing companies can also use inventory management to bootstrap their businesses. Inventories comprise both raw materials used to manufacture the product and finished goods that are waiting to be shipped to customers. Poorly managed inventories of both types can tie up large amounts of cash. *Just-in-time* is one method of inventory management that keeps on hand only inventory that is needed for the current jobs being processed. To successfully implement just-in-time, the entrepreneur must have the cooperation of suppliers (raw material inventory) and customers (finished goods inventory) to ensure that product will be delivered as needed. In addition, the business must develop four key elements:

- A continuous inventory update system to ensure that inventories are always at the proper level to meet immediate production and shipping schedules.
- High standards for on-time shipping to minimize the cost of back orders and keep raw materials at proper levels.
- A tracking system to monitor the time it takes to fill back orders from suppliers when they occur and to communicate data to suppliers to facilitate improved performance.
- Tracking customer complaints as a percentage of orders shipped to monitor timeliness and quality of finished goods.

Even small companies need to use cost accounting to manage inventories (see Chapter 5). Accurate knowledge of the costs associated with manufacturing each product the company makes will help ensure acceptable return on investment for the cash that is invested in inventory. Small companies can benefit from keeping their inventories simple. For example, a small printing company realized it had colors and grades of paper that were almost never used. It aggressively trimmed inventory to only the most popular colors and grades, with no negative reaction from the customers. This example also illustrates the importance of tracking the usage, or turnover, of each item in the inventory (see Chapter 7). It is important to communicate inventory reports to all key managers (finance, production, and sales) and to analyze them frequently.

There also are opportunities to bootstrap a service company. A method that has proven successful in keeping costs down for service businesses is to create a so-called *virtual company*. The story of Allen Shatto earlier in this chapter is a good example of a virtual company. During the start-up, Shatto's workers all operated out of their own home offices, thus avoiding the need to rent space. In setting up a virtual service company, communication and coordination are two of the biggest challenges. The entrepreneur should establish daily communication as one of the major priorities. Telephones, e-mail, and even Internet instant messaging can be used as the communication system, and all employees should be trained in the proper use of such systems. As a company grows, some elements of the virtual company may be continued by having some staff engage in telecommuting, which has proved popular with many employees and can actually improve recruitment of new staff.

BOOTSTRAP MARKETING

> If I had one dollar left to spend on my business, I would spend it on marketing.
> —Charles Hagood, cofounder of The Access Group
> and Healthcare Performance Partners

In a new venture the entrepreneur must find the right product or service for the right customer group at the right price. That is, the entrepreneur must be effective at marketing. The goal of bootstrap marketing is to achieve the desired impact on customers, getting them to buy a product or service, by using the least possible amount of resources. Levinson and Godin (1994) identify several basic principles that guide bootstrap marketing:

1. *Know the customer.* To market to their customers effectively and efficiently, entrepreneurs should seek to understand their customers' needs and expectations and how they make decisions to purchase.
2. *Focus on the impact of the message, not volume.* The budgets of large corporations allow for mass promotion and advertising of their products. Their advertising campaigns reach many people who are not, and never will be, customers. These large companies understand that this overkill in advertising is just a cost of doing business. Entrepreneurs, however, cannot afford to waste their message on those it is not intended for, if it can be avoided.
3. *Focus on benefits that the product or service brings to the customer.* In many cases, special benefits offered by the product, the way the product is delivered to the customer, and services that go with the product are the entrepreneur's strongest competitive advantage. Although entrepreneurs cannot match dollar-for-dollar the advertising spent by larger competitors, they can provide the product in a way that will attract and keep customers.
4. *Understand the market niche.* Many entrepreneurs have discovered the significant advantage of gaining control of a small, often undiscovered or underserved segment (niche) in the market. The ultimate goal of the market niche strategy is not to be noticed, thus not attracting competition. For example, an entrepreneur recognized that all the charter boats operating on a local lake catered to large groups of fifty or more people. His research revealed that many smaller groups of ten to fifteen people wanted to book a charter boat but were not being served in this market. Recognizing this unserved market, the entrepreneur began what became a successful charter business designed for these smaller groups.
5. *Spend marketing dollars wisely.* At times it may be possible to achieve remarkable results while spending little or no money. Other times, as will be seen in the following discussion of bootstrap marketing techniques, it is essential to spend enough money to get the quality needed to be effective. A careful plan can avoid wasted resources.
6. *Understand that marketing is a process, not an event.* Many entrepreneurs concentrate on marketing their businesses only during the start-up and when revenues slow down. To be cost-effective, marketing should be a continuous part of doing business.

THE BASIC BOOTSTRAP MARKETING TOOLS

A single chapter cannot capture all the creative tools and techniques that entrepreneurs have developed to market their businesses to their customers, so the focus here will be on the most commonly used tools and techniques.

Word of Mouth

Using customers to spread information about a business is known as *word-of-mouth marketing*, which is probably the oldest and most commonly used form of bootstrap marketing. Sernovitz and Kawasaki define word-of-mouth marketing as simply "everything you can do to get people talking" about a business (2006, 3). One recent poll found that 82 percent of small businesses use word of mouth to grow their business and that 15 percent rely almost exclusively on word of mouth (NFIB 2008). Kevin Jennings, cofounder of soundAFX in Nashville, Tennessee, describes the benefits of word of mouth for his sonic branding company this way: "Word of mouth is an incredible way to market. The more people I meet, the more connections are formed. People know people who know people who know people. If you are good at what you do, people will refer you to others."

Social networking through the various forms of social media has proven to amplify and accelerate the spread of word of mouth. Blogs, Twitter, and Facebook have all become media that allow consumers to talk about products and services. A study by Jansen et al (2009) found that about 19 percent of all microblogging comments made on Twitter have some mention of an organization or product brand in some way. Of those that mentioned a brand in this study, 20 percent offered an opinion on that brand. Not only do people talk about brands in social media, others listen to what they have to say. A marketing industry study by Morepace found that two-thirds of Facebook users said that a friend referral would increase their chances of purchasing a product or visiting a retailer.

However, whether it is counting on traditional word of mouth from person to person or via social media, many entrepreneurs fall into the myth of "if we build it, they will come." They fail to understand that spontaneous word of mouth rarely just happens. Most consumers find it hard to identify a specific product or business that they could not wait to talk about with friends, family, and even strangers. Successful word-of-mouth promotion requires entrepreneurs to actively find ways to motivate customers to talk about a business in a positive way.

The following are some of the most reliable ways to encourage word of mouth marketing:

- *Motivate customers to talk about your company through excellence in customer service.* Customer service is not what it used to be, so if you can create an exceptional experience, people will tend to talk about it. The service must be consistent, genuine, and enthusiastic.
- *Create incentives for customers to spread the word through a referral thank-you program.* Offer customers a future discount or send them a small thank-you gift, such as a gift card, for each new customer they send your way.

- *Ask the customer to "sell" for you.* There are certain businesses that the customers desperately want to see succeed. This most often happens when you fill a niche that has not been addressed in the market. In this case, ask your customers to spread the word. Let them know that you cannot succeed without their help bringing in new customers. This is something that can be done using a Facebook page if a strong brand loyalty exists with customers.
- *Create a "buzz campaign."* It is possible to mimic word-of-mouth marketing by getting friends, family, and employees to actively create a "buzz" about your business. In effect, they try to create demand for the business by word of mouth. This strategy is used quite often in the entertainment industry. Fan groups are actively enlisted to get the word out about an artist. A buzz campaign also can be done through a user group, which, in exchange for free service, support, and education, can become a "sales force" for your business. Social media can greatly increase the speed and reach of a buzz campaign.

Although word of mouth is often considered "free advertising," it is most effective when some time, energy, and even a few marketing dollars are committed to it.

Business Cards

One of the most important, and often one of the first, marketing tools for any entrepreneur is the business card. It is still a standard part of business etiquette around the globe. The entrepreneur must decide on the design, the paper, the colors, and the content. Because the business card often provides the first contact and the first impression, these decisions are important. Following is a list of considerations for creating a business card:

1. *Design.* Experts tend to agree that a professional designer should do the design of a business card. Although this may cost several hundred dollars, it is money well spent given the importance of first impressions. A professional designer can provide valuable input into decisions regarding logos, white space, font, and so forth.
2. *Data.* Business cards should include all-important contact information, but only if it is useful. For example, in today's digital business world, many businesses have contact with clients only by e-mail and phone. Therefore, it may not be necessary to include such things as a mailing address.
3. *Paper.* Top quality paper is important. A card printed by a home computer on perforated paper tends to make the business appear as if it is not permanent nor even a "real" business. A professional printer using the best paper that the entrepreneur can afford should do printing. This is another example of when it is important to spend money, but spend it wisely.
4. *Color.* Colored ink can make a card stand out. Most experts suggest using at least two colors of ink. Additional colors are more expensive, and it is questionable how much benefit is gained by adding a third or fourth color. Standard colors are much less expensive than custom blended colors, so it

may be advisable to stick to standard colors offered by the printer. With digital printing, full-color pictures on business cards have become much more affordable for even small businesses.

5. *Description or slogan.* Most cards have room to include a brief description of the business or a slogan. Because cards may be one of the only forms of advertising for a new business, it is recommended that such information be included on the card.

6. *Using both sides.* Remember, a business card has two sides. The front is for the entrepreneur's basic contact information. If getting more content onto the business card is important, it is possible to include additional information on the back—for example, pricing, a map with directions, or a photo of the product. Slogans and descriptions of the business also can be moved to the back if necessary.

Blogs

Blogs have become a major bootstrap marketing tool. One recent survey found that 10 percent of small businesses were using or were planning to use blogs for their businesses (NFIB 2008). Blogging allows for a highly targeted personal contact with a customer base. If done properly, a blog can build strong customer loyalty and name recognition for the entrepreneur's business.

Blogging can be a good public relations tool. It can set the entrepreneur apart as an expert in the field, leading reporters to the blog site when looking for content for articles. Here are some suggestions and cautions to maximize the effectiveness of blogging as a bootstrap marketing tool (Cornwall 2009):

- Be consistent in blogging. Most experienced bloggers find that multiple posts each week are required to build a loyal following.
- Do not use the blog merely to promote the business. If the blog seems too self-serving or self-promoting, blog readers will not come back to the site for very long. Develop content that is interesting and lively enough to keep people coming back day after day.
- Take the time to do the blog well. Most regular bloggers spend several hours each week to do research and to write.
- Be patient. Building an audience will take time. Build awareness by developing relationships with reporters, other bloggers, and customers. Use e-mail to promote the blog.
- Be cautious about what you write. The whole world can read what you have written. This includes employees, bankers, and your competition.

Facebook Pages and Twitter Followers

Many businesses now find Facebook pages to be as essential as a website to promote their business. In fact, there are an increasing number of new businesses that forego a website and only use a Facebook page and/or Twitter as their web presence. People who are fans of your brand are more likely to purchase from you in the future. A study released jointly by marketing firms Chadwick Martin Bailey and iModerate Research Technologies (2010) found that "60 percent of Facebook fans and 79 percent of Twitter followers are more likely to recommend those brands since becoming a fan or follower." But people most often need a reason to become a Facebook fan or a follower on Twitter. Studies show that receiving discounts is the primary reason driving people to become fans or to follow a company.

Brochures

Traditionally, brochures were a way to communicate with customers in print. While printed brochures are still widely used, there are now many options for electronically producing and distributing brochures. Most basic Web sites are nothing more than electronic brochures. The same information can also be disseminated using other media, such as DVDs and e-mail lists. No matter what the format, it is important to spend wisely and know the customers' expectations. It is easy to both underspend and overspend on design and production.

Banners and Signs

Entrepreneurs can use a variety of banners and signs to bring attention to their businesses. Banners and signs can draw attention to the business location, promote special offers, highlight new products, and announce grand openings. Such tools are typically used in retail businesses whose customers come directly to the place of business. Banners and signs also can be used by service companies to highlight jobs that these businesses are currently doing—for example, lawn signs used by home repair companies or signs on the trucks and equipment of a landscaping business that are parked at a job site.

Newsletters

Another basic marketing tool is a customer newsletter. Most newsletters are now sent electronically. To increase the likelihood that the newsletter is read by the customer, it should be made interesting, informative, and educational. The content can be a mix of articles related to the entrepreneur's industry, some that highlight the company itself, and some that highlight customers. Many companies manage e-mail newsletters for other businesses. These companies can manage the e-mail lists and help in designing the look of the newsletter. Newsletters should be sent every one to three months. Once a business starts a newsletter, there should be a commitment to continue it over time. Customers can become disaffected when a newsletter that they have grown to anticipate stops arriving in their e-mail inbox.

Direct Mailing and E-Mailing

Mailing lists are a means for contacting existing and potential customers using a variety of techniques. Mailings can be done through traditional postal services or through e-mail lists. Coupons or other special offers can be mailed that encourage potential customers to try the business. Existing customers can be sent items that reinforce loyalty and increase frequency of purchase. This can be done by sending out greeting cards at holidays, giveaways with the company name and logo, copies of articles that might interest customers or that feature them in the news, thank-you notes for large orders or referrals, and special promotions, including preferred customer discounts or special sales.

While lists can be purchased, many entrepreneurs bootstrap this process by creating their own lists. Sources of information for a direct mail or e-mail database include creating a new customer form to collect contact information, using fishbowl contests for a free prize to collect business cards, or gathering names from other free lists such as the Yellow Pages or online directories.

Publicity

When a newspaper, blog, television news broadcast, or other media run a story on a business, it is called publicity. It is, in effect, free advertising. Therefore, finding ways to get stories in the paper, on radio, or on television can be an effective means of bootstrap marketing. Most stories about businesses start with a press release sent to various media outlets. In effect, much of the news written about businesses is written by those very businesses in their news releases. Although public relations firms can be hired to write and distribute news releases, many entrepreneurs are successful at creating publicity on their own behalf. It may be necessary to build a relationship or educate people in the media to get their attention before sending news releases about the business. Once a news release is sent, a follow-up phone call to see if there are any questions may help increase interest in running the story.

THE ETHICS OF BOOTSTRAPPING

In a study of start-up ventures, Winborg and Landstrom (1997) identify entrepreneurs who bootstrap using delaying techniques. That is, these entrepreneurs delay payments to vendors and other creditors as a management practice in their businesses. This approach to bootstrapping, used by entrepreneurs who are desperate and some who are not so desperate, has been generally criticized in the entrepreneurship literature. These entrepreneurs are using other peoples' resources, most often without their permission or consent, to offset their own lack of resources. Certainly many entrepreneurs find themselves in times of limited cash flow, which may require that difficult decisions be made. However, to intentionally delay payment as a bootstrapping technique creates serious ethical and moral issues. In some cases, entrepreneurs are using something that is not their own, cash flow and other resources, without permission. In other cases, deliberately delaying payment creates an exchange (e.g., inventory for account receivable) in which the entrepreneurs have no intention of meeting the terms of that exchange (i.e., payment within the agreed-upon time). Such behavior can become standard practice for an entrepreneur, creating a climate of unethical and immoral actions.

Bootstrapping should not be practiced in such a way that it intentionally harms other businesses. If delays in payment become necessary due to circumstances outside an entrepreneur's control, creditors should be approached openly and honestly about payments due. If problems in making payments are anticipated, creditors should be made aware so that they can consent to working with the entrepreneur, if they so choose, in order to weather the difficult time.

SUMMARY

This chapter has explored a variety of tools and techniques—collectively known as bootstrapping—that can significantly reduce expenses and cash flow requirements in entrepreneurial ventures. Bootstrap marketing allows a company to be highly effective at reaching the customer while keeping marketing expenses much lower than those of traditional marketing methods. Bootstrapping also can be applied to manage the expenses associated with staffing, administrative functions, and the operations of the business. With bootstrapping techniques implemented and cash flow well managed, the amount of outside funding required can be significantly reduced. However, many businesses will still need to raise external funding. Chapters 12 to 14 present the various sources of external funding and their uses.

DISCUSSION QUESTIONS

1. Discuss the potential advantages and disadvantages of bootstrapping a new business venture.
2. What are the four rules of bootstrapping? Discuss how each helps control scarce resources.
3. What are the principles behind bootstrap marketing? Give examples of why each principle is important.
4. What are the ethical concerns that apply to the various bootstrapping techniques discussed in this chapter?
5. Why is it critical to examine overhead expenses carefully in a new business venture with limited resources?
6. What are the advantages and disadvantages of equity compensation methods?

OPPORTUNITIES FOR APPLICATION

1. Interview entrepreneurs to find examples of bootstrapping techniques they have used in their businesses.
2. Develop a bootstrap marketing plan for a new business idea you currently have under development.
3. Design a business card, brochure, Web page, blog, and Facebook page for your new business idea.

REFERENCES

Berkus, D. 2006. *Extending the Runway.* Boston: Aspatore Books.
Bhide, A. 1992. "Bootstrap Finance: The Art of Start-Ups." *Harvard Business Review* (November–December): 109–117.

Caggiano, C., and J. Finegan. 1995. "Bootstrapping: Great Companies Started With Less Than a Thousand Dollars." *Inc.* (August): 38.

Chadwick, Martin Bailey, and iModerate Research Technologies. 2010. Press release, March 10.

Cornwall, J. 2009. *Bootstrapping.* Englewood Cliffs, NJ: Pearson/Prentice-Hall.

Cornwall, J., and M. Naughton. 2008. *Bringing Your Business to Life.* Ventura, CA: Regal Books.

Ebben, J., and A. Johnson. 2006. "Bootstrapping in Small Firms: An Empirical Analysis of Change over Time." *Journal of Business Venturing* 21(6): 851–865.

Fenn, D. 1999. "Grand Plans." *Inc.* (August 1): 24.

Finegan, J. 1995. "Bootstrapping Tactics: A Bootstrapper's Primer." *Inc.* (August). http://www.inc.com/magazine/19950801/2365.html.

Godin, S. 1998. *The Bootstrapper's Bible.* Chicago: Upstart.

Jansen, B.J., Zhang, M., Sobel, K., and Chowdury, A. 2009. "Twitter Power:Tweets as ElectronicWord of Mouth." *Journal of the American Society for Information Science* 60(11): 2169–2188.

Larson, K. 1999. "Don't Leave Home Without It." *Inc.* (October). http://www.inc.com/articles/1999/10/14732.html.

Levinson, J., and S. Godin. 1994. *The Guerrilla Marketing Handbook.* Boston: Houghton Mifflin.

National Federation of Independent Business (NFIB). 2008. "Small Business Polls." http://www.nfib.com/object/sbPolls.

———. 2010. "Consumers Follow Social Brand Referrals." eMarketer.com (April 14). http://www.emarketer.com/Article.aspx?R=1007630 (accessed Janaury 2, 2012).

Ries, E. 2011. *The Lean Startup.* New York: Crown Business.

Sernovitz, A., and G. Kawasaki. 2006. *Word of Mouth Marketing: How Smart Companies Get People Talking.* Chicago: Kaplan.

Winborg, J., and H. Landstrom. 1997. "Financial Bootstrapping in Small Businesses: A Resource-Based View on Small Business Finance." In *Frontiers of Entrepreneurship Research,* ed. P.D. Reynolds et al., pp. 471–485. Babson Park, MA: Babson Center for Entrepreneurial Studies.

12 External Sources of Funds: Equity

Chapter 10 discussed using what are generally considered internal sources of funding—the entrepreneur's own funds, and money secured from family members and friends. Funding from the entrepreneur, family members, and friends can be structured as either debt or equity. Chapters 12–14 examine external sources of funding through either debt or equity. Debt financing, the topic of Chapter 13, involves a contractual, temporary use of funding provided by an outside person or entity. Debt creates an obligation to repay the funding provided to the business. Equity financing, the topic of this chapter and Chapter 14, creates a more permanent relationship in which ownership interests are transferred to the person or entity providing funds.

Equity in a business reflects the owners' investment in a business. Equity is comprised of capital invested by the owners and through profits generated by the business, less any distribution of profits taken by the owners. In the accounting equation (see Chapter 3), equity equals assets minus liabilities. From a financing perspective, equity also can refer to the actual market value of a business if it were to be sold to new owners on the open market. *Equity funding* of a business is the exchange of a share of ownership in return for a capital investment, which an entrepreneur may use during the start-up of a business. But it also can be a source of funding to support the growth of business during periods of significant expansion.

Equity funding is generally an investment that is made with the expectation of a return on that investment. Such returns can come from future cash flows from the business, from selling the business, from taking a business public, or from the repurchase of stock. Equity investors generally hope to realize a certain return on their investment, but because the investment is in equity and is fully at risk, no formal expectation of a return can be provided.

This chapter examines the basic approaches to equity financing, including angels, strategic partners, private placements, crowdfunding, and small business investment companies (SBICs). As seen in Figure 12.1, these sources of financing are available to an entrepreneurial venture from start-up through the growth phase. Discussion will include how each equity strategy works and the best uses for each approach. Venture capital financing, which is also a form of equity funding generally reserved for use with high-growth ventures, will be discussed in detail in Chapter 14.

Figure 12.1 **Equity Financing**

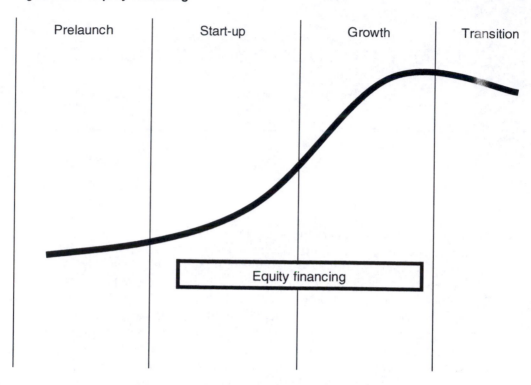

| Prelaunch | Start-up | Growth | Transition |

Equity financing

ANGEL INVESTORS

Angels are individuals who invest directly in entrepreneurial ventures. Angels have enough personal wealth to invest part of their personal portfolios, typically between 1 and 10 percent, in risky investments directly into start-up or growing companies. Angels may have inherited their wealth or earned it as professionals, such as physicians, attorneys, or accountants, as executives in large corporations, or from being successful entrepreneurs. What angels share is a desire to invest directly in companies that have the potential for a higher rate of return than traditional equity investments in publicly traded companies. Most angels are sophisticated investors who understand the risks they are assuming with this type of investment.

Angels are generally willing to provide seed funding for start-ups or second-stage funding that will provide capital to help an early-stage business grow. In 2007 angel investors placed 39 percent of their investments in seed-stage investments, 35 percent in post–start-up businesses, and 21 percent in later-stage business deals. A survey by Pepperdine University found that over two-thirds of the deals they invested in were within 100 miles of their office. Angels generally do not like retail businesses unless they have the potential to grow into multiunit operations. Some angels tend to specialize in an industry that they have knowledge about or experience in for their investments. Others may look for opportunities in a "hot" industry. For example, it was relatively easy to find angel investors in the health-care industry during the late

1980s and early 1990s, but by the late 1990s technology was the favored industry. A 2007 survey of angel investors (Sohl 2008) found that their investments were in the following industries at the percentage shown:

- Software: 27 percent
- Health-care services and medical devices and equipment: 19 percent
- Biotech: 12 percent
- Manufacturing and energy: 8 percent
- Retail: 6 percent
- Media: 5 percent

The 2011 Pepperdine survey found that clean tech investments were the fastest growing industry segment for angel investment.

Most angels are interested in a deal size between $50,000 and $1 million. Larger deals will attract only a small number of angels, since funding a $1 million deal typically suggests a net worth of up to $100 million. Also, angels often are involved in multiple ventures, so the investment in any one deal will not reflect the total funding they are willing to put into entrepreneurial ventures. Increasingly, angel investors are joining together to invest in deals, thereby spreading the risk of each deal among several investors. This practice also allows angels to get involved in larger deals—which are sometimes later-stage investments—by pooling their money.

Some joint investments are informal, but angels also join together into formal angel investor networks. The Pepperdine survey found that 62.8 percent of angel investors belong to formal angel networks. Such networks typically have a small staff that makes all initial contact with entrepreneurs. When working with an angel network, the entrepreneur should anticipate the following steps:

1. The entrepreneur submits a formal business plan to the angel network staff. The staff may have asked the entrepreneur to submit the plan, the plan may have been referred by a professional, or the entrepreneur may send the plan to the network directly. Many angel networks have Web sites through which entrepreneurs can submit their business plans. Also, the network may host business plan competitions or other events to boost the number of deals for the angels to consider.
2. The network staff screens the plans to find those that it believes have legitimate potential and meet the investment goals and preferences of the angels who are members of the network.
3. The staff works with the entrepreneur to refine and improve the business plan and sharpen the presentation.
4. Once the staff believes the plan is ready, it will arrange for the entrepreneur to present the plan to any interested members of the angel network. Typically, more than one entrepreneur will present a plan to this group of angels.
5. If the plan is of interest to the angel investors, they will negotiate with the entrepreneur regarding the terms and expectations of any investment. In some cases, networks will pool funds from several angels to make the investment, but it is most common for wealthy angels to make individual decisions.

6. Once the plan is funded, the entrepreneur will either be accountable to the angel investor or to the angel staff as agents of the investors.

In addition to formal angel networks, several other ways to find angel investors have emerged over the past few years. Bill Clark (2011) identified the following approaches to connecting with investors:

1. Several groups have formed within the social media site LinkedIn to help connect potential investors with possible deals. Since LinkedIn has emerged as one of the most used sites for business professionals, it can prove to be an effective tool for connecting with angel investors seeking new deals to invest in.
2. Entrepreneurship networking events are held in almost every major city.
3. Crowdfunding sites have emerged as a means of connecting start-up entrepreneurs with multiple smaller investors. These sites are best for entrepreneurs seeking smaller amounts of seed capital. Examples of crowdfunding sites include Kickstarter (www.kickstarter.com) and IndieGoGo (www.indiegogo.com).
4. Start-up incubators offer not only resources for start-ups, but also work to get the businesses they support investor-ready. Examples include Y Combinator (www.ycombinator.com) and TechStars (www.techstars.com).

There are still a significant number of angel investors who do not participate in angel networks. Finding those angel investors who have chosen not to be part of an angel network can be a significant challenge for the entrepreneur. As one angel said, "You're not going to find me in the Yellow Pages." In fact, many angels closely guard their privacy to avoid being overwhelmed by entrepreneurs looking for funding. To illustrate, one of the authors of this book was interviewed by a local newspaper for a story on angel investors. Only one brief quote was used in the article, but that quote generated dozens of calls from entrepreneurs asking for help finding investors. So where and how are angels found? First, many angels work through their attorneys, accountants, bankers, or other professional advisers to identify possible investment opportunities. Therefore, entrepreneurs must develop a network that will gain visibility with this group of intermediaries in their local community. These intermediaries may then be willing to make a referral, which is the preferred method of contact for most angel investors (Kelly and Hay 1996). Second, many programs for connecting entrepreneurs and angels are sponsored by universities or other neutral institutions. Third, some business brokers or small investment bankers specialize in connecting angels with entrepreneurs. However, this approach can require large fees that will add to the cost of finding an investor. Finally, some entrepreneurs find angels though matchmaking Websites and magazines that present profiles of businesses for angels to review. One matchmaking source is Active Capital (http://activecapital.org), a nonprofit originally established by the Small Business Administration (SBA), to help entrepreneurs and qualified investors network with each other over the Internet. Generally, entrepreneurs have to pay a fee, either directly or indirectly, to get their business profiled with any of these matchmakers.

Once contact is initiated between a potential angel investor and an entrepreneur, an initial meeting will be set up to help both sides begin to gauge the fit between the angel and the entrepreneur and the business. Most angels report that these initial meetings are primarily to help them evaluate the entrepreneur more than the business. As one angel said, "I invest in people, not in businesses." Entrepreneurs also must understand that this is their opportunity to assess the angel as a person. An angel who invests in the business will become one of the owners of the business, a new partner. The same angel advised entrepreneurs to consider that "angels are not just a source of cash like a bank. The entrepreneur should make sure that the angel is someone they want to be in business with."

If initial meetings generate continued interest by both sides, then more detailed discussions can ensue about the business itself, the angel's expectations, and, eventually, a general agreement on a deal structure for the investment. The structure of any deal varies based on the type of business, but many angels will want preferred stock if possible to provide a little more protection for their investment. Some angels will want to have a position on the board of directors or at least some decision-making role, such as veto power over major decisions. Communication is an important part of the entrepreneur's relationship with an angel, and specific expectations for information may be formalized in the deal itself. In almost all situations, the angel will not want to be involved in day-to-day operations. As one angel put it, "I want to own the restaurant, but I don't want to flip hamburgers." Generally, angels will provide a much quicker decision about their investment than other equity sources. The final steps involve the angel conducting due diligence on the investment (i.e., verifying the key information supplied by the company) and the entrepreneur's attorney creating the legal documents needed to complete the investment.

Most angels look for a payoff within three to seven years. Payoff to the angel investor typically comes through an exit event. Angels do not desire year-to-year distribution of profits and in fact may view such a distribution negatively as they generally want profits to be retained to fund growth. Since the passage of Sarbanes-Oxley in 2002, 65 percent of exit events in businesses with angel investments came through mergers and acquisitions (Sohl 2008). The entrepreneurial venture is typically purchased by either a publicly traded corporation or a private venture that has a large amount of cash to invest in acquisitions. Angel investors hope to realize a 20 to 50 percent annual return, depending primarily on the level of risk they perceive in the entrepreneurial investment. And the risk for angel investors is real, as 27 percent of deals they invest in go bankrupt (Sohl 2008).

For example, assume an angel is interested in investing $100,000 in a fairly new venture that has growth potential. This angel is willing to leave the money in this business for about five years and is hoping for an annual rate of return of about 30 percent. The following equation provides a quick estimate of what the angel hopes to see in five years:

Amount invested × (Expected annual rate of return on investment to the power of the Expected number of years invested) = Expected return in dollars
$$\$100,000 \times (1.3)^5 = \$371,293.$$

The angel will want to see that there is an exit strategy that will allow for cashing out of the investment within five years. This exit can occur though the sale of the business, the repurchase of the angel's stock by the company, second-stage investment by a venture capital firm, or a public offering of the company. The angel also will try to determine an estimate of the value of the business in five years in order to negotiate enough ownership in the business to realize the desired return. Assume that, based on the business plan, a reasonable estimate of the value of the business in five years is $3 million. The angel investor will probably want a percentage of ownership based on the following:

$371,293 desired return / $3 million estimated value = 12.38% ownership.

Much of this calculation is based on estimates and assumptions, so the angel may try to negotiate for a number of shares of stock that roughly represents that percentage of ownership.

In reality, determining the future value of a company that may not have yet sold a single product can be a significant challenge and a point of serious disagreement between the angel and the entrepreneur. If both parties can agree, for example, that a business is worth $4 million before an investment is made and the investor puts in $1 million, the business is now worth $5 million. The investor will probably get stock worth 20 percent ownership in the business ($1 million / $5 million = 20 percent). However, valuing a business during the seed round of funding has been compared, by some, to trying to measure the exact speed of the wind by holding up a wet finger in the air! It is just too hard to assess value in a brand-new business that needs seed funding. So how, then, do the parties determine the percentage of ownership that the angel should get when putting seed funding into a relatively new business that may have no revenues as yet?

In many instances, the answer to the question is that they do not try to estimate a value of the business entity before it becomes operational. A common approach to valuation for seed financing is to use a *convertible promissory note*, which is a loan that will be converted into equity at a later date. So the angel investor in this case does not receive actual ownership in the business during the initial financing. Any need to value the business is delayed until there is clearer information to use for valuation, which happens after the business begins to sell product and a clearer picture of the size of the market is known. Until the note converts to equity, it will accrue interest (the interest is added to the loan) at a predetermined interest rate.

The angel will convert the convertible promissory note from debt to equity after sales have begun and later stage investments come in (Series A investment—discussed in more detail in Chapter 14). The convertible promissory note agreement with the angel investor includes a multiplier that gives the angel some added value for taking a risk with the start-up of the venture.

For example, assume a start-up needs $1 million in seed funding. The angel investor issues a convertible promissory note with a 10 percent interest rate and with a 1.25 conversion multiplier. At the time of the Series A investment, which in this example we will assume is a $5 million venture capital investment one year later, the conversion occurs and the angel converts the promissory note into equity and gets shares that are equivalent to the original $1 million seed money times the 1.25 multiplier plus accrued interest on the original loan. So a year later the seed investor gets shares that would be the same as if $1,375,000 ($1,000,000 × 1.10 × 1.25) had

---

Box 12.1
In Their Own Words . . . An Angel Investor

Although people have been investing in private ventures for as long as there have been entrepreneurs starting businesses, angel investors recently have become more widely recognized as a source of equity financing. Here is a description of what an angel investor looks for when working with entrepreneurs in his own words:

"When an entrepreneur is deciding to work with an angel, he should make sure that their strategy is the same: when to get in, how to run the business, and when to exit. Deciding on the exit strategy beforehand is crucial. I have seen many times the entrepreneur wanting to build the business beyond what the angel wants. This should all be resolved in the beginning.

"Angels are looking to make a substantial return in a potentially risky investment. One thing entrepreneurs imagine about angels is that they have so much money that their investments don't matter to them. This couldn't be farther from the truth. We care a lot about who and what we invest in. We want to work with someone who has a well-thought-out-plan and understands what it is going to take to become successful. One of the biggest mistakes entrepreneurs make is in their presentation to an angel investor. Most entrepreneurs when they come and do a presentation (you will get about a thirty-minute attention span from an angel) make the mistake of spending twenty-five of those minutes talking about how good their widget is and the other five minutes talking about the financial implications. What the entrepreneur should do is concentrate his time on what the investment is, what the person is going to get out of it, and what the return is going to be in a certain period of time. He should then spend the rest of the five minutes on proving how great his product is. If entrepreneurs do it the other way around, the angel's mind begins to wander because he has no idea what he has to put in, what the returns are going to be, and what he is going to get out of it. You have to remember angels are out to make a risk-reward return. They don't fall in love with a widget; they are investing in a product and expect a return for their money."

Interview with John M. Morrison, angel investor, Minneapolis, MN

---

been invested. Again, the logic is that by the time the business is ready for larger investments (in this case another $5 million), there is a clearer basis for valuation. Product sales have begun, the size and scope of the market are better defined, there are time lines for product sale, and so forth.

STRATEGIC PARTNERS

Certain businesses may be interested in providing equity financing to entrepreneurs because of their close business relationships or the potential for mutually beneficial working relationships in the future. Businesses with such close relationships are known as *strategic partners* or *strategic alliances*. Strategic partners can be suppliers, customers, or other businesses operating in the same industry.

For example, a supplier may decide to invest in a new company that can help get its products distributed into a new market. A large company may provide investment capital to help entrepreneurs open distribution companies or retail outlets, or a large manufacturing company may move backward in the distribution chain by investing in start-up suppliers of raw materials or packaging.

Strategic partnerships are also used by large companies in the same industry investing in a start-up company that has a completely new product or service. This is quite common in the pharmaceutical industry where large companies use strategic investments in small start-ups to secure control of additional new drugs to put into their pipeline. The need for new drugs has grown due to the limited time the large pharmaceutical companies can protect each drug before generic equivalents are allowed to come to the market. Companies such as Twitter, Facebook, and Amazon are active in providing strategic investments in technology start-ups.

Most strategic partners have lower expectations for financial returns than investors such as angels. These firms expect a closer relationship if the venture begins to succeed, which will create market advantages. For example, pharmaceutical companies that invest in start-ups may plan to purchase the business if it succeeds or at least have the ability to market any new drugs that are developed, which can create a long-term profit for the larger company. Clearly, an advantage of a strategic partner is that it knows the business and can make a quick decision with less development work. The costs associated with strategic partner investments are often quite a bit lower than other forms of equity investment.

Many strategic partners are companies with which the entrepreneur is already doing business, so initiating contact is rather simple. If the potential strategic partner is a new contact for the entrepreneur, it is relatively easy for both sides to learn more about the other through industry contacts. It is important for both sides to take the time to determine their level of comfort with the new possible relationship as business partners. The corporate cultures of the two businesses should be evaluated to determine if they might clash, creating difficulty in working together over the long term. Also, it is important to understand expectations on both sides for governance and control. Some strategic partners play a very hands-off, passive role in companies in which they invest, while others will expect a seat on the board of directors or other significant roles in decision making. The exit plan should be clearly discussed to prevent avoidable surprises in the future.

PRIVATE PLACEMENT

Individual or small groups of investment angels may not always be an option for an entrepreneurial venture. In such situations, it may be necessary to offer equity investments to a wider group of people who would consider making smaller individual investments in the firm. It is possible to raise equity capital through a process of offering unregistered securities to a certain type of investor. This form of equity financing is known as a *private placement* or a *private offering*. Any placement that goes beyond the regulatory and legal limits of a private offering must follow the full registration process for public offerings. The registration process is costly and leads to significant public reporting requirements for the company as long as it is considered a publicly held business.

The Security and Exchange Commission (SEC) has set specific limitations on private stock offerings. Private placements usually have lower expectations of return on investment than some other forms of equity financing, particularly venture capital, and therefore will result in less dilution of the entrepreneur's equity. In other words, as will be discussed in Chapter 14, venture capitalists often require high-equity stakes in a business in order to realize the high returns that they expect from their investments. Transaction costs in private placements tend to be among the highest of all forms of equity financing due to legal compliance requirements, and the relative time to raise funds can be quite lengthy.

A private offering can be made only to what is known as either a *qualified* or an *accredited* investor. Qualified investors must be able to demonstrate knowledge, financial strength, and investment experience that prove they can tolerate the risk of such an investment. For example, a health-care company was established in a southeastern state to build a contracting network for health-care providers wanting to contract with large insurance companies and self-insured employers. The company needed to raise about $800,000, which was to be used to pay for professional management and staff to build the network and to develop software systems. Potential investors for this venture included individual physicians and health-care companies, such as labs, clinics, and hospitals in the region. All the investors were wealthy, experienced, and had a good understanding of the industry.

An accredited investor must be one of the following:

1. Any national bank.
2. Any corporation or business trust with assets in excess of $5 million.
3. Any insider of the issuing company (officer, director, or owner).
4. Any individual with income over $200,000 or couple with income over $300,000 (must have two years of income at these levels and reasonable expectations for the continuation of this level of income).
5. Any individual with net worth in excess of $1 million.

The amount of capital that can be raised through a private placement varies based on the number and mix of investors. These restrictions are spelled out in what are known as safe-harbor exemptions. SEC Rule 504 applies to offerings up to $1 million. Under this rule, the restrictions of the private placement are the most flexible. Under Rule 505, private offerings can be up to $5 million, but they must meet more restrictive requirements to still be exempt from registration. Under Rule 506, it is possible to raise more than $5 million, but again the requirements are even more specific and restrictive. Under all these exemptions, no public advertising is allowed. Other exceptions to stock registration allow for offerings over the Internet and offerings to employees, all of which have very specific limitations and requirements. All exemptions have specific requirements for reporting to the SEC to ensure compliance with the various rules.

Because advertising and formal promotion of private offerings are prohibited, potential investors are generally found through personal networking, which can be a very time-consuming process of building referral upon referral. The entrepreneur initially supplies basic information on the business to determine the general comfort level and fit of each potential investor. If interest seems significant, additional information is supplied, which must comply with any formal requirements of a private placement. It should be made clear to the investors how they will be represented on the board of directors and what routine communication will be supplied to shareholders.

The primary disadvantage of this strategy is the complexity it can create for the entrepreneur. Even a fairly limited private offering can create a large number of shareholders to whom the entrepreneur is now accountable as fellow owners of the business. Because the transfer of stock is usually restricted, any shareholder problems will be long-term, for a disgruntled investor cannot simply dispose of the stock, as is the case in a publicly traded company. Management of the board of directors becomes a much more formal, complex, and even political process that can take up much of the entrepreneur's valuable time. The founder of the health-care company discussed above reported that he spent as much as one to two days a week just on shareholder and board-related issues during the first two years of operation.

CROWDFUNDING

Using the Internet and social media to rally a large number of people to offer financial support, usually in small increments, is known as *crowdfunding*. It has been used by musicians, artists, political candidates, and others to try and get financing for their project or cause. In return, those who contribute a donation or make a small loan are usually given something nominal in return. For example, musicians often offer a free download of a song to those who help give support through crowdfunding. Kickstarter.com is an example of a Web site that has helped to organize this type of crowdfunding around creative projects.

In 2012 new legislation was passed, called Jumpstart Our Business Startups (JOBS) Act, with the intent of expanding the use of Internet portals for crowdfunding to support small businesses. Before this legislation passed, crowdfunding for small businesses was possible, but just like crowdfunding for creative projects, it required giving something of value in return. For example, a restaurant start-up could offer coupons or discounted meals to people willing to "donate" or lend a small amount money to help support the start-up. The reason for this limitation on businesses using crowdfunding is the requirement of the Security and Exchange Commission (SEC) that investors in an entrepreneurial venture must be accredited investors, as discussed earlier in this chapter. The intent of the JOBS Act is to open up funding of start-ups to a much broader group of investors, particularly those who do not meet the criteria set up to be considered an accredited investor.

Businesses that are eligible for this type of crowdfunding, called an emerging growth company (EGC), must be below $1 billion in revenues. An EGC can raise up to $1 million from a crowdfunding offering each year. Investments must come from individuals who meet the following criteria (Winterfeldt and Kilgore, 2012):
- for those whose annual income or net worth is less than $100,000, the greater of $2,000 or 5 percent of the investor's annual income or net worth
- for those whose income is $100,000 or more, 10 percent of the investor's annual income or net worth up to a maximum of $100,000.

Although the JOBS Act exempts eligible businesses from certain provisions of Sarbanes-Oxley and other securities regulations, the SEC will provide regulatory oversight that dictates the process of pursuing crowdfunding under this law. For example, there are explicit graduated financial reporting requirements based on the amount of funding raised through crowdfunding. Entrepreneurs should not attempt to crowdfund completely on their own. They need to follow specific legal requirements and processes, and should be guided by an experienced attorney or other recognized expert.

SBIC

A small business investment company (SBIC) is a privately owned and managed investment company that is licensed by the SBA. There are over 300 licensed SBICs in operation. SBICs can provide a combination of equity investments and long-term loans to small businesses (see Box 12.2). Because the funding is, in part, backed by the federal government, the risk is much lower to the investors in the SBIC. Therefore, the rate of return expected by the SBIC is much lower than the rate for angel, private placements, or venture capital investment. This opens SBIC funding up to much smaller businesses with more limited growth potential. The SBA provides up to three times the capital invested in the SBIC through guaranteed notes to leverage the funding in order to help more small businesses. The limitations and restrictions on the small businesses supported through the SBIC are similar to those found in SBA loan programs (see Chapter 13).

THE DOWNSIDE OF EQUITY FINANCING

Equity financing can be an effective source of funding for entrepreneurial ventures. This is particularly true for businesses that cannot meet the funding requirements to use only debt financing or that need more capital than can realistically be raised through debt. However, entrepreneurs should understand some cautions about equity financing before deciding to raise money using this method of funding.

A common concern with equity financing is dilution, which was discussed previously in this chapter. Equity financing reduces the ownership percentage of the founding entrepreneurs, thus reducing their share of any profits and any wealth created through the venture. The business must get that much larger for them to reach the financial goals that they established for their business. However, they may need to create a much bigger pie to have any chance at all of reaching their personal goals. Therefore, dilution may be a necessary aspect of their business and financing models.

Some entrepreneurs who are desperate to raise money for their businesses end up taking equity funding from unscrupulous individuals, sometimes called *sharks*. Sensing the entrepreneur's vulnerability, these investors will demand much more of an ownership stake than the deal actually requires, based on their investment. For example, one entrepreneur had developed a process to turn corn waste products into fuel pellets. Eager to start the business, he rushed into a financing arrangement with a small group that demanded 90 percent ownership in the venture. However, if the typical rate of return for such an angel investor were applied, the entrepreneur should have given up no more than 30 percent or at the very most 40 percent ownership to these investors. Also, the investors had voting control of the company and within six months fired the entrepreneur from his own company. By the time he sought advice from his local Small Business Development Center, it was already too late for him to save his interest in the company. Unfortunately, analysis of the original deal showed that this could have been a fundable deal with more reasonable terms if only the entrepreneur had more fully understood financing and had been more patient to find the right investors.

When using equity funding strategies, the entrepreneur is adding on new partners or shareholders in the business. Even if the original ownership structure had more than one owner, adding on more can create interesting dynamics. Many entrepreneurs report that partnership relationships can be as complex as a marriage. The commitment is long-term and, in reality, indefinite. It also involves sharing something, the venture, which can elicit strong emotional reactions from the founding entrepreneurs. For example, a group of three entrepreneurs had been in business together for several years. Although their relationship had been at times quite volatile, they had matured into a strong working partnership. The opportunity for significant growth had led them to bring in an angel investor. "The balance that the three of us had developed in our working relationship was instantly torn apart," reported one of the entrepreneurs. "Although the investor was a great guy, it created a whole new set of relationships among the four of us to be worked out, even though he was not very active in day-to-day operations. It took us several more years to reestablish the trust and positive relationships that the three of us had developed before our new partner came in."

The Recession of 2008 changed the expectations of equity investors. Because their overall investment portfolios have declined, they have become much more cautious with their investments. This has resulted in generally more challenging relationships between entrepreneurs and investors. It has become harder to get initial seed money, and less likely that investors will be willing to provide follow-up investments even if they do make the initial investment. They have also been more closely monitoring the businesses they invest in and are much less patient with underperformance.

WORKING WITH OUTSIDE INVESTORS

Standard procedures are typically followed when working with debt financing. For example, although each bank may have different forms and procedures, most banks follow very similar processes when making loans. Equity financing, particularly through sources other than venture capitalists (Chapter 14), has no real standard procedures or processes. Each deal and each equity investor can vary significantly. However, there are some common elements to equity financing negotiations, particularly regarding the key documents that are used with most potential equity investors. The specific requirements may vary, but most investors will require the following items.

BUSINESS MODEL AND BUSINESS PLAN

The business model has become a more common step of the investment process with the wide adoption of business modeling tools (see Chapter 6). Many investors prefer to prescreen deals using tools such as the Business Model Canvas (Osterwalder and

Pigneur 2010). This is particularly true for deals that come out of incubator programs or are part of large-scale pitch events. For some investors business models that include robust financial forecasts, such as those that can be developed using the financial forecast template that goes along with this book, may replace the need for a more formal business plan presentation.

But for many investors, a formal business plan is still the primary tool they use to perform their initial assessment of a potential deal. The business plan can take many forms and use different formats depending on the audience and intended use of the document. Almost any business plan will include a discussion of the various component plans, including the marketing, financial, operating, and staffing plans. Equity investors expect four specific elements in addition to the traditional parts of the plan. First, the business plan should include a clear description of the company, including its history, developmental stage, and goals. The discussion should be an honest appraisal and not a sales pitch. For example, if there is only a limited probability that the goals will actually be met, that should be stated in this plan. Second, the product and market description should be factual and cautious. Overselling potential will only lead to problems with investors later. A thorough, factual description of competition also should be included. Third, there should be a realistic description of the management team, including any specific deals or commitments made to these individuals by the company, such as stock options or profit sharing. Finally, a clear, factual assessment of all risks should be fully disclosed. Experienced investors understand that any entrepreneurial venture has risk and uncertainty associated with it. The business plan should provide them with as full and complete a description of the potential downside of the venture as possible, allowing them to assign the true risk of the deal in negotiating an ownership stake in the company. Rather than scaring these investors away, such a description shows that the venture has been fully thought through. Although experienced investors realize that surprises will occur, they do not want any information withheld that is known by the current ownership, because once the investment is made, they are part of that very group.

CONFIDENTIALITY AGREEMENT

Before any detailed information is shared, a confidentiality agreement should be signed by the entrepreneur and the potential investor. Experienced investors often will have their own form of confidentiality agreement. Any confidentiality agreement should be reviewed or written by the entrepreneur's attorney. In fact, it is advisable that an attorney with expertise in mergers and acquisitions be used throughout negotiations for equity investments. Confidentiality agreements for equity investments typically bind both parties to limit the sharing and use of any information used in discussions and negotiations. The entrepreneur needs to protect proprietary competitive information and the investors will most often seek to keep their financial information secret. Most agreements will require that any written information that is shared be returned if the deal does not go through. Violation of the terms of a confidentiality agreement used in equity financing can have significant consequences. Therefore, agreements should be entered into carefully and with complete understanding of the terms.

LETTER OF INTENT

If the investor is interested in pursuing ownership in the venture and if the basic terms of the investment are agreed upon, a letter of intent is usually issued by the investor and signed by the entrepreneur. This letter commits both parties to take the necessary steps to complete the deal, including full disclosure of required information. However, such negotiations often fail, and the letter allows for both parties to withdraw under reasonable circumstances. Such a letter usually restricts the entrepreneur from negotiating with other potential investors while current negotiations are under way. Although a letter of intent is a commitment to negotiate a deal *in good faith*, the majority of deals will fail before they reach a final agreement.

MODIFICATIONS OF SHAREHOLDER AGREEMENTS

If an agreement for a private investor to invest in a venture is reached, modification of existing shareholder or partnership agreements is usually required. For example, the investor may require participation as a member of the board of directors, there may be limitations on distribution of earnings until certain milestones are reached, or there may be a change in the decision-making responsibility of the chief executive officer, allowing more authority to the board for strategic decisions and for commitment to purchase significant new assets such as a new factory building.

COMMUNICATION WITH SHAREHOLDERS

The level and means of communication with the new shareholders or partners should be agreed upon fully and clearly from the beginning. Investors have their own criteria to determine when they want to be notified outside of normal meetings and reports to shareholders. Some investors require regular updates and notification if any variations from the plan arise. Others want to be notified only if significant events occur, good or bad. The definition of *significant* should be clear to both parties. For example, one angel investor considered any event that could end up in the newspaper or in court as being significant. For anything else he would wait until the normal monthly reports were given at the meeting of the board of directors. The most important thing to remember is that the investor is now, in most cases, a full partner in the business and should be treated with the honesty and integrity that a partner deserves. The investment is based in large part on trust, and that trust should be respected and valued by the entrepreneur.

SUMMARY

The typical sources of external equity investing are strategic partners, angel investors, private placements, and SBICs. Equity financing, although an effective means of raising funds for many entrepreneurial ventures, brings with it some disadvantages such as dilution, shark investors, and additional business partners. The process of working with equity investors varies significantly, but most deals share basic documentation including a business model and the business plan, a confidentiality agreement, and a letter of intent.

DISCUSSION QUESTIONS

1. Discuss the various types of external equity financing. What are the best uses for each type? What should an entrepreneur do to establish each form of equity financing?
2. What is an angel investor? Summarize the types of deals in which they invest. Describe the process that leads to an equity investment by an angel investor.
3. How does a strategic partner become an equity investor in an entrepreneurial venture? What are the motivations and expectations of the strategic partner?
4. What are the key steps in the private placement process? Be sure to discuss any limitations or restrictions on this equity strategy.
5. What are the roles of the SBIC and the government in the SBIC program?
6. Discuss the advantages and disadvantages of equity financing for entrepreneurial ventures.

OPPORTUNITIES FOR APPLICATION

1. Choose one form of external equity financing. Conduct two interviews, the first with a person who is a source of such financing and the second with an entrepreneur who used such financing. Describe the form of equity financing from both the source's and the entrepreneur's point of view.
2. Write a plan to build relationships with the sources of equity financing for a new business venture you are developing.

REFERENCES

Bagley, C., and C. Dauchy. 1998. *The Entrepreneur's Guide to Business Law.* New York: West.

Blechman, B., and J. Levinson. 1991. *Guerrilla Financing.* Boston: Houghton Mifflin.

Clark, B. 2011. "7 Resources for Startup Investment Opportunities." http://mashable.com/2011/05/18/startup-investment-resources/ (accessed on December 29, 2011).

Freer, J., J. Sohl, and W. Wetzel. 1996. "Technology Due Diligence: What Angels Consider Important." In *Frontiers of Entrepreneurship Research*, ed. P.D. Reynolds et al., pp. 359–360. Babson Park, MA: Babson Center for Entrepreneurial Studies.

Kelly, P., and M. Hay. 1996. "Serial Investors: An Exploratory Study." In *Frontiers of Entrepreneurship Research,* ed. P.D. Reynolds et al., pp. 329–343. Babson Park, MA: Babson Center for Entrepreneurial Studies.

Osterwalder, A, and Y. Pigneur. 2010. *Business Model Generation.* Hoboken, New Jersey: Wiley.

Pepperdine University Graziadio School of Business and Management. 2011. "Pepperdine Private Capital Markets Project." Survey Report IV (Winter).

Small Business Administration. "Financial Assistance." http://www.sba.gov/services/financialassistance/index.html.

Sohl, J. 2008. "The Angel Investor Market in 2007: Mixed Signs of Growth." Center for Venture Research, University of New Hampshire. http://www.wsbe.unh.edu/files/2007%20Analysis%20Report_0.pdf.

Winterfeldt, D., and Kilgore, C. 2012. "United States: US Securities Law Update: Jumpstart Our Business Startups Act 2012." http://www.mondaq.com/unitedstates/article.asp?articleid=176256&login (accessed May 22, 2012).

13 External Sources of Funds: Debt

Almost every business uses some form of debt in a variety of ways and from a variety of sources. Businesses use debt to support day-to-day operations and also to purchase long-term assets such as land, buildings, and equipment. Debt can be created simply by buying raw materials from a supplier on credit. On the other hand, debt also can include extremely complex instruments that finance business expansion through acquisitions. It is important to create a plan for the use of debt in any business. Typically, this plan will involve the use of several different types of debt from several different sources.

Accountants recognize two basic categories of debt or liabilities: short-term and long-term. (The terms *debt* and *liabilities* are basically synonymous and will be used interchangeably throughout this chapter.) Many different types of liabilities fall into each of these categories. However, for the purposes of debt planning, these liabilities in these categories share a fundamental characteristic: timing of the repayment. This chapter provides an overview of the various types of debt, examining how each type of debt works and for what it is best used.

SHORT-TERM DEBT

Any liabilities that are expected to be paid within one year are considered short-term debt. Examples include outstanding invoices from a supplier, wages that are payable to employees for hours already worked between paydays, lines of credit from banks, and payroll taxes that are due within a few days after payroll is paid.

Typically, short-term liabilities are those that arise in the day-to-day operations of a business and that reflect the timing differences between business activities and cash flow. For example, an entrepreneur needing to purchase inventory for a retail store would contact the supplier and place an order. If the entrepreneur has established credit with the supplier, that supplier may be willing to ship the inventory with the understanding that the goods will be paid for within a short period of time, usually under thirty days. In another example, a computer consulting business has credit established with a bank. This credit may be used from time to time to cover payroll because it may take until the completion of a consulting job for the entrepreneur to get paid by the customer. The bank would therefore lend the money to cover payroll, expecting the entrepreneur to pay the borrowed money back after receiving payment for the consulting job. Again, this is a liability that will be paid back within a few days, weeks, or months.

TRADE CREDIT

The type of debt most commonly used by entrepreneurs is called *trade credit*, which is debt that arises from credit extended by suppliers and other vendors. For example, an entrepreneur first starting a business may determine that he needs business cards, so he places an order with a local printer. When picking up the order, he is surprised that the printing company wants immediate payment, since he had assumed that a bill would be sent and the cards could be paid for when he ran checks at the end of the week. The entrepreneur inquires why other business owners seem to be able to pick up their printing orders without immediate payment. But those other business owners have already established their creditworthiness. What the entrepreneur has not considered is that expecting the printer to send an invoice for the business cards is incurring debt. The entrepreneur must establish creditworthiness, since the printer is taking a risk by extending credit. The printer's demand for immediate payment is not a personal slight; it is just good business.

It is not unusual for entrepreneurs to have difficulty establishing trade credit with suppliers and vendors, particularly early in the life of a new business. Even service providers, such as accountants and lawyers, may require payment in advance. The entrepreneur must establish a trust that the business is sound and will be able to pay its bills. This may take time. The entrepreneur will need to build relationships with vendors before most will consider extending even very short-term credit for inventory, supplies, or services. It is important to address this difficulty in a business plan. Entrepreneurs often fail to understand that, for many new ventures, building relationships with suppliers and vendors can be just as important as building relationships with the customers (see Box 13.1). This process may require sharing information, such as a basic business plan, financial statements, credit references, letters of credit, and even personal financial information—a requirement that the entrepreneur may at first resist. Once credit is established, the vendors and suppliers will monitor payment history to determine if they are willing to continue extending credit to the entrepreneur.

Trade credit is normally extended for only a few days or at most a few weeks. Sometimes a business needs to finance operations over a longer period of time. Cash flow coming into businesses can often be anything but steady. Cash may come in only during certain times of the year or periodically throughout the year due to any number of factors. For example, many retail stores are highly seasonal businesses that sell eighty percent of their goods during the Christmas rush, which may last only six weeks. These retailers still need to build and maintain inventory and pay rent, employees, payroll taxes, and the light bill throughout the year. However suppliers, employees, landlords, and the Internal Revenue Service are not willing to wait for payment until the cash starts coming in during the Christmas buying rush. Therefore, these retailers need to use a different

---

Box 13.1
In Their Own Words . . . A Supplier

Establishing trade credit with suppliers is not an automatic a process, as is assumed by many new entrepreneurs. Here is a description of what a small manufacturer looks for when working with entrepreneurs in his own words:

"Establishing trade credit with a supplier can be a very long task, especially to new businesses. It can take anywhere from six months to four or five years. The main thing suppliers want to know before working with a small business is what the business's cash flow is so they know that it can afford to pay them for their supplies. In order to take in account if a smaller company can foot the bill, we look at all sorts of things, such as tax reports, statements of how long it has been in business, and number of employees in the company in relationship to the sales generated. We will also look at an entrepreneur's business plan to make sure that he isn't just flying by the seat of his pants. We find with many entrepreneurs that they don't have business plans. They have a great idea that has just kind of grown. This is great at the present time, but we want to know their plan for the future. We want to know how they are going to keep their sales up so they can afford to buy from us. Another point about establishing trade credit with a company that some entrepreneurs don't realize involves how many orders a year they place. If a small business only orders once a year, it will take that business several years to build up trade credit verses a company that orders twice a week.

"The best advice for a small business that is having problems obtaining credit from a company is to continue to buy from the company. The small business will have to do this on a cash-only basis. They will then start to build a history with the company, which should make it easier to gain credit with that supplier in the future.

"If a small business ever gets in trouble and can't pay their supplier, I suggest that they immediately sit down with not only their supplier but also with their banker. The small business should first sit down with their banker and figure out a plan. They should then sit down with their supplier and let them know the plan that was figured out at the bank and start to form their own plan with the supplier."

Interview with Robert Cornwall, former president, Rotocast Plastics Products Inc., Miami, FL

---

type of short-term liability to finance this part of their day-to-day operations—that is, to help cash coming in match the cash that must go out of the business. Typically, this cash will come from bankers and other institutional creditors.

INSTITUTIONAL CREDITORS

Institutional creditors, including banks, require a more formalized credit relationship than loans from family and friends. Sources of short-term debt to manage cash flow include banks, asset lenders, and factors. Each of these types of creditors will be willing to take differing levels of risk on the businesses they will fund. With more risk, the cost of financing can increase significantly. Therefore, it is important for the entrepreneur to use the lowest cost creditor possible given the risk that the business presents to the creditor.

To a creditor, *credit risk* is the assessment of the probability that a client will not repay borrowed money and interest owed on that money. Credit risk is assessed based on several objective and subjective criteria. Although these criteria may vary from creditor to creditor, there are basic factors that most creditors will assess.

The most basic objective criterion is the ability of the business to generate cash to repay the money borrowed. Creditors will determine the history of cash flow generated and used by the business as well as future cash flow that will be generated by current customers. Having long-term relationships with customers and having contracts in hand for future orders reduces credit risk. Objective criteria also include the amount of assets that can be quickly turned into cash, such as accounts receivable and finished inventory. Accounts receivable from large, creditworthy customers reduces credit risk. Creditors also will examine the personal assets of the entrepreneur. If the entrepreneur has personal wealth that could easily be turned into cash, such as publicly traded stocks, this also might reduce credit risk if the entrepreneur is willing to pledge those assets against business liabilities. Most banks require pledging personal assets, which will be discussed later in this chapter. Finally, the amount of debt already incurred is another key objective factor used to evaluate the overall credit risk of a business.

There also are more subjective criteria that creditors will assess to determine the degree of credit risk of a business. Most of these criteria are based on perceptions of the creditor rather than on hard financial data. The reputation and history of both the entrepreneur and the entrepreneur's business will be assessed. An entrepreneur who has started successful business ventures in the past will have less credit risk, as will a business with a profitable operating history. A sound business plan also can reduce the perception of credit risk. Doing business in a thriving industry is another positive factor considered by some creditors. On the other hand, a business in an industry that is experiencing general decline may actually increase the perception of credit risk even if other factors are all positive.

If a business is initially evaluated as a poor credit risk, the entrepreneur can take specific actions to alleviate the problem. For example, an entrepreneur may be able to obtain letters of commitment for future business from customers to reduce some of the perceived risk. Family members with sound financial records may guarantee debt if the entrepreneur and the business are unable to repay the loans. Establishing credibility with creditors may require several interactions that provide additional documentation and evidence to support the creditworthiness of the business. The most common types of institutional creditors and the role each can play in creating a financing plan for the entrepreneur are discussed next.

Banks

The institutional creditor that is generally least willing to take credit risk even on short-term lending is a bank. Banks face strict regulation and must meet demanding credit standards imposed by federal regulators. Over time, banks will take on slightly more or less credit risk based primarily on the overall strength of the economy. However, the range of risk-taking for all banks during any given economic climate is firmly rooted on the conservative side.

Some banks—generally referred to as *aggressive banks*—are more willing than others to work with entrepreneurs. These banks have a reputation for working effectively with entrepreneurs and may focus much of their marketing efforts toward attracting small and growing businesses. Often, small, locally owned, community banks are most interested in working with entrepreneurial ventures (Lange, Warhuus, and Levie 1998). Because these banks are rarely able to compete for larger corporate business, they try to match their own small business culture with small businesses in the community. These banks can generally handle the size of the relatively small loans needed by the entrepreneur. The majority of small business owners in one recent survey reported that they bank with a small bank (NFIB 2005a). The bad news is that since the financial crisis of 2008, the number of banks willing to take on such an aggressive role has been greatly diminished.

Banks are best suited for certain types of short-term credit. Lines of credit, for example, are one of the most common types of loans that banks can offer to entrepreneurs for the short-term cash flow needs of their businesses. A *line of credit* is a loan that can be used to smooth out cash flow. The money is loaned against accounts receivable that are expected to be collected in the near future; it may also be loaned against inventory that is likely to be sold in the near future. A line of credit is negotiated for a maximum amount, or credit limit, that can be borrowed by the entrepreneur as the need arises. Because the loan is already approved, it provides quick, easy access to cash for the entrepreneur. A phone call to the loan officer can provide funds from the line of credit, often on the same day that the request is made. As described previously in this chapter, the entrepreneur will have already incurred expenses associated with business activity (e.g., payroll, rent, raw materials), and the line of credit provides cash until the payment for goods and services is actually received from the customer.

The bank typically will charge interest on a line of credit that is based on its *prime rate*, which is the rate charged to its best corporate customers. The bank will set a rate that reflects the level of risk it perceives it is taking with the loan. A very low-risk line of credit to an entrepreneur may be priced only slightly above the bank's prime rate, possibly only a fraction of a percent higher. Higher credit risks, but ones that still fall within the bank's comfort level, may be charged several percentage points higher than the bank's prime rate. However, lines of credit have become less available since the financial crisis of 2008. Therefore, entrepreneurs must rely on personal financing (Chapter 10) and bootstrapping (Chapter 11) to offset the lack of available working capital through bank lines of credit. Also, the terms associated with lines of credit have become more stringent as a result of the banking crisis that began in 2008, according to a 2011 survey by the National Federation of Independent Business (NFIB).

A bank will require that certain conditions be met or maintained by the business as part of the loan agreement. The bank often will ask to receive monthly verification of accounts receivable and/or inventory balances to ensure that the assets that secure the loan are at an adequate level. Assume, for example, a bank has issued a line of credit to a business for up to $50,000. The loan agreement states that the bank is lending this amount against 70 percent of the accounts receivable that are under ninety days old. If the entrepreneur submits a report that indicates that 70 percent of the accounts receivable under ninety days old is actually only $42,000, the bank will not lend the full amount, but only up to $42,000. If the entrepreneur has already borrowed more than $42,000, the bank can, and probably will, require the entrepreneur to pay the principle balance down to $42,000.

Banks place such limits on lines of credit in order to manage their credit risk. Bankers have learned that not all accounts receivable will be collected, thus the 70 percent limit in this example. They also know that older accounts receivable are the most difficult to collect, thus the 90-day limit on receivables. In addition, banks will often require that the principle of a line of credit be paid in full at least once during the year and may require that the principle be zero for at least thirty consecutive days at least once a year. These demands assure the bank that the line of credit is really being used to fund temporary shortages in cash flow. The topic of how entrepreneurs effectively work with bankers will be discussed in more detail a little later in this chapter.

Asset-Based Lenders

Institutional creditors that can take a higher level of credit risk on short-term lending are commonly referred to as asset-based lenders. These lenders are not banks, although bank holding companies may own this type of entity. Asset-based lenders also lend money against accounts receivable and sometimes against inventory. Asset-based lenders do not face the same regulatory constraints as a bank. However, since they work with businesses that have a high risk of defaulting on the loan, they will often charge much higher interest rates than a bank—sometimes six to ten percentage points above the prime rate charged by a bank. Unlike banks, asset-based lenders do not examine as many other factors when lending money (see Box 13.2). They are primarily concerned with the value of the assets they are lending money against. Therefore, these lenders are more likely to quickly seize the assets they back if the loan becomes at all distressed (i.e., if the loan payments are late). Many asset-based lenders view their role as a temporary one, providing financing until a business is able to secure bank financing. They will work with start-ups more readily than most banks. They also will work with businesses that banks are no longer willing to serve due to poor financial performance.

Factors

A final source of short-term financing is not really a lender of funds at all. It is a form of "financing," called *factoring*, used by entrepreneurs who have an extremely high level of credit risk. A factor does not lend against assets, as does a bank or an asset-based lender, but actually purchases certain accounts receivable from the entrepreneur. Factors are used by businesses that are considered too much of a credit risk for either bankers or asset-based lenders.

Using a factor requires that both the entrepreneur and the entrepreneur's customers agree to the sale of these receivables. Such a sale can strain the relationship between

---

Box 13.2
In Their Own Words . . . An Asset Lender

Asset-based lenders offer an alternative for entrepreneurial ventures that may not be "bankable" under normal criteria for bank lending. Here is a description of what an asset-based lender looks for when working with entrepreneurs in his own words:

"The customer that we see typically is experiencing some sort of financial distress, but this is not always the case. As an example, often owners of privately held companies will take out substantial sums of money, leaving the company in a highly leveraged position. Highly leveraged companies are not a good fit for a traditional bank lending arrangement, but do present an opportunity for asset-based lenders. When a company transitions to an asset-based lender, there is significantly more structure to their transaction and it will generally cost them more. Our structure would include reporting as frequently as daily, quarterly collateral audits, and advance rates typically lower than what traditional banks would offer. Generally speaking, the closer we are to cash, the happier we are. Advance rates tend to decline as the time it takes to convert the asset to cash increases. Prior to issuing a proposal we will conduct an audit of the company's records and procedures. Advance rates for accounts receivable are set with consideration of the audit findings concerning billing practices, aging stratification, concentrations, dilution, contras, and other factors. Inventory advance rates are often set based on appraised forced liquidation value or in consideration of type and category, turns, price and test count results, and prior liquidation results. Advances against fixed assets are typically tied to some percentage of appraised value with much shorter loan amortizations than what would be available from a traditional bank lender. Depending on the size and complexity of a transaction, rates can vary from slightly below prime to 7 or 8 percent over prime."

Interview with Terry Jackson, vice president, Wells Fargo Business Credit, Minneapolis, MN

---

the entrepreneur and the customers by causing a perception, often correct, that the future of the entrepreneur's business is questionable. Some customers will cut back on or even stop doing business with a company that uses a factor to advance money. Therefore, it is important for an entrepreneur to communicate directly with customers about why the company is using a factor and what the long-term outlook for the business is actually expected to be.

Factors are a very costly source of funding. Depending on the risk they perceive in a business, they will charge from 4 to 7 percent of the accounts receivable they purchase. Since the Recession of 2008, most factors are trending toward the higher end of this range for their fees. So, for a $10,000 receivable from a customer, it will likely only result in an advance of only $9,300 to the entrepreneur from the factor. The highest-risk businesses may face even further limitations and charges from factors. Although the 4 to 7 percent fee may not seem to be that high, it is actually the equivalent of a bank charging an annual rate of 50 to 85 percent on a line of credit! Given the high cost and problems that can be created in customer relations, factors are

---

Box 13.3
In Their Own Words . . . A Factor

Although factors are sometimes thought of as a financial last resort for desperate businesses, factors view themselves as key lifelines for new or struggling businesses. Here is a description of how a factor views his role in his own words:

"Cash is key in a business. We, as factors, mainly work with businesses that are new, growing, or that have run into trouble by providing them with cash for their receivables. We can give them tomorrow's money today so they can concentrate on selling their product and turning their operating cycle more quickly to become profitable.

"Most businesses that choose to work with a factor work with us on a short-term basis. Most factors in the field generally require a minimum of six months to a year agreement and a $10,000 a month minimum of a company's receivables before we'll work with them. When it comes to an issue of who will qualify for financing, we can usually work with most businesses as long as they have bona fide commercial receivables that can be collected. Some exceptions to this rule, however, would be if the business doesn't have a creditworthy customer, if the business doesn't have enough receivables, or if the business only has one customer. These are all situations in which we might turn down working with a business.

"A lot of people have questions about what happens to a receivable that doesn't get paid. Factors will either buy receivables with recourse or without recourse. When a factor buys a receivable with recourse, that means if the receivable is not collected, it will be returned to the business. Buying without recourse means that if the receivable is not paid it is the factor's responsibility. Some factors are reluctant about buying without recourse because they want to be able to collect the receivable and will usually only do this for very creditworthy customers.

"The bottom line for deciding if factoring is an option for you is if you need immediate cash because you are a start-up business or you have gotten into a difficult situation or for some other reason you need cash fast; we can give you the money you need and get it to you immediately."

Interview with Rick Yunger, president, GreenBridge Finance, Minneapolis, MN

---

generally a funding source of last resort that should be used only for a short period of time and, in many cases, only as an emergency source of funding for a business that is not likely to survive without a quick infusion of cash (see Box 13.3). The entrepreneur should develop a plan to make a transition from the factor to an asset-based lender or even a bank.

LONG-TERM DEBT

Any liabilities that a business expects to pay off in a time frame beyond one year are considered long-term debts. Long-term debt is most often used to fund the purchase of assets that are to be kept and used over a long period of time rather than consumed in the course of day-to-day business. Unlike inventory or office supplies, these *fixed assets* will remain with the company for more than one year, often indefinitely. Examples of fixed assets are equipment, automobiles and other vehicles, land and buildings, and finishing work such as constructing new walls and other modifications to rented space with a multiyear lease. Credit risk is a critical issue with long-term debt just as it is with short-term debt. In fact, it can become an even greater issue because the money is being lent over a much longer period of time. Therefore, the lender may place much more severe restrictions and conditions on such loans. There are various types of long-term lenders. Like short-term lenders, long-term lenders vary by the types of lending they will engage in, ranging from a generalist such as a bank that will lend against a variety of assets to a specialist that may lend only against one type of asset, such as real estate.

BANKS

Banks face the same basic restrictions and limitations in long-term lending as they do in short-term lending. Because banks limit their credit risk, they offer the lowest costs for this type of lending. The type of loan that a bank uses to finance these types of assets is called a *term loan*. A term loan agreement is written so that it is paid back over a specified period of time, known as the term. Typically, the term is no longer than, and often less than, the expected useful life of the asset being financed. For example, the term for land and buildings loans may be as long as ten to thirty years, whereas loans to purchase computers are likely to have only a two- to three-year term based on the equipment's expected useful life. The specific assets being funded are used to secure the term loan. However, bank term loans are generally subject to additional conditions and restrictions that protect the bank, as will be discussed later in this chapter.

Some term loans will be structured with a *balloon payment*, which gives the bank the option of ending the term loan before the actual number of years used to structure the payments. For example, a bank may offer a term loan for a building that is amortized over a period of fifteen years. However, the actual term of the loan is only three years. At the end of the three years, the loan shows the entire remaining balance due in a balloon payment. If the company is doing well, the bank may consider renewing the loan for another period of time should the bank's capital adequately be sufficient at that point in time. However, if conditions for the business *or the bank* have changed and the credit risk is no longer acceptable to the bank, the balloon allows the bank to get out of the loan by not renewing it at that point. A business with a very low credit risk may be able to negotiate for no balloon payment, but such clauses are a common technique used by bankers to reduce their credit risk.

LEASING COMPANIES

Almost any asset can be leased, and leasing should be considered as just one more option for financing asset purchases. Leasing is often used for equipment purchases, especially for equipment that has a limited useful life, such as computers. Ownership of the asset is maintained by the company leasing it to the business. However, the obligation for the lease is with the entrepreneur for the life of the contracted period.

Real Estate Lenders

The purchase of land and buildings can be funded through real estate lenders. Real estate lenders can be stand-alone companies that specialize in this type of loan, or they can be the investment departments of insurance companies or pension funds. These lenders can be very competitive with banks if the credit risk is low, but they also are able to lend money to much higher-risk entrepreneurial ventures than can a bank. Therefore, the terms and conditions of loans from real estate lenders are as varied as the customers they serve. However, since the real estate mortgage bubble, their ranks have been substantially reduced. Most experts do not expect the national commercial real estate market to improve for many years to come. It should be noted that this varies significantly by geographic region.

Forms of Debt Overlooked by Entrepreneurs

Some liabilities that a business will incur may be overlooked by an entrepreneur and may not even show up as specific items on internal financial statements. Nevertheless, these are liabilities that the business owes and that will affect its overall credit risk. For example, property leases for office space, warehouses, or manufacturing space are liabilities for the business. Although notations may be made about such leases on an audited financial statement, these liabilities generally do not show up on a standard balance sheet. However, such leases are often entered into for several years and create large liabilities for the business over that period of time. For example, if a service business leases office space at a rate of $3,000 per month for a five-year lease, the business has effectively created a long-term liability of $36,000 per year for five years, or a total of $180,000. It is not uncommon for an entrepreneur to think of the lease as only a monthly obligation of $3,000. However, in thinking of it this way they are overlooking the real debt they have incurred by signing the lease. In this example the true debt incurred is $180,000, which is how banks and other lenders will view the financial impact of this lease.

Another business activity that can create a liability is an employee contract. For example, some employment contracts guarantee payment even if the employee is terminated, while others have guaranteed severance packages for termination. Such contracts create liabilities for the company that might not show up on standard financial statements.

Credit card debt is sometimes not carried "on the books" of an entrepreneurial start-up, but may obligate the entrepreneur to significant and often expensive debt.

Government Funding Through SBA

Many entrepreneurs are able to secure debt financing through loans guaranteed by the Small Business Administration (SBA), an agency of the federal government. The

Box 13.4
In Their Own Words . . . An SBA Lender

Loans using the Small Business Administration's programs are a common tool of emerging and growing entrepreneurial ventures. Here is a description of what an SBA lender looks for when working with entrepreneurs in her own words:

"SBA loans are for entrepreneurs who have financing needs that cannot be met by conventional bank financing. My advice to them is to go to their bank and request a small business loan. If the request is turned down, they should ask for an SBA loan.

"I can't stress enough that prior to applying for an SBA loan the entrepreneur should have a business plan that includes financial projections that they understand and can explain. I like to review all aspects of the plan and in particular the business's financial projections with them. Sometimes they will underestimate the costs of operating the business and overestimate revenue growth. They will also underestimate their cash flow needs. They don't take into account the relationship between expenses and income that typically results in a cash shortfall. This is particularly important for start-up businesses because in my experience entrepreneurs often fail to fully understand their financial needs. If they do have a need for more cash and they have an existing SBA loan, they can request that the bank increase their loan or they can consider applying for a new SBA loan.

"Although the business plan is important, the most critical factor affecting a loan approval is the entrepreneur's personal credit history. Personal credit must be clean for the bank and the SBA to approve a loan request.

"Prior to applying for an SBA loan some people think it is necessary to go to a loan packager, who would put the loan documents together. However, this is not a requirement of the bank. The fact is entrepreneurs simply need to make sure their loan application forms are accurately completed. If they do need assistance with the loan package or with developing a business plan, there are a number of organizations that can help: SCORE, Small Business Development Centers, etc.

"Entrepreneurs should realize one thing: the SBA and the bank want to help their businesses to succeed; they just have to take the right steps to get the loan."

Interview with Tammy Hambrook, assistant vice president, SBA portfolio banker, Wells Fargo Bank, Minneapolis, MN

SBA does not itself provide funding or grants to businesses. Rather, the entrepreneur works with a traditional lender, usually a local bank, to apply for an SBA guarantee of a loan issued by the bank. Many banks have loan officers or even lending departments that focus on SBA-guaranteed loans. These lenders work with entrepreneurs to complete all necessary forms.

The SBA has two basic types of loan programs. In addition, it also has equity programs, which were discussed in Chapter 12. The 7(a) Loan Guarantee Program is the most commonly used SBA program. Through 7(a) loans, the SBA will guarantee up to $1 million (the actual loan amount can be up to $2 million). SBA loans require that the entrepreneurs also make an equity contribution. For smaller loans, under $150,000, the SBA will guarantee 85 percent. For loans over that amount, the

SBA will guarantee 75 percent. The 7(a) loans must be used for business purposes, including land and buildings to house operations of a business, renovations of the business facilities, furnishings and fixtures, machinery and equipment, inventory, and working capital to support cash flow fluctuations.

A second loan program offered by the SBA is its Certified Development Company (504) program. A certified development company (CDC) is a nonprofit corporation set up to support economic development in a region. There are almost 300 CDCs nationwide (the SBA Web site, www.sba.gov/services/financialassistance/index.html, lists specific CDC locations). The 504 loans fund land and buildings for a small business venture with the specific purpose of creating or retaining jobs. In fact, the proposal must demonstrate that one job will be created or retained for every $35,000 guaranteed by the SBA. In a typical 504 arrangement, the bank will issue a loan that covers 50 percent of the project, the entrepreneur must contribute equity equal to 10 percent, and the CDC will lend 40 percent. The SBA guarantees only the CDC's portion of the project; it does not guarantee the bank's loan to the entrepreneur.

The SBA has established certain eligibility criteria for its loan programs. The business must operate for profit, do business in the United States, have reasonable equity invested by the owners of the business, and use other types of financing, including personal assets of the entrepreneurs (see Box 13.4). The SBA also has certain size requirements that companies must meet in order to qualify for its programs. The size of the business requirements include both an upper limit and a lower limit. For small businesses, the SBA has the MicroLoan Program, ranging from $100 to $25,000. The SBA makes funds available for microloans through nonprofit economic development agencies. Microloans generally require only that the assets funded be used as collateral and that the owners personally guarantee the loans. Some types of businesses are ineligible for SBA loans, including real estate investment companies, companies engaged in lending activities, companies in the gambling industry, pyramid sales companies, and businesses engaged in illegal activities. The SBA's Website provides complete information on all its programs and services (www.sba.gov).

WORKING WITH BANKERS

One of the most important relationships that an entrepreneur can have is the one with the banker. Bankers can be a source of critical financing at several key junctures in the growth of a business, providing several types of both short-term and long-term financing. Therefore, understanding how banks make business loans and how to establish and nurture a good relationship with the banker should be part of the entrepreneur's financing plans.

A myth held by many first-time entrepreneurs is that bankers lend based on collateral. That is, if the business has assets to pledge, the banker will lend money without any question. Nothing could be further from the truth, especially since several banks have recently been substantially hurt by loaning against assets that were at their peak of a bubble. The ability of the business to generate enough cash flow each month to easily make payments of interest and principal is the primary factor that a bank will use to determine if it is willing to make a business loan (Petty, Upton, and Griggs

Figure 13.1 **Debt Financing**

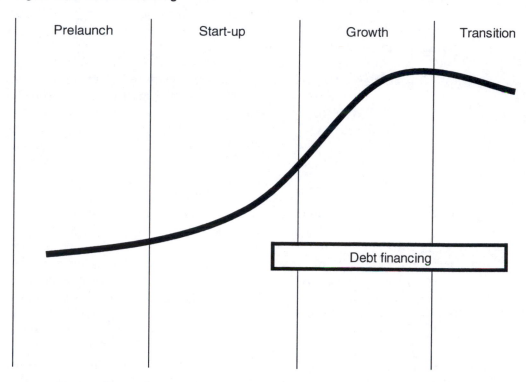

1997). That is why banks are generally unwilling to lend money to a true start-up venture. A history of positive cash flow is a fundamental condition for most bank loans. Such cash flow does not occur in most businesses until well after the initial start-up, which explains why bankers generally lend money only to businesses later in the life cycle, as seen in Figure 13.1.

Next, the banker evaluates the entrepreneur's ability to personally pay back the loan if the business fails. One study found that 96 percent of bankers consider personal guarantees of business loans a requirement of lending to entrepreneurs (Petty, Upton, and Griggs 1997). The bank may eventually lift this requirement, but only after the business reaches a point where the positive cash flow is so substantial that the business no longer carries significant credit risk. The banker will ask for personal financial statements from all shareholders in the business. These documents include a personal balance sheet, which shows personal assets and liabilities, and a personal income statement or tax return. The bank will focus primarily on what it considers liquid assets, such as cash and marketable securities, and free cash flow from each shareholder. The bank needs this information because it will almost always require that the entrepreneurs personally guarantee the business loans. That is, if the business fails, the bank wants a legal right to pursue full payment of the loan from the entrepreneurs. Even if the business enters bankruptcy and closes its doors, the banks want the ability to pursue repayment from the guarantors.

Box 13.5
In Their Own Words . . . A Banker

Although financial data are critically important to bankers, other factors and characteristics can become important. Here is a description of what two community bankers look for when working with entrepreneurs in their own words:

"A key aspect we look for is how long the entrepreneur has kept his key employees. If the employees working for the company have been working there for ten or fifteen years, the person must be a pretty good manager. This would lead us to be more willing to work with them. If the entrepreneur is willing to take more risk than the bank, such as in risking their house, this tells the bank how dedicated an entrepreneur is, therefore improving their chances of getting a loan. The interview with the banker is very important for an entrepreneur. I find that when people meet with a banker, they often tend to be a little defensive, not because they don't like the bank but because they are in an uncomfortable situation and that comes across. To alleviate this, don't come into an interview with a banker with any preconceived notions. Come into the meeting thinking of it as a financial partnership. This can get rid of some of the defensiveness. Also, in these interviews it is the little things that count. Be on time and be organized. Have all of the tax returns, financial statements, and your business plan ready. No one reason leads us to not work with entrepreneurs. If we don't work with one, it may be because the deal itself didn't make sense, lack of collateral, or the individual is not prepared. If an entrepreneur comes into a meeting with a banker and he isn't prepared, chances are his business is not prepared. We are not only getting the feel for you in this interview as a person but also we are getting a feel for how the business might operate. Usually the two are one and the same. Within meetings with a banker it is a lot of the small things that in the course of a half-hour interview stay with you other than the numbers."

Interview with Robert Vogel, president, and Daniel Ringstad, vice president, New Market Bank, Lakeville, MN

The final primary consideration is assets to serve as collateral to back the loan. Bankers have little interest in taking over distressed businesses and even less interest in selling assets they can seize to pay off defaulted loans. Even if a business has valuable assets—for example, a building and land that are owned without any encumbrance of debt—most banks will not lend money unless the business is profitable and generating strong cash flow. Most banks will pursue repayment from the shareholders rather than seize the assets of the business, if at all possible.

If the primary criteria are met, the bank also will evaluate secondary criteria before committing to a loan. Secondary factors that may be considered include the entrepreneur's character, management capability, and personal funds invested as equity in the business. Loans issued with SBA guarantees must meet these same primary and secondary criteria.

The relationship with a bank involves not just the activities related to securing the loan. Before a bank makes a loan, certain information will need to be shared. And after a bank makes a loan, the relationship with the banker must be maintained for the long term (see Box 13.5).

Initial Contact With Bankers

There are three phases of the relationship between an entrepreneur and a bank. First impressions *do* count when making contact with a banker. Even though financial analyses are the primary criteria used by bankers, their perception of the character and professionalism of the entrepreneur does come into account in their evaluation. The entrepreneur should be fully prepared to provide all the information needed to make a lending decision even at the initial meeting. The banker will be evaluating the entrepreneur's own understanding of the financial data and the assumptions used in generating projected financial statements. Bankers prefer relationships with an entrepreneur who has been referred by someone they know and trust, such as an accountant, attorney, or successful entrepreneur with whom they already work (Smeltzer, Van Hook, and Hutt 1991).

It is important for the entrepreneur to manage the relationship with the banker actively from the very beginning. Many entrepreneurs become frustrated by the banker's seemingly cold, analytical approach. One of the biggest frustrations is that the banker has not taken the time to get to know the entrepreneur's business (NFIB 2005b). One entrepreneur said, "I always take the time to tell my story before I give one piece of financial information to a prospective banker. If the banker is not interested in hearing my story first, I move on to the next banker because to me it is important for the banker to be excited about my business as a business. There's a bank on every corner."

Bankers will sometimes give preference to certain industries or types of businesses. This preference is guided by their experiences with these industries. If they have had favorable experience with other companies in an industry, their perception reduces the credit risk of the next company in that industry. Conversely, if bankers are relatively unfamiliar with an industry, their perception of credit risk is increased. Information and experience reduce uncertainty for bankers. Therefore, it is advisable for an entrepreneur to research which banks currently lend money to businesses in the same industry because the chances of a favorable response may be higher.

Preparation of Key Loan Documents

Loan Proposal

The first document generated by the bank is often a loan proposal, also referred to as a *commitment letter.* The loan proposal outlines the general terms and conditions of the loan, including loan amount and interest rate, purpose of the loan, payment schedule, fees, collateral, conditions to be met before loan closing, restrictions and reporting expectations, loan guarantees, and events that are considered a default on the loan. An officer of the bank, officer(s) of the company, and the guarantors of the loan are usually all asked to sign the loan proposal. Before signing, the entrepreneur may try to negotiate certain items in the proposal.

Loan Document

Once the loan proposal is agreed to by both parties and fully executed, the bank will create the actual loan document, which is the legal documentation of the loan. It will contain all the general terms, conditions, restrictions, and performance requirements agreed to in the loan proposal. The loan document may also contain additional terms and conditions that the entrepreneur should carefully evaluate. Although bankers hesitate to change the standard format of a loan document, there can be negotiation at this point as well, even on the standard contract language on the back of any standard form the bank uses. The entrepreneur should consider every aspect of the loan document very carefully, as it may have a significant impact on the operation of the business. For example, a loan agreement may include a standard clause that prohibits a company from buying any assets costing more than $50,000 without written permission of the bank. Given the cost of even some office equipment and vehicles, this restriction could become a significant constraint to doing everyday business.

Personal Guarantees

As discussed earlier, most loans made to entrepreneurial ventures will require that the shareholders or owners personally guarantee the loans. The document that creates this personal obligation is called the *personal guarantee.* In most cases, the guarantee will be what is called a *joint and several guarantee*, which means that all shareholders are responsible for their share of the loan (several liability) and that each shareholder can be held responsible for the entire loan (joint liability). In some cases, the bank may allow only several liability, in which case each shareholder is responsible for only his or her share of the liability based on percentage of ownership in the company. The personal guarantee may allow the bank to require the guarantors to pay off a loan without any notice if concerns arise about increasing credit risk, even if the loan payments are being made on a regular and timely basis. Also, all beneficiaries can be held to the guarantee if the entrepreneur should die before the loan is paid. All collection and attorney fees incurred in collecting money from guarantors can be added to the loan balance that is due. Fortunately, very few guarantors are called upon to pay off a loan.

ONGOING COMMUNICATION AFTER THE LOAN IS MADE

There is an old adage that says, "Bankers hate surprises." Loans are made to an entrepreneurial venture based on future performance, which is reflected in its projected financial statements. As was discussed in Chapters 4 and 5, projected financial statements are created in large part by generating any number of assumptions regarding both revenues and costs. It is the entrepreneur's responsibility to provide information to the banker on progress toward the projected financial performance. Banks will require certain financial statements at predetermined intervals (i.e., monthly, quarterly, annually). To assist the banker in understanding the actual financial statements, the entrepreneur also should provide updates on the key assumptions behind the projected financial statements so that any variances can be understood.

If assumptions prove to be significantly wrong or if certain factors require assumptions to be changed, the entrepreneur should inform the bank as soon as possible about the changing conditions, their impact on the business, and any steps the business is taking to adjust for them. For example, one group of entrepreneurs faced a market in which their three largest customers merged within a period of six months. The newly merged customer, now representing 80 percent of the entrepreneurs' revenues, was able to demand significant price concessions from the entrepreneurs. The entrepreneurs informed their banker about the change in projected revenues caused by this event, the short-term impact on profitability, and steps that were already under way to cut costs and return the business to its targeted profitability. All this information was provided before the bank received any periodic financial statements that reflected the actual impact of these events. Although the bankers paid closer attention to this business during the next few months, they considered this communication an indication of the strength of management, and the relationship between the bank and the company remained strong. Had the entrepreneurs not provided the information when they did, the bank would have received the financial statements showing much lower profits without understanding why this occurred and what was being done to alleviate the situation. In situations such as this, bankers also may be able to provide valuable assistance, such as help in finding new customers, management advice, or even contacts with other sources of capital if necessary. Regular communication with the banker may take both written and verbal forms. Such updates can provide the banker with a better understanding of the variations in performance that inevitably occur (Binks and Ennew 1997).

THE DOWNSIDE OF DEBT

Debt is certainly critical to almost any business venture. However, debt can create some risks and concerns that should always be taken into account. If a business has relied heavily on debt to finance the operation, it can become much more susceptible to downturns in the economy. If a downturn occurs and profits decline, large payments on loans can become difficult or impossible to meet. A similar business with less debt will have more excess cash flow, without the large debt payments, to cushion the blow of declining revenues and profits.

Lenders, particularly bankers, can impose many restrictions on a company as part of the terms of the loan. These restrictions may limit the entrepreneur's freedom to make decisions on major issues affecting the business, such as expansion, payment of dividends to shareholders, or compensation of management.

Additionally, since some forms of debt require personal guarantees by both the entrepreneur and his or her spouse, increasing use of debt can create tension or conflict in the entrepreneur's family. Guarantees of debt may not be a significant issue when a business is young and the entrepreneur has little real wealth, but as the business grows and succeeds, the entrepreneur can amass real wealth that is at risk if the business suddenly begins to falter.

Finally, when a business is sold, the buyer may not be willing to assume all, or even any, of the debts of the business. This refusal will require the entrepreneur to pay off all debts before any money can be distributed to the owners. Because taxes owed on the proceeds of a sale are typically calculated without consideration of any debt that must be paid off, entrepreneurs who have relied heavily on debt may have little or no money left after the sale of their businesses. The exit process will be discussed in more detail in Part IV of this book.

DEVELOPING A FINANCING PLAN

The vast majority of entrepreneurs use some combination of debt financing and the equity funding strategies discussed in Chapter 12. An effective financing plan is derived from realistic, complete forecasts. Knowledge of all fixed assets needed by the business and the cash flow projections showing operating cash flow shortfalls during start-up are critical for the development of financing plans. The tools and techniques discussed in Chapters 4 to 6 should give a reasonable view of the financing that is required. The assumptions used in financial forecasts can be more important than the actual statements produced in the forecasting process, so these assumptions should be clearly outlined and then measured to assess their accuracy.

Since entrepreneurs rarely raise all the funding they initially think they must have for their ventures, a clear understanding of priorities for funding should be developed. What expenditures are critical—that is, those without which the business will never get started? This category could include key equipment or money to pay the salary of key staff. As discussed in Chapter 11, overhead expenses can be the undoing of many start-ups. Initial funding should be targeted for the operation of the business, and any nonessential expenses should be delayed, which may require operating out of a basement, bedroom, or garage. Effective bootstrapping, which can drastically reduce the actual need for financing, should be part of the financial planning process.

While the entrepreneur may initially assume that a single source will provide funding, the reality is that most ventures are funded by an array of sources. In their book *Guerrilla Financing,* Blechman and Levinson (1991) recommend that an entrepreneur first create a list of all assets that can directly or indirectly be funded through debt. The entrepreneur should then match those assets with the most appropriate source of funding, which may include either debt or equity investment.

For example, Sally Warner, an entrepreneur, estimates that she will need $500,000 to start her business. She derives this estimate from talking to other entrepreneurs with similar businesses. In developing her financing plan, she determines what assets her business will have to fund her venture. Table 13.1 displays her list of assets and the loans that they may help to support. These loans may come from a variety of sources. For example, the entrepreneur may be able to get a bank to issue a line of credit based on accounts receivable and customer purchase orders, a real estate lender to finance land and buildings, and a leasing company to fund equipment purchases. In this example, the entrepreneur is able to fund, through various sources of debt, as much as $214,000 of the $335,000 in assets that the business owns or will own once operational.

Table 13.1

Example of Assets and Potential Funding Generated

Asset	Estimated value	Percent financed	Potential funding generated
Customer purchase orders	$50,000	70	$35,000
Accounts receivable (< 60 days)	$80,000	70	$56,000
Inventory	$20,000	30	$6,000
Leasehold improvements	$10,000	50	$5,000
Building	$120,000	70	$84,000
Undeveloped land	$40,000	40	$16,000
Equipment	$15,000	80	$12,000
Total of business funding sources	$335,000		$214,000

The forecasted financial statements developed for Sally Warner's business show cash flow projections that include both operating cash flow needs and assets that will need to be purchased. She has carefully evaluated these projections and determined there is some room for bootstrapping her venture during start-up. The total financing required is thus determined to be about $380,000, rather than the $500,000 initially estimated.

The entrepreneur's personal assets (such as bank accounts, retirement accounts, and publicly traded stocks) are worth another $150,000, and another $120,000 can be borrowed by pledging these assets. Therefore, between debt financing of $214,000 using the various business assets, and investing personal equity of $120,000 raised from her personal assets, she will have $334,000 of the $380,000 to fund the venture, which leaves $46,000 in equity that needs to be raised to fund the assets of the business. She is reasonably confident that she can go to friends and family for this amount of funding. This example demonstrates the variety of funding sources that can go into the financing plan of a single deal.

SUMMARY

This chapter has discussed external debt as a source of funding for entrepreneurial ventures. Sources of short-term debt include trade debt, bank debt, asset-based lenders, and factors. Sources of long-term debt include banks, real estate lenders, and leasing companies. The Small Business Administration can guarantee bank loans for some small business uses. Entrepreneurs must learn to develop a good working relationship with their bankers and create a strategy that can include an array of sources of debt funding. Finally, debt, although used by almost all businesses to some degree, requires prudent and careful planning. The next chapter will examine venture capital equity funding, which is available only for those few ventures that are considered high-growth, high-potential businesses.

DISCUSSION QUESTIONS

1. Discuss the various types of short-term credit. What are the best uses for each type? What should an entrepreneur do to establish each form of short-term credit?
2. How can entrepreneurs manage their own business' credit risk?
3. Discuss the various types of long-term credit. What are the best uses for each type? What should an entrepreneur do to establish each form of long-term credit?
4. What are the roles of bankers and the government in the SBA lending process?
5. Discuss the advantages and disadvantages of debt financing for entrepreneurial ventures.

OPPORTUNITIES FOR APPLICATION

1. Choose one form of debt financing and conduct two interviews: the first with a person who is a source of such financing; the second with an entrepreneur who used such financing. Describe the form of debt financing from both the source's and the entrepreneur's point of view.
2. Write a plan to build relationships with various sources of debt financing (bankers, suppliers, etc.) for a new business venture you are developing.
3. Write an overall financing plan (including all sources of debt and equity financing) for a new business venture you are developing.

REFERENCES

Binks, M., and C.T. Ennew. 1997. "The Relationship Between U.K. Banks and Their Small Business Customers." *Small Business Economics* 9: 167–178.

Blechman, B., and J. Levinson. 1991. *Guerrilla Financing*. Boston: Houghton Mifflin.

Dennis, Jr., W.J. 2011. "Financing Small Businesses: Small Business and Credit Access." National Federation of Independent Business Research Foundation report, January.

Lange, J., J. Warhuus, and J. Levie. 1998. "Entrepreneur/Banker Interaction in Young Growing Firms: A Large-Scale International Study." In *Frontiers of Entrepreneurship Research*. Babson Park, MA: Babson College Press.

National Federation of Independent Business (NFIB). 2005a. "Bank Competition." *Small Business Poll* 5 (8). http://www.411sbfacts.com/sbpoll.php?POLLID=0043.

———. 2005b. "Evaluating Banks." *Small Business Poll* 5 (7). http://www.411sbfacts.com/sbpoll.php?POLLID=0049.

Petty, J., N. Upton, and J. Griggs. 1997. "The Entrepreneur and the Banker: A Comparative Study of Factors Affecting the Relationship." In *Frontiers of Entrepreneurship Research*. Babson Park, MA: Babson College Press.

Small Business Administration. "Financial Assistance." http://www.sba.gov/services/financialassistance/index.html.

Smeltzer, L., Van Hook, B., Hutt, R. 1991. "Analysis of the Use of Advisors as Information Sources in Venture Startups." *Journal of Small Business Management* 29: 10–20.

14 Financing the High-Growth Business

Entrepreneurs with ventures that have the potential for high growth can face major challenges in financing the operating and capital needs that these businesses face throughout their development. Although high-growth ventures are relatively rare, their impact can be significant. Companies such as Dell, Intel, Microsoft, and Gateway have not only created wealth for their founders and investors, but also created thousands of jobs that have transformed their home communities. Some high-growth ventures have even created entirely new industries. High-growth ventures most often require financing on the scale of millions of dollars, which normally is the domain of equity investors such as private equity funds and venture capitalists (see Box 14.1). They both operate under the same overall principle of managing a fund of investments. The fund pools investments from a variety of large investors, such as pension funds, life insurance companies, and even some very wealthy individuals. The purpose of the fund is to invest in high-growth and high-potential companies. Because these investments carry significant risks, the investors' expectations of returns may exceed 70 percent capital appreciation annually.

Since the Recession of 2008 there has been a dramatic change in the venture capital Industry. According to the National Association of Venture Capital, the ability of venture capital firms to raise money dropped by about 50 percent between 2007 and 2011. This inability of fundraising has decreased deal flow from venture capitalists to entrepreneurial firms by about a third over this same time period. And venture capitalists remain skeptical about the future as the economy continues to suffer from the effects of the recession that began in 2008. However, although they are less active than they have been in recent years, venture capitalists play an important role in funding businesses with the potential for high growth.

Venture capitalists have to provide value to companies or else they would not exist. What they provide could be called the four Cs: capital, contacts, counsel, and credibility. *Capital* is obviously the first thing that comes to mind as it helps firms expand to the next level and achieve their goals. *Contacts* are the financial and general business relationships that can assist the firm in marketing its products and services, perhaps outsourcing expensive, non-core functions, and finding optimal personnel. *Counsel*

Box 14.1
In Their Own Words . . . A Venture Capitalist

Venture capitalists are often closely linked to high-growth entrepreneurial ventures. Here is a description of what a venture capitalist looks for when working with entrepreneurs in his own words:

"Venture capitalists look to invest in companies that are trying to make a major advance in their market by developing a product or service that is fundamentally better, faster, or cheaper than the alternatives. We typically invest in a company when they are still in the development stage and have yet to make a sale or validate their product. In exchange for taking the risk associated with investing at this early stage, investors in venture capital funds expect to generate compound annual returns well above what is offered in the broader public markets—typically targeting 20 percent or more across the portfolio of companies.

"To find these returns, venture capitalists screen for several key attributes. First, we like to see a large and growing market opportunity, typically in excess of a billion dollars at maturity. Large markets are more likely to support new company formation and generate large returns. The rate of growth is also an important measure of the value creation potential that exists in the market—when a small company catches or creates a rapidly growing wave, great things can happen.

"The second area of focus for venture capitalists is on the management team. We are looking for an entrepreneurial team with the skills, experience, passion, and chemistry necessary to build a great business. There is much more art than science involved in management assessment, but most venture capitalists would agree that the quality of the team is a critical factor in shaping their interest in an opportunity.

"Finally, we are looking for companies that possess some form of enduring competitive advantage. In order to achieve market leadership, an emerging company must have something special that will allow them to prevail in the market. Their advantage could come in the form of differentiated technology, a unique team, or other relationships that contribute to a compelling offering. We spend a great deal of time during due diligence in testing and validating the degree to which this advantage exists."

Interview with Michael Gorman, St. Paul Venture Capital, St. Paul, MN

---

provides the CEO and board with legal advice to which a start-up firm would typically not have access. Finally, *credibility* refers to validating the company's potential valuation so that wealth can eventually be realized by the investors and founders. Without this validation, markets would tend to price firms at a discount from their true value.

INTEGRATING PROFITABILITY INTO THE BUSINESS PLAN

Raising money for a high-growth venture is one of the most difficult activities that an entrepreneur can undertake (Figure 14.1). When making a request, the entrepreneur should be aware that the potential investor's time is just as valuable as the money. Because venture capital and private firms have such high expectations of returns on

Figure 14.1   **Financing a High-Growth Venture: Venture Capital**

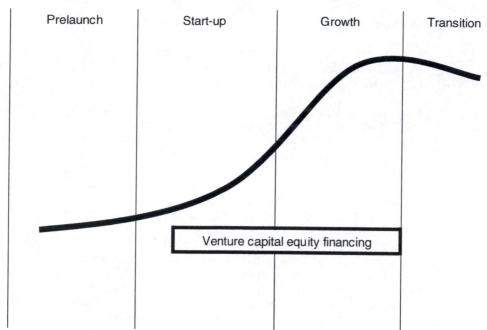

their investments in growing companies, it is critical to integrate these expectations into the financial forecasts in the business plan. Therefore, before approaching a venture capitalist or any other financing source, the entrepreneur should revisit the business plan applying a technique called the *reverse income statement*, which is based on the discovery-driven planning model first discussed in Chapter 1.

The concept of the reverse income statement is to start with the required level of profit and work backward. The required level of profit is the minimum profit necessary to pay an adequate return to the investors.

Minimum rate of return × amount invested = required level of profit

Once this required level of profit is approximated, the forecasting template that is included with this book can be used to determine the assumptions that will be necessary for the enterprise to generate that level of profit. These assumptions can be identified by first inserting into the template the assumptions that the user believes are supportable and seeing if the spreadsheet model generates an income greater than the required level. If it does, this part of the exercise is finished. If not, then the entrepreneur must experiment by changing assumptions until the spreadsheet eventually records a projected profit that is greater or equal to the required level. All the assumptions that have been made in order to achieve this calculated level of profit should be recorded and compared to experience or double-checked with other sources to see if they are reasonable. If they are not, the endeavor should not be pursued because the firm will not be able to earn an adequate return for the investors. If a reasonable and supportable set of assumptions generates the required level of profit, then the entrepreneur can undertake the pursuit of funds. It cannot be overemphasized, however, that this is not a process of "making the numbers work." It is a process of discovering the necessary conditions for success. If the conditions do not exist, then the entrepreneur knows to back up and not pursue this particular financing source.

Venture capitalists operate in an environment where investment proposals are based more on assumptions than historical facts because the high-growth firms are not traditional, mature enterprises. Therefore, the potential investors will be especially interested in the underlying assumptions of the proposal. If unreasonable assumptions have to be created to make a proposal profitable, the venture capitalists will probably not be willing to take the risk. The economic uncertainty that began in 2008 has only increased the perceived risk that venture capital firms see in most deals, which has contributed to the decrease in deal flow in recent years.

STAGES OF THE FIRM

Entrepreneurs, especially inexperienced ones, face some very serious risks when it comes to raising money. Without a track record of success in creating other companies, the job of convincing potential investors that this particular opportunity is an excellent use of funds becomes more difficult. Raising funds is a lot like being a salesperson. The entrepreneur should expect to be told "no" a number of times before getting a "yes." Even if an entrepreneur does have a track record of success, the task still is not easy:

1. The economic window of opportunity may pass before the funds can be raised.
2. Key employees may not be willing to start work until funding is secured.
3. Sharing information with a potential investor may expose a company's trade secrets.

This last issue, protecting intellectual property associated with a new business venture, can be one of the most contentious. An entrepreneur is probably not going to have a successful high-growth venture if the plan is to start a firm in a preexisting industry and do what everyone else does. Typically, an opportunity exists because entrepreneurs believe that they have discovered a new market that few people know about or a new way to do business in an established market. In other words, a successful business must have some sort of competitive advantage. This advantage could be technological, strategic, or geographic, and it must be of a nature that is unique to this company. However, if that advantage is fully exposed, then the door is open for others to do the same thing, thus eliminating the advantage. In a perfect world, an entrepreneur would have to share the secret with only one investor and raise a sufficient amount of money at that time. However, it is more likely that several sales pitches will have to be made before fund-raising is successful, and, with each sales pitch, the circle of people who now know of the firm's competitive advantage gets wider.

Typically, funds are raised in stages and not in one lump sum at the front end. Staging of financing allows investors to deal with the uncertainty of the validity of the idea and the untested nature of the management in the enterprise. Stages of funding are typically tied to stages of business development, which generally progress as follows:

1. *Pre–start-up.* In the pre–start-up stage, the focus is on product research and development. The firm is not ready to invest in infrastructure or employees to actually produce or distribute the product. The firm generates no revenues and has a negative net income and cash flow. Cash flow will continue to be negative as the firm invests in development equipment and pays development-type employees, such as engineers and designers.

2. *Start-up.* The start-up phase occurs when the company purchases equipment and hires the employees who will actually produce and distribute the product. Net income and cash flow are still negative as investments in manufacturing equipment and working capital are made. Working capital consists of the increases in inventory and other current assets. This expense is in addition to the salaries, space rent, and utilities that must be paid during this phase.

3. *Early growth.* During the early growth stage, cash flow and net income are still negative. Revenue is now being generated, and potentially the rate of revenue growth could be quite high in percentage terms. However, the actual dollar amount of revenue is low relative to the expenses and investments in working capital, such as accounts receivable, and inventory.

4. *Rapid growth.* This stage is similar to early growth in the sense that cash flow is still negative. However, the negative cash flows will be much higher. A high sales growth rate in percentage terms calculated on a much larger starting base of sales in dollar terms would require very large financing amounts immediately, thanks to the immediate expenses and working capital that are required now to satisfy the larger volume of sales that are anticipated to occur in each succeeding sales period.

5. *Mature growth.* The mature growth phase is a point where the market has become saturated with the product so that the rate of growth, while still positive, is much lower. In this situation, the net income and operating cash flow are ideally positive. The revenues generated in a particular month should be sufficient to cover the investment in working capital necessary to get the firm through the next month and so forth. Some entrepreneurs choose not to operate their firms in this phase. They may hire professional managers to take over at this point, or instead they may choose to jump to the next phase.

6. *Exit or harvesting.* The exit or harvesting phase is a time when the purpose of the firm is to generate cash flows and returns for the investors. There are two ways to get cash flow to the investors. One method is to sell all or part of the firm to other investors or to another company. Another strategy to generate cash flow for the investors is to operate the firm in such a way as to maximize available cash and allow the investors to take this cash out of the firm through dividends. With this kind of strategy, only the minimal necessary expenditures for working capital and investments in replacement equipment are made. Ironically, a firm can generate its

maximum amount of cash during a period of declining sales. Generating cash flow by killing the firm with a slow death is unlikely to be popular with firms that used a number of outside stockholders in the earlier stages. This is because entrepreneurs cannot attract outside investors without a concrete or at least reasonably thought-out exit strategy spelled out for the investors at the time the pitch for funding is made.

STAGES OF BUSINESS FUNDING

Funding for high-growth ventures typically parallels the development of new ventures as they emerge and grow. There are four generally recognized stages of funding for such ventures:

1. *Initial-stage financing.* The first stage of the firm may have to be initially financed by the founder. Sometimes this stage is financed simply with sweat equity and a lot of creative bootstrapping. Angel investors often will play an important role in this stage of a high-potential business. In this seed round, the firm is still a very early start-up. Initial funding is generally tied to the first one or two stages of business development. Beyond this very initial stage, a high-growth venture may require a much more formal request for funding from a venture capital fund.

2. *First-round financing.* For the first round, the company should have refined its business plan, established some of its management team in place, and started development of products and sales. The first round of financing could be large enough to cover the first two stages of business development: the pre–start-up and early start-up.

3. *Second-round financing.* For this round of financing, the company should have made acceptable progress toward achieving the goals and benchmarks described in its business plan. For instance, at this point the company's sales should have started to increase and the business should be expanding. This round of financing should involve an amount that is consistent with the early and rapid growth phases of the business.

4. *Late-round financing.* At this point, the company should have been successful in selling to the market and its product should be refined. The goal of this round of financing is to prepare the firm for an eventual exit through an initial public offering or some other major development.

As was stated earlier, in raising funds for a new venture, an entrepreneur does not have the same access to the liquidity and past history that a publicly traded firm would. Therefore, benchmarks/milestones have to be used in place of statistically based risk and return measures to assess performance. If a firm can achieve the milestones that it set for itself in the previous stage of financing, then it will have increased its odds of successfully convincing investors to supply funds for the next round of financing. These benchmarks can be quantitative goals, such as the volume of sales to be achieved by a particular date, or specific accomplishments.

The types of goals that are appropriate in a funding request depend upon the stage of development and the corresponding financing round. Here are some possible milestones:

1. Initial-stage funding
   - File for incorporation
   - Write business plan
   - Find office and development space
   - Complete initial design
   - Hire key development personnel
   - Complete prototype unit
   - Complete prototype testing
2. First-round financing
   - Secure key vendors
   - Hire key service or manufacturing personnel
   - Rent or build manufacturing facility
   - Purchase manufacturing equipment
   - Do market testing
   - Obtain first sales contract
   - Produce first manufactured unit
   - Produce first 100, 1,000, 10,000 units, etc.
3. Second-round financing
   - Achieve breakeven level of sales
   - Develop next generation of product
4. Late-round financing
   - Stage initial public offering or sale of business

THE DARK SIDE OF VENTURE CAPITAL FINANCING

Venture capitalists are only really interested in projects that have an extremely large potential payoff. This is because venture capitalists may take on several proposals, of which only a minority will succeed. Therefore, the returns of the one that does succeed must cover the costs of the ones that do not. The pressure to realize the returns expected by the fund investors can create significant conflict between the entrepreneur and the venture capitalist, influencing decisions about staffing, product design, marketing strategy, quality, and rate of growth.

To achieve the desired returns, venture capitalists may insist upon a very large percentage of ownership of the company, leaving the founders with only a minority stake. Venture capitalists want a large percentage of ownership for two reasons: (1) if the company succeeds, the venture capitalist will get a large proportion of the return, and (2) a venture capitalist who loses confidence in the management team will be able to take control to protect the investment. And this is the rub. The entrepreneurs who founded the venture may soon find themselves on the outside of their own venture if the venture capitalists are not satisfied with their management of the business. It is not unusual for founders to find themselves out of a job if later-stage financing results in ownership that is not pleased with their management of the company and its lack of financial performance compared with expectations.

However, there are also examples of businesses that fail because they are *not* willing to take the risk of working with venture capitalists. One of the authors of this book once tried to help some research chemists who claimed to have developed an extremely cheap and extremely fast test for the existence of gram-negative bacteria such as E. coli, Salmonella, and antibiotic-resistant superbugs. The standard test requires an incubator, a laboratory, and twenty-four hours. The chemists' new test supposedly required a solution that could be squirted on a sample of food or water and a paper test strip that would change color if the bacteria were present. This test could be done in less than ten minutes at a cost of pennies per trial. The failure to arrange financing that was acceptable to the researchers arose from their unwillingness to accept less than 50 percent ownership under any situation. The funding sources rightly saw that neither the chemists nor their board of directors had a history in entrepreneurship. They also had no established system of distribution. In addition, the chemists refused to disclose the formula for their solution or release a sufficient quantity of the solution for outsiders to test because they feared reverse engineering by competitors. Hence, the unwillingness of both sides to give up control prevented this business from moving beyond the most preliminary stages.

INITIAL CONTACT WITH A VENTURE CAPITALIST

Venture capitalists are bombarded with as many proposals from hopeful entrepreneurs as a Hollywood agent is bombarded with scripts from would-be screenwriters. Therefore, to avoid wasting their time, an entrepreneur should do some homework to see which type of venture capitalist is right for a particular proposal. For instance, venture capitalists tend to specialize in particular industries. If the entrepreneur intends to start a manufacturing company, it would do no good to approach a venture capitalist who concentrates exclusively on computer software. Likewise, if a firm is needs late-stage financing, there is little value in approaching a venture capitalist who specializes in seed-round financing.

Once appropriate potential venture capital firms are identified, the following checklist of information should be created in anticipation of the venture capitalists' requests:

1. *Funding amount.* Be specific about the net amount of the loan or equity. Stipulate the actual net amount needed in your hands at drawdown. Be prepared to demonstrate milestones for when additional funds are to be injected.
2. *Duration.* Although venture capital is an equity investment, the fund managers will want to understand the time frame of their commitment to the deal. A clear exit plan is essential. This will generally be tied to either an initial public offering or some type of sale. No venture capital firm is looking for long-term investments. Three to seven years is the expected duration for most deals.
3. *Summary of the project.* Give a brief but factual, detailed summary of the project or transaction. This is most often the executive summary of a fully developed business plan.

4. *Use of the funding.* Write a clear summary of how the funds will be used and over what period of time. Show milestones when funds are to be injected.

5. *Confirm a plan on how the transaction will be harvested/exited.* One of the foremost thoughts in an investor's mind is, "How am I going to get my money back?" Be able to show the investor that this has been worked out. The investor might be more inclined to invest if there was not only an exit strategy but also back-up strategies. To put the investor's mind at rest that this investment will likely reach the harvest/exit stage, it might be helpful to include the following details for the first five years:
   a. Projected revenue stream
   b. Projected cost of goods sold
   c. Projected gross profit
   d. Projected overheads and expenses
   e. Projected net profit
   f. Net present value of future expected cash flows
   g. Sinking fund or reserve that will be available out of retained profits to repay principle, interest, and so on
   h. Exit strategies for equity investors (initial public offering, buy-back, merger, etc.)

6. *Investment in the project.* State how much money has already been invested in the project to date and how the funding was used.

7. *Bankers, lawyers, accountants, and consultants.* Provide the names, addresses, telephone and fax numbers, and e-mail addresses of other people involved in the transaction.

8. *Unusual or sensitive information.* Be aware that it will be necessary to provide any additional information in support of the application that may be relevant or unique. Disclose negative factors that could affect the project. If requests for funds have been made to other sources and were rejected, be prepared to answer why. Due diligence will probably reveal problems anyway.

Standard due diligence as performed by venture capitalists often includes a market review of the product, a background check on the principal agents of the company, a look at competing companies, interviews with potential customers, financial projections, and an analysis of the firm's management. In addition to standard due diligence, a formal legal due diligence will take place as well. A prospective entrepreneur should develop good filing and document-management skills so that when prospective funding sources request documents, the entrepreneur can have them ready. Among the documents to keep handy are the company's business plan, sales contracts, lease contracts, employment agreements, confidentiality agreements, the corporate charter and bylaws, and any intellectual property documents such as patents and copyrights. In addition, the minutes and the resolutions of the board of directors should also be available.

Once a venture capitalist is satisfied with the information that the entrepreneur has provided, a term sheet may be issued. A term sheet is a list of proposed terms and provisions for investing. It is not a legally binding contract, but it does show a rather serious level of interest on the part of the venture capitalist. The term sheet could include the following terms or conditions:

1. The amount of money that the venture capitalist wishes to invest.
2. The percentage of ownership, or at least the number of shares out of the total, that would belong to the venture capitalist.
3. The nature of the investment, such as a loan, stock, or warrants (i.e., long-term stock options).
4. The rights of the venture capitalist vis-à-vis the board of directors.
5. The right of the venture capitalist to eventually register shares for a public offering.
6. Any remaining conditions that have to be met by the entrepreneur, such as periodic reports and financial statements.
7. An estimate of valuation of the company.
8. Any specific requirements about what the money is to be used for or specific assets that must be purchased with the funds.

After both parties agree to the terms of the sheet, the next step is the preparation of the stock purchase agreement. The venture capitalist's attorney typically prepares this document. The stock purchase agreement will be more detailed, outlining who is required to pay or be reimbursed for various legal fees and costs. Unlike the term sheet, the stock purchase agreement is official and legally binding.

INITIAL PUBLIC OFFERING

Engaging in an initial public offering (IPO) means that some of the company's stock will now be sold to outside investors through the public stock markets. An IPO is a frequent goal of an entrepreneur, but it is not an absolute requirement. The decision whether to do an IPO depends on weighing the various pros and cons.

ADVANTAGES OF AN IPO

1. *Diversification and liquidity*. These are the main reasons that most entrepreneurs would like to bring their firms to an IPO. Typically, the original founders of a company find almost all their wealth tied up in one enterprise. An IPO allows the original founders to diversify a portfolio and thus reduce investment risk by selling some stock to others and then reinvesting that cash into other investment vehicles. Selling stock directly to another investor is not as easy as selling stock directly into an actively traded market where the value of the company is determined by the market rather than individually negotiated.

2. *Ability to raise new cash for the company*. If new opportunities present themselves to a company that is still closely held, the ability to raise money can be constrained by the inability of the original owners to supply more of their own cash, the regulatory restrictions placed on insiders to transact with others to raise cash, and the general level of outsider skepticism about investing in a closely held company. If the firm

transacts an IPO, then the increase in liquidity and reporting requirements of a public market can reassure investors and provide more opportunities in the future for cash to be raised.

3. *Valuation.* Having an established market determine a valuation for a company can be useful for raising funds in the future, assessing the performance of the company, determining tax issues, and providing incentives to key employees through stock options.

4. *Future business deals.* Being publicly traded can assist in finding potential business partners through stock swaps or even mergers that can be paid for with stock.

5. *Publicity.* A publicly traded company gains visibility that not only can help its stock to be sold, but can also transfer into a larger awareness of the firm's product.

DISADVANTAGES OF AN IPO

1. *Reporting costs.* This is the major downside of "going public," especially since the adoption of the Sarbanes-Oxley Act of 2002 (sometimes referred to as "Sox"). It has been estimated that the provisions of this Act have approximately doubled the average cost of going public to $2.5 million annually. Even to be listed with the smallest stock markets can be extremely expensive in direct accounting and legal costs compared with staying privately held. If a firm is listed on a major exchange like the New York Stock Exchange (NYSE), with the reporting and regulatory requirements can theoretically add an additional $10 million or more in annual costs compared with a privately held firm.

2. *Disclosure of information.* Closely held companies have a flexibility of operation that is sometimes not appreciated by entrepreneurs until after they have gone public. First, the formal disclosure of information to the stock market also means that the information is available to competitors as well. Second, internal transactions, say between founding family members, that are possible in a private company to minimize tax liability may no longer be an option. Third, since the theoretical purpose of the rules of disclosure is to release information to all potential investors as simultaneously as possible, the company's employees may have to undergo an extreme behavioral adjustment—such as forgoing the practice of talking shop with others—because it could result in an unintentional but illegal release of information. Fourth, the need to maintain investor relations may require further changes in behavior. Top managers in the company frequently find their job descriptions changing dramatically. In addition to performing their regular duties, top executives will now have to budget substantial amounts of time to deal with major stockholders and influential stock analysts.

3. *Maintenance of control.* Just like the previous stages of financing, an IPO results in a further reduction in the voting rights of the original founders and therefore in their ability to unilaterally run the company. Indeed, the process of going public, especially under the Sarbanes-Oxley Act requirements, now affects almost every aspect of managing a company. As discussed previously, the company now has to submit to regulations on how to disclose information. Sarbanes-Oxley also places more legal liability on the CEO and CFO, dictates the makeup of the audit committee (all members must be independent and at least one must be a financial expert),

limits company loans to officers and directors, and severely restricts stock trading by insiders and increases the requirements of reporting such trading. The legislation also places substantial restrictions on the destruction of documents.

4. *Weak IPO market.* One of the consequences of the economic downturn that began in 2008 is that the market for IPOs has significantly weakened. The volatility of the capital markets has made IPOs a risky strategy. This has resulted in a reluctance to pursue IPOs due to soft demand in the equity markets and depressed prices for those companies that do pursue a public offering.

THE PROCESS OF THE IPO

STEP 1. SELECTING AN INVESTMENT BANKING FIRM

Once a company chooses to go public, it must select an investment banking firm. If a company has used venture capital funding at an earlier stage, it might be an extremely good idea to use the investment banker that is recommended by the venture capitalist, especially if the venture capitalist and the investment banker have substantial experience working together. Theoretically, it would be desirable to have all the investment bankers lay out proposals and fee schedules, allowing the offering firm to pick the most economical one. However, the only instance where a competitive bid process of side-by-side comparisons of investment banking fees and terms is possible is when the instruments being sold are extremely standardized (certain debt issues) and there is very little risk. The typical IPO does not fall into this situation. The actual process can take several months before an offering can be made, and full disclosure of information is not physically possible until the process is almost completed. Typically, this means that the entrepreneur has no choice but to make a commitment to "dance with the one who brought you." Switching relationships at midstream and constantly being on the hunt for the best deal is not a good option because of time constraints caused by either running out of cash or having the financial market conditions change before the offering can take place. In addition, such an action would be hard on the offering firm's reputation among investment bankers. Therefore, capitalizing on an existing relationship between the venture capital firm and the investment banker is typically the best and most seamless option.

In the absence of a relationship between the venture capitalist and an investment banker, the entrepreneur must do some shopping. A beginner might be tempted to take the preliminary valuations from various investment bankers and choose the highest one. However, a preliminary valuation is just that, preliminary. Frequently, the final offering price is quite different from the preliminary valuation because of the information that is gleaned through the due diligence process combined with the changing conditions in the financial markets. As a result, the entrepreneur should select an investment banker on the basis of qualitative factors such as these:

1. Relationship with the venture capital firm that handled the company's earlier financing.

2. Experience with doing IPOs for companies in that same industry.
3. Reputation for "making things happen" and following through on offerings.
4. Reputation for being aboveboard in all dealings (e.g., no investigations by the Securities and Exchange Commission).
5. Respected research staff that has the ability to make clear presentations during the road show for firms that have unique proposals.
6. Ability to organize syndicates of the necessary size to match the needs of offerings.

The market-making capability of the investment bank is a key consideration. If the IPO is to be conducted on an exchange that is not as large and famous as the NYSE, then secondary market liquidity becomes even more crucial in attracting investors to the offering. An investment banker provides the following benefits in the IPO process:

- *Pool of investors.* The investment bank can provide a mechanism to sell stock because it has a large pool of existing customers. This pool may consist of certified investors; that is, investors who have a level of wealth and income to invest in above-average risk investments. Institutional investors such as mutual funds can also be a part of the pool.
- *Analysts.* When an investment bank agrees to take on a firm as a client, it also agrees to supply an analyst so that its brokerage arm will have regularly distributed reports for investors. The involvement of a highly respected analyst can be helpful in promoting an active secondary market to provide liquidity, which in turn encourages investment.
- *Certifying the stock price.* By assessing a value for the IPO, the investment bank is attempting to convince its investors that the stock is not overpriced. Theoretically, what the investment bank is providing is an assurance that if investors buy this stock, they are likely to earn a good return. The investment banker therefore has an incentive to at least slightly underprice the offering. This, of course, is not what is best for the firm pursuing the IPO.

STEP 2. DECIDING WHETHER TO UNDERWRITE

Underwriting means to make explicit and implicit representations to investors about the value of the shares. It could mean that the investment banker directly purchases the shares and then resells them to the market. This is a very dramatic way to help an issuing firm deal with risk, and it is usually not done during IPOs. In IPOs, underwriting usually means that a syndicate has agreed to buy the entire security offering. This protects the firm pursuing the IPO by guaranteeing that the funds will be raised. An alternative approach is called "best efforts," in which there is no guarantee that the issue will be completely sold out. Everything else being equal, a company would obviously prefer underwriting, but things are not always equal and the investment banking fees as a percentage of cash raised will be quite a bit higher under an underwritten offering.

STEP 3. GETTING THE PAPERWORK IN ORDER AND CERTIFYING THE PRICE OF THE OFFERING

The Securities and Exchange Commission (SEC) has jurisdiction over all public stock offerings. Therefore, at least twenty days before a public offering, a registration statement called Form S-1 must be filed. The purpose of this document is to disclose legal and financial information to the SEC. Another document, a prospectus, also needs to be prepared. The prospectus is a summary of the S-1 meant for potential investors.

To properly complete these documents, a substantial process of due diligence and price certification must take place in which an investment banker plays the role of intermediary between the issuing firm and the investing public. Generally, the price of securities rises after an IPO, thereby suggesting that offerings are typically undervalued. This price behavior comes from the asymmetry of information between the seller of shares and the buyers of shares. The seller naturally would like to raise funds with the least loss of company control. Buyers of shares know much less about the company than the issuer but are aware of this informational disadvantage. Therefore, they have an incentive to demand a discount in purchase price. This discount can be considered analogous to the discounts offered by a used car dealer. Some used cars are mechanically sound and some, known as "lemons," are defective. If there is no way to fully inform potential buyers which are which, then a natural result will be a pricing discount on all used cars because every car purchased carries a risk of being a lemon. The better the information shared with the potential car buyers, the smaller the discount from fair value.

In the IPO market, this same situation occurs. When an investment banker with a good reputation conducts a thorough due diligence, the size of this pricing discount is reduced from what it theoretically could have been if the investment banker did not exist. Even with an investment banker, a small discount always exists on because it is impossible to share all relevant information with all potential investors. This is especially true when intellectual property is the competitive advantage. Nevertheless, reducing the problems caused by information asymmetry is part of the intermediary role that an investment banker plays. Due diligence helps to ensure that the investment banker uncovers any information that would have a negative effect on the buyer and hence on the valuation. Frequently, the due diligence process is sufficient to scare off charlatans from issuing securities in much the same way that a certified mechanical inspection would keep a car seller from lying about whether a particular vehicle is a lemon.

Most of the work to certify the price is done in this third step of the IPO process, but it also continues through later steps as more feedback is obtained. Generally, the pricing process runs concurrently with the other steps of the IPO process:

1. Company and investment banker meet and explore whether there is a good fit between the two of them. If the answer is a potential "yes," then they continue.
2. The investment banker gathers data.
3. The investment banker finds valuations of comparable firms that are already publicly traded.

4. The investment banker compares this IPO with similar IPOs that have recently been completed.
5. The investment banker estimates future cash flow for the entity and performs several discounted cash flow valuations.
6. The information gathered in the second item above is used to create a preliminary estimate of value.
7. The offering company decides whether to formally commit to using the investment banker.
8. Due diligence commences and new information is gathered from the financial markets.
9. The investment banker issues a preliminary filing range (possible values) in a preliminary prospectus.
10. The road show takes place. This is done to market the offering and gauge demand for the shares. At the same time as the road show, the investment banker is also watching the financial markets for any possible changes.

The final issuing price and amount to be raised is reported in the final prospectus. The valuation and the amount of funds to be raised can be quite different from what was perceived in the third item above, depending upon changes in the financial markets in recent months, the facts discovered during due diligence, and the perceptions of demand from the road show.

STEP 4. PRESENTING THE ROAD SHOW

At this point, the top management and lawyers of the company, along with the investment bankers, make a series of presentations to potential investors. Usually these investors are large clients of the investment bank. The presentations may be given as frequently as twice a day in many different cities for up to two weeks. A crucial aspect of the road show is that the managers are not legally allowed to say anything that is not in the registration statement (Form S-1). This "quiet period," mandated by the SEC, is required to last from the day the registration is effected to a period twenty-five days after the stock has begun trading. It does not stop the potential investors from asking many questions during the presentation.

STEP 5. DETERMINING THE SIZE OF THE BOOK

The investment banker tabulates the information gathered up to this point. During the road show, information on the demand for the offering was gathered through nonbinding requests from possible investors. However, the price certification process must eventually come to an end and a formal offering price must be declared, given all the information gathered from the due diligence process, the nonbinding indications of interest from the road show, and any other information that comes to light. After the road show, the investment banker asks potential investing clients if they are interested in buying shares, a process called "book building." A positive response may result in the offering being oversubscribed, meaning that more shares are desired for purchase than are currently offered. The night before the offering, the investment banker should have the offering price officially set.

STEP 6. THE FIRST DAY OF TRADING

In a typical offering, there will be a significant price run-up during the first day of trading. This is because the market is aware of the incentive for the investment bank to at least slightly underestimate the initial offering price in order to guarantee that the stock actually gets sold.

SUMMARY

As was stated at the start of this chapter, raising funds is one of the most difficult activities that an entrepreneur must perform. The type of financing requested depends upon the stage of development of the firm, so, as a result, the funding is typically provided in stages that have milestone goals used as indicators of success or failure. Venture capitalists are active players in the financing of new firms and, like any potential investor, demand a substantial amount of information and control from the firm. The end point of the investment for some of these investors is an IPO, which can be a very involved and expensive process but one which allows the initial founders to diversify their holdings.

DISCUSSION QUESTIONS

1. What is a reverse income statement and what is its relevance to raising funds?
2. Why do the financial markets traditionally raise funds in stages rather than supply the whole amount to an entrepreneur at the start?
3. In what funding stage is angel financing most likely to occur, and why?
4. Why are venture capitalists interested in owning a large percentage of a business?
5. What issues should a firm consider when choosing a venture capitalist?
6. What is the relevance to entrepreneurial finance of having an exit or harvesting strategy?
7. What reasons could make a firm desire to undergo an IPO?
8. Why is due diligence such a crucial activity?
9. When various investment bankers offer preliminary valuations for a company that wishes to do an IPO, the investment banker with the highest valuation is not necessarily the best choice. Why not?
10. What causes the disparity between the initial offering price and the trading price afterward?

OPPORTUNITIES FOR APPLICATION

1. Conduct two interviews, the first with a person who is a source of venture capital financing and the second with an entrepreneur who used such financ-

ing. Describe the venture capital financing from both the venture capitalist's and the entrepreneur's point of view.

2. Write a plan to build relationships with venture capitalists for a new business venture you are developing.

REFERENCES

Batterson, L. 1986. *Raising Venture Capital and the Entrepreneur.* Englewood Cliffs, NJ: Prentice-Hall.

Churchill, N., and V. Lewis. 1983. "Five Stages of Small Business Growth." *Harvard Business Review* (May–June): 2–11.

Higashide, H., and S. Birley. 2002. "The Consequences of Conflict between the Venture Capitalist and the Entrepreneurial Team in the United Kingdom from the Perspective of the Venture Capitalist." *Journal of Business Venturing* 17 (1): 59–81.

Lander, G.P. 2004. *What Is Sarbanes-Oxley?* New York: McGraw-Hill.

McGrath, R., and I. MacMillan. 1995. "Discovery-Driven Planning." *Harvard Business Review* (July–August): 4–12.

National Venture Capital Association. 2011. "Venture Capital Disbursements (MoneyTree Data)." http://www.nvca.org/index.php?option=com_content&view=article&id=344&Itemid=103 (accessed December 28, 2011).

Prentice, Robert. 2005. *Student Guide to Sarbanes-Oxley Act.* Stamford, CT: Thomson West.

Smith, J., and R. Smith. 2000. *Entrepreneurial Finance.* New York: Wiley.

PART IV

PLANNING FOR THE ENTREPRENEUR'S TRANSITION

15 Business Valuation

Entrepreneurs do not have the time to read a thick, technically oriented book on business appraisal nor the excess cash to hire a professional appraiser on a whim. As a result, proposals for sale or investment are frequently rejected or accepted on the basis of some vague valuation ratio or, absent that, emotions. The purpose of this chapter is to provide a brief synopsis of valuation so that an entrepreneur can economically and rapidly determine which offers are unreasonable and which are worthy of further consideration.

It must be stressed that an appraisal is an estimate or opinion. Business valuation is not an exact science. Instead, it might be called an art because a certain amount of judgment must be used in conjunction with the mathematical principles. The techniques learned in this chapter should help the entrepreneur to use judgment to separate the relevant information from the irrelevant.

GENERAL CONCEPTS THAT GUIDE THE DETERMINATION OF VALUE

There are seven general principles that should govern any valuation:

1. Fair market value
2. Going-concern value
3. Highest and best use
4. Future benefits
5. Substitutes and alternatives
6. Discounted cash flow analysis
7. Objectivity

This section will examine each of these principles in detail.

FAIR MARKET VALUE

Having a clear definition of value is important during negotiations because the other side may try to justify its proposed price by referring to comparable firms that have been recently sold. However, just because someone else sold a company does not mean that the price received is directly related or relevant to another business.

The definition of fair market value as used in this chapter comes from the Institute of Business Appraisers. This definition also seems to be consistent with general legal precedents and rulings of the Internal Revenue Service (IRS). Fair market value means the price, in cash or equivalent, that a buyer could reasonably be expected to pay and a seller could reasonably be expected to accept, as long as the property is exposed for sale on the open market for a reasonable period of time, and both buyer and seller are in possession of the pertinent facts, with neither being under compulsion to act.

Therefore, a price is *not* fair market value if any of the following conditions applies:

1. *The payment is not made in cash on or near the date of the deal.* If payment were to be deferred, for instance, then the amount received was probably adjusted to allow for the time value of money. In other words, if the buyer is going to give the seller a note that promises to make payment at some future date, then the total amount that the entrepreneur receives should be greater than the fair market value to allow for the interest that could have been earned. This does not rule out seller-financed arrangements; it simply means that the parties should use the cash equivalent price as the starting point for negotiation.

2. *It is a less than arm's length transaction.* For example, a transaction between two family members cannot be used as the basis for a market comparison. Such situations are not open markets.

3. *The offering period is excessively short.* Suppose an entrepreneur offers a firm for sale for such a brief period of time that only a person with beforehand knowledge could have submitted a bid. This would roughly be the equivalent of insider trading—not a fair open market.

4. *Information is withheld or not pursued by one or both parties.* This situation does not necessarily nullify the agreement to buy or sell at the specified price (unless criminal intent was involved). All it means is that the acquisition might not be taking place at a price that fully reflects fair market value in the conceptual sense.

5. *One of the parties is operating under duress or is legally required to consummate the agreement regardless of the terms.* A price cannot be deemed a fair market value unless the parties have the right to reject an offer or bid. For instance, some partnerships have a legal agreement that forbids selling a share of the business to anyone other than a partner. In this case, the buyout price should probably not be used as a market comparison. Another example would be a seller who is forced into a quick sale rather than face a probable bankruptcy. However, it should be noted that dire financial distress, by itself, does not automatically mean the same as "under compulsion to act" or that the price is not fair market value. It could be that *all* sellers in that industry are desperate, so reasonable buyers and sellers would expect a low price. This was highly evident after the Recession of 2008 when the value of many businesses were substantially depressed relative to their previous history.

GOING-CONCERN VALUE

Going-concern value is the value of a business as an operating concern rather than the sum value of all the individual assets that are owned by the firm. Another way to explain going-concern value is to view buying a business as if it were a traditional investment that will be paying income. Most businesses are purchased based on the anticipated cash flows. Therefore, the purchase price would be based on the value of the income to be generated by the business rather than on the resale value of the inventory, office furniture, and so on that make up the firm.

The approach of valuing the real assets of a business sometimes is referred to as *liquidation value.* This implies that the equipment and property of the firm are sold individually. For the sake of brevity, we offer no advice on how to estimate liquidation value. Volumes could be written on this topic alone because the individual markets for real estate and used equipment would have to be studied to arrive at this value.

As a side note, if a business is being sold, it is important for the entrepreneur to be aware that potential buyers sometimes try to use liquidation value as a rationale for suggesting that the price should be lower. In most cases where the firm is a going concern, the estimation of liquidation value is merely an attempt to distract the negotiation discussions away from the potentially higher going concern value.

HIGHEST AND BEST USE

The concept of highest and best use means that the price paid for a business should be based on the activity or use of the company's assets that generates the highest economic value. For example, suppose the business in question is a shop that repairs eight-track cassette tapes (an obsolete activity) in downtown Manhattan. It would be safe to assume that the going-concern value would probably be much less than the value of the real estate upon which the shop sits (liquidation value). Therefore, the highest and best use would be to sell the real estate of the business rather than to value the business on the basis of its income.

FUTURE BENEFITS

While historical information is very useful for valuing a traditional business, it may be a luxury not available to an entrepreneur. In addition, even if a firm does have a track record, it is irrational for a buyer to pay extra for *past* good performance if the economic conditions have changed. For instance, a business may have had a long string of successes because there was no other competition in town. If new competitors have now moved in, the owner should not expect those large cash flows to continue and neither should a potential buyer. Another case where this "looking forward" approach can substantially affect value is when the state of the world economic outlook can changes dramatically. When economic expansion seems the norm, the value of most businesses will be high, but,during times when overall economic growth is perceived to be low for the future, the value of business will fall today. The technique of discounted cash flow is consistent with this concept of future benefits because it attempts to value the firm on the basis of the future prospective cash flows. Multiplying historical profits or revenues by valuation multiples should be viewed as a reality check rather than a definitive valuation technique. This is a "quick and dirty" method of valuation that should be used only for a rough estimation of the potential value of a business. Again, it is the *future* potential benefits that should determine the value of a business, not its past benefits.

SUBSTITUTES AND ALTERNATIVES

This principle means that the value of a business is related to the value of alternative investments. The process of selling a home offers a good example of this principle. Home appraisals are conducted on the basis of how much money similar homes sell for in the same neighborhood. As applied to business, there are many techniques that borrow valuation ratios (such as price to earnings ratios of companies in that same industry) to assist in valuing a particular company. While substitute or alternative investment is the basis for these techniques, we will see later in this chapter that it is extremely difficult to apply these so-called market comparison techniques without violating this principle. At the very least, the buyer should keep in mind that buying that *one* particular business is *not* the only alternative. The buyer will always have the option of taking that same money and investing it in something else with a comparable or even lower level of risk. For instance, if higher returns were available from risk-free U.S. government securities than from owning a business with an exponentially higher probability of default, why would someone buy it under this principle?

DISCOUNTED CASH FLOW ANALYSIS

Discounted cash flow analysis is a technique that intrinsically incorporates all the previously mentioned principles. It builds on the capital budgeting techniques found in a traditional corporate finance textbook. This process uses the current income of a business as a starting point. Income is almost always measured using earnings before interest, taxes, depreciation, and amortization (EBITDA). EBITDA creates a consistent measure of profits that removes the specific income tax situation and financing strategy from valuation, as these vary widely from firm to firm and do not really reflect the true performance of a business entity. EBITDA also removes the noncash items of depreciation and amortization from net income, as investors are interested in assessing the future *cash flow* that a business can generate. Therefore, it is important for entrepreneurs to keep track of the EBITDA measure of profits in their businesses.

Using EBITDA as the starting point, the entrepreneur then estimates as objectively as possible what the cash flows should be over the next five years. A key element of discounted cash flow analysis is choosing accurate assumptions; for instance, a sales growth rate of 5 percent, salaries increasing or decreasing based on hiring plans, and the planned replacement of a machine during a specific year.

Box 15.1
A Lesson in the Principle of Objectivity

"From the buyer's perspective I know all too well how difficult it can be to pass over a 'dream.' I had the opportunity to conduct a leveraged buyout (LBO) of a firm that was located in the town where I grew up. Moving back and taking over the company would have offered an exceptional quality of life in addition to the 'psychological benefits' of serving my home community. Most exciting of all, my partner could have raised the necessary financing for us without putting a large sum of my personal funds at risk. Despite all of this, I had to honestly admit to myself and to my partner that the firm would not be able to repay the debt holders and other investors who would be part of this transaction. In addition, there were forty other offers to buy this firm so there was a strong likelihood of the 'winner's curse' taking place. In other words, the entity that purchased this firm by beating out all other offers probably would be paying too much and would have an even harder time paying off all of the creditors. As a result, I had to pass on this deal because the objective facts required me to."

David Vang

At the end of the five-year forecast, a terminal value of the firm is estimated that represents the approximate value of all the cash flows expected to be generated beyond the fifth year. The five years of forecasted cash flows and the terminal value are then adjusted through the discounting process to determine what those future cash flows are worth as of today's date. The value of those cash flows as of today's date is called *net present value.* The process of calculating net present value requires the use of a rate of return that would represent appropriate compensation for the business's risk.

The end result of this process is a value calculated in today's dollars that would be a fair price in exchange for all the estimated cash flows that this particular business is expected to generate in the future. Therefore, the technique should represent the concepts of fair market price, going-concern value, future benefits, and substitutes and alternatives. The issues of whether going-concern is the highest and best use and whether the cash flows have been estimated objectively will have to be determined by the entrepreneur. A full discussion of the method for computing discounted cash flow, including examples, will be presented later in this chapter.

OBJECTIVITY

To perform a valuation, it is absolutely essential for both seller and buyer to be objective in confronting the reality of the situation. A buyer must never allow the dream of business ownership to cloud sound judgment. A seller must accept the fact that the buyer will be interested only in the economic value of the business. The entrepreneur may have worked very hard to build the business, taking great risks along the way, but none of that will be relevant to a potential buyer. Only supportable data should be used to assure a consistent and objective analysis of business valuation. Box 15.1 and Box 15.2 offer examples of this principle in action.

Box 15.2
A Second Lesson in Objectivity

"Another experience, this one from my consulting practice, highlights the importance of objectivity from the seller's perspective. I was hired as a valuation consultant to a corporation that was contemplating the acquisition of a family-owned business. During this assignment, the patriarch and other members of the family consistently demanded a price that was 50 percent over the maximum possible value that our analysis could determine. Since it appeared that no deal would take place anyway, I suggested that the corporation disclose to the family all of its information and its process for valuation to show that the difference between our bid and their offer was not due to any sort of negotiating strategy. Even with all of this information supplied to them, this family still could not calculate a value on their own that was anywhere near ours. I discovered at a much later date that members of the family had serious health issues that would not allow them to run the business in the future. Nevertheless, they turned down what was a more than fair offer (which I can attest to) with no guarantee that a similar offer would ever be extended again. While it is perfectly okay to turn down a fair offer for whatever personal reasons one may have, in this particular case, the other party's emotions did not allow them to even recognize that the offer was fair. This was borne out one year later. During this time period the family had invested a tremendous amount of energy and money to make their business 30 percent larger. Due to the above mentioned health issues they wound up recontacting my client and selling their much larger business for roughly the same price that was offered before. It took the passage of time before they could emotionally 'let go' of the firm, and the result was that they gave away 30 percent of their business for free."

David Vang

BASIC INFORMATION REQUIRED FOR A VALUATION

The following is a checklist of the basic requirements for performing an effective valuation of a business venture:

1. *Income statements and/or tax returns.* A general rule of thumb in business valuation is to ask for copies of financial statements from the most recent five years (or from every year of its existence if the firm is less than five years old), including statements of cash flow if possible. If the firm is a sole proprietorship, it may not have official income statements. In this case, tax returns combined with other information may have to be used to estimate the firm's actual cash flow so that the discounted cash flow technique can be used.

2. *Balance sheets and/or list of assets and liabilities.* The request for five years of financial statements should include both income statements and balance sheets. If the firm does not have a balance sheet, then one may have to be constructed from a compiled list of the assets owned by the firm and the liabilities that the firm owes.

Table 15.1

Information Checklist for Management Interviews

1. A list of employees and salaries.
2. A list of all personal expenses that the owner(s) may have loaded into the company.
3. A summary of any equipment that may need to be fixed or replaced in the near future.
4. A discussion of which key employees will stay with the company and how the firm usually recruits new staff.
5. A list of all judgments or potential judgments against the firm. For example, does the firm have possible problems with OSHA, the IRS, the EEOC, or potential lawsuits?
6. A list of receivables that is unlikely to be collected.
7. A list of payables that are past due.
8. The owners' opinion on why customers choose their product or service and what expectations must be met to keep their customers satisfied.
9. What are the most common problems that the owners must deal with?
10. Do they have cost accounting capabilities to estimate cost per unit?
11. What is the outlook for the industry?

3. *Rates of return that are consistent with the risk level.* This is the kind of information that will be needed so that the valuation analysis is consistent with the principle of substitutes and alternatives. In other words, this information will help determine whether the potential business owner will get a return that will be commensurate with the amount of risk undertaken. The process of estimating a firm's specific required rate of return will be discussed later in this chapter.

4. *Interviews with current owners and staff.* For privately owned companies, access to the owners and staff will be essential to obtain information that does not show up on financial statements. Table 15.1 displays a checklist of the type of information that is often required during interviews with staff. Some business owners run expenses through their company that are not 100 percent essential for the business in order to reduce taxes. Providing information on items such as (1) and (2) would generally be in the seller's interest because removing such expenses from the estimate of cash flows would increase the assessed value of the firm. For example, it is unreasonable to expect the new owner to continue employing Uncle Bill as the receptionist at three times the going wage or paying the previous owner's life insurance. For items (3) through (11), however, the seller may not have an incentive to be quite as open with the buyer. In this case, the buyer may have to get outside confirmation from someone familiar with the industry, a professional appraiser, or an experienced acquisition attorney.

5. *An assessment of the future business environment for this firm.* Such an assessment should begin with a thorough analysis of competitors and potential competitors. Is the industry shrinking or growing? Is the number of competitors increasing? Where does this particular firm fit in the industry? Picking up the lunch tab for other people in the industry is a small price to

pay for such insight. If the business is local in nature, then the local chamber of commerce or the city development office might have information on the economic outlook for that community. For broader-based information, possible contacts are the Chamber of Commerce of the United States, the National Association of Manufacturers, the National Federation of Independent Business, the Small Business Administration, and industry trade associations.

DISCOUNTED CASH FLOW

With an income-oriented approach to valuation, a company can be viewed as an income-generating machine. What a buyer is willing to pay for this machine depends upon how much income it can produce. Discounted cash flow analysis estimates the value of the income a business can produce. As was mentioned earlier, EBITDA in most cases is a closer representation of the actual cash flow of the firm than taxable income.

For example, suppose that Widgets Inc. has a constant EBITDA every year. The value of the firm could be found by dividing the EBITDA of the firm by a rate of return that represents a fair compensation rate for the risk of the firm.

$$\text{Value of Widgets Inc.} = \frac{\text{EBITDA}}{\text{Rate of return}}$$

If the Widgets, Inc., is capable of generating $27,000 per year in income as measured by EBITDA and if a 27 percent rate of return is required to compensate for the level of risk of this investment, then

$$\text{Value of Widgets Inc.} = \frac{\$27,000}{0.27} = \$100,000$$

The most that a buyer should be willing to pay for Widgets Inc. is $100,000 because $100,000 placed in an investment of equal risk that earns 27 percent would generate just as much income per year.

There are two components to this valuation—the numerator (EBITDA) and the denominator (the rate of return). The annual income measured with EBITDA should reflect the expected future annual income rather than past income. A more accurate measure for estimating future EBITDA would be to add back all the nonbusiness expenses that the previous owner loaded into the firm. This would give the true level of income that the owner actually received. At this point, a judgment also must be made as to whether this level of income is sustainable in the future.

The other component for estimating value is determining the appropriate rate of return with which to capitalize Widgets Inc.'s future sustainable income. The rate of return required on the buyer's equity is not something that can be looked

Table 15.2

Perceived Expected Long-Run Annualized Returns (in percent)

Publicly traded companies	12–18
Privately held companies (with substantial history)	20–35
Angel investors	20–50
Venture capitalists	35–80

up in some official publication, but it can be inferred from the rate that could be earned on other opportunities. At a minimum, it should be several percentage points above the calculated, long-term rate of return on a common stock mutual fund that is devoted to small company stocks. A rate of such magnitude, given the principle of substitutes and alternatives, should be relevant because of the following issues. First, equity ownership is more volatile in terms of rate of return than government securities, hence the use of a small company mutual fund as a starting benchmark rather than a treasury rate. Second, the diversification effect of a mutual fund invested in many different companies would cause it to have a much lower overall risk than the "all-your-eggs-in-one-basket" position the buyer would have with direct investment in just one company. Third, a mutual fund is a liquid investment that can be easily sold on the investor's whim. Direct ownership in a company, on the other hand, may take months or more to liquidate. Because of these last two items, an owner should demand a rate of return that exceeds the return on the previously mentioned mutual fund.

Long-term returns on stock indexes such as the Standard and Poor's 500 or the New York Stock Exchange are occasionally published in periodicals such as *Barron's* and the *Wall Street Journal*. However, these indexes represent only large companies. For small company stock returns, an excellent source that can be found at most libraries is *Stocks, Bonds, Bills and Inflation* by R.G. Ibbotson and R.A. Sinquefield (1989). This source has calculated stock returns measured over periods of sixty years or more. Typically, when measured over long periods of time, small company tradable stocks have an average return between 12 and 18 percent. This return should be adjusted to deal with the observation that investment values are frequently reduced by between 10 and 50 percent in the absence of a liquid market in which to sell them. Furthermore, the value of an investment can fall even more if it is not of a diversified nature. Table 15.2 displays general guidelines for expected returns of different types of investments.

Suppose an appraiser consults *Stocks, Bonds, Bills and Inflation* and finds that small company stocks had an average return of 18 percent over the past ten to twenty years. The appraiser believes that this rate should be increased by about a total of 50 percent (30 percent to reflect a lack of liquidity premium and another 20 percent to reflect that Widgets, Inc., will not be a diversified investment like a mutual fund). So, the required return on equity in this example should be

$$18\% \times 1.50 = 27\%$$

The reader should be aware that this is a crude approach to approximating the required return on equity. It is a tremendous simplification of the process that a professional appraiser would and should perform. Many volumes of research have been written on this topic, and part of the reason that an appraiser should be hired is that professionals are familiar with the most recent findings. However, under the assumption that the buyer has chosen not to hire a professional, the practice of adding a premium that doubles or more than doubles the stock fund rate would not be unreasonable. For instance, if an investment has a value 50 percent less than a similar but liquid investment, its ratio of profit to price will result in a rate of return that is double the liquid investment.

The moral to entrepreneurs is that a direct purchaser of their business will not be shy about demanding a rate of return in the range of 20 to 70 percent (about two to three times the rate on the stock market) on the equity that has been invested. On the other hand, if the purchaser is a large corporation with publicly traded stock or if stock is sold directly into a well-established market (i.e., an IPO), then investors might not demand such a high liquidity or risk premium, which would result in a higher value for the business. For instance, if investors demanded only a 20 percent rate of return, then Widgets Inc., would be worth

$$\$27,000/0.20 = \$135,000$$

Notice the inverse relationship between required rates of return and value. When investors demanded a lower rate of return, the value increased by $35,000 (from $100,000 to $135,000).

This simple example demonstrates the forward-looking aspect of valuation. However, the use of a single number to represent average future income may be too simplistic to accurately capture the specific circumstances of the firm. We can now add more sophistication.

Instead of using a single number to represent future earnings, it might be better to estimate the annual cash flow for a number of years (usually five or more) into the future. These estimated cash flows are then discounted at the appropriate rate to determine their present value (today's cash equivalent). In addition, a *terminal* or *ending value* of the investment is estimated at the end of this forecasted time period. This terminal value also is discounted back to today's cash equivalent, just like all the other cash flows. The terminal value represents the value of all cash flows expected to continue beyond the end of the analysis period. The sum of these discounted cash flows represents the cash value of Widgets Inc. as of today. Financial calculators, spreadsheets, or regular calculators can rapidly perform such calculations. The following example will demonstrate how.

Suppose a more thorough valuation of the Widgets Inc. firm is desired. It is discovered that 5 percent growth in sales per year is a reasonable expectation, but the future beyond five years is totally indeterminate. In addition, Widgets Inc. has a machine that will wear out in two years and will cost $20,500 to replace. Given these assumptions, the next five years' worth of cash flows (CFs) can be estimated as follows.

Today + 1 year	$27,000 × (1.05)	= $28,350 CF1
Today + 2 years	$28,350 × (1.05) – $20,500	= $ 9,268 CF2
Today + 3 years	$29,768 × (1.05)	= $31,256 CF3
Today + 4 years	$31,256 × (1.05)	= $32,819 CF4
Today + 5 years	$32,819 × (1.05)	= $34,460 CF5

In other words, each year's cash flow is 5 percent larger than the previous year's, except for the second year, when $20,500 is subtracted to represent the cost of replacing the machine at that time. Cash flows in years 6, 7, and so on are assumed to be the same as in year 5, based on the belief that growth beyond year 5 is indeterminate. The valuation technique discussed previously can be used plus the assumed rate of return of 27 percent to estimate what the Widgets Inc. theoretically could be sold for five years from now (i.e., its terminal value):

$$\frac{\text{Cash flow, year 6}}{\text{Rate of return}} = \frac{\$34,460}{0.27} = \$127,630 = \text{terminal value}$$

The next step is to discount all these cash flows back to a cash equivalent in today's dollars using the 27 percent rate of return. If a regular calculator is used, the math would be as follows:

Year 1	$ 28,350 / (1.27)	= $ 22,323
Year 2	$ 9,268 / (1.27)2	= $ 5,746
Year 3	$ 31,256 / (1.27)3	= $ 15,259
Year 4	$ 32,819 / (1.27)4	= $ 12,616
Year 5	$ 34,460 / (1.27)5	= $ 10,430
Terminal	$127,630 / (1.27)5	= $ 38,631
Total cash equivalent value		$105,005

If a financial calculator is used, the typical keystrokes would be as follows:

0	CF$_0$	
28,350	CF$_i$	
9,268	CF$_i$	
31,256	CF$_i$	
32,819	CF$_i$	
162,090	CF$_i$	(162,090 is equal to 34,460, the year 5 cash flow, plus the terminal value of 127,630)
27	I	(I is the interest rate button on the calculator)
		(The NPV button calculates the net present value or sum of all presently valued cash flows)
NPV		(Answer would be displayed as 105,005)

(If the answer is not reasonably close to this, double check to see that the calculator is set on END mode, the display is set to four or more decimal places, and the calculator is set for annual, not monthly, compounding.)

Thus, the estimated value of Widgets Inc. according to the discounted cash flow method is $105,005 compared with the crude estimation of $100,000. The difference of $5,005 is the result of the ability of the discounted cash flow approach to incorporate the additional information learned about this company. The output of this analysis is only as precise as the assumptions that went into its calculation, of course, but the advantage of discounted cash flow analysis is the ability to re-estimate values by varying the assumptions. For instance, the analysis could be repeated using a range of growth rates from 3 to 10 percent. The actual price to be offered within this range would depend upon the perceived likelihood of sales growth being above or below 5 percent. As was mentioned earlier in this chapter, business valuation is an art, not an exact science.

The basic view that someone *should have* when buying a small business is "How much should I be willing to pay to get a decent salary (if I were to run the business myself) *and* a reasonable return on my investment?" Of all the techniques for valuation, the discounted cash flow approach is the best at answering this question. The only way to make a fully informed decision is to formally calculate the level of cash flow of the firm to see if it currently is providing an appropriate salary and return on investment. The market comparison approach of multiplying a ratio by one piece of business information would not automatically provide such insight.

Performing a discounted cash flow analysis is a worthwhile activity for both buyers and sellers. Buyers should know whether the firm will provide sufficient personal income, and sellers should know whether they are being too generous to the buyer. This analysis also provides a nice, direct rule for the buyer. If the net present value of the estimated cash flows is greater than the offering price, buy the company. If the net present value is less than the offering price, do not buy.

DEFINITION OF CASH FREE FLOW

Free cash flow represents the cash that is left over *after* covering operating costs, debt repayment, capital expenditures such as asset replacement, *and* paying the owner/manager an economically reasonable wage.

This definition fits in nicely with the principle of substitutes and alternatives and the concept of future benefits because one alternative to buying a business is to get a job working for an established company. The supposed economic benefit of owning a business, however, is that buyers should get an income in excess of what they would get working for someone else. Sometimes people refer to buying a business as "buying yourself a job." In principle, it does not make sense to pay a huge sum of money just to "buy yourself a job." But, it does make economic sense to pay money (i.e., make an investment) to have incremental income above and beyond the market value that the buyer can earn in the open job market. Therefore, free cash flow must be carefully estimated so that the buyer is not paying for the following:

1. Cash flow that could have been gotten without the risk of business ownership (the income from working for a company).
2. Cash flow that must be paid to the bank, lender, or equipment dealer for future asset replacements that will be the responsibility of the new owner.

3. Cash flow that must be used to pay the normal expenses that allow the business to run on a day-to-day basis, such as salaries to employees, production costs, and the light bill.

In other words, a firm could be generating large annual revenues, but the amount that the owner can consider discretionary income might be only a very small percentage of that revenue. It is very likely that this amount is very different from the reported EBITDA. Indeed, a firm may officially be making a profit but have a negative cash flow. This situation frequently occurs in years when the company has to make major asset purchases.

ESTIMATING FREE CASH FLOW FOR A PARTICULAR YEAR

To determine what the free cash flow for a business is in any particular year, the entrepreneur would start with the official operating profit or EBIT (earnings before interest and taxes) of the business and make the following six adjustments:

1. Add back the owner's salary and benefits.
2. Subtract out a more reasonable compensation for the work performed by the owner.
3. Add back any of the owner's personal expenses that have been run through the company.
4. Add back any depreciation and amortization expenses that were claimed this year. Remember, these are noncash expenses. They are not actual payments made to someone, but merely a number from a table or formula that the IRS allows the owner to subtract out before the calculation of the firm's taxable income.
5. If a major piece of equipment or asset is intended to be purchased in this particular year, then subtract this amount.
6. Subtract the amount of money it would take to bring the inventory of the company up to a reasonable level. For instance, sometimes when a business owner knows that the company will be sold, he may "sell out of inventory" rather than reorder new inventory. Therefore, by the time the new owner takes possession, there may be nothing on the shelves to sell. As a result, the new owner may need to invest in inventory or other types of working capital *before* the business is able to operate and generate income. An analogy might be the way that people sell their cars. They typically do not pay for new tires, a brake job, a battery, a tune-up, and a tankful of gas the day before a car is sold.

ESTIMATING FREE CASH FLOW OVER A SIX-YEAR PERIOD

Let us suppose the following situation:

1. A potential buyer is interested in purchasing a company called MacroTech from an owner whose financial statements report that this year's EBIT was $200,000.

2. Other information gathered reveal that the owner paid himself salary and benefits of $100,000 when a more reasonable compensation, given the local job market, was $50,000.
3. There was $20,000 in depreciation expense this year.
4. The owner had $10,000 in personal expenses such as lease payments on a Lexus that he called a "company" car.
5. The firm will need a net investment of $200,000 next year to replace worn-out equipment. Buying this new equipment will cause depreciation expense to increase by $50,000 each year for four years.
6. It is believed that EBIT will increase by 7 percent per year for the next five years given the productive capacity of the firm and the nature of the product market. Beyond five years, a reasonable estimate of growth is neither possible nor relevant because the buyer should not have to pay for growth that would come from his own efforts and future investment.
7. The firm has an outstanding loan of $500,000.
8. The cost basis of the firm is $100,000. In other words, the original owner has $100,000 of his money invested in the company. If the firm sells for more than $100,000, the difference between the selling price and the $100,000 invested would be considered income to the seller. Further suppose that the original owner would fall in a combined state and federal tax bracket of 40 percent.
9. MacroTech has a history of maintaining an average inventory balance of $80,000. Since MacroTech first appeared on the market for sale, the owner has not purchased any new inventory and has allowed the level to drop to $65,000, thus suggesting that the buyer will probably need to invest $15,000 in inventory just to bring the firm's inventory back up to a safe level.

Given all the above information, Tables 15.3 through 15.9 demonstrate how to construct a forecast of cash flows for the next six years. Table 15.3 determines the cash flow for this year (year zero), the year that MacroTech is sold, as a baseline starting point. The first cash flow to be received by the buyer will be cash flow for year 1.

So, if MacroTech were purchased, it could theoretically have the following cash flows:

First year	+ 79,000
Second year	+ 308,980
Third year	+ 321,509
Fourth year	+ 334,915
Fifth year	+ 349,259

and an approximate amount per year thereafter of +$349,259.

Notice that EBIT was *never* equal to the actual cash flow. Also note that, even though EBIT was growing at 7 percent per year, cash flow did not steadily increase at that

Table 15.3

Year 0

Official EBIT	$200,000
Add back owner salary	+100,000
Subtract out more reasonable salary	−50,000
Add back depreciation for this year	+20,000
Add back "personal" expenses	+10,000
Estimated EBITDA	$280,000
Subtract new equipment purchased	0
Subtract inventory investment	0
"Free Cash Flow" vs. Accounting EBIT $200,000	= +$280,000

Table 15.4

Year 1

Official EBIT	$214,000[a]
Add back owner salary	+100,000
Subtract out more reasonable salary	−50,000
Add back depreciation for this year	+20,000
Add back "personal" expenses	+10,000
Estimated EBITDA	$294,000
Subtract new equipment purchased	−200,000[b]
Subtract inventory investment	−15,000
"Free Cash Flow" vs. Accounting EBIT $214,000	= +$79,000

[a]This number is last year's official EBIT multiplied by 1.07 to represent a 7 percent growth (200,000 × 1.07).

[b]This represents the purchase of the new equipment needed this year.

Table 15.5

Year 2

Official EBIT	$178,980[a]
Add back owner salary	+100,000
Subtract out more reasonable salary	−50,000
Add back depreciation for this year	+70,000[b]
Add back "personal" expenses	+10,000
Estimated EBITDA	$308,980
Subtract new equipment purchased	0
Subtract inventory investment	0
"Free Cash Flow" vs. Accounting EBIT $178,980	= +$308,980

[a]This number is last year's EBIT of $214,000 multiplied by 1.07 to represent 7 percent growth, then subtract the extra $50,000 in depreciation.

[b]This is last year's depreciation plus $50,000 from the newly purchased equipment.

Table 15.6

Year 3

Official EBIT	$191,509[a]
Add back owner salary	+100,000
Subtract out more reasonable salary	−50,000
Add back depreciation for this year	+70,000
Add back "personal" expenses	+10,000
Estimated EBITDA	$321,509
Subtract new equipment purchased	0
Subtract inventory investment	0
"Free Cash Flow" vs. Accounting EBIT $191,509	= +$321,509

[a]This is the previous year multiplied by 1.07 (178,980 × 1.07).

Table 15.7

Year 4

Official EBIT	$204,915[a]
Add back owner salary	+100,000
Subtract out more reasonable salary	−50,000
Add back depreciation for this year	+70,000
Add back "personal" expenses	+10,000
Estimated EBITDA	$334,915
Subtract new equipment purchased	0
Subtract inventory investment	0
"Free Cash Flow" vs. Accounting EBIT $204,915	= +$334,915

[a]This is the previous year multiplied by 1.07 (191,509 × 1.07).

Table 15.8

Year 5

Official EBIT	$219,259[a]
Add back owner salary	+100,000
Subtract out more reasonable salary	−50,000
Add back depreciation for this year	+70,000
Add back "personal" expenses	+10,000
Estimated EBITDA	$349,259
Subtract new equipment purchased	0
Subtract inventory investment	0
"Free Cash Flow" vs. Accounting EBIT $219,259	= +$349,259

[a]This is the previous year multiplied by 1.07 (204,915 × 1.07).

Table 15.9

Year 6

Official EBIT	$269,259[a]
Add back owner salary	+100,000
Subtract out more reasonable salary	−50,000
Add back depreciation for this year	+20,000[b]
Add back "personal" expenses	+10,000
Estimated EBITDA	$349,259
Subtract new equipment purchased	0
Subtract inventory investment	0
"Free Cash Flow" vs. Accounting EBIT $269,259	= +$349,259

[a]This is the same official EBIT as year 5 (zero growth) because it is difficult to reasonably predict what will happen in the marketplace after five years. To this amount, however, we added $50,000 to represent that the equipment we purchased in year 1 will now be fully depreciated (219,259 + 50,000) in accounting terms, but it is operationally still useful.
[b]A reduction of $50,000 to reflect equipment that is now fully depreciated.

Table 15.10

Relationship of Price and Net Present Value

Price > net present value	Buyer earns less than the required rate of return.
Price < net present value	Buyer earns more than the required rate of return.
Price = net present value	Buyer earns exactly the required rate of return.

same rate. In fact, cash flow actually dropped significantly in the first year from what it was originally.

It is from these cash flows that the new buyer will have to recover the purchase price of the firm. If these cash flows have a discounted present value that is less than the seller's proposed purchase price, buyer should *not* buy this firm. Such a situation means that the cash flows are not sufficient to do all the following at the same time:

1. Pay back the debt part of the financing that would be used to purchase the firm.
2. Earn an acceptable return on the personal equity investment that would be used to purchase this firm.
3. Pay the buyer a reasonable compensation for his own labor.

Suppose that the required rate of return is still 27 percent. If the preceding information is accurate and reasonable, then the potential value of the expected future cash flows of this firm can now be calculated.

The first step is to find the year 5 terminal value by using the investment value approach:

$$\frac{\text{Terminal value at year 5}}{\text{Cost of financing}} = \text{Cash flow, year 6} = \frac{\$349,259}{0.27} = \$1,293,552$$

The next step is to discount all the cash flows back to a cash equivalent in today's dollars using the 27 percent rate of return:

Year 1	$ 79,000 / (1.27) = $62,205
Year 2	$ 308,980 / (1.27)² = $191,568
Year 3	$ 321,509 / (1.27)³ = $156,957
Year 4	$ 334,915 / (1.27)⁴ = $128,742
Year 5	$ 349,259 / (1.27)⁵ = $105,713
Ending	$1,293,552 / (1.27)⁵ = $391,530
Total cash equivalent value as of today:	$1,036,715

Using a financial calculator, the typical keystrokes would be as follows:

0	CF0	
79,000	CFi	
308,980	CFi	
321,509	CFi	
334,915	CFi	
1,642,811	CFi	(1,642,811 is equal to 349,259 cash flow plus the terminal value of 1,293,552)
27	I	
NPV		(Answer would be displayed as 1,036,715 allowing for rounding differences)

By using different sales growth assumptions that can be considered reasonable, the value of this MacroTech, if purchased today, is in a range with a reasonable middle value of $1,036,715. If the seller is absolutely adamant about a price that is significantly greater than $1,036,715, then the potential buyer should probably refuse. The cash flows that have been estimated perfectly correspond to a 27 percent rate of return if the company is purchased for $1,036,715. If the company is purchased for more than $1,036,715, the buyer will be earning less than 27 percent. In other words, if more than $1,036,715 is paid, the buyer would not be able to pay the principle and interest on the money borrowed, get a reasonable rate of return on the equity investment, and receive the reasonable salary of $50,000 all at the same time. Something has to give, and mostly likely it will not be the banker—it will be the buyer. Likewise, the lower the price, the easier it will be to accomplish all these things.

Now let us look at the seller's perspective. He has received $1,036,715 from the sale of MacroTech. Out of this amount he can now pay off the outstanding $500,000 loan (see assumption number 8). However, he had a cost basis of $100,000 and sold the business for $1,036,715. In the eyes of the IRS, he just made income of $936,715. Given a tax rate of 40 percent, the seller now owes $374,686 in taxes. Altogether,

Proceeds from sale	$1,036,715
Minus debt to be paid	−500,000
Minus income tax	−374,686
= Net proceeds	$162,029

At this point the potential seller of MacroTech should go back to Chapter 2 of this book and see if achieving a wealth of only $162,029 is sufficient to allow him to achieve his personal goals.

VALUATION ANALYSIS WHEN EQUITY IS NOT THE ONLY FUNDING SOURCE

Let us suppose that MacroTech was to be purchased by a mixture of different sources of financing. For instance, if the buyer can get 25 percent of the financing from debt at a rate of 15 percent, this would change the effective discount rate used to value the cash flows of the firm and therefore the potential purchase price. If the equity providers do not change their required rate of return of 27 percent (which they might, given that more debt can sometimes lead to more risk), then the discount rate becomes what is referred to in finance as the weighted average cost of capital (WACC):

$$W_d R_d (1 - T) + W_e R_e = WACC$$

where W_d = weight (percentage) of debt used (25 percent)
W_e = weight (percentage) of equity used (75 percent)
R_d = interest rate on debt financing (15 percent)
R_e = required rate of return on equity (27 percent)
T = tax rate (assumed to be 40 percent)

Since cash flows were forecasted on an after-tax basis, an after-tax discount rate must be used for evaluation. Equity is a non-tax-deductible form of financing and debt is deductible; therefore, $(1 - T)$, is multiplied only against the cost of debt, R_d. However, the cost of equity financing, R_e, is already an after-tax rate of return. Therefore, the WACC for this firm would be 22.5 percent:

$$(25\%) (15\%)(1 - 0.40) + (75\%) (27\%) = 22.5\%$$

Valuing the above company using a combination of 25 percent debt and 75 percent equity would require the following changes to the valuation of the firm's cash flows:

$$\text{Terminal value at year 5} = \frac{\text{Cash flow, year 6}}{\text{Cost of financing}} = \frac{\$349,259}{0.225} = \$1,552,262$$

Using a financial calculator, the typical keystrokes would be as follows:

$$
\begin{array}{rl}
0 & \text{CF}_0 \\
79{,}000 & \text{CF}_i \\
308{,}980 & \text{CF}_i \\
334{,}915 & \text{CF}_i \\
1{,}901{,}521 & \text{CF}_i\dagger \\
22.5 & \text{I} \\
& \text{NPV}
\end{array}
$$

321,509 CF_i

(1,901,521 is equal to 349,259 + 1,552,262, which is the year 5 value cash flow plus the terminal value)

(Answer would be displayed as 1,283,336 allowing for rounding differences)

MacroTech's value is now higher ($1,283,336 versus $1,036,715) because a lower discount rate was used in its calculation (22.5 percent versus 27 percent). Of the potential $1,282,336 value of the company, $320,584 is debt that must now be paid back because the firm is 25 percent debt financed. The remaining value after subtracting the debt is the equity value of the firm—which is also 75 percent of the company value.

Value of company	–	Amount of debt	=	Value of equity
$1,282,336	–	$320,584	=	$961,752

Therefore, while the total value of MacroTech is higher, the resulting dollar value that equity investors get is less because equity investors are no longer entitled to 100 percent of the cash flow.

SUMMARY OF THE DISCOUNTED CASH FLOW APPROACH

The basic view that potential *buyers* should have when valuing a business is, "How much should I be willing to pay to get a decent salary and a reasonable return on my investment?" The only way to make a truly informed decision is to formally calculate the level of free cash flow of the firm to see if it can provide for repayment of debt, an appropriate salary, and an appropriate return on investment. If the calculated net present value of the cash flows is less than the offering price, the answer is no, it cannot. If the net present value is more than the offering price, the answer is yes, this firm can provide these amounts. Potential *sellers* should consider the effect of debt repayment and income taxes in order to determine if the size of the wealth accumulation from the sale of the business is significant enough for them to achieve their personal goals.

MARKET COMPARISON TECHNIQUES

There are a number of different techniques for valuing companies, but, in determining going-concern value, these techniques fall into two broad areas—those that use

Table 15.11

Possible Ratio Formulas for Market Data Approach

Variable	Ratio
1. Net income	1. Price\Earnings
2. Earnings per share	2. Price\Earnings
3. Pretax earnings	3. Price\Pretax earnings per share
4. Cash flow	4. Price\Cash flow
5. EBITDA	5. Price\EBITDA
6. Dividends	6. Price\Dividends
7. Gross revenue	7. Price\Sales
8. Total assets	8. Price\Assets
9. Book value per share	9. Price\Book value per share
10. Number of total customers	10. Price\Customer
11. Industry-specific measurements	11. Price\Unit

some sort of market comparison and those that discount future earnings or cash flow. While the latter approach is advocated in this chapter, information on market comparison techniques is included because of their widespread use. Ideally, this section will give businesspeople the necessary ammunition to recognize the reasonable from the unreasonable when approached with market comparison ratios.

The market comparison approach goes by many different names in the literature of business valuation—market multiples, market data, market comparables, sales comparison, and so on. Regardless of the terminology, the general process is to identify recent company sales or use publicly traded prices of companies that are comparable to the specific company to be valued. If the companies used for comparison are not 100 percent comparable to the firm of interest, then those prices must be adjusted. The adjusted selling prices of the comparable firms are now used as the basis for estimating the value of the company in question. Usually, this is done through some sort of ratio formula.

Table 15.11 displays a list of possible variables and corresponding ratios that may be used in conjunction with company acquisitions or stock prices to estimate values according to the market data approach.

Not all of these variables are used in every valuation. Which ones are used would depend upon the kind of sales data collected and industry convention. For instance, if data are available for actual purchases of companies in the industry, the selling price would be divided by the respective net income for each company. The result is a series of total-price-to-total-net-income ratios that can be multiplied by the net income of a particular firm to estimate its possible value.

The underlying principle of the market comparison approach is the concept of substitutes and alternatives. The use of market comparisons as sanity checks or a quick and dirty way to assess offers comes from the idea that if the calculation uses firms from the same industry, then their risk should be approximately equal to the risk of the firm to be valued. Therefore, the company is valued by using the values of what should be equally desirable substitutes. Thanks to the common-sense appeal of this general approach, it is frequently used by valuation experts and courts of law. The actual application of the market comparison approach, however, is fraught with difficulties. For instance, its successful use depends on having access to information on several different company acquisitions. Furthermore, its validity depends upon these sales being sufficiently comparable to a given situation.

The first difficulty with market comparisons is access to information. There are data files of recent sales of companies, but access is usually reserved for professional appraisers who pay fees for memberships in organizations such as the Institute of Business Appraisers. Another source might be industry trade journals, but again there is usually an annual fee for a subscription. For laypeople, access to such information can be very difficult, and even professional appraisers may have trouble. One reason is that data are usually collected only on very large company transactions. Also, most data are recorded in summary fashion rather than being fully detailed.

The market comparison approach has a second potential difficulty: the occasional need to adjust for comparability even when information is available. This is an area where objectivity, the seventh general concept discussed at the beginning of this chapter, is sometimes tainted. Box 15.2 discussed a family that refused a more than fair offer because they were unable to recognize it as such. One of the reasons was their insistence on using the price-to-earnings ratio of the purchasing corporation to value their own firm without allowing for any differences. The purchasing corporation had three different divisions, and a single division was more than thirty times larger than the family firm. In addition, the corporation's stock was traded on a major stock exchange. In other words, the family ignored three issues of comparability. First, they were comparing their company to a firm that was approximately a hundred times larger. Second, they ignored the difference in risk between the diversified corporation and their single-product firm. Last, they ignored the difference in liquidity between a publicly traded stock on a major exchange and ownership in a family business. In other words, they probably should have adjusted the price-to-earnings ratio downward three times before they applied it to their company.

Using a market comparison approach is not as simple as it first seems because of the potential need for value adjustment. Many possible issues can interfere with finding a set of truly comparable company sales. Truly comparable company sales would involve firms that have these same basic characteristics:

1. *Line of business.* This item may be extremely obvious, but finding a comparable type of business may be difficult because many small businesses operate in niche markets for which there is no direct comparison.
2. *Geographic area.* As an example, a gas station that operates in a large city by any measure would probably sell for more than a similar firm in a rural area because of the difference in the number of potential customers. In other

cases, the value may be different because of geographic differences in the cost of financing or the cost of living.

3. *Production process and age of assets.* If a firm operates with an outdated technology, it should not be expected to sell at a price similar to that of a firm that has recently modernized. If the firm needs new equipment in the near future, this will reduce the future cash flows of the enterprise.

4. *Listing status or form of ownership.* Firms whose stock is traded on a major stock exchange are highly liquid; that is, investors can change their minds every day about whether to own the stock or not. As a result, investors are willing to pay extra for ownership in such a firm compared with the illiquid investment in a company that is not listed on the stock exchange. There can even be differences in liquidity between different stock exchanges.

5. *Costs of inputs or other competitive advantages that affect the level of profitability.* Because of the principle of future benefits, valuation ratios that do not directly relate value to cash flow or profits should probably be viewed with skepticism. It may seem like common sense that when the cost of servicing the customer exceeds the revenue collected, there is no value. Despite this simple logic, false industry conventions sometimes arise, such as valuing firms as a multiple of total revenue, total assets, or some other basis that does not allow for any difference in profitability.

6. *Level of establishment, name, trademark, or industry position.* Direct comparisons between a firm that has a 1 percent market share and another that has a 75 percent market share would probably not be appropriate because the latter has the economic power to influence product price and industry behavior while the former does not. Likewise, a firm with a widely recognized trademark or a historically recognized location has an advantage over a recently started company. For instance, one of the authors of this book had consulting client whose company used to experience a slight increase in sales whenever a competitor ran TV ads because of its location, name recognition, and the fact that it was listed alphabetically before all its competitors in the Yellow Pages. Obviously, an upstart company should not be given a comparable value in this market.

7. *Sale terms.* Buying or selling a business is more confusing than buying a car or a house. Theoretically, the starting point of negotiation should be the cash price, with further negotiations dealing with the terms of the sale. In reality, terms may be so important that the cash equivalent price need only be an approximation rather than a precisely determined number. Sale terms may include issues such as how payments should be timed, who absorbs the financing fees, whether it is an asset purchase or an equity purchase, and so on. Just as in real estate, there may be advantages to rolling some of these issues into the purchase price rather than dealing with them separately. As a result, the official "price" that gets quoted may not be very close to the true cash price equivalent.

8. *Standing of ownership.* This issue deals with whether a purchaser is buying all or most of the company (majority ownership) or a minor holding in the company (minority interest). A direct value comparison should not be made

between an acquisition of a minority interest—say 5 percent—and the total acquisition of a company because a majority owner would have control over how the firm operates, whereas a minority owner generally does not. For example, if the interest is 5 percent of the company, the buyer does not calculate the total value of the firm and pay 5 percent of that amount. Instead, the price should be less than that amount because the future benefit of that 5 percent ownership stake depends upon the continuing wisdom, fairness, and general good management of the controlling majority owner.

9. *Size of the business.* Depending upon the valuation measure, small companies usually sell for a discount compared to large companies due to many of the previously mentioned issues such as differences in risk, profitability, industry standing, and economies of scale.

10. *Financing.* Buying a business can be similar to buying a house in that when interest rates go down, buyers can afford to spend more. As a result, firms that have been purchased with low-cost financing may have a higher price than similar companies for which the buyers could not access cheap financing.

11. *Time period.* Economic conditions can change substantially over time. Therefore, a company purchase that was recorded more than a year or two ago probably would not be a good comparison because the conditions for economic growth and the level of interest rates could be very different than today's growth and rates.

12. *Similar buyer.* The value of a particular business can be different for different types of buyers. To illustrate, if the only buyers are individuals who need to retain the company's entire staff in order to run the business, then the fair market price probably would be less than in another time or place where the buyers are all large corporations who have the luxury of laying off redundant personnel. An organization that already owns one or more businesses in the industry may assess a value that is more than the fair stand-alone value for a company because of potential synergies, economies of scale, or both.

SUMMARY OF THE MARKET COMPARISON APPROACH

To summarize this discussion of the market comparison approach, it should be said that valuation techniques that use price-to-earnings ratios or other market comparison measures are susceptible to large errors unless the companies used for comparison are very similar to the company of interest. If the companies are not almost identical, then subjective judgment must be inserted into the process to adjust the values. At this point the objectivity of the valuation becomes highly suspect. On the plus side, such techniques have two advantages. First, they are mathematically simple. Second, they have a wide range of acceptance by the general, though not necessarily informed public.

SUMMARY

The ability to estimate the valuation of a business is a crucial skill needed by entrepreneurs to make decisions as to whether or not to sell or otherwise harvest wealth from their business enterprise that he has created. Likewise, a person who wants to become an entrepreneur by buying a preexisting company needs these skills to make sure he does not pay too much. The basic principles of valuation are fair market value, going-concern value, highest and best use, future benefits, substitutes and alternatives, discounted cash flow analysis, and objectivity. Of the different methods of valuation, the technique of discounted cash flow analysis is the most detailed and most consistent with all the principles of valuation. The market comparison approach attempts to follow the principles of valuation but its simplistic nature causes it to frequently fail.

DISCUSSION QUESTIONS

1. How does the discounted cash flow approach incorporate many of the other principles of valuation?
2. Market comparables are theoretically based on the principle of substitutes and alternatives. What are some of the ways that market comparables actually contradict this principle?
3. Explain why liquidation value is typically not the method that should be used for evaluation of the exit/harvesting strategy for a company.
4. Under what conditions would the concept of highest and best use be in conflict with the concept of discounted cash flow?
5. What will the effect be on valuation if the discount rate is too high? What if it is too low?
6. Give some examples of how income in accounting terms can be different from cash flow.
7. What are some of the reasons that return on U.S. Treasury bills should not be used as the discount rate in valuation of a business?
8. Why would two businesses that are identical except for the fact that one is publicly traded and one is privately owned have two different values?
9. If a transaction took place three years ago, why would it not necessarily be applicable to a business sale that is taking place today?
10. Is it possible for an entrepreneur to experience a reduction in wealth when a business is sold even though the value of the business is much greater than the amount invested? Under what conditions would this take place?

OPPORTUNITIES FOR APPLICATION

1. Suppose a firm generates an annual cash flow of $100,000, has zero growth, and has a required rate of return of 15 percent. If the offering price is $50,000, should you buy it?
2. You believe you need a 50 percent return on equity to compensate you for risk. How would this affect the value of the firm in problem 1?
3. Your firm had an EBIT of $105,000 last year this year. You have $15,000 in personal expenses annually paid by the company. Depreciation expense was $2,000, and you will purchase new office equipment at a cost of $5,000. You paid yourself a salary of $200,000, but you know you could hire someone

else to be a manager for $75,000. What was your EBITDA and estimated free cash flow this year?

4. A company has free cash flow: year 1, $100,000; year 2, $90,000; year 3, $110,000; year 4, $120,000; year 5, $125,000; year 6 and beyond, $125,000. The required rate of return on equity is 30 percent. What is the most a buyer should pay for this firm?

5. Redo problem 4 under the assumption that the firm has $65,000 in debt that must be paid off. What will the seller's proceeds be from the sale of the business after paying off the debt, but before paying income taxes on the gain?

6. Redo problem 5 under the assumption that the tax rate is 40 percent, and the cost basis of the business is only $10,000. What will the net proceeds be after the payment of the debt and the taxes?

7. Your firm's free cash flow per year is as follows:

Year 1	= $120,000
Year 2	= $140,000
Year 3	= $150,000
Year 4	= $160,000
Year 5	= $170,000

The cost of capital is 20 percent.
   a. What would the terminal value be at year 5 if there is no growth expected beyond the fifth year?
   b. What is the present value of the free cash flow for the first five years?
   c. What is the value of the firm today?

8. A business has an EBITDA of $220,000. If a comparable firm recently sold at a price-to-EBITDA ratio of 2.1, what would be the theoretical value of this business using the market comparables approach?

9. A privately held business has the same EBITDA as a publicly traded one. It is assumed that the liquidity discount is 25 percent. What theoretically should be the value of the privately held business if the publicly traded one is worth $1,500,000?

10. A firm's discounted cash flow value is $1,600,000. Its market comparables value is $1,550,000, and its liquidation value is $100,000. Using only an average of techniques based on the principle of highest and best use, what should a valuation report claim as this firm's value?

REFERENCES

Damodaran, A. 2002. *Investment Valuation.* 2d ed. New York: Wiley.

Ibbotson, R.G., and R.A. Sinquefield. 1989. *Stocks, Bonds, Bills and Inflation.* Ontario: Irwin.

Mills, R.C. 1984. *Basic Business Appraisal.* New York: Wiley.

Pratt, S. 2008. *Valuing a Business:* The Analysis and Appraisal of Closely Held Companies, 5th ed. New York: McGraw-Hill.

Sherman, A.J. 2001. "Methods of Company Valuation." http://www.entrepreneurship.org/Resources/Detail /Default.aspx?id=10822.

16 Exit Planning

At some point in time, the founding entrepreneur will leave the venture. This can happen in a variety of ways, including selling the business, transitioning to the next generation in a family business, bankruptcy, or through the death of the entrepreneur. The process of preparing for the transition of both the entrepreneur and the business is called *exit planning*. This chapter presents a model of exit planning that ties back to the self-assessment first presented in Chapter 2. Many experts believe that exit planning should begin at the very inception of the business; that is, a person should plan for the end of the business from the very beginning. Taking this approach, the exit planning process integrates the personal aspirations of the entrepreneur with the starting point of the exit planning process. This chapter will examine the various options for the actual exit process.

SELF-ASSESSMENT REVISITED

The first major component of an exit plan is an assessment of the wealth the entrepreneur aspires to realize from the sale of the business. As stated throughout this book, the entrepreneur is best served by integrating his wealth and income goals into the planning process. Wealth in a business is created by excess cash flows that potential buyers believe will continue into the future and provide an adequate return on their investment. Achieving this goal requires a history of positive cash flow, an industry that holds the promise for continued growth or stability, and, most often, a business that can continue after the entrepreneur exits the firm. This last item is why many small service businesses have very little value in a sale. Because the owner is the main source of revenue, that revenue is dependent on his reputation and business relationships. The promise for continued cash flow is not there. Therefore, entrepreneurs should make sure that their aspirations match reality and that they do not have unrealistic expectations of wealth based on their exit from the business. An understanding of valuation, as presented in the previous chapter, is beneficial to creating realistic wealth objectives.

For example, a husband and wife team ran a successful commercial landscaping company for over two decades. Although during the peak season they employed dozens of seasonal workers, there were only four full-time, year-round employees, including the two of them. The business had several hundred thousand dollars of profit every year. When the owners started the process of selling their business, they thought they could sell it for several times their annual profit. However, potential buyers consistently shied away from serious negotiations. All saw a problem that the owners failed to recognize. All the contracts the business had were based on long-term personal relationships the couple had with a few customers. None of the potential buyers believed that these customers would stay on once the company was sold. This is an example of a service business that is too dependent on the entrepreneur to have much value once the owners exit the business.

Another key part of exit planning involves the issue of timing. First, entrepreneurs have to consider their personal preferences based on their own life and career planning. When does the entrepreneur want to retire? Does she want to participate in more start-ups? Would she enjoy a change in career after leaving the venture, such as consulting, teaching, or working with other entrepreneurs on their ventures? Second, entrepreneurs have to consider the market opportunity for a sale. In some industries, the sale of a business is a fairly rational and consistent process over time. In other industries, periods of consolidation may be episodic, requiring quick decisions about selling because the next opportunity for the desired price may be far in the future, if it occurs at all. This has been the case in many emerging industries, such as personal computers in the 1980s, managed health-care in the early 1990s, and Internet companies in the late 1990s. Many entrepreneurs in these industries failed to understand that the sustainability of these industries, or at least the sustainability of their growth, would not last indefinitely. Many held on to ownership of their businesses well beyond their real peak in value, hoping that the value would continue to go up. After high-growth industries reach their peak, the subsequent drop in value can be so rapid that many entrepreneurs fail to implement an exit strategy in time to get any real value out of their ventures. Knowing when to exit, therefore, requires attention to both personal and market factors, and these two factors do not always intersect. Ignoring either one can result in exiting too early or too late.

As discussed in Chapter 2, the process of self-assessment plays an important role throughout the life of an entrepreneurial venture. Aspirations for income and wealth can change over time due to changes in the entrepreneur's family situation, situations where ventures either exceed or fall well short of initial expectations, or dramatic changes in market conditions. Such changes will have an impact on the expectations these entrepreneurs have when exiting their businesses. The exit process, if well executed, relies on careful, thoughtful self-assessment throughout the growth and development of a business venture. Exit planning should be an ongoing process because most business exits do not happen as the entrepreneur originally intended.

For example, market fluctuations dramatically changed the exit plans of a group of entrepreneurs in the health-care industry. During start-up, they envisioned building a modest business that would generate strong cash flow for about twenty years until the time came for the partners to retire. However, their concept caught fire in the marketplace and the business appeared to have potential well beyond even their most optimistic start-up assumptions. Realizing that their initial exit plan failed to account for the wealth generated by the value of their growing venture, the entrepreneurs changed their plans and their expectations. Their time frame for exit decreased by a decade to roughly ten years due to the newfound potential of their business. Then a major change developed in the health-care industry. Large sums of money flowing in from public offerings persuaded these companies to go on an acquisition binge. The entrepreneurs realized that their window for exit had just shortened to about three years, and they began to prepare their business for sale. They no longer believed the company could grow as large as they once thought, but they could realize a good return from a sale. Again, they had to adjust their expectations to be consistent with the new reality.

Economic changes also affect exit strategies. For example, many entrepreneurs who had planned to exit from their businesses and retire in the late 2000s had to postpone their plans due to the Recession of 2008. Such financial downturns can reduce valuations due to declining profit margins suffered by many businesses. Valuations can also decline in a recession due to fewer potential buyers for their businesses. Companies or individuals who may in the past have had interest in buying a business may no longer have the ability to finance the deal or may just be more reluctant due to economic uncertainty. Even if valuations do not diminish, entrepreneurs postpone their exit as their own personal financial portfolios suffer with recessionary conditions. With a declining stock market, the entrepreneur may be forced to hold off and wait for a higher valuation for their business to offset the loss in wealth in their overall portfolio.

Not all changes in exit plans are financial in nature. For example, a highly successful retail coffee store chain was sold because the owner's wife became seriously ill. The entrepreneur wanted to care for her and be more available to parent their teenage child. Up until his wife's illness, the entrepreneur had no intention of selling his business.

When a business has more than one owner, the challenge is to consider the potentially differing aspirations of the various partners. The self-assessment process becomes not just an individual activity but also one that all the partners should share openly with each other. An example of such a challenge can be seen in an engineering firm in which the three partners had quite different aspirations and expectations. One was interested in building a large, possibly national company. The second wanted to create a sustainable business and possibly move into other ventures. The third hoped simply to harvest as much wealth as possible, as quickly as possible. The partners did not openly discuss these differences during the start-up phase. When a consolidation period began in their industry, an opportunity arose to sell the business for an excellent return. This caused the partners to squabble, however, because one was anxious to sell, one was not at all ready to exit, and one was uncertain and hesitant. The potential buyers were worried by the dissent among the owners and eventually walked away from the deal. The partner who wanted a quick exit grew bitter over the failed sale, and the three never fully regained their earlier trust in each other. Clearly, a full, frank discussion of aspirations before they started and throughout their growth could have prevented this unfortunate situation.

THE ETHICAL SIDE OF THE ENTREPRENEUR'S TRANSITION

Much of the focus on exit up to this point has been on financial matters. After all, the basic purpose of the exit is to execute a transition in the ownership of the busi-

Figure 16.1   **The Exit Planning Process**

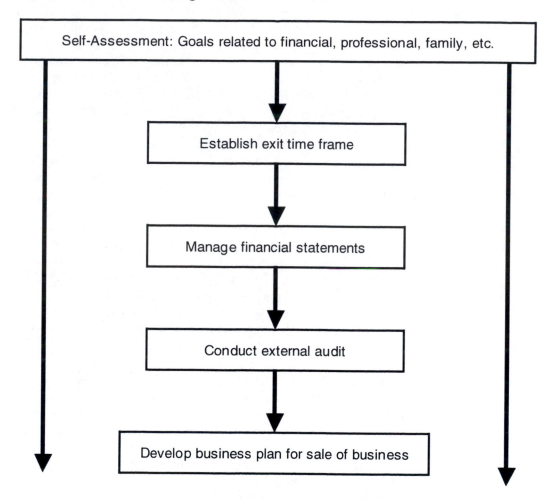

ness. However, the entrepreneur still retains the opportunity to fulfill the original vision during this final transition. That is, the culture and the values the entrepreneur brought to the business can be factored into the exit process. Who is chosen to be the next owner and how the transaction is structured can be deliberate decisions made in a way that is consistent with the entrepreneur's values. Some entrepreneurs take great care to find buyers for their businesses who espouse cultures consistent with their own. Their intent is to ensure that employees, customers, and other stakeholders will continue to be treated as they have been under the original ownership. These entrepreneurs believe in a commitment to these stakeholders even as they leave the business. Factoring in these types of considerations can limit the number of potential buyers, however, and the law of supply and demand suggests that such an exit strategy can reduce the ultimate sale price.

    A decision not to take the venture public can result in even more money being left on the table in an exit. While public offerings can create tremendous wealth, they often create a fundamental shift in the business to a more financially based culture due to the pressures for financial returns in the public equity market. For example, when Dale Merrick, Bob Wahlstedt, and Lee Johnson started Reell Precision Manufacturing (RPM), a small Midwestern company, they envisioned a very specific culture they wanted to foster in their business. When they decided to exit the firm they founded, they could have easily taken their business public or sold it to a public firm, but they wanted to make sure that the unique culture they had created in their business would continue for the benefit of their employees and customers. With that goal in mind, they opted to pursue an employee stock ownership plan (ESOP) that resulted in the founders realizing only a fraction of the value they could have received with other exit strategies. Their feeling of obligation toward those who helped them build their company was more important than the money they earned from the sale. The exit process can require courageous acts if the entrepreneur intends to focus on more than just the financial considerations of the exit transaction.

A MODEL OF EXIT PLANNING

Several additional steps are involved in an exit plan beyond the setting of goals and time frames through the self-assessment process as discussed thus far in this chapter. Figure 16.1 displays a model of exit planning.

MANAGE FINANCIAL STATEMENTS

Analysis of the balance sheet may reveal several items that can impact the exit process. If possible, reducing outstanding loans is advantageous. In most business sales, the seller uses the proceeds to pay off any outstanding loans. Even if the buyer agrees to assume the liabilities, bankers can be hesitant to assign loans to a new entity with which they have no history. To illustrate this point, assume that three different businesses—Company A, Company B, and Company C—are being sold at a price of $1 million each. All three are subchapter S-corporations and none has significant assets that could be subject to the capital gains tax. That is, the proceeds of the sale will pass through to the owner as regular income (not an unusual situation for a service-related business). Two of the owners have used bank debt to fund their business and still have balances on their loans. Company A's sale is a distress sale, and it still owes the bank $750,000. Company B owes $250,000. Both companies borrowed for working capital using accounts receivable as collateral.

	Company A	Company B	Company C
Sale price	$1,000,000	$1,000,000	$1,000,000
Loans due	750,000	250,000	-0-
Gross proceeds	$250,000	$750,000	$1,000,000
Personal tax (assume 40% rate)	400,000	400,000	400,000
Net proceeds	(150,000)	350,000	600,000

Taxes on all three sales are based on the proceeds of the sale and do not take into account any outstanding liabilities. Company B's owner will receive only 35 percent of the sale price; Company C's owner will receive 60 percent. Company A is a distress sale and its owner will owe more tax on the sale than she received after paying off its loans!

Certain assets can actually be a detriment to a sale. Any nonproductive assets—buildings, vehicles, or equipment not in use—should be sold off prior to entering into the sale process. Nonproductive assets lower the buyer's perception of the potential return on the investment. Moving property and buildings into a separate entity may also be beneficial, because many buyers do not want to own real estate. The entrepreneur can then either keep the property and buildings and receive rental income or sell the property to someone who specializes in owning commercial real estate. If the buyer wants the property, the seller can sell both the operating and the property businesses in the same transaction.

Any property leases should be kept short-term toward the time of a sale. Such leases are considered liabilities that must be assumed by the buyer and can actually reduce the cash flow value to the buyer. The buyer may already have space in which to consolidate operations or may have other, cheaper space in mind.

The income statement and statement of cash flows should be monitored to ensure that progress is being made toward the desired level of profitability. Remember that the key objective is to maximize cash flow because EBITDA is the main component of valuation. Minimizing nonproductive overhead can also be a significant benefit, for example, keeping administrative staff as small as possible and not overspending on space for administrative offices. Furthermore, unless it is essential to the operations or perceived quality of the business, expensive office space should be avoided so that the maximum amount of cash flows to the bottom line.

CONDUCT AN EXTERNAL AUDIT

Most buyers will request three years of financial statements audited by an outside public accounting firm. A review of the financial statements is cheaper and usually adequate for bankers, but most buyers will want an audit. However, this is generally not the case for small businesses, especially those with sales under $500,000. Audits cost about $10,000 to $25,000 for businesses under $10 million in sales if they are performed each year. A retroactive audit (one going back in time at the time of sale) for three years is much more expensive. If the business has significant inventory, it will need a supervised inventory count for at least a few years even if a retroactive audit is completed. It is a good idea to begin the audit process if a sale is expected to occur in the next few years.

Chapter 7 contained suggestions for hiring and managing outside accountants. The same suggestions apply when hiring and managing an audit firm. It is wise to get bids from two or three auditors as their fees and procedures can vary significantly. Price is not the only factor to consider; a good personality match with the business and its team is also important. The auditors' understanding of the industry can also have a major impact on the quality and cost of the audit. During negotiations, billing procedures and any concerns over charges should be discussed openly and honestly. To use resources efficiently, the business's own staff should handle the most routine tasks rather than incur unnecessary auditing expense.

DEVELOP A BUSINESS PLAN FOR THE SALE OF THE BUSINESS

A well-developed business plan can assist the process of selling the venture. What is being purchased, in effect, is the potential of the firm. If that potential can be supported and substantiated by a business plan, the buyer may be willing to pay more for the business. The plan should be comprehensive, including a thorough industry analysis, marketing plan, financial plan, and operating plan for at least three to five years in the future. Of particular interest to the potential buyers are the marketing plan and its link to future revenue forecasts, as discussed in Chapter 4. If the plan strongly supports future growth, the seller may be able to negotiate for a higher multiple. In addition to most-likely-case forecasts, the plan should include a best-case scenario to show the upside potential of the venture and all assumptions tied to this scenario.

EXIT OPTIONS

An entrepreneur may consider a number of different exit options before choosing one. Often, several of these options may present themselves simultaneously. The notion of transfer of ownership most likely emerges when an entrepreneur thinks about an exit strategy. However, some options may not represent such a clean transition, and a few involve the business simply ceasing operations entirely. A variety of factors should be considered when evaluating each alternative exit strategy. Which gives the best financial return? Which generates the most cash to the entrepreneur? How do the various options fit with the nonfinancial aspects of the entrepreneur's aspirations? Are there overriding tax implications that come into play? How can the entrepreneur ensure that the vision, culture, and values nurtured in the business continue beyond the present ownership and control? Table 16.1 summarizes the options discussed in this section.

OWNERSHIP TRANSFER

The most common form of ownership sale is an *asset sale*. In an asset sale, the buyer purchases all the assets tied to the operations of the business, usually excluding cash and accounts receivable. The liabilities remain the responsibility of the seller. Buyers usually prefer an asset sale because they can depreciate many of the assets they purchase, thus reducing future taxes. Buyers also have a desire to avoid any unknown liabilities, including such items as unforeseen tax assessments or lawsuits that may be filed after the closing. There are some disadvantages to the seller in an asset sale. First, any taxes owed by the seller that arise from the sale of the business accrue at the time of the sale in their entirety. In some types of transactions, some of the tax liability can be deferred. Also, the price in an asset purchase is usually less at face value than with other kinds of transactions. The advantages to the seller are that the

Table 16.1

Summary of Exit Options

Type of exit	Advantages to the seller	Disadvantages to the seller
Ownership transfer		
Asset sale	Cash sale	Immediate tax on full sale
	Clean break for entrepreneur possible	Lower face value sale price
	Earn-out possible if price disagreement cannot be resolved	
Stock sale	Higher face value of sale price	If sale of stock is for stock in the acquiring company seller's actual proceeds are subject to the price volatility of the stock received and there may be restrictions on the sale of the stock
	No future liabilities related to the business	
Partial or limited transfer		
Merger	Potential synergies of companies brought together	Cultures may clash
	Tax deferment of sale price	Limited opportunities to receive immediate cash
IPO	Taking some cash out of business possible	Limits on sale of stock
	Can use funds to bring in professional management	
Strategic alliance	Reduces risk to existing value of business	May take a long time, if at all, to actually exit
ESOP	Can maintain culture of business	May take a long time, if at all, to actually exit
Family business transfer	Can maintain culture of business	Challenges of generational succession
Bankruptcy as exit	Orderly end to business	Ethical challenges
		Results in no realization of wealth from business
		Can hurt entrepreneur's ability to fund future deals
Liquidation	May result in more value, especially for service business	No value for going concern
		Can be viewed as "failure"

sale is usually for cash and allows the entrepreneur to make a clean break from the business if both sides agree.

In some asset sales, the buyer and seller cannot agree on a price, but both sides are eager to move ahead with the transaction. In such cases, the deal can be structured with an earn-out option. With an earn-out, a base price is mutually determined. Then, if the business that was purchased realizes the growth that the seller predicted, the buyer pays an agreed-upon premium or bonus. However, if the business fails to meet expectations, the price that was paid probably reflects a fair price. Both sides can thus benefit from an earn-out. Earn-out agreements need to be carefully structured to avoid potential lawsuits resulting from the seller's belief that the buyer ran the business in such a way as to compromise the seller's opportunity to achieve the earn-out.

Another form of ownership transfer is with a *stock sale.* In a stock sale the buyer purchases the stock in the selling company. The advantage to buyers is that they are purchasing an ongoing business with employees, customers, locations, and immediate cash flow. The advantage to sellers is that they will typically get a much higher valuation than they would with an asset sale. The seller also has no potential future liability for anything related to the business. The buyer may pay for the business in cash or in stock of the buyer's company. The advantage of cash is that the seller knows exactly what the purchase price is. However, if the payment is in stock there may be an opportunity to recognize even more proceeds from the transaction if the buyer is a publicly traded company with an appreciating stock price. On the other hand, a significant disadvantage to the seller involves potential volatility in the buyer's stock. There are usually restrictions on the sale of the stock in the buyer's company now held by the seller. There can be restrictions on how many shares can be sold at a time and when they can be sold. Thus, stock sales can hold considerable risk for the seller. For example, a publicly traded company called Coastal Health Care used its company stock in the late 1980s and early 1990s to purchase physicians' medical practices. The stock showed many months of consistently increasing prices, which was very attractive to physicians wishing to realize an even greater return for the sale of their practice. Some saw the value of the stock they now owned in Coastal double in value in only a few months after they closed their sale to Coastal. However, the Coastal stock began to fall into disfavor and experienced a sudden, dramatic fall in market price. Many sellers were unable to sell their Coastal stock before it had lost most of its market value. Consequently, the high prices they thought they had received for the sale of their businesses vanished.

This is not a unique story. A major bust occurred in a speculative health-care stock market during the early 1990s, and an even bigger bust emerged in the speculative bubble of dot-com stocks in the late 1990s. Many sellers in this industry never truly realized the gains they thought they had received on the sale of their business due to the crash in the dot-com equity market.

PARTIAL OR TRANSITIONAL TRANSFER

Several exit strategies do not involve a complete or at least an immediate transfer of ownership. These strategies are varied in their structure and intended outcomes, yet all of them typically include an ongoing ownership and often a management role for the entrepreneur.

In some instances, two or more businesses are brought together to form an entirely new entity, a transaction called a *merger.* A merger may be preferred if both entities are approximately the same size and the owners desire to demonstrate that neither side is taking over the other's business. The shareholders of both entities trade their stock for stock in the new company at a predetermined ratio based on the relative value of each company. For example, assume that Company A is valued at $4 million and Company B at $5 million and that both have the same number of shares outstanding. The owners agree that Company A shareholders will receive four shares in New Company for each share they currently own, and Company B shareholders will get five shares in New Company for each of their Company B shares.

One major challenge in the merger of two companies is blending two distinct cultures that may be very different. This has certainly been the experience in the merger of large corporations. The merger of Chrysler and Daimler-Benz resulted in many clashes between two entrenched and proud corporate cultures. Even in smaller companies, mergers can be traumatic. Cultural fit should be examined during negotiations and due diligence for any potential merger. In fact, both parties should recognize cultural fit as a deciding factor in whether or not to proceed with the merger. Otherwise, mergers can go terribly awry. For example, two service companies were considering a merger; we will refer to them as Company X and Company Y. Company X had a strong market position in two states, and Company Y in three neighboring states. Company X was known for its marketing strengths, and Company Y for its operating efficiencies. The lead entrepreneurs of both companies believed the complementary nature of the fit between the two companies was compelling. Because they were of comparable size, both having revenues between $10 and $20 million, a merger was considered to be the best form of integrating the two companies. Additionally, because the owner of Company X was interested in phasing out his day-to-day operation of the company, management control was not a contentious issue. However, as the negotiations began to move to detailed discussions and disclosures, it became clear that the businesses had fundamental cultural differences. In Company X, the financial function was viewed as a supporting system aiding managers to make quality decisions, while in Company Y it was a watchdog that constantly challenged even the smallest expenditures and used the budget to keep operating units under its control. Company X sought out new opportunities, but only after detailed planning and evaluation. Company Y preferred taking risks and was consequently willing to start new ventures with little or no formal planning. Company X had a decentralized structure; Company Y had a highly centralized and formalized structure. Even the boards of directors, which would be merged in the new company, operated differently. In the end, the companies realized that trying to blend two opposite cultures would create overwhelming obstacles to a successful merger, and the negotiations were terminated.

Another strategy for ownership transfer is an initial public offering (IPO), discussed in Chapter 14. With an IPO, the founding entrepreneurs may have the opportunity to move out of day-to-day management if they so choose or if it is in the best interests of the shareholders. An IPO also can provide the founding entrepreneurs with the chance to take some money out of their business. Entrepreneurs will normally be limited to how much and how often they can sell stock, however, and the market will likely look negatively or suspiciously on those who sell too many shares. Nevertheless, an IPO can mark the beginning of a transitional time for many entrepreneurs.

Some entrepreneurs find a *strategic alliance* to be a useful transitional strategy. A typical strategic alliance is a long-term fixed contract between two companies to engage in a defined business relationship. An entrepreneur may make a strategic alliance with a much larger firm that could result in a sale of the entrepreneur's business to that company at some point in time. Sometimes a strategic alliance involves some equity investment in the entrepreneurial venture by the larger firm. Large companies use the strategic alliance to help in new product or market development. For example, Vical is a company located in San Diego, California, that is currently developing new DNA-based pharmaceuticals. Large drug manufacturing companies like Merck were among the early investors in Vical. A strategic alliance like the one between Vical and Merck can provide an entrepreneurial venture access to capital and expertise from the larger company. No matter what the structure of the strategic alliance is initially, the larger company often decides to purchase the entrepreneurial venture outright should its product become marketable or shows signs of rapid growth.

An employee stock ownership plan (ESOP) is a tax-advantaged mechanism whereby employees become owners of the company. Employees can use the company's pretax dollars to fund the plan or to support an ESOP loan. The Internal Revenue Service and the Department of Labor tightly regulate ESOPs, so care must be taken to properly structure and administer the program. There are reasons beyond the financial advantages for using an ESOP as an exit strategy. For example, Reell Precision Manufacturing established an ESOP to ensure the continuation of the culture and values that the founding partners had established for the business. Many of the employees had come to work for Reell because of its appealing culture, and the founders wanted to create an exit strategy for themselves that would allow these employees to carry this culture well into the future. After several years, the ESOP still does not have total ownership but shares it with the founders and their families. An ESOP is not a strategy that leads to a quick and clean exit for the entrepreneur, but it does create a mechanism to begin to liquidate the founders' ownership in the firm.

The owners of family businesses often desire to pass on ownership and control of a venture over multiple generations. By definition, family businesses face transitions as they pass from generation to generation. In some family businesses, the transition involves a buyout and transfer of control from one generation to the next. In others, the process is more gradual and integrates estate planning in the transition of ownership. No matter what the planned transition strategy, a succession plan is essential, as it not only designates who will succeed the current generation's management, but how those successors will become prepared to fill the leadership role. This often includes a policy requiring family members to work outside the family business for a number of years.

BANKRUPTCY AND TERMINATION OF OPERATIONS

Some entrepreneurs do not have the opportunity to take an exit strategy that provides for the realization of wealth from their businesses. Due to a variety of causes that are not always within the control of the entrepreneur, a business may no longer have the viability to continue into the future. Typically, the business faces *insolvency* when its ability to meet future liabilities is in doubt. Some entrepreneurs find that the process of bankruptcy is the best method for facing this problem. A business bankruptcy can take two basic forms. The first, known as a Chapter 11 bankruptcy, allows a business to reorganize. The terms of its debts are changed, and a plan is submitted to a bankruptcy court that will allow the business to again become a going concern. Management keeps control of the assets necessary to ensure the operation of the business. The court protects the company from any attempts by its creditors to collect debts outside of the plan. Under the second type, a Chapter 7 bankruptcy, the court appoints a trustee to oversee the liquidation of the assets of the business, the proceeds of which are used to pay its creditors. Under a Chapter 7 bankruptcy, the business ceases operations. Ethical issues come into play with a bankruptcy, and the entrepreneur should not use bankruptcy as a convenient option to reduce debt obligations. Many of the creditors involved in a bankruptcy are likely to be entrepreneurs and small business owners themselves; they can be adversely affected by a nonpayment of money owed to them. One entrepreneur noted in a speech to a class of young entrepreneurs that he was now a millionaire, but it took him three bankruptcies to get rich. What he did not acknowledge is the damage he caused to others on his path to financial success.

Some entrepreneurs exit their businesses through a planned liquidation without the need of bankruptcy protection. This strategy is most effective if the parts of the business—that is, its assets—are worth more than selling the company as a going concern. The entrepreneur sells off the assets, pays off any outstanding debts, and then keeps any residual proceeds as the wealth taken out of the venture. Many service businesses find that their ventures have very little value as going concerns. The owner of a successful landscaping company with over $2 million in revenues, for example, found that the value of his business as a going concern was less than he was able to get by selling off his equipment and buildings separately.

Figure 16.2 displays a checklist that summarizes the exit planning process. The next section will discuss the specific process of selling a business, should that become the exit option of choice for an entrepreneur.

THE PROCESS OF SELLING A BUSINESS

When contemplating the sale of a business as a going concern, some entrepreneurs mistakenly look to their book value or retained earnings to assess value. However, as discussed in Chapter 15, valuation is based on the buyer's expectations of future cash flows. Even historic cash flow matters only to the degree that it predicts future cash flow. For example, a corrugated box manufacturer decided to sell his business after learning that a large national company was going to build a plant in his geographic market. Although his company was historically quite profitable, the national competitor was likely to have a devastating impact on his sales because he would be unable to compete on price. When he decided to sell his company, he tried to value the business based on a steady record of historically positive cash flow. As soon as potential buyers learned of the new competition in his market, however, their interest immediately vanished. A purchase is based on future cash flow, and this business's future was clearly in jeopardy. A realistic estimation of value should be the starting point for any attempt to sell a business. Figure 16.2 displays the sale process.

Figure 16.2 **Sale Process of a Business**

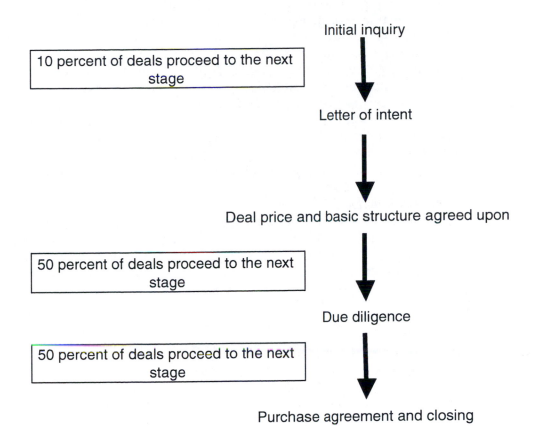

The sale process normally begins with an initial inquiry by a prospective buyer. The entrepreneur's potential interest in selling is determined, and some basic information is exchanged. Until a confidentiality agreement is signed, only general, nonfinancial information should be shared. Only about one in ten inquiries typically goes to the next stage, the letter of intent. This stage generally begins with both sides entering into a confidentiality agreement. The letter of intent includes a proposed initial price and will require a right to exclusive negotiations in return for the costs the potential buyer will incur related to the potential acquisition. The sale of a business is usually characterized by tough negotiations. Initial offers are not always close to true value. Once a price and basic deal structure are agreed upon, the deal moves into a more complex stage. However, about half of all prospective deals never get beyond the letter of intent.

In the next stage, the parties enter into due diligence. At this point, it is no longer possible to keep the sale secret from employees because of the process itself. In due diligence, all details of the company are disclosed, including an analysis of accounts, inventory, contracts, and employee records. The seller needs to honestly disclose everything, even possibly embarrassing details, because surprises that are discovered without being disclosed first can adversely affect the sale price or even derail the deal. The price can change significantly during due diligence based on the information that is disclosed. The seller also should use this time to learn about the buyer by contacting other companies purchased by the buyer and gathering data to assess the culture of the buyer. Again, about half of the remaining deals do not proceed past the due diligence stage of negotiation.

In the final stage, attorneys will develop the purchase agreement and prepare for closing. Even at this late stage, about half of the remaining active deals will end before the final closing due to disagreements over document language and specific terms of the purchase agreement, which means that less than 1 percent of inquiries ultimately result in a closed deal. Therefore, it is important to continue to run the business wholeheartedly because the entrepreneur will own it up until closing, which may never happen.

Transaction costs to sell a business are high. Most experienced entrepreneurs and experts will recommend that only an attorney with expertise in mergers and acquisitions should handle the sale. However, they also will recommend that the entrepreneur make sure to stay in control of the process. In complex businesses or in highly emotional situations, the entrepreneur may want to engage a business broker or investment banker to handle the negotiations.

Postexit Issues

Obviously, life does not end for the entrepreneur after exiting the business. Many entrepreneurs experience what is known as *seller's remorse*. That is, they have second thoughts about the wisdom of selling the business, the specific terms of the deal, or the way that the new owners are running the venture. One entrepreneur reported feeling quite depressed after realizing that she would never be able to just walk into her business any time she felt like it—because it was no longer hers! Experts in mergers and acquisitions find that seller's remorse is actually quite a common feeling, and they will often warn their clients that they will probably experience some degree of remorse when they sell their businesses.

These same experts also caution their clients to take time before starting new endeavors. Just like a jilted lover, entrepreneurs can make impulsive decisions on the rebound from selling their business. By taking the time to do periodic self-assessments and by remembering their personal aspirations, entrepreneurs will be more likely to make wise and reasoned choices about their next steps. Making sure that career choices are part of a broader life plan can keep such decisions in perspective.

Summary

This chapter presented a model for exit planning. By preparing well in advance of the actual sale of the venture, the entrepreneur has a better chance of meeting the objectives for the business. The process of exit planning includes doing ongoing self-assessment, determining the desired time frame of the exit, managing the financial statements, hiring an external auditor, and developing a business plan for the sale. Entrepreneurs can pursue a variety of exit options based on the situation and their personal and professional goals. These options include a complete or partial transfer of ownership or the possibility of simply ceasing operations. Whichever option is finally chosen, it is important for entrepreneurs to use their personal aspirations as a guide to this critical process.

DISCUSSION QUESTIONS

1. Why is timing such an important issue in planning to exit a business?
2. Discuss the factors that entrepreneurs should consider when planning their exit strategies.
3. Discuss the advantages and disadvantages of the various exit options. Give specific examples of each.
4. Examine the ethical issues related to the exit options discussed in this chapter.

OPPORTUNITIES FOR APPLICATION

1. Interview an entrepreneur to determine what exit planning has been done for the business. Evaluate any gaps that exist in the exit plan and how those gaps may be remedied.
2. Write an exit plan for a new business venture you are developing. Reflect on the self-assessment you completed in Chapter 2 to understand specific goals and aspirations that shape your plan. Make sure to examine any postexit plans that you can or should make at this time. Remember, it is never too early to begin exit planning, even during the start-up process!

REFERENCES

Bagley, C., and C. Dauchy. 2007. *The Entrepreneur's Guide to Business Law.* 3d ed. New York: West.

"Bankruptcy Basics." http://bankruptcy.findlaw.com/bankruptcy/bankruptcy-basics.

Fenn, D. 1997. "Business 101: Family-Business Planning." *Inc.* (July). http://www.inc.com/articles/1998/07/14582.html.

Foundation for Enterprise Development. http://www.fed.org.

Fraser, J. 1999. "What Do Buyers Really Want?" *Inc.* (July). http://www.inc.com/articles/1999/07/13637.html.

Gabriel, C. 1998. "Selling Your Business." *Inc.* (November). http://www.inc.com/magazine/19981101/1035.html.

Payne, W. 2002. "Choosing Your Exit Strategy." http://www.entrepreneurship.org/Resources/Detail/Default .aspx?id=10672.

Rosen, C. 1998. "Employee Ownership: The Basics." *Inc.* (September). http://www.inc.com/articles/1998/09/15799.html.

Savage, D. 2000. *Cases on Reell Precision Manufacturing.* Unpublished.

Vical. "Shaping the Future of Vaccines." http://www.vical.com.

Index

Italic page references indicate boxed text.

Access Group, 161
Accountants, working with, 137–138, 278
Accounting as language of business, 3–4, 49
Accounting equation, 31–32, *33*
Accounts payable, 34, *36*, 37, *38*, 47
Accounts receivable, 37, *39*, 44–45
Accounts receivable turnover ratios, 132
Accredited investors, 201
Accrual-based income statement, 141
Accumulated depreciation, 41
Acid test ratio, 131
Active Capital (nonprofit), 196
Activity ratios, 132
Administrative costs, 89
Administrative expenses and overhead, 73, 179–181
Administrative salaries, 181
Advertising tools, 186–190
Aggressive banks, 212
American One-Way Inc., 66, *67*, 68
Angel investors, 69, 194–199, *199. See also*
    Investors
Aspirations, entrepreneur's financial, 22, 86–87,
    159–160
Assessment of risk sensitivity, 92–93
Asset-based lenders, 213, *214*
Asset sale, 279–281
Asset turnover, 134
Assets
  on balance sheet, 45–47, *45*
  categories of, 34, *35*

Assets *(continued)*
  current, 44, 47, 129–131
  in exit planning, 278
  intangible, 46–47
  long-term, 44, 48
  noncurrent, 46
  owner's equity and, 32, *33*, 41, *42*
  required rate of return and, 11
  return on, 134–135
Assumptions, entrepreneur's
  inventory of, 88–89
  tracking, 123–125, *125*
Audit, external, 278–279

"Back-of-the-envelope" type of calculation,
    77–78
Bagley, C., 137
Balance sheet, 41, 44–48, *45*, 89, 252
Balloon payment, 216
Bankers, working with, 219–224, *220*, *221*
Bankruptcy, 283–284
Banks
  investment, 239–240
  long-term debt and, 216
  short-term debt and, 211–213
  start-up business and, 157–158
Banners, advertising, 189
Best-case scenario, creating, 57–58, 92
Betas, 10–11
Billing
  by the hour, 60–61
  by the job, 61–62

Blechman, B., 225

Blogs, 188

"Book building" process, 242–243

Book value of company, 32, *33*, *37*, 41, *42*, 48

Bookkeeper, 137

Bootstrapping
  administrative overhead and, 179–181
  defining, 83, 176–179, *179*
  employee expenses and, 181–183
  ethical issues, 190–191
  expense forecasting and, 83
  lean start-ups, 177
  life cycle of business venture and, 178, *179*
  marketing, 185–190
  operating expenses and, 183–184
  overview, 176, 191

Breakeven analysis, 77–78

Brochures, advertising, 189

Brown, Mike, 161

Burn rate, 91

Burton, Sally, 125–126

Business cards, 187–188

Business funding, stages of, 233–234

Business model
  business plan and, 25–26
  diversity of, 158–159
  entrepreneurial financial management and, 25–26
  outside investors and, 204–205

Business Model Canvas, 204–205

Business plan
  business model and, 25–26
  entrepreneurial financial management and, 25–26, *27*
  family and friends financing and, 171–172
  integrated financial model and, 93
  marketing mix and, 55, *55*
  outline, *27*
  outside investors and, 204–205
  for selling business, 279
  venture capital financing and, 229–231, *230*

Business valuation
  discounted cash flow and, 254–266
    analysis, 250–251
    overview, 254–258, 266
    when equity isn't the only funding source, 265–266
  financing sources and, multiple, 265–266

Business valuation *(continued)*
  formal, 18–19
  free cash flow and
    defining, 258–259
    estimating for a year, 259
    estimating over six-year period, 259–260, *261*, *262*, 263–265, *263*
  information required for, basic, 252–254, *253*
  initial public offering advantage and, 238
  market comparison techniques, 266–270
  overview, 247, 270–271
  principles guiding
    discounted cash flow analysis, 250–251
    fair market value, 247–248
    future benefits, 249–250
    going-concern value, 249
    highest and best use, 249
    objectivity, 251–252, *251*
    overview, 247
    substitutes and alternatives, 250
  "quick and dirty" method of, 18–20, 87

Business ventures. *See also specific type*
  bootstrapping throughout cycle of, 178, *179*
  life cycle of, 22–24, *22*, 160, *179*, *180*
  types of
    high-growth, high-potential business, 159, 162–163, *163*
    lifestyle businesses, 158–159
    nonprofits, 89, 112, *113*, 114–115, *116–117*, 118–120
    small businesses, 159, 161–162, *162*

Capital, 228

Capital expenditures, 46, 73

Capital financing, 7

Capital leases, 47

Capital markets, 7

Capitalization policy, 46

Carter, N., 24

Cash, 34, *35*, 37, *38*, 44, 91–92

Cash conversion cycle, 151–152

Cash flow forecasts, 58–59

Cash flow management
  accrual-based income statement and, 141
  cash conversion cycle, 151–152
  effective, 149–152
  emotional aspects of, 152–153, *153*

Cash flow management *(continued)*
  entrepreneurial financial management and, 6
  measuring cash flow and, 141–142, *143*, 144
  negative operating cash flow and, 148
  net income and, 140–141
  operating cash flow and sales, 151
  overview, 6, 140, 153
  problems, 149–152
  Statement of cash flows
    components of, 141–142, *143*, 144
    creditors' use of, 148–149, *149*
    defining, 41, 48
    direct method of preparing, 144–145, *145*, *146*
    indirect method of preparing, 145–148, *147*
    investors' use of, 148–149, *149*
    of nonprofits, 89
Cash flow measurements, 141–142, *143*, 144
Cash flow statement. *See* Statement of cash flows
Certified Development Company (504) program, 219
CFO, 137
Change in net assets, 89
Changes in owner's equity statement, 41, 48
Chapter 7 bankruptcy, 284
Chapter 11 bankruptcy, 284
Chief financial officer (CFO), 137
Chrysler (car company), 282
Clark, Bill, 196
Coastal Health Care, 281
Collecting receivables, 149
Commission-based selling firms, 64–65, 81–82, *82*
Commitment letter, 222
Committed fixed costs, 75–76
Compensation, equity, 182–183
Competitive analysis, 56–57, *57*, 66
Confidentiality agreements, 205
Contracts, 228
Contribution format, 87
Contribution margin, 78
Controller, 137
Convertible promissory note, 198
Cornwall, J., 21, 24, 96
Corporate culture, 282
Corporate scandals, 5
Cost behavior
  expense forecasting and, 73–77
  fixed costs, 75–76, *75*

Cost behavior *(continued)*
  mixed costs, 76–77, *77*
  overview, 73
  variable costs, 73–74, *74*
Cost of goods sold, 34, *36*, 45–46, 72
Costs. *See also* Expenses
  administrative, 89
  defining, 72–73
  direct labor, 78, 88
  discretionary fixed, 76
  fixed, 75–76, *75*
  of goods sold, 34, *36*, 45–46, 72
  labor, 78, 88
  materials, 74, 78, 88
  mixed, 76–77, *77*
  program, 89
  raw material, 78, 88
  reporting, of initial public offering, 238
  variable, 73–74, *74*
Counsel, 228–229
Coverage ratios, 129, 135–136
Credibility, 229
Credit card debt, 217
Credit policies, 149
Credit risk, 211
Crowdfunding, 202–203
Culture, corporate, 282
Current assets, 44, 47, 129–131
Current liabilities, 44, 47, 130–131
Current maturities of long-term debt, 47
Current ratio, 130–131
Customer, knowing, 185
Cyclical sales firms, 65, 82–83

Daimler-Benz, 282
Danko, W., 18
Dauchy, C., 137
Days in payables, 152
Days sales outstanding (DSO) ratios, 132
Debt, 217. *See also* Liabilities; Long-term debt; Short-term debt
Debt financing
  bankers and, working with, 219–224, *220*, *221*
  debt overlooked by entrepreneurs, 217
  financing plan and, 225–226, *226*
  government funding through Small Business Administration, 217–219, *218*

Debt financing *(continued)*
  liabilities and, 208
  in life cycle of business, 220, *220*
  limitations of, 224–225
  loan documents, 222–224
  long-term debt
    banks, 216
    leasing companies, 216–217
    overview, 215–216
    real estate lenders, 217
  overview, 208, 226
  short-term debt
    institutional creditors, 210–215, *214*, *215*
    overview, 208–209
    trade credit, 209–210, *210*
Debt ratios, 136–137
Debt to equity, 136
Deferred revenues, 48
Depreciation, 46, 141
Dilution, 177
Direct labor costs, 78, 88
Direct mail marketing, 189–190
Direct method of preparing Statement of cash flows, 144–145, *145*, *146*
Disclosure of information, 238
Disconnect rate, 62–63
Discounted cash flow
  analysis, 250–251
  free cash flow and
    defining, 258–259
    estimating for a year, 259
    estimating over six-year period, 259–260, *261*, *262*, 263–265, *263*
  overview, 254–258, 266
  when equity isn't the only funding source, 265–266
Discretionary fixed costs, 76
Distribution place, 54–55
Diversifiable risk, 10
Diversification, 237
Dot.com businesses of 1990s, 5
DSO ratios, 132
Due diligence, standard, 236
DuPont model, 135

E-mail marketing, 189–190
Earnings Before Interest and Taxes (EBIT), 43, 87–88, 128

Earnings before Interest, Taxes, Depreciation, and Amortization (EBITDA), 18–19, 44, 147–148, 250, 254, 278
EBIT, 43, 87–88, 128
EBITDA, 18–19, 44, 147–148, 250, 254, 278
Education Foundation (NFIB), 140
EGC, 202
E.I. duPont de Nemours & Co., 135
Emerging growth company (EGC), 202
Employee contracts, 217
Employee expenses, 181–183
Employee leasing, 182
Employee stock ownership plan (ESOP), 277, 283
Ending value of investment, 256
Entrepreneurial financial management. *See also* Self-assessment
  business model and, 25–26
  business plan and, 25–26, *27*
  cash flow management and, 6
  components, 5–7
  defining, 5–7
  ethical decision making and, 12–14, *13*
  exit planning and, 7, 24
  financial goals and, 6
  financial reports and, 6
  financial statements and, 6
  financing sources and, 6
  forecasting and, 6, 52
  historical data and, lack of, 8
  investors' perspective and, 8
  model of, 7, *7*, *17*, *52*, *72*
  overview, 14
  risk and return concepts and, 9–12
  stakeholder analysis and, 12–14, *13*
  traditional finance and
    differences from, 8–11
    similarities to, 7–8
Entrepreneurial Mind blog, The (Cornwall), 96
Entrepreneurs
  assumptions
    inventory of, 88–89
    tracking, 123–125, *125*
  bankers and, working with, 219–224, *220*, *221*
  debt overlooked by, 217
  financial aspirations and, 22, 86–87
  language of business and, 3–4
  lifestyle changes and, 22

Entrepreneurs *(continued)*
  personal transactions and, *32*
  success of, measuring, 4–5
Entrepreneur's Guide to Business Law, The (Bagley
    and Dauchy), 137
Equipment, 34, *35*, 41, 73, 141, 180–181
Equity compensation, 182–183
Equity financing
  angel investors, 194–199, *199*
  crowdfunding, 202–203
  defining, 193
  in life cycle of business venture, 193, *194*
  limitations of, 203–204
  outside investors and, 204–206
  overview, 193, *194*, 206
  private placement, 200–202
  small business investment company, 193, 203
  strategic partners, 199–200
ESOP, 277, 283
Ethical decision making, 12–14, *13*
Ethical issues
  bootstrapping, 190–191
  exit planning, 275–277, *276*
Exit planning
  assets in, 278
  defining, 24, 273
  entrepreneurial financial management and, 7, 24
  ethical issues, 275–277, *276*
  issues after exit, 286
  model
    conduct external audit, 278–279
    develop business plan for sale of business, 279
    income statement, 278
    manage financial statements, 277–278
    overview, 277
    statement of cash flows, 278
  options
    bankruptcy, 283–284
    overview, 279
    ownership transfer, 279–281
    partial transfer, 281–283
    selling business, 284–286, *285*
    termination of operations, 283–284
    transitional transfer, 281–283
  overview, 7, 273, 286–287
  process, 274, *276*
  self-assessment and, 273–275

Expense forecasting
  bootstrapping and, 83
  breakeven analysis and, 77–78
  business type and
    commissioned-based sales firms, 81–82, *82*
    cyclical sales firms, 82–83
    manufacturing firms, 78–79
    recurring revenue firms, 80–81
    seasonal sales firms, 82–83
    service firms, 79–80
  cost behavior and, 73–77
  defining costs and, 72–73
  financial statements and, 6
  importance of, 73
  overview, 72, 83
Expenses. *See also* Costs
  administrative, 73, 179–181
  capital, 46, 73
  defining, 37
  employee, 181–183
  general, 73
  on income statement, 43
  interest, 44
  operating, 183–184
  selling, 72
External audit, 278–279
External financing sources. *See* Debt financing;
    Equity financing
External funds, 176. *See also* Debt financing;
    Equity financing

Facebook pages, 188–189
Factoring, 213–215, *215*
Fair market value principle, 247–248
Family and friends financing
  boundaries, keeping, 172
  business plan, 171–172
  information about business, providing accurate,
    172
  motivations, determining true, 171
  overview, 169–171
  tax planning, 172–174
FIFO, 45
Financial aspirations, 22, 86–87, 159–160
Financial goals. *See also* Self-assessment
  business model and, 25–26
  business plan and, 25–26, *27*

Financial goals *(continued)*
  entrepreneurial financial management and, 6
  income and, 17–20
  nonfinancial goals and, 20–21
  overview, 6, 17, 26
  revenue goals and, 6
  stages of funding and, 234
  wealth and, 17–20
Financial markets, 7
Financial performance, monitoring
  accountants, working with, 137–138
  assumptions, tracking, 123–125, *125*
  financial statement analysis, 127–129, *127*, *128*
  milestones, establishing, 125–126
  numbers, 123, 126, *127*
  operating cash flows and sales, 151
  overview, 123, 138
  ratio analysis, 129, 131–137
Financial reports, 4, 6
Financial statements. *See also specific type*
  accounting equation and, 31–32, *33*
  analysis, 127–129, *127*, *128*
  basic types
    balance sheet, 41, 44–48, *45*
    cash flow statement, 41, 48
    changes in owners' equity, 41, 48
    income statement, 41, 43–44, *43*
    overview, 41
  entrepreneurial financial management and, 6
  example, 32, *33*, 34, *35–36*, 37, *38–40*, 41
  in exit planning model, 277–278
  expense forecasting and, 6
  importance of, 3
  limitations of, 48–49
  overview, 31, 49
Financing activities, 142
Financing over life of business venture
  high-growth, high-potential business, 162–163, *163*
  misconceptions about, common, 157–158
  nature of business financing, 158–160
  overview, 157, 163–164
  small business with modest growth potential,
    161–162, *162*
Financing plan, 225–226, *226*
Financing sources. *See also* Bootstrapping; Debt
    financing; Equity financing; Start-up financing;
    Venture capital financing

Financing sources *(continued)*
  banks, 157–158
  business model and, 158–159
  entrepreneurial financial management and, 6
  financial aspirations and, 159–160
  fitting pieces together and, 160
  government funding through Small Business
    Administration, 217–219, *218*
  government grants, 158
  overview, 6
  personal assets, 166–167
  personal cash, 165–166
  personal credit, unsecured, 166–167
  relying on more than one, 158
  second job, 167
  second mortgage on property, 167
  seed financing, 161
  Small Business Administration, 158
  stage of business venture and, 160
  venture capitalists, 157, 163
First-in, First-out (FIFO), 45
First-round financing, 233–234
Fixed costs, 74–76, *75*
Flamholtz, E., 23
Forecasting. *See also* Expense forecasting; Revenue
    forecasting
  cash flow, 58–59
  entrepreneurial financial management and, 6, 52
  integrated financial model and, 90–91
  mistakes, 52–54
  overview, 6
  quantitative techniques, 65–66, *67*, 68
Form S-1 (SEC), 241–242
Formal business valuation, 18–19
4 Cs of venture capitalists, 218–229
4 Ps of marketing, 54–55, *55*
Free cash flow
  defining, 258–259
  estimating
    for one year, 259
    over six-year period, 259–260, *261*, *262*,
      263–265, *263*
Funding document, 93
Funds needed, determining, 89–90. *See also*
    Financing sources
Furnishings, office, 180–181
Future benefits principle, 249–250

GAAP, 34, 44, 47, 140
General expenses, 73
Generally Accepted Accounting Principles (GAAP), 34, 44, 47, 140
Godin, S., 185
Going-concern value principle, 249
Good faith, dealing in, 206
Goodwill, 47
Government funding, 217–219, *218*
Government grants, 158
Gross profit, 43
Growing Pains (Flamholtz and Randle), 23
Growth stage of business venture, *22*, 23–24
Guerrilla Financing (Blechman and Levinson), 225

Hagood, Charles, 161, 185
High-growth, high potential businesses, 159, 162–163, *163*, 230, *230*, 232–233. *See also* Venture capital financing
Highest and best use principle, 249
Historical data in measuring risk, 8, 11–12
Hockey stick forecast mistake, 53

Ibbotson, R.G., 255
Income, 17–20
Income statement
  accrual-based, 141
  for business valuation, 252
  contribution format, 87
  in exit planning model, 278
  expenses on, 43
  of merchandising company, 76, *77*
  of nonprofits, 89
  overview, 41, 43–44, *43*
  revenue on, 43
  reverse, 230
Independent contractors, 182
Indirect method of preparing statement of cash flows, 145–148, *147*
Industry trends, 55
Initial public offering (IPO)
  advantages of, 237–238
  disadvantages of, 238–239
  Form S-1 and, 241
  overview, 237
  ownership transfer of business and, 282

Initial public offering (IPO) *(continued)*
  process of
    certify price of offering, 241–242
    decide whether to underwrite, 240
    determine size of book, 242–243
    get paperwork in order, 241–242
    present road show, 241
    select investment banking firm, 239–240
    trade on first day, 243
Initial-stage financing, 233–234
Insolvency, 283–284
Institute of Business Appraisers, 268
Institutional creditors, 210–215, *214*, *215*
Intangible assets, 46–47
Integrated financial model
  assumptions and, inventory of, 88–89
  business plan and, 93
  EBIT and, 87–88
  financial aspirations and, 86–87
  forecasting and, 90–91
  funding document and, 93
  funds needed, determining, 89–90
  income statement and, 87
  overview, 86, 93–96, *94–95*
  risk sensitivity and, assessing, 92–93
  social ventures and, 89
  template spreadsheets
    nonprofit model, 112, *113*, 114–115, *116–117*, 118–120
    overview, 96
    product model, 96, *97*, 98–101, *102–103*, 104
    service model, 105, *106*, 107–108, *109–110*, 111–112
  time out of cash and, 91–92
Interest expense, 73
Interest income, 73
Interest rate, 212
Internal funds, 178
Internal Revenue Service (IRS), 151, 174, 248, 283
Interns, student, 182
Inventory
  asset, 34, *36*
  assumptions, 68
  control, 133
  management, 150, 184
  turnover ratios, 133
Investing activities, 141–142

Investors. *See also* Angel investors
  accredited, 201
  crowdfunding, 202–203
  in joint ventures, 195
  outside, 204–206
  perspective of, 8
  private placement, 200–202
  qualified, 201
  revenue forecasting and, 69
  strategic partners, 199–200
IPO. *See* Initial public offering
IRS, 151, 174, 248, 283

Jansen, B.J., 186
JOBS Act (2012), 202–203
Johnson, Lee, 277
Joint guarantees, 223
Joint investments, 195
Jumpstart Our Business Startups (JOBS) Act
    (2012), 202–203
Just-in-time inventory management, 184

Kawasaki, G., 186

Labor costs, 78, 88
Landstrom, H., 190
Language of business, 3–4, 49
Language of numbers, 3–4
Last-in, First-out (LIFO), 45–46
Late-round financing, 233–234
Lean start-ups, 177
Leasing, 47
Leasing companies, 216–217
Letters of intent, 206
Levinson, J., 185, 225
Liabilities
  on balance sheet, *45*, 47–48
  current, 44, 47, 130–131
  debt financing and, 208
  long-term, 44, 48
  overlooked by entrepreneurs, 217
  owners' equity and, 32, *33*, 41, *42*
Lifestyle businesses, 158
Lifestyle changes, 22
LIFO, 45–46
Line of credit, 212
Linear forecast mistake, 52–53

Liquidation value, 249
Liquidity, 44, 237
Liquidity ratios, 129–132
Loan documents, 222–224
Loan Guarantee Program, 218
Loan proposal, 222
Long-term assets and liabilities, 44, 48
Long-term debt
  current maturities of, 47
  financing
    banks, 216
    leasing companies, 216–217
    overview, 215–216
    real estate lenders, 217
Long-term returns, 255
Lopez, Carlos, 124

Manufacturing firms, 59–60, 78–79
Market comparison techniques, 266–270
Market niche, 185
Market research, 55–56
Market risk premium, 11
Market trends, 55
Marketing, bootstrap, 185–190
Marketing mix, 54–55, *55*
Marketing plan
  revenue forecasting and, 54–57, *57*
  revenue goals and, 6
Marketing tools, 186–190
Maturity stage of business venture, *22*, 24
Merchandising company's income statement, 76, *77*
Merger, 281–282
Merrick, Dale, 277
Message, marketing, 185
Milestones, establishing, 125–126
Millennial generation, 5
Millionaire Next Door, The (Stanley and Danko), 18
Mirror stock, 183
Mixed costs, 76–77, *77*
Money markets, 7
Most-likely scenario, creating, 58, 92

National Federation of Independent Business
    (NFIB), 140, 212
Naughton, M., 21
Negative operating cash flow, 148
Net assets, 32, *33*, *37*, 41, *42*, 48

Net income, 140–141

Net present value, 251

Newsletters, 189

NFIB, 140, 212

Noncurrent assets, 46

Nondiversifiable risk, 10

Nonfinancial goals, 20–22

Nonmonetary benefits, 183

Nonprofits
  administrative costs of, 89
  balance sheet of, 89
  cash flow statement of, 89
  change in net assets and, 89
  function of, 89
  general costs of, 89
  income statement of, 89
  integrated financial model template of, 112, *113*, 114–115, *116–117*, 118–120
  program costs of, 89

Notes payable, 34, *35*

Numbers and financial performance, 123, 126, *127*

Objectivity principle, 251–252, *251*

Operating activities, 141

Operating cash flows and sales, 151

Operating expenses, 43, 183–184

Operating income, 89

Operating leases, 47

Operating loss, 89

Operating margin, 87

Orfalea, Paul, 4

Osterwalder, A., 26

Ottenheimer, J., 126

Outside accountants, working with, 137–138, 278

Outside investors, working with, 204–206

Outsourcing production, 183

Overhead, administrative, 179–181

Owner's equity, 32, *33*, 37, 41, *42*, 48

Ownership transfer of business, 279–281

Partial transfer of business, 281–283

Partnership assessment, 24–25, 29–30

Pass-through entities, 172–174

Payroll, 150

Payroll taxes, 150–151

Performance dashboard, 124

Personal assets financing, 166–167

Personal cash financing, 165–166

Personal credit financing, unsecured, 166–167

Personal guarantees, 223

Personal transactions, *32*

Phantom stock, 183

Pigneur, Y., 26

Postexit issues, 286

Pre-launch stage of business venture, *22, 23*

Premium, risk, 11

Pricing, 54

Prime rate, 212

Private offering, 200–202

Private placement, 200–202

Product benefits, 185

Product model of integrated financial statements template, 96, *97*, 98–101, *102–103*, 104

Product positioning, 54

Profit multiple, 19

Profit targeting, 87

Profitability ratios, 129, 133

Profits, 4–5, 19, 43

Program costs, 89

Promissory note, convertible, 198

Promotion, 54–55

Property leases, 217, 278

Publicity, 190, 238

Qualified investors, 201

Quantitative forecasting techniques, 65–66, *67*, 68

Quantity, 54

"Quick and dirty" method of business valuation, 18–20, 87

Quick ratio, 131

"Quiet period," 242

Randle, Y., 23

Rate of return, 230, 253

Ratio analysis, 129, 131–137

Raw material costs, 78, 88

Real estate lenders, 217

Realization of wealth, 87

Recession (2008), 140, 204, 214, 228, 275

Recurring revenue firms, 62–64, 80–81

Reell Precision Manufacturing (RPM), 277

Regression analysis, 65–66

Relevant range of activity, 75

Reporting costs of initial public offering, 238

Required rate of return, 11
Return and risk, 9–11
Return on assets (ROA), 134–135
Return on sales, 133–134
Revenue forecasting
  business type and
    commissioned-based selling firms, 64–65
    cyclical sales firms, 65
    manufacturing firms, 59–60
    overview, 59
    recurring revenue firms, 62–64
    seasonal sales firms, 65
    service firms, 60–62
  cash flow forecasts and, 58–59
  financial goals and, 6
  forecasting mistakes and, 52–54
  importance of, 68–69
  investors and, 69
  marketing plan and, 54–57, *57*
  overview, 52, 69
  quantitative forecasting techniques and, 65–66, *67*, 68
  scenarios and, creating, 57–58, 92
  space and, 68
  staffing and, 68
Revenue goals and marketing plan, 6
Revenues, 43, 48
Reverse income statement, 230
Risk
  credit, 211
  debt ratios and, 136–137
  diversifiable, 10
  historical data in measuring, 8, 11–12
  nondiversifiable, 10
  premium, 11
  return and, 9–12
  sensitivity, assessing, 92–93
  total, 9–10
Risk-free rate, 11
RMP, 277
ROA, 134–135
Robert Morris Associates, 59
Rule 504 (SEC), 201

Salaries, administrative, 181
Sarbanes-Oxley law (2002), 197, 202
SBA loans, 158, 196, 217–219, *218*

SBIC, 193, 203–204
Seasonal sales firms, 65, 82–83
Seasonality of sales, 149–150
SEC, 201–203, 241–242
Second job financing, 167
Second mortgage on property financing, 167
Second-round financing, 233–234
Security and Exchange Commission (SEC),
    201–203, 241–242
Seed financing, 161
Self-assessment
  entrepreneurial financial management and, 21–22
  exit planning and, 273–275
  importance of, 21–24
  individual, 25, 28–29
  process, 24–25
Self-financing
  advantages of, 167–169, *169*
  disadvantages of, 167–169, *169*
  overview, 165–167
Seller's remorse, 286
Selling business
  business plan for, 279
  process of, 284–286, *285*
  seller's remorse and, 286
Selling expenses, 72
Sernovitz, A., 186
Service firms, 60–62, 79–80
Service model of integrated financial statements
    template, 105, *106*, 107–108, *109–110*,
    111–112
Several guarantees, 223
Shareholder agreements, 206
Shareholder assessment, 24–25, 29–30
Shatto, Allen, 184
Short-term debt
  asset-based lenders, 213, *214*
  banks, 211–213
  factoring, 213–215, *215*
  institutional creditors, 210–215, *214*, *215*
  overview, 208–209
  trade credit, 209–210, *210*
Signs, advertising, 189
Singleton, Kate, 5
Sinquefield, R.A., 255
Small Business Administration (SBA) loans, 158,
    196, 217–219, *218*

Small business investment company (SBIC), 193, 203–204

Small businesses, 159, 161–162, *162*

Social entrepreneurship, 96. *See also* Nonprofits

Social venture model of integrated financial statements template, 112, *113*, 114–115, *116–117*, 118–120

Social ventures. *See* Nonprofits

Solvency ratios, 129, 135–136

Space, 68, 180

Staffing and revenue forecasting, 68

Stakeholder analysis, 12–14, *13*

Stand-alone risk, 9–10

Standard deviation, 9

Stanley, T., 18

Start-up businesses
  banks and, 157–158
  lean, 177

Start-up financing
  family and friends
    business plan, 171–172
    information about business, providing accurate, 172
    motivations, determining true, 171
    overview, 169–171
    tax planning, 172–174
  overview, 165, *166*, 174–175
  self-financing
    advantages of, 167–169, *169*
    disadvantages of, 167–169, *169*
    overview, 165–167
  structure of funds invested, 174

Start-up stage of business venture, *22*, 23

Statement of cash flows
  components, 141–142, *143*, 144
  creditors' use of, 148–149, *149*
  defining, 41, 48
  direct method, 144–145, *145*, *146*
  in exit planning model, 278
  indirect method, 145–148, *147*
  investors' use of, 148–149, *149*
  of nonprofits, 89

Statement of Changes in Owners' Equity, 41, 48

Stefansic, Jim, 5

Stock options, 183

Stock sale, 281

Stockholders' equity, 32, *33*, 37, 41, *42*, 48

Stocks, Bonds, Bills, and Inflation (Ibbotson and Sinquefield), 255

Straight-line depreciation, 46

Strategic partners, 199–200, 282–283

Student interns, 182

Subprime mortgage meltdown (2007–2008), 5

Substitutes and alternatives principle, 250

Success, measuring entrepreneurial, 4–5. *See also* Self-assessment

Tax planning, 172–174

Tax returns, 252

Temporary employees, 182

Term loan, 216

Terminal value of investment, 256

Termination of operations of business, 283–284

Thompson, Bob, 4–5

Time out of cash, 91–92

Times interest earned, 136–137

Total risk, 9–10

Trade credit, 209–210, *210*

Traditional finance and entrepreneurial financial management
  differences from, 8–11
  similarities to, 7–8

Transitional transfer of business, 281–283

20/80 versus 80/20 forecast mistake, 53–54

Twitter followers, 188–189

Underwriting initial public offerings, 240

Unearned revenues, 48

U.S. Department of Labor, 283

Variable costs, 73–74, *74*

Variance, 9

Variation in sales, 149–150

Venture capital financing
  business plan and, 229–231, *230*
  dark side of, 234–235
  4 Cs and, 228–229
  initial contact with venture capitalist and, 235–237
  initial public offerings and, 237–243
  life cycle of firm and, 231–233
  overview, 228–229, *229*, 243
  Recession of 2008 and, 228
  stages of business development and, 232–233

Venture capital financing *(continued)*
  stages of funding, 233–234
Venture capitalists, 69, 157, 163, 228–229,
    235–237. *See also* Investors
Virtual company, 184

Wages payable, 37, *40*

Wahlstedt, Bob, 277
Warner, Sally, 225–226
Wealth, 17–20, 86–87
What-if analysis, 92–93
Winborg, J., 190
Word-of-mouth marketing, 186–187
Working capital, 44, 90, 129–130, 158
Worst-case scenario, creating, 58, 92

About the Authors

Jeffrey R. Cornwall is the inaugural recipient of the Jack C. Massey Chair in Entrepreneurship at Belmont University in Nashville, Tennessee. He also serves as the director of the Center for Entrepreneurship. He has a DBA and an MBA from the University of Kentucky.

In the late 1980s, Jeff left academics to become the cofounder, president, and CEO of Atlantic Behavioral Health Systems, which operated a variety of health-care facilities and programs. After nine years of rapid growth, he and his partners negotiated the sale of most of their corporations' business interests, and Jeff returned to academics.

Jeff was awarded the Presidential Faculty Achievement Award from Belmont University in 2010. He received the 2008 National Model Undergraduate Entrepreneurship Program Award from the U.S. Association of Small Business and Entrepreneurship. He won the same award while teaching at the University of St. Thomas in 1999, as well as the 2002 National Outstanding Entrepreneurship Course Award. He was inducted as a Justin G. Longenecker Fellow of the U.S. Association of Small Business and Entrepreneurship in 2006.

He has published five other books: *Organizational Entrepreneurship, The Entrepreneurial Educator, From the Ground Up: Entrepreneurial School Leadership, Bringing Your Business to Life,* and *Bootstrapping.* He does research in various areas of entrepreneurship and in business ethics. His blog, *The Entrepreneurial Mind* (www.drjeffcornwall.com), is one of the most popular small business blogs on the Web. He is the editor and author of the monthly *Entrepreneurship Educator Newsletter.*

David O. Vang is a professor of finance in the Opus College of Business at the University of St. Thomas in St. Paul, Minnesota. He received a bachelor's degree, summa cum laude, from St. Cloud State University in Minnesota with majors in economics and political science. He holds a PhD in economics, concentrating in finance, from Iowa State University. He teaches and researches in the areas of finance, economics, and real estate. Dave is a winner of the Iowa State Outstanding Educator Award. He has served as the CFO for a high-technology start-up company and has performed over seventy different consulting assignments for several organizations in areas such as derivatives, acquisitions, leveraged buyouts, product and service costing, and corporate finance.

Jean M. Hartman began her career in public accounting at Arthur Andersen & Co. After three years, she ventured into her first entrepreneurial experience, operating a grocery store in Iowa. She subsequently served as controller of entrepreneurial companies, including Knox Lumber Company, a home improvement business, and 10,000 Auto Parts, a leveraged buyout venture. She then joined Carlson Marketing Group, a division of Carlson Companies in Minneapolis, Minnesota. In 1992, she joined academia, teaching at Hennepin Technical College and then the University of St. Thomas, both in Minnesota. In 2003 she became the Chief Financial Officer for the Sisters of St. Benedict of St. Paul's Monastery in Minnesota. For the next six years she worked with the Sisters to sell their large monastery to an organization providing shelter for victims of domestic abuse and to sell the adjacent land for affordable and senior housing. She then oversaw the construction of a smaller, more efficient monastery. Jean currently provides financial guidance working for a nonprofit organization that serves the chronically homeless.

Jean's areas of interest include working with entrepreneurs and nonprofits to develop their understanding of financial statements and the critical importance of cash flow while applying ethical business practices. Jean holds a BA in business administration and accounting from Southwest Minnesota State University and an MBA from the University of St. Thomas. She is a certified public accountant.